CW00967859

Compensation for Stress at Work

Compensation for Stress at Work

David Marshall
Partner, Anthony Gold Solicitors

JORDANS

Published by
Jordan Publishing Limited
21 St Thomas Street, Bristol BS1 6JS

Copyright Jordan Publishing Limited 2009

All rights reserved. No part of this publication may be reproduced, stored in a retrieval system, or transmitted in any way or by any means, including photocopying or recording, without the written permission of the copyright and database right holder, application for which should be addressed to the publisher.

British Library Cataloguing-in-Publication Data

A catalogue record for this book is available from the British Library.

ISBN 978 1 84661 148 3

Typeset by Letterpart Ltd, Reigate, Surrey

Printed in Great Britain by CPI Antony Rowe, Chippenham, Wiltshire

PREFACE

This work aims to provide a comprehensive guide to bringing claims for compensation for stress and bullying at work, looking at both personal injury law and employment law remedies. Inevitably, given the experience of the author, it is written from the perspective of a solicitor for claimants, but aims to provide an overview of the relevant law and practice for anyone in the field.

Work-related stress is now the second most common reason given for absence from work. Whilst the 16 propositions of Hale LJ in *Hatton v Sutherland* have sometimes been viewed as hurdles for employees to jump, our knowledge of the causes of stress and of the policies and procedures best able to prevent or minimise it have improved greatly over the last decade. All of the employees in the *Hatton* appeals left their jobs more than 10 years ago when the causes of stress at work were much less widely understood. The *Hatton* propositions, although widely admired and applied, have now been the subject of considerable judicial consideration. In the autumn of 2008 alone, whilst this book was being written, Smith LJ severely criticised the formulation of *Hatton* proposition 14 in respect of apportionment of injury, but the High Court dismissed the latest attempt in *Patterson* to get around *Hatton* on foreseeability by means of the Management Regulations 1999. This is cutting edge law with many opportunities for practitioners.

I have tried to set out all the options that might be open to the claimant. I have assumed some basic knowledge and understanding of personal injury law and employment law. Although I have tried to amplify the relevant principles where appropriate, some matters are beyond the scope of this work (eg the detail of pension loss claims) and readers are advised to consult appropriate specialist works on these subjects. Most readers will primarily specialise in one field or the other. Although it is one of the aims of this work to introduce relevant employment law principles to personal injury lawyers and vice versa, in this 'cross-over' work it is essential to develop referral mechanisms between different teams within a firm.

I have generally used the phrase 'stress at work' as shorthand for 'stress and bullying at work'. The situations in law are generally synonymous and I have sought to distinguish them when they are not. I have used the masculine pronoun throughout for the sake of brevity only and it is intended to include the feminine pronoun.

I thank my partners and other colleagues at Anthony Gold for their support. I am very grateful to my publisher Jordans and, in particular, Tony Hawitt, for his enthusiasm for this book and for all his support during the course of writing it. I thank Cheryl Prophett of Proof Positive and also my wife, Aileen Marshall, who nobly assisted me with correcting the proofs and by challenging my opinions. I also thank Aileen and our children Alexander and Helena for all their support with this project and for their considerable forbearance.

This area of law is complex with new law being made regularly by the courts. The variety of factual situations is limitless and advice should be carefully tailored to the circumstances of the case. Any errors or omissions are my own and, generally, the law is stated as at 16 February 2009.

David Marshall
Anthony Gold, Solicitors
The Counting House
53 Tooley Street
London SE1 2QN

CONTENTS

TABLE OF CASES

References are to paragraph numbers.

Marshall v Southampton and South West Hampshire Health Authority, No 2 (Case C-271/91) [1994] 1 AC 530n, [1994] 1 All ER 736n, [1994] 2 WLR 392, [1994] ICR 242n, HL, [1994] QB 126, [1993] 4 All ER 586, [1993] ECR I-4367, [1993] 3 WLR 1054, [1993] 3 CMLR 293, [1993] ICR 893, [1993] IRLR 445, ECJ, *Referred from* (1991) 14 October, unreported, HL, *On Appeal from* [1990] 3 CMLR 425, [1991] ICR 136, [1990] IRLR 481, 134 Sol Jo 1368, CA, *affirming* [1989] 3 CMLR 771, [1990] ICR 6, [1989] IRLR 459, EAT, *Reversing* [1988] 3 CMLR 389, [1988] IRLR 325, Ind Trib 7.4.4

Mattis v Pollock (trading as Flamingos Nightclub) [2003] EWCA Civ 887, [2004] 4 All ER 85, [2003] 1 WLR 2158, [2003] ICR 1335, [2003] IRLR 603, (2003) *The Times*, 16 July, 147 Sol Jo LB 816, [2003] All ER (D) 10 (Jul), CA, *reversing* [2002] EWHC 2177 (QB), [2002] All ER (D) 373 (Oct), QBD 4.3

McAdie v Royal Bank of Scotland Citation [2007] EWCA Civ 806, [2008] ICR 1087, [2007] IRLR 895, [2007] NLJR 1355, [2007] All ER (D) 477 (Jul), CA, *affirming* [2006] All ER (D) 393 (Nov), EAT 5.2

McCabe v (1) Cornwall County Council (2) Governing Body of Mounts Bay School [2002] EWCA Civ 1887, [2003] ICR 501, [2003] IRLR 87, [2003] PIQR P19, [2003] 09 LS Gaz R 27, (2002) *The Times*, 28 December, [2002] All ER (D) 294 (Dec), CA 2.4.3.3, 8.5.2.2

McDonald or Cross v Highlands and Islands Enterprise [2001] IRLR 336, 2001 SLT 1060, 2001 SCLR 547, [2000] Scot CS 307, OH 11.2.1.2

McGhee v National Coal Board [1972] 3 All ER 1008, [1973] 1 WLR 1, 13 KIR 471, 116 Sol Jo 967, HL 6.1.1

McLoughlin v Grovers (a firm) [2001] EWCA Civ 1743, [2001] All ER (D) 335 (Nov) 11.1.6

McLoughlin v O'Brian [1983] 1 AC 410, [1982] 2 All ER 298, [1982] 2 WLR 982, [1982] RTR 209, 126 Sol Jo 347, [1982] LS Gaz R 922, HL, *affirming* [1981] 1 QB 599, [1981] 1 All ER 809, [1981] 2 WLR 1014, [1982] RTR 209, 125 Sol Jo 169, CA 7.1

Meikle v Nottinghamshire County Council, *sub nom* Nottinghamshire County Council v Meikle [2004] EWCA Civ 859, [2004] 4 All ER 97, [2005] ICR 1, [2004] IRLR 703, 80 BMLR 129, (2004) *The Times*, 15 July, 148 Sol Jo LB 908, [2004] All ER (D) 123 (Jul), CA, *affirming* [2003] All ER (D) 06 (Oct), EAT 2.4.3.1, 5.4.2

Melhuish v Clifford (unreported) 18 August 1998 2.5.2

MG v North Devon NHS Primary Care Trust [2006] EWHC 850, [2006] All ER (D) 267 (Apr), QBD 3.5.1, 3.5.2, 6.1.3, 7.1.1.2, 7.1.2.3, 7.1.3.1, 11.2.1.1

Midland Bank Trust Co Ltd v Hett, Stubbs & Kemp (a firm) [1979] Ch 384, [1978] 3 All ER 571, [1978] 3 WLR 167, 121 Sol Jo 830, Ch D 11.1.6

Miller Steamship Co Pty Ltd v Overseas Tankship (UK) Ltd, R W Miller & Co Pty Ltd v Overseas Tankship (UK) Ltd, *The Wagon Mound* (No 2) [1963] 1 Lloyd's Rep 402, NSW SC, [1967] 1 AC 617, [1966] 2 All ER 709, [1966] 3 WLR 498, [1966] 1 Lloyd's Rep 657, 110 Sol Jo 447, [1967] ALR 97, [1966] 1 NSWR 411, PC, On Appeal from [1963] 1 Lloyd's Rep 402, NSW SC 3.1.1, 3.5.1

Ministry of Defence v Cannock [1995] 2 All ER 449, [1994] ICR 918, [1994] IRLR 509, EAT 7.4.4

Minto v Revenue and Customs Comrs [2008] STC (SCD) 121, [2007] SWTI 2124, SPC00625 (23 April 2007) LTL 4/9/2007, SCD 11.4.3

Morgans v. Alpha Plus Security Ltd [2005] 4 All ER 655, [2005] ICR 525, [2005] IRLR 234, [2005] All ER (D) 229 (Jan), EAT 9.4

Mullins v Laughton [2002] EWHC 2761 (Ch), [2003] Ch 250, [2003] 4 All ER 94, [2003] 2 WLR 1006, [2003] 05 LS Gaz R 30, (2002) *The Times*, 27 December, 147 Sol Jo LB 56, [2003] BPIR 674, [2002] All ER (D) 326 (Dec), Ch D 2.5.2

Myatt and Others v National Coal Board (Nos 1 and 2) [2007] EWCA Civ 307, [2007] 4 All ER 1094, [2007] 1 WLR 1559, (2007) *The Times*, 27 March, [2007] All ER (D) 301 (Mar), CA 10.7.4

TABLE OF STATUTES

References are to paragraph numbers.

TABLE OF STATUTORY INSTRUMENTS

References are to paragraph numbers.

TABLE OF EUROPEAN MATERIALS

References are to paragraph numbers.

CHAPTER 1

STRESS AND BULLYING AT WORK

1.1 DEFINITIONS

1.1.1 Occupational stress

The Health and Safety Executive (HSE) define occupational stress as:[1]

> 'The adverse reaction people have to excessive pressure or other types of demand placed on them.'

It should be noted, firstly, that the emphasis is on '*excessive* pressure'. Secondly, stress also requires an 'adverse' reaction to the pressure. Even excessive pressure does not inevitably lead to occupational stress. Whether the excessive pressure will lead to such a reaction is dependent not only upon the pressure, but also upon the nature of the individual concerned.

In this connection, ACAS say:[2]

> 'Don't confuse positive pressure, which can create a "buzz", and the harmful effects of pressure that is beyond a person's ability to cope.'

And the Chartered Institute of Personnel and Development (CIPD) say:[3]

> 'There is sometimes confusion between the terms pressure and stress. It is healthy and essential that people experience challenges within their lives that cause levels of pressure and, up to a certain point, an increase in pressure can improve performance and the quality of life . . .
>
> The pressures of working life can lead to stress if they are excessive or long-term. Examples of long-term or chronic stress are the fear, frustration and anger that may be produced by an unhappy relationship with one's boss or with a difficult customer, and the unhappiness of an unsuitable job.'

---

1 See www.hse.gov.uk.

2 ACAS advice leaflet 'Stress at work', August 2006 at www.acas.org.uk.

3 CIPD factsheet 'Stress at work', December 2008 at www.cipd.co.uk/subjects/health/stress/stress.htm.

The Court of Appeal in *Hatton v Sutherland*[4] were clearly aware of the distinction between stress and pressure, Hale LJ quoting from guidance from the HSE in 'Stress at Work' (1995):

> 'Stress is not therefore the same as ill-health. But in some cases, particularly where pressures are intense and continue for some time, the effect of stress can be more sustained and far more damaging, leading to longer-term psychological problems and physical ill-health.'

In the context of establishing the legal liability of an employer in court proceedings (although not in the employment tribunal), it is also necessary for the 'adverse reaction' to lead to a recognised psychiatric injury.[5]

1.1.2 Bullying and harassment

1.1.2.1 Bullying

Bullying is not defined anywhere in the legislation. However, the Andrea Adams Trust, who are a 'not for profit' sector charity lobbying and educating to prevent workplace bullying, state:[6]

> 'When we talk about bullying at work we are referring to an abuse of power or position. It is offensive discrimination through persistent, vindictive, cruel or humiliating attempts to undermine, criticise, condemn, and to hurt or humiliate an individual or group of employees.'

ACAS have produced a leaflet for employees about bullying and harassment. As they point out:[7]

> 'These terms are used interchangeably by most people, and many definitions include bullying as a form of harassment. Harassment, in general terms is unwanted conduct affecting the dignity of men and women in the workplace. It may be related to age, sex, race, disability, religion, sexual orientation, nationality or any personal characteristic of the individual, and may be persistent or an isolated incident. The key is that the actions or comments are viewed as demeaning and unacceptable to the recipient.'

They go on to say that:

> 'Bullying may be characterised as offensive, intimidating, malicious or insulting behaviour, an abuse or misuse of power through means intended to undermine, humiliate, denigrate or injure the recipient.'

---

4 *Hatton v Sutherland*; *Barber v Somerset County Council*; *Jones v Sandwell Metropolitan Borough Council*; *Bishop v Baker Refractories Ltd* [2002] EWCA Civ 76, [2002] 2 All ER 1, [2002] ICR 613, [2002] IRLR 263, 68 BMLR 115, [2002] All ER (D) 53 (Feb), CA.

5 See **7.1**.

6 www.andreaadamstrust.org (viewed January 2009).

7 'Bullying and Harassment at Work – Guidance for employees', November 2008 at www.acas.org.uk.

They give a useful checklist of examples of behaviour they consider 'bullying and harassment' to include:

- 'spreading malicious rumours, or insulting someone by word or behaviour (particularly on the grounds of age, race, sex, disability, sexual orientation and religion or belief)
- copying memos that are critical about someone to others who do not need to know
- ridiculing or demeaning someone – picking on them or setting them up to fail
- exclusion or victimisation
- unfair treatment
- overbearing supervision or other misuse of power or position
- unwelcome sexual advances – touching, standing too close, the display of offensive materials, asking for sexual favours, making decisions on the basis of sexual advances being accepted or rejected
- making threats or comments about job security without foundation
- deliberately undermining a competent worker by overloading and constant criticism
- preventing individuals progressing by intentionally blocking promotion or training opportunities.'

The mental health charity MIND say:[8]

> 'Bullying behaviour is not about being bossy. It's not about the occasional, angry outburst on the subject of meeting work targets or reaching and maintaining standards. It's about persistent criticism and condemnation.
>
> If you tell someone often enough that they are stupid, hopeless and not up to the job, they are likely to start believing it, and to imagine that it's entirely their own fault. Workplace bullying occurs when someone persistently acts in a discriminatory way towards an employee which hurts, criticises or condemns them . . . These attacks on someone's performance are unpredictable, unreasonable and often unseen, creeping up on the person long before they are aware of what's happening. It wears the employee down, making them feel belittled and inadequate, and gradually makes them lose faith in themselves. It causes constant stress and anxiety, which can cause ill health and mental distress.'

And they helpfully consider an often raised defence by asking the question 'how does it differ from strong management?':

> 'Although bullying is not the same as strong management, it often spreads downwards from a senior manager taking what they feel is a "strong line" with employees . . .
>
> The line is crossed between strong management and bullying when there is a purposeful, malicious intent. It happens when hurting an employee or

---

8 MIND information booklet 'How to deal with bullying at work', first published by MIND in 2001 and revised in 2008 at www.mind.org.uk.

colleague by intimidating, upsetting, embarrassing, humiliating, offending or ultimately destroying them is more important than getting the task done.

Bullying can easily become part of the culture in companies that pride themselves on their strong, robust management. Employees may assume that management allows and even condones such behaviour unless it takes action against it . . .'

1.1.2.2 Harassment as discrimination under the equality legislation

Insofar as the bullying amounts to discrimination under the equality legislation, the wording generally used in statute is:[9] 'unwanted conduct' 'which has the purpose or effect of violating the employee's dignity' or 'creating an intimidating, hostile, degrading, humiliating or offensive environment for the employee'.

This harassment must be in respect of one of the grounds protected by the discrimination legislation (namely, sex, transgender status, race, disability, religion or belief, sexual orientation or age).

It is not enough that 'bullying' behaviour is simply directed at a person who is potentially protected by statute. If the employer can establish that the reason for the bullying does not relate to the protected ground then the remedy will not lie in a claim for discrimination under the equality legislation in the employment tribunal. However, the employer may still be liable under the common law[10] or under the Protection from Harassment Act 1997 (PFHA 1997).[11]

1.1.2.3 Non-discriminatory harassment

There is no tort of harassment or bullying (and hence no definition) at common law, unless the behaviour constitutes the tort of assault or of intentional infliction of harm.[12]

The state has, however, legislated against specific forms of harassment falling within the definition set out in the PFHA 1997. This outlaws a 'course of conduct' (which is defined[13] as meaning at least two incidents) causing 'harassment' where the person alleged to be harassing:[14]

> '. . .ought to know that it amounts to harassment of another if a reasonable person in possession of the same information would think the course of conduct amounted to harassment of the other.'

---

9 See **5.3.1**.

10 See Chapter 3.

11 See **1.1.2.3** and Chapter 4.

12 See **4.1**.

13 PFHA 1997, s 7(3).

14 PFHA 1997, s 1(2).

This is a rather flexible definition, but there is no doubt that bullying in the workplace can constitute harassment under the PFHA 1997.[15]

1.2 THE SCALE OF THE PROBLEM

Occupational stress is undoubtedly a significant issue in the workplace and has been so for the last two decades. It is a substantial cause of loss of productivity in the workplace and ill-health. However, many commentators still see it as 'all in the mind' and, because it does not (usually) involve physical injury, less serious.

In seeking to establish the extent of the problem, a study by the HSE[16] analysed the data from two different kinds of sources:

(1) the self–reporting by the population, through the Psychosocial Working Conditions (PWC) and the Stress and Health at Work (SHAW) studies and, most importantly, the Labour Force Surveys (LFS) which 'provides the most broadly based estimate of the overall prevalence and incidence of work-related stress in Britain, and also the resulting working days lost'; and

(2) reports by specialist physicians through the HSE's occupational disease surveillance schemes (THOR).

The HSE study concludes that:

> 'Results from all surveys consistently indicate that stress and related conditions form the second most commonly reported group of work-related ill-health conditions after musculoskeletal disorders.'

And that specifically:

> 'In 2007/08 an estimated 442 000 individuals in Britain, who worked in the last year, believed that they were experiencing work-related stress at a level that was making them ill, according to the Labour Force Survey (LFS).'

Such figures are backed up by the PWC:

> 'The 2007 Psychosocial Working Conditions (PWC) survey indicated that around 13.6% of all working individuals thought their job was very or extremely stressful.'

This led to an estimated 13.5 million working days lost in 2007. There has not been a recent upsurge in stress-related conditions:

---

15 See further Chapter 4.

16 HSE study 'Stress-related and psychological disorders', updated 25 November 2008 at www.hse.gov.uk/statistics/causdis/stress.

> 'LFS survey data suggests the incidence rate of self-reported work-related stress, depression or anxiety has been broadly level over the years 2001/02 to 2007/08, with the exception of 2005/06 where the incidence rate was lower than all other years.'

The HSE do say that their THOR surveillance suggests that the number of new cases of work-related mental health problems in 2007 was much lower (approximately 5,750), but conclude:

> '…this almost certainly underestimates the true incidence of these conditions in the British workforce.'

The data shows that there is a 'statistically significant' greater likelihood of women suffering from occupational stress, although interestingly the data also shows that women are more likely to be referred to, and be reported by, occupational health physicians whilst men were more likely to be referred to, and be reported by, psychiatrists. With regard to age, the highest incidence is in the 35–44 and 45–54 age groups.

The survey also identified the occupations which were most likely to be affected:

> 'Occupation groups containing teachers, nurses, and housing and welfare officers, along with certain professional and managerial groups have high prevalence rates of self-reported work-related stress according to the LFS. The LFS also shows people working within public administration and defence to have high prevalence rates of self-reported work-related stress. The THOR datasets . . . also report high incident rates of work-related mental illness for these occupational groups, along with medical practitioners and those in public sector security based occupations such as police officers, prison officers, and UK armed forces personnel.'

The Samaritans' survey in 2007[17] found:

> 'Significant proportions of workers feel work rules their life (39% UK, 47% ROI)
>
> Over half of people feel their jobs are just going to get more stressful (52% UK, 55% ROI)
>
> A quarter of all UK workers (22%) and one third in Ireland (34%) take sick leave due to stress.'

By contrast, ACAS focus on the costs to business of occupational stress:[18]

> 'Stress is costly, especially for small firms where cover for sick employees is difficult to arrange. Stress can reduce the effectiveness of employees and lead

---

17 The Samaritans 'Stressed Out: a study of public experience of stress at work', December 2007 at www.samaritans.org.

18 ACAS advice leaflet 'Stress at work', August 2006 at www.acas.org.uk.

> to higher rates of absence. Research estimates that 12.8 million working days were lost to stress, depression and anxiety in 2004/5. Each new case of stress leads to an average of 29 days off work. Work-related stress costs society about £3.7 billion every year (at 1995/6 prices).'

So far as bullying is specifically concerned, the statistics are more controversial. The Samaritans' survey[19] in 2007 found:

> 'Almost everyone claims to have been bullied at some point in their careers (81% UK, 86% ROI). Alarmingly bullying is a weekly or daily cause of stress for one in four people (22% UK, 27% ROI).'

However, commenting to the BBC News website[20] the Confederation of British Industry (CBI) challenged these findings:

> 'Responding to the research, the employers' group the CBI acknowledged that workplace stress was an important issue, but said the Samaritans' findings were significantly out of step with official statistics.
>
> "Workplace bullying should never be tolerated and most employers have policies to prevent and deal with it," said senior policy advisor Marion Seguret.
>
> However, she added: "It is important not to exaggerate the problem – government data shows that less than 4% of employees have experienced bullying in the workplace in the last 2 years."'

Digital Opinion conducted a survey[21] on behalf of the Andrea Adams Trust which focused on the nature of workplace bullying as reported by victims of bullying:

> 'The feedback indicates that workplace bullying is perpetrated by a range of individuals, from directors to reports, with immediate managers being cited most often. It takes a variety of forms. Unfair criticism and intimidating behaviour are the most commonly cited examples, while some respondents indicate that they have been the victims of physical abuse.
>
> Just over half of victims of bullying said that they had been bullied for over a year. Almost 23% had been bullied for 6 to 12 months . . .
>
> People respond to workplace bullying in different ways. 75% say that they discussed it with family or friends while 58% talked with colleagues. Just 32% made a formal complaint. 53% say that they started looking for another job and 22% took legal advice.

---

[19] Samaritans press release 'Workplace bullying rife', January 2008.

[20] 'Charity warns on bullying at work', 17 January 2008 at www.news.bbc.co.uk.

[21] 'National Workplace Bullying Survey' at www.andreaadmastrust.org.

5% of respondents say that their actions solved the problem, while 31.5% say that they achieved a partial solution. Unfortunately, over 38% say that their actions had no effect, while a quarter of victims say that they actually made the situation worse.'

1.3 WHAT SHOULD EMPLOYERS BE DOING?

1.3.1 The legal framework

The legal framework is set out in detail in Chapter 2.

In brief, an employer may be liable:

- under European law, particularly the directives requiring governments to protect the health and safety of workers and the directives requiring equal treatment;
- under statutory law separate from European obligation (eg PFHA 1997); and
- under common law duties imposed by contract and tort.

Where a claim is brought in contract or tort, the employer will generally be liable only if a reasonable employer would not have behaved in that way.[22]

Reasonableness is judged by the standards of the time and not with hindsight. It is therefore important to consider the state of general industry knowledge at various key dates.

1.3.2 Health and Safety Executive Guidance

1.3.2.1 Industry knowledge at the date of Walker

The judgment in *Walker v Northumberland County Council*,[23] the first reported successful claim for compensation for stress at work, was handed down on 16 November 1994. Mr Walker's first breakdown had led him to leave work in November 1986. His second and final breakdown led him to cease employment permanently in September 1987.

In his judgment, Colman J does not refer at all to any generally publicly available materials in respect of occupational stress in support of his conclusion that, in respect of the second breakdown, the employer was in

---

22 See **3.5.1**.

23 [1994] EWHC QB 2, [1995] 1 All ER 737, [1995] ICR 702, [1995] ELR 231, [1995] IRLR 35, [1995] PIQR P521.

breach of its duty of care towards Mr Walker and that it was reasonably foreseeable that he would suffer psychiatric injury as a result.

The judge's findings were based on the particular evidence of the facts of that case – namely, the employer's knowledge of the particular stresses of Mr Walker's work and its knowledge that Mr Walker, having suffered one breakdown, was vulnerable to another one.

1.3.2.2 Industry knowledge at the date of Hatton

The Court of Appeal handed down its seminal decision in *Hatton*[24] on 5 February 2002. As the House of Lords pointed out in *Barber*,[25] the only appeal from its decision, the judgment is 'practical guidance' and does not have 'statutory force'. In particular, by stressing the primacy of *Stokes v Guest, Keen Nettlefold (Nuts and Bolts) Ltd*,[26] it should be noted that the common law test is as follows:

> '. . . the overall test is still the conduct of the reasonable and prudent employer, taking positive thought for the safety of his workers in the light of what he knows or ought to know . . .'

and such knowledge is not set in stone:

> '. . . where there is developing knowledge, he must keep reasonably abreast of it and not be too slow to apply it . . .'

It is now 7 years since the Court of Appeal handed down its judgment regarding the behaviour expected of a reasonable employer in the light of available knowledge about stress at work at the relevant time. Indeed, of course, the conjoined appeals in *Hatton* were decided at first instance even earlier than 2002 and involved judging the action or inaction by employers in the light of knowledge at the time of the breach in each case. The following table sets out the dates of cessation of employment in each of the conjoined appeals:

---

24 Ibid.

25 *Barber v Somerset County Council* [2004] UKHL 13, (2004) 77 BMLR 219, [2004] 1 WLR 1089, [2004] 2 All ER 385, [2004] ELR 199, [2004] ICR 457, [2004] IRLR 475, [2004] PIQR P31.

26 [1968] 1 WLR 1776, 112 Sol Jo 821, 5 KIR 401.

Case	Employment ceased
Jones v Sandwell Metropolitan Borough Council	20/1/1995
Hatton v Sutherland	16/11/1995
Barber v Somerset County Council	12/11/1996
Bishop v Baker Refractories Ltd	25/2/1997

The HSE[27] helpfully summarise the historical picture during the 1990s. They conclude that:

> 'The public profile of work-related stress increased dramatically across the decade as demonstrated by a steep increase in the number of UK national newspaper articles on work stress, and over that time became an issue of public discussion and controversy. This increase in profile is related to the very large changes in working conditions over the same period, including programmes of downsizing and reorganisation, an increase in short-term contracts, outsourcing and the introduction of new technology.'

They also point out that during that decade the self-reporting of work-related stress increased significantly until it levelled off towards the year 2000. However, as the overall prevalence of mental health illness was constant over that decade they suggested that the increase in reported occupational stress could 'partly be due to a shift in attribution'.

This suggests that the judges at first instance in the conjoined *Hatton* appeals were dealing with cases at a time of flux in public awareness and attitudes towards occupational stress.

In *Hatton*, with regard to the then publicly available literature on occupational stress, the Court of Appeal refers only to the Report of a working party of the Health Education Authority entitled 'Stress in the public sector – Nurses, police, social workers and teachers (1988)', the Report of the Education Service Advisory Committee of the Health and Safety Commission entitled 'Managing occupational stress: a Guide for Managers and Teachers in the Schools Sector (1990)' and, most importantly, a general booklet of guidance from the Health and Safety Executive entitled 'Stress at work (1995)'.

It should be noted that the HSE guidance, which was the first published specifically on the subject of occupational stress, only appeared in 1995

27 HSE study 'Stress-related and psychological disorders', updated 25 November 2008 at www.hse.gov.uk/statistics/causdis/stress.

the year in which two of the employees in the *Hatton* appeals ceased employment. The other two employees ceased work within a year or two of its publication.

Employers' knowledge and understanding as to the causes of occupational stress and how it might be avoided would have been necessarily more limited then than now.

The first version of the Management of Health and Safety at Work Regulations ('the Management Regulations') had come into force in 1992.[28] However, these do not expressly deal with stress at work and, importantly, did not give rise to civil liability until the revised Management Regulations 1999[29] were amended to that effect in 2003.[30]

1.3.2.3 Industry knowledge today

Since *Hatton* was decided, as we have seen,[31] the prevalence of occupational stress has been widely recognised and reported.

In addition, since 1995 the HSE and other bodies have issued a plethora of guidance aimed at educating employers with a view to reducing work-related stress.

First, in 2001 the HSE published a guidance pack for employers entitled 'Real Solutions, real people: a manager's guide to tackling work related stress'.[32]

The HSE say[33] that the evidence collated since 1995 has been used to formulate their Stress Management Standards (which were first published in November 2004):

> 'There is a growing body of epidemiological evidence indicating working conditions that lead to work stress. This information has been condensed within HSE's Management Standards for Stress . . .
>
> In general factors intrinsic to the job such as demand, control, support, job role ambiguity, work relationships and changes at work are reported as participating factors for most of the cases of mental ill-health reported. This is consistent with epidemiological evidence linking working conditions to work stress and relates well to HSE's six stress management standards of Demand, Control, Support, Role, Relationships and Change.'

---

28 SI 1992/2051.

29 SI 1999/3242.

30 Management of Health and Safety at Work and Fire Precautions (Workplace) (Amendment) Regulations 2003, SI 2003/2457. See **2.2.1**.

31 See research referred to at **1.2**.

32 London, HSE, 2003, ISBN 0717627675.

33 HSE study 'Stress-related and psychological disorders'.

The problems of occupational stress for business are now well-recognised. For example, the CIPD state:[34]

> 'It is well recognised that stress reduces employee well-being, and that excessive or sustained work pressure can lead to stress. Occupational stress poses a risk to most businesses and compensation payments for stress-related injuries are rising. It is important to meet the challenge by dealing with excessive and long-term causes of stress.'

And ACAS[35] concur, stressing the growing awareness of a long-established problem:

> 'There is a growing awareness of the importance of health and safety and recognition that healthy employees make a greater contribution to a business. People are more aware of the harmful effects of stress in workplaces but it is not new – psychologists have been studying stress since the 1950s.'

The CIPD also state:[36]

> 'Stress in the workplace has to be properly managed if it is to be controlled. CIPD believes that:
> - people work more effectively within a participative management style
> - people are better motivated when work satisfies economic, social and psychological needs
> - motivation improves by paying attention to job design and work organisation.
>
> We have been working with the HSE on a project to develop practical help for HR and line managers to tackle the issue of workplace stress. In March 2007 we produced initial guidance for HR managers and line managers including a competency framework enabling line managers to work on the skills required to reduce and prevent stress at work. Phase 2 of the project was completed in 2008 and we have now refined and updated the guidance and framework.'

The HSE first launched 'Management Standards for Work-related Stress' in November 2004. The approach is to encourage employers to take preventative measures through risk assessment. The standards are voluntary. They focus on the areas of work with the highest reported incidence of occupational stress, namely health, education, central and local government, and the financial services sector.

The HSE Management Standards consider six key words or concepts: 'demands, control, support, relationship, role and change'.

---

34 CIPD factsheet 'Stress at Work', December 2008 at www.cipd.co.uk/subjects/health/stress/stress.htm.

35 ACAS advice leaflet 'Stress at Work', August 2006 at www.acas.org.uk.

36 CIPD factsheet 'Stress at Work', December 2008 at www.cipd.co.uk/subjects/health/stress/stress.htm.

Demands

'Demands' include 'workload, work patterns, and the work environment'. The standard is that:

> '• Employees indicate that they are able to cope with the demands of their jobs; and
> • Systems are in place locally to respond to any individual concerns.'

To achieve this the employer should show that:

> '• The organisation provides employees with adequate and achievable demands in relation to the agreed hours of work
> • People's skills and abilities are matched to the job demands;
> • Jobs are designed to be within the capabilities of employees; and
> • Employees' concerns about their work environment are addressed.'

The ACAS advice leaflet states in this connection:[37]

> 'Demands: employees often become overloaded if they cannot cope with the amount of work or type of work they are asked to do:
> • make sure employees understand what they have to do and how to do it;
> • meet training needs;
> • consider whether working flexible hours would help employees to manage demands.'

Control

'Control' includes 'how much say the person has in the way they do their work'. The standard is that:

> '• Employees indicate that they are able to have a say about the way they do their work; and
> • Systems are in place locally to respond to any individual concerns.'

To achieve this the employer should show that:

> '• Where possible, employees have control over their pace of work;
> • Employees are encouraged to use their skills and initiative to do their work;
> • Where possible, employees are encouraged to develop new skills to help them undertake new and challenging pieces of work;
> • The organisation encourages employees to develop their skills;
> • Employees have a say over when breaks can be taken; and
> • Employees are consulted over their work patterns.'

ACAS say in this connection:[38]

---

37 ACAS advice leaflet 'Stress at Work', August 2006 at www.acas.org.uk.
38 Ibid.

'Control: employees can feel disaffected and perform poorly if they have no say over how and when they do their work:

- involve employees in the way work is carried out
- consult employees about decisions
- build effective teams with responsibility for outcomes
- review performance to identify strengths and weaknesses.'

Support

'Support' includes 'the encouragement, sponsorship and resources provided by the organisation, line management and colleagues'. The standard is that:

'• Employees indicate that they receive adequate information and support from their colleagues and superiors; and
- Systems are in place locally to respond to any individual concerns.'

To achieve this the employer should show that:

'• The organisation has policies and procedures to adequately support employees;
- Systems are in place to enable and encourage managers to support their staff
- Systems are in place to enable and encourage employees to support their colleagues;
- Employees know what support is available and how and when to access it;
- Employees know how to access the required resources to do their job; and
- Employees receive regular and constructive feedback.'

ACAS say in this connection:[39]

'Support: levels of sick absence often rise if employees feel they cannot talk to managers about issues that are troubling them:

- give employees the opportunity to talk about issues causing stress
- be sympathetic and supportive
- keep employees informed about what is going on in the firm.'

Relationship

'Relationship' includes 'promoting positive working to avoid conflict and dealing with unacceptable behaviour'. The standard is that:

'• Employees indicate that they are not subjected to unacceptable behaviours, e.g. bullying at work; and
- Systems are in place locally to respond to any individual concerns.'

To achieve this the employer should show that:

---

[39] Ibid.

- ‘The organisation promotes positive behaviours at work to avoid conflict and ensure fairness;
- Employees share information relevant to their work;
- The organisation has agreed policies and procedures to prevent or resolve unacceptable behaviour;
- Systems are in place to enable and encourage managers to deal with unacceptable behaviour; and
- Systems are in place to enable and encourage employees to report unacceptable behaviour.’

ACAS say in this connection:[40]

> ‘Relationships: a failure to build relationships based on good behaviour and trust can lead to problems related to discipline, grievances and bullying
> - have clear procedures for handling misconduct and poor performance
> - have clear procedures for employees to raise grievances
> - tackle any instances of bullying and harassment and make it clear such behaviour will not be tolerated.’

Role

‘Role’ means ‘whether people understand their role within the organisation and whether the organisation ensures that the person does not have conflicting roles’. The standard is that:

- ‘Employees indicate that they understand their role and responsibilities; and
- Systems are in place locally to respond to any individual concerns.’

To achieve this the employer should show that:

- ‘The organisation ensures that, as far as possible, the different requirements it places upon employees are compatible;
- The organisation provides information to enable employees to understand their role and responsibilities;
- The organisation ensures that, as far as possible, the requirements it places upon employees are clear; and
- Systems are in place to enable employees to raise concerns about any uncertainties or conflicts they have in their role and responsibilities.’

ACAS say in this connection:[41]

> ‘Role: employees will feel anxious about their work and the organisation if they don’t know what is expected of them:
> - carry out a thorough induction for new employees using a checklist of what needs to be covered
> - provide employees with a written statement of employment particulars
> - give employees clear job descriptions

---

40 Ibid.

41 Ibid.

- maintain a close link between individual objectives and organisational goals.'

Change

'Change' includes 'how organisational change (large or small) is managed and communicated in the organisation'. The standard is that:

'• Employees indicate that the organisation engages them frequently when undergoing an organisational change; and
- Systems are in place locally to respond to any individual concerns.'

To achieve this the employer should show that:

'• The organisation provides employees with timely information to enable them to understand the reasons for proposed changes;
- The organisation ensures adequate employee consultation on changes and provides opportunities for employees to influence proposals;
- Employees are aware of the probable impact of any changes to their jobs. If necessary, employees are given training to support any changes in their jobs;
- Employees are aware of timetables for changes;
- Employees have access to relevant support during changes.'

ACAS say in this connection:[42]

> 'Change: change needs to be managed effectively or it can lead to uncertainty and insecurity:
> - plan ahead so changes can be signposted and managers and employees are prepared
> - consult with employees about prospective changes so they have a real input and work together with you to solve problems.'

The HSE also launched a brand new dedicated stress website in February 2009.

1.3.3 Action in practice

1.3.3.1 Do nothing?

Notwithstanding the legal requirements,[43] many employers have historically taken the view, and some may still take the view, that they wish to take no proactive action in respect of managing workplace stress and bullying. Although such an attitude might be unlawful, they may consider that prosecution by the HSE is unlikely and that given the difficulties in successfully pursuing stress and bullying at work claims through the courts, the risk of a successful claim is very small. They

42 Ibid.
43 Outlined in **1.3.1** and dealt with more fully in Chapter 2.

subscribe to the view that pressure is good for business performance and efficiency and that, if there are consequences, then these are 'all in the mind'. The longer-term and hidden 'iceberg' effect on productivity of work-related stress is ignored in favour of the short-term economic gain achieved by their employees working longer hours.

For a common law claim to succeed an employee will usually have to establish that the possibility of psychiatric injury was foreseeable. Employers may well take the view that in most cases where no vulnerability has been declared or made obvious, foreseeability of injury will be hard for the employee to establish. And, notwithstanding the legal protections contained in the Disability Discrimination Act 1995 (DDA 1995), employees are often reluctant to disclose potential psychiatric vulnerability fearing the potential impact on their career.

And so far as the stricter duties under European law are concerned (e g to proactively assess and act to eliminate or minimise risk), until 2003 there was no potential civil liability in respect of a failure to undertake a risk assessment. Even now, the recent decision in *Paterson v Surrey Police Authority*[44] shows just how little effect the Management Regulations have had in practice. It is very unfortunate that the way in which the Management Regulations have been interpreted by the courts, particularly in the field of occupational health, has had the effect of reducing their impact in changing employer behaviour to improve workplace health.

Pragmatically it might also be argued that if the employer takes some action in the form of an inadequate risk assessment, the court will look at how far that action falls short of what was required, whereas if he takes no action at all he may escape criticism for the inaction because the court may hold that injury was not foreseeable.

Similarly, some of the 'second breakdown' cases have been successful where an employer has allowed a managed return to employment, but has then failed to manage it. Pragmatically, if an employer refuses to allow an employee to return to work following a breakdown (albeit risking a DDA 1995 claim), he will avoid the risk of a stress at work claim following a second breakdown.

However, ACAS advises:[45]

> **'Is my firm required by law to tackle stress?**
>
> As an employer you have duties under health and safety law to assess and take measures to control risks from work-related stress.
>
> You also have a duty under common law to take reasonable care to ensure the health and safety of your employees. If one of your employees suffers

44 [2008] EWHC 2693 (QB). See **2.2.1**.

45 ACAS Advice leaflet 'Stress at Work', August 2006 at www.acas.org.uk.

from stress related ill-health and the court decides that you should have been able to prevent it, then you could be found to be negligent. There is no limit to the compensation your employee could get from this.

HSE Management Standards and supporting guidance aim to help and encourage employers to meet their legal obligations.

If you dismiss an employee because they have work-related stress, then an employment tribunal will treat this as unfair dismissal unless you can show that you acted reasonably. The Acas Advisory handbook – Discipline and grievances at work gives practical advice on handling problems which may give rise to disciplinary action or dismissal.'

As we have seen,[46] the landscape has completely changed over the past two decades. It will be increasingly difficult for an employer to argue that he had no knowledge or understanding of the risk of occupational stress and workplace bullying. This is particularly so in the case of larger employers with professional managers.

1.3.3.2 Policies

Many larger employers have now adopted stress policies, although this is by no means required. The CIPD state:[47]

'While many organisations have developed stress policies, others have found that a well-being policy is much more effective in recognising the need to maximise the well-being of their employees rather than merely reduce their level of stress. This approach is in line with that taken by the World Health Organisation (1990).'

However, where an employer chooses to adopt a stress policy as part of its method of dealing with occupational stress, the CIPD helpfully point out common matters to be addressed by each employer:

'The policy should

- begin with a clear statement which shows that the organisation is committed to developing a working environment that promotes the health and well-being of the organisation and its employees
- be supported by senior management
- be kept under constant review, together with other company policies, procedures and initiatives to ensure that they maximise employee well-being
- provide for identification of and a regular review of the key well-being indicators
- ensure the provision of effective advice, support, counselling and training to enhance employee well-being

---

46 See **1.3.2.3**.

47 CIPD factsheet 'Stress at Work', December 2008 at www.cipd.co.uk/subjects/health/stress/stress.htm.

- incorporate the process for evaluating the effectiveness of all well-being initiatives.'

The CIPD also list possible signs of employee stress under the headings 'work performance', 'regression' (ie immature behaviour), 'withdrawal' (ie avoiding social contact), 'aggressive behaviour' (including shouting and bullying), 'physical signs' and other out-of-character behaviour.

So far as bullying is concerned, the CIPD state:[48]

> 'A well-designed policy statement is essential in addressing harassment. Policy statements should be agreed with union or employee representatives. A policy does not automatically change attitudes and behaviours. All corporate communication tools should reflect a zero tolerance of bullying and harassment and managers should have clear targets for ensuring that this is not a factor in their teams.'

The same factsheet then sets out the matters which a bullying policy should contain:

'Policies should:
- give examples of what constitutes harassment, bullying and intimidating behaviour including cyber-bullying, work-related events and harassment by third parties
- explain the damaging effects and why it will not be tolerated
- state that it will be treated as a disciplinary offence
- clarify the legal implications and outline the costs associated with personal liability
- describe how to get help and make a complaint, formally and informally
- promise that allegations will be treated speedily, seriously and confidentially and that you prevent victimisation
- clarify the accountability of all managers, and the role of union or employee representatives
- require supervisors/managers to implement policy and ensure it is understood
- emphasise that every employee carries responsibility for their behaviour.'

An employer might forget that he also has legal obligations towards those accused of harassment or bullying. Being accused of harassment or bullying, whether or not the complaint is genuine, is in itself stressful. It is essential that the employer takes care to explain to those who face such allegations why they have to investigate and then deal with this swiftly. Particularly if the policy is contractual, there is always the risk to the employer that breach of procedures might lead to a claim in respect of occupational stress from the alleged bully.

---

[48] CIPD factsheet 'Harassment and Bullying at Work', April 2008 at www.cipd.co.uk/subjects/dvsequl/harassmt/harrass.htm.

1.3.3.3 Risk assessment

As far as the Management Regulations and indeed the HSE are concerned, the key to dealing with occupational stress is risk assessment. For occupational stress this follows the traditional HSE pattern:[49]

- Step 1 Identify the hazards
- Step 2 Decide who might be harmed and how
- Step 3 Evaluate the risk and take action
- Step 4 Record your findings
- Step 5 Monitor and review

The HSE publication 'Management standards for work-related stress' specifies how these can impact specifically on risk assessment for occupational stress.

With regard to 'Step 1 – Identify the hazards' is concerned, the HSE say inter alia:

> 'The starting point is the content of the six Management Standards themselves. It is important to become familiar with these and how they apply in, and translate to, the local context of your workplace. There will be organisational "hot-spots" but these can only be identified by undertaking a systematic risk assessment . . .
>
> The Standards help you to measure performance in managing work-related stress. Each standard provides simple statements about good management practice in each of the six areas . . .
>
> HSE does not expect every employer to meet all the Standards at their first attempt. The Standards are goals that employers should be working towards through an ongoing process of risk assessment and continuous improvement.'

With regard to 'Step 2 – Decide who might be harmed and how', the HSE say inter alia:

> 'Your organisation may already collect information that can be used to obtain an initial broad indication of whether stress is a problem for your organisation. For example:
>
> - High levels of sickness absence may indicate a potential problem area. Checking the reasons given for absence may help identify the cause.

[49] HSE guidelines 'Management standards for work-related stress' at www.hse.gov.uk/stress/standards/standards.htm.

- Being open and honest about stress helps to reduce the perceived stigma and improve the reliability of the reasons staff give for absence.
- Low productivity can be an indicator of problems. Talking to employees should help you explore the reasons behind this.
- High employee turnover could be an indication of high stress levels. Investigate why people are leaving – conducting exit interviews is one way of doing this . . .
- Performance appraisal could offer an opportunity to have a one-to-one discussion about work and to explore whether people in your team are experiencing excessive pressure.
- Team meetings and focus groups can help you assess current performance. They allow you to explore issues in considerable depth and are particularly useful if you want to find out what specific groups of people think about their work. Further information on how to run a focus group is available at the end of this section.'

However, if this is not adequate the HSE provide an 'indicator tool' for conducting an employee survey in respect of working conditions and then provide another tool for the analysis which shows where the individual firm stands in comparison to other organisations.

With regard to 'Step 3 – Evaluate the risk and take action', the HSE say inter alia:

> 'Developing solutions is often the most difficult part of tackling the possible causes of work-related stress. Each workplace and each worker is different, meaning that it is not possible to describe one set of solutions for all circumstances. There are some good examples of what other organisations have done to successfully deal with problematic working conditions that could help you and your employees . . .
>
> The overall aim of each focus group is to draw up recommendations in the form of an action plan (see step 4). It is reasonable that employers/senior management may have to prioritise solutions from the different action plans, but they should communicate back to staff the general results of the risk assessment and their plans for continuous improvement, with dates for review.'

With regard to 'Step 4 – Record your findings', the HSE say inter alia:

> 'If your risk assessment has identified areas of concern and you have taken steps to develop some solutions, it is important that you record your findings.
>
> The best method of achieving this is to write and disseminate an action plan . . .
>
> There is no prescribed method or format for an action plan. However, this site includes a template and worked example you may want to use. The action plan needs to be agreed with employees, senior management and employee representatives. The final plan should be shared with employees.'

With regard to 'Step 5 – Monitor and review', the HSE say inter alia:

> 'It is essential that you review any action you take to tackle stress. There are two elements to this:
>
> - Monitor against your action plan to ensure the agreed actions are taking place.
> - Evaluate the effectiveness of the solutions you implement.
>
> It is important to remember that the Standards are about making steady improvements in the way you manage stress. It is critical that you are committed to continuously working with employees to identify and address the problems in your workplace that could lead to stress-related ill health.'

As can be seen, the HSE guidance for employers in respect of risk assessment for occupational stress is now relatively straightforward to understand and is easy for employers to access online or in print and to implement.

1.3.3.4 External assistance

Employers might bear in mind the availability of external assistance to assist them to comply with their legal duties. Feelings often run high on both sides in stress at work cases and there is often a practical break down in trust and confidence, whether or not that in law constitutes a breach of the implied contractual term to that effect. Employees are often suspicious of dealing with both human resources staff and occupational health.

Many employers offer counselling services for employees. It is important that confidentiality is assured and also that employees understand the extent to which they can be accessed and any limitations (eg if the employee is contemplating legal action). One of the commercial confidential 'whistleblowing' hotline services might be more appropriate for larger employers than traditional counselling services via occupational health. In *Hatton,* the court implied that provision of a confidential counselling service might operate as a complete defence to a stress claim.[50] Although this has been doubted in subsequent cases,[51] there is no doubt that a prudent employer will see the benefit of independent counselling both as a line of defence to a court claim, but also as a way of avoiding or at least minimising stress claims in the first place.

So far as bullying and harassment are concerned, these issues are particularly sensitive and can detrimentally affect working relationships beyond the alleged bully and victim. There is obviously a role in larger employers for external counselling and whistleblowing services. In addition, large employers might consider training staff to be 'harassment

---

[50] See **3.5.4**.

[51] For example, *Dickins v O2 plc* [2008] EWCA Civ 1144, [2009] IRLR 58. See **3.5.4**.

advisers'[52] to provide expert, but informal, advice and sometimes resolution. It may even be appropriate to engage an external mediator to try to resolve conflicts within a team.

1.4 THE FUTURE

1.4.1 Trends

It would seem that occupational stress is likely to remain a significant cause of work related ill-health in the twenty-first century. It is already the second most common cause of absence after musculoskeletal injuries. The HSE have identified this and have produced good, effective guidance on risk assessment. The emphasis is on prevention rather than enforcement through prosecution. However, it will take a considerable time for attitudes to change.

The level of work-related stress has reached a plateau, but there is no sign yet of any fall, notwithstanding the efforts of the HSE. Preventative measures proposed by the HSE are likely to take a considerable time to make any impact as what is required is a significant change in culture and attitude.

1.4.2 Development of the law

As we shall see, the courts have been ambivalent towards common law claims for occupational stress and bullying. The ordinary principles of employer's liability in tort and contract apply, so claims for compensation can be brought. However, having opened the door, the courts seem very concerned to avoid opening the floodgates for large numbers of such claims to succeed. The 16 propositions in *Hatton*, and particularly the emphasis on foreseeability, have certainly made it much more difficult for claimants to succeed.

The European approach to health and safety is to deal with this by introducing the principles of assessment and elimination (or minimisation) of risk and increasingly strict liability of employers for breach. In theory this should go a long way towards improving the prospects of successful claims. However, as we will see, progress has been slow. This is the result of a combination of government reluctance to enable employees to utilise the benefits of the European approach (by failing to allow claims for civil liability for breach of the Management Regulations between 1992 and 2003) and the interpretation of the European directives by the courts with an English gloss of 'reasonable practicability' watering down any stricter liability.

[52] See www.andreaadamstrust.org.

However, the recent House of Lords judgment in *Robb v Salamis Limited*[53] suggests that this attitude may be shifting. It is also becoming harder for employers to argue that they are unaware of the extent and consequences of work-related stress. The HSE materials advising employers how to identify and deal with risk are now easily available. The more recent stress cases of *Intel Incorporation (UK) Ltd v Daw*[54] and *Dickins v O2 Plc*[55] suggest the courts are becoming increasingly impatient with larger employers who do not effectively deal with occupational stress. And, it is submitted, the impact of the Management Regulations must increase with time making it more difficult for employers to escape liability by arguing that injury as a result of occupational stress was not foreseeable.

---

53 [2006] UKHL 56.

54 [2007] EWCA Civ 70, [2007] 2 All ER 126, [2007] ICR 1318, [2007] IRLR 355.

55 [2008] EWCA Civ 1144, [2009] IRLR 58.

CHAPTER 2

THE EMPLOYER'S DUTIES

2.1 SOURCES OF LEGAL LIABILITY

As we have seen,[1] occupational stress is common in the UK. However, the employee has no remedy unless the employer is in breach of a legal duty that has caused injury to him.

Such duties can arise as the result of a number of different kinds of obligation.

First, as a member state of the European Union (EU) the British Government is required to implement directives of the EU into domestic law. With regard to compensation for stress at work, this falls into two distinct categories: the directives requiring governments to protect the health and safety of workers and the directives requiring equal treatment.

Secondly, there is statutory law separate from European obligation. Both health and safety at work law and discrimination law originally had their origins in British statutes rather than in Europe, but are now largely governed by European directives. However, the Protection from Harassment Act 1997 (PFHA 1997) is an example of a British statute imposing civil liability which creates duties on employers.[2]

Thirdly, there are the common law duties imposed by contract and tort.

Some claims might involve overlapping duties in common law, statute and legislation deriving from EU directives.[3]

2.2 EUROPEAN LAW AND STATUTORY DUTIES

As a member state of the EU the UK is required to implement directives of the EU. This is by way of statute or secondary legislation (ie regulations). Very often these simply repeat the wording of the directives, but sometimes this is varied by the government and may lead to

---

1 See **1.2**.

2 See Chapter 4.

3 See Chapter 8 for the opportunities and difficulties this can create.

arguments about whether the government has properly implemented the directive, which in turn can lead to decisions of the European Court of Justice (ECJ) which are binding on the UK.

The courts are required to take a 'purposive approach' to interpretation of regulations deriving from European directives. In essence, this means that in interpreting the wording of regulations, the courts must not simply look at the meaning of the words in isolation but have regard to the purpose of the underlying directive. In particular, in the case of duties to employees, it must be remembered that the purpose of the directive is expressed to be the promotion of health and safety in the workplace and the promotion of equal treatment.

2.2.1 Health and safety at work

Article 118a of the Treaty establishing the European Economic Community (EEC) provides that the EU shall adopt through directives minimum requirements for encouraging improvements, especially in the working environment, to guarantee a better level of protection of the safety and health of workers.

Article 1(2) of the Council Directive[4] of 12 June 1989 on the introduction of measures to encourage improvements in the safety and health of workers at work provides:

> '... general principles concerning the prevention of occupational risks, the protection of safety and health, the elimination of risk and accident factors, the informing, consultation, balanced participation in accordance with national laws and/or practices and training of workers and their representatives, as well as general guidelines for the implementation of the said principles.'

Article 6 sets out the general obligations on employers:

> 'Within the context of his responsibilities, the employer shall take the measures necessary for the safety and health protection of workers, including prevention of occupational risks and provision of information and training, as well as provision of the necessary organization and means.
>
> The employer shall be alert to the need to adjust these measures to take account of changing circumstances and aim to improve existing situations.'

Article 6(2) expands on this by setting out the 'general principles of prevention':[5]

4 Council Directive 89/391/EEC.

5 Repeated as Sch 1 to the Management of Health and Safety at Work Regulations 1999, SI 1999/3242.

'(a) avoiding risks;
(b) evaluating the risks which cannot be avoided;
(c) combating the risks at source;
(d) adapting the work to the individual, especially as regards the design of work places, the choice of work equipment and the choice of working and production methods, with a view, in particular, to alleviating monotonous work and work at a predetermined work-rate and to reducing their effect on health.
(e) adapting to technical progress;
(f) replacing the dangerous by the non-dangerous or the less dangerous;
(g) developing a coherent overall prevention policy which covers technology, organization of work, working conditions, social relationships and the influence of factors related to the working environment;
(h) giving collective protective measures priority over individual protective measures;
(i) giving appropriate instructions to the workers.'

The only potential derogation from the directive is provided by Art 5(4):

> 'This Directive shall not restrict the option of Member States to provide for the exclusion or the limitation of employers' responsibility where occurrences are due to unusual and unforeseeable circumstances, beyond the employers' control, or to exceptional events, the consequences of which could not have been avoided despite the exercise of all due care.'

A whole host of specific health and safety provisions are incorporated in the so-called 'six-pack' regulations (eg work equipment, protective equipment, working at heights and so on). None is usually directly relevant to stress at work claims, other than the regulations governing management of health and safety in the workplace. The Management of Health and Safety at Work Regulations 1992[6] came into force on 1 January 1993 and were replaced by the Management of Health and Safety at Work Regulations 1999 ('the Management Regulations') on 29 December 1999.[7]

The Management Regulations provide:

'3.—(1) Every employer shall make a suitable and sufficient assessment of—
(a) the risks to the health and safety of his employees to which they are exposed whilst they are at work; and
(b) the risks to the health and safety of persons not in his employment arising out of or in connection with the conduct by him of his undertaking,

for the purpose of identifying the measures he needs to take to comply with the requirements and prohibitions imposed upon him by or under the relevant statutory provisions.'

---

6 SI 1992/2051.
7 SI 1999/3242.

Regulation 4 requires employers to carry out preventive and protective measures on the basis of the 'general principles of prevention' in the Directive[8] which are set out in Sch 1 to the Regulations. Paragraphs (d) and (g) are of most interest in respect of stress at work claims.

Regulation 6 additionally imposes a requirement of 'health surveillance':

> '. . . as is appropriate having regard to the risks to their health and safety which are identified by the assessment.'

This may be of particular use to show that the employer ought to have been aware of levels of stress within the organisation.

In addition Regulation 13 provides:

> '(1) Every employer shall, in entrusting tasks to his employees, take into account their capabilities as regards health and safety.
>
> (2) Every employer shall ensure that his employees are provided with adequate health and safety training—
> (a) on their being recruited into the employer's undertaking; and
> (b) on their being exposed to new or increased risks because of—
> (i) their being transferred or given a change of responsibilities within the employer's undertaking,
> (ii) the introduction of new work equipment into or a change respecting work equipment already in use within the employer's undertaking,
> (iii) the introduction of new technology into the employer's undertaking, or
> (iv) the introduction of a new system of work into or a change respecting a system of work already in use within the employer's undertaking.
>
> (3) The training referred to in paragraph (2) shall—
> (a) be repeated periodically where appropriate;
> (b) be adapted to take account of any new or changed risks to the health and safety of the employees concerned; and
> (c) take place during working hours.'

All of these training requirements may be of importance where stress at work arises from change in the workplace or new methods of working.

So far as derogation from the requirements is concerned, Regulation 5 provides:

> 'Every employer shall make and give effect to such arrangements as are appropriate, having regard to the nature of his activities and the size of his undertaking, for the effective planning, organisation, control, monitoring and review of the preventive and protective measures.'

---

8 Directive 89/391/EEC, Art 6(2).

It will be noted that this appears to be wider than the corresponding provision in Art 5(4) and the reference to 'nature of his activities and the size of his undertaking' appears to open the door to a defence of 'reasonable practicability'. Whether or not the government has adequately implemented the directive in this regard may have to be litigated in the ECJ in due course.

The Management Regulations have not yet generated the same interpretative case-law as their fellow six-pack regulations. The reason for this is quite simple. Both the Management Regulations of 1992 and 1999 provided:[9]

> 'Breach of a duty imposed by these Regulations shall not confer a right of action in any civil proceedings.'

Presumably under pressure from the EU to implement the directive fully (by giving workers the ability to enforce their rights under it), the government eventually introduced the Management of Health and Safety at Work and Fire Precautions (Workplace) (Amendment) Regulations 2003[10] which provide with effect from 27 October 2003:

> 'For regulation 22 there shall be substituted the following regulation—
>
> > "Restriction of civil liability for breach of statutory duty
> >
> > 22. Breach of a duty imposed on an employer by these Regulations shall not confer a right of action in any civil proceedings insofar as that duty applies for the protection of persons not in his employment."'

So, for employees, a breach of the Management Regulations is now actionable in civil proceedings. This is not, however, in any way retrospective. In *Sayers v Cambridgeshire County Council*[11] Ramsay J held:

> 'I do not consider that the 2003 amendment regulation which came into effect on 27 October 2003 had retrospective effect. Even on the most purposive construction of the Regulations, it does not impose retrospective liability on employers …
>
> I note that this was the conclusion which was reached in *Westwood v. Accantia* (Unreported, 29 April 2005) at paragraphs 145 and 146 in relation to the effect of the 2003 amendment on the 1992 Regulations. In considering an application for permission to appeal, albeit by reference to the task of applying the 2003 amendment to the 1992 Regulations, Rix LJ considered it an "impossible task" in the absence of an express provision.'

---

9 Management of Health and Safety at Work Regulations 1999, SI 1999/3242 (as originally passed), reg 22.

10 SI 2003/2457.

11 [2006] EWHC 2029; [2007] IRLR 29.

In theory at least, the Management Regulations impose a degree of strict liability for breach on the employer. However, because of the traditional approach to employers' liability claims before introduction of the European directives, the courts are often reluctant to construe them other than in accordance with the way in which they construe ordinary English statutes. Therefore, for example, 'reasonable practicability' is often used to qualify duties even though this is not expressly stated in the regulations.

However, in connection with risk assessments (albeit not for stress) in *Robb v Salamis Limited*[12] Lord Hope said:

> 'The risk that a person may fall from a ladder if it slips because it is not fixed securely is a known risk. The question is whether that risk was foreseeable in this case. The issue of whether there was a risk that the ladder might not be replaced properly ought to have been examined as a matter of generality. This was an exercise which the Extra Division expressly rejected: see para 110. But generality is what a risk assessment exercise of the kind referred to in regulation 4(2) requires. The scope of the exercise is no less exacting than that required at common law. The employer must anticipate that it may not be possible to predict the precise ways in which situations of risk may arise, especially where the risk is created by carelessness. The employer is liable even if he did not foresee the precise accident that happened . . .'

This might be applied in stress at work claims where a general risk assessment on the stresses faced by employees has not been properly carried out or the findings of a risk assessment have not been implemented.

The claimant must still prove that the breach of statutory duty caused the injury. Contributory negligence will apply in the same way as for claims for breach of the common law duty of care.[13]

Because the Management Regulations did not provide for a civil remedy for breach at the time of the facts giving rise to the claims, the Court of Appeal decisions on stress claims have focussed on the extent of the common law duties. It has been suggested that these decisions would have been decided differently had the Management Regulations given rise to civil liability.[14] Whilst the statutory requirement to undertake risk assessments certainly gives a new dimension to claims, it is still necessary for the claimant to show how the risk assessment would have made a difference, which is not always straightforward. Furthermore the wording of Regulation 5 might in effect re-introduce a defence of reasonable practicability not very different to that in common law.

---

12 [2006] UKHL 56.

13 See **3.6**.

14 See, for example, A Buchan 'Stress at work: is Hatton v. Sutherland still good law?', Proceedings of the Industrial Law Society, 2006 at www.industriallawsociety.org.uk.

In *Paterson v Surrey Police Authority*[15] the judge was not impressed. Mr Paterson was employed as the estate manager of a large site. He argued that he suffered a nervous breakdown as a result of stress at work caused by excessive hours and irregular call outs night and day. No formal risk assessments were carried out. He argued that there had been a breach of the Management Regulations. However, in dismissing the claim the judge held:

> 'The provisions of the 1999 Regulations which I have quoted seem to be vague. There is no definite requirement as to when an assessment for the purposes of Regulation 3(1) ought to be undertaken. It seems that the assessment does not have to be undertaken in any particular form, for example by compiling some sort of document. All that is required, in the case of an employer employing five or more employees, is that the significant findings of the assessment, and any group of employees identified as being especially at risk, be recorded. The form of the required record is not specified. In any event the purpose of the assessment is to consider risks to health and safety to which employees are exposed whilst at work for the purpose of identifying steps to be taken to comply with the requirements and prohibitions imposed by other, unidentified, statutory provisions. Thus what appears to be necessary is to consider any applicable statutory provisions contravention of which would expose an employee to risks to health or safety and then to consider what measures should be taken to avoid contravention. There does not seem to be a requirement in Regulation 3 to consider the health and safety of an employee more generally or to identify steps which might protect the health and safety of the employee, rather than steps to secure compliance with other statutory provisions. In the present case the "relevant statutory provisions" for which Miss Hobhouse contended were the material provisions of the 1998 Regulations, to which I shall come. However, the effect of the position adopted by Miss Hobhouse, I think, was that it was contended that the Authority should have considered the risks to the health of Mr. Paterson if it did not comply with the provisions of the 1998 Regulations.'

It is submitted that this is not an appropriate approach to the Management Regulations. To understand the purpose of a risk assessment, the court can consider an 'Approved Code of Practice' or 'Management Standards'. And with a view to a purposive interpretation, the directive itself shows that it is aimed at improving health and safety. The approach taken by the judge would certainly not be acceptable in respect of risks of physical injury and, it is submitted, is not in accordance with the comments of the Lords in *Robb v Salamis*. However, the judgment gives an indication of how the judiciary might view such claims in practice.

The Working Time Regulations 1998[16] which implemented Council Directive 89/391/EEC do not expressly provide for a civil remedy for

---

[15] [2008] EWHC 2693 (QB).

[16] SI 1998/1833, amended by SI 2002/3128 and SI 2003/1684.

breach. In *Barber v RJB Mining (UK) Ltd*[17] and *Sayers v Cambridgeshire County Council*[18] two High Court judges have held that non-compliance does not in itself establish a cause of action for breach of statutory duty. This issue has also been considered by the Court of Appeal in *IRC v Ainsworth and others*[19] where they held:

> 'It is that the Working Time Regulations were plainly intended to provide a single and exclusive regime for the enforcement of the new statutory rights.'

However, it should be noted that Maurice Kay LJ was rejecting an argument that rights under the Wages Act 1996 could be applied to the Working Time Regulations as:

> '. . . I do not consider that in 1996, Parliament can have intended to refer to a subsequently created statutory right which comes with its own enforcement regime.'

IRC v Ainsworth was not related to a claim for compensation for stress at work. In *Hone v Six Continents Retail*,[20] where the employee was working well in excess of the limits imposed by the Working Time Regulations, at first instance the claim was pleaded at common law and no claim was brought for breach of statutory duty. In the Court of Appeal the employee's claim was upheld at common law on the ground that he had established reasonable foreseeability,[21] and the Court of Appeal recorded that the employee would also if necessary:

> '. . . have sought to argue that a breach of the Working Time Regulations of itself gave rise to a discrete civil claim against the defendants either for breach of statutory duty or for breach of an implied term of the contract of employment or both. As I say, we have heard no argument on that point.'

This point might therefore be open to argument in a subsequent claim.

2.2.2 Equal treatment

The other duty imposed by European law on employers, breach of which might lead to claims for psychiatric injury caused by work-related stress, is that of the requirement for equal, non-discriminatory treatment. The UK had already introduced its own statutory duty not to discriminate on the grounds of sex (Sex Discrimination Act 1975) or race, nationality or ethnic origin (Race Relations Act 1976) before the requirements imposed by the EU came into effect.

---

17 [1999] ICR 679.
18 [2006] EWHC 2029 (QB).
19 [2005] EWCA Civ 441.
20 [2005] EWCA Civ 922.
21 See discussion at **3.4.6**.

However, the various Equal Treatment Directives[22] now govern this field and UK domestic legislation has had to be amended accordingly.

The European Treaty provides for equality between women and men as a fundamental principle[23] and imposes a positive obligation on the EU to promote it in all its activities. Article 141 of the Treaty deals specifically with equal opportunities and equal treatment of men and women in matters of employment and occupation.

With regard to sex discrimination the amending Equal Treatment Directive[24] was made on 23 September 2002 and was designed to modernise the earlier Equal Treatment Directive.[25] Importantly for stress at work claims the new directive incorporated the following definitions:

> 'harassment: where an unwanted conduct related to the sex of a person occurs with the purpose or effect of violating the dignity of a person, and of creating an intimidating, hostile, degrading, humiliating or offensive environment
>
> sexual harassment: where any form of unwanted verbal, non-verbal or physical conduct of a sexual nature occurs, with the purpose or effect of violating the dignity of a person, in particular when creating an intimidating, hostile, degrading, humiliating or offensive environment.'

The new directive expressly provided that:

> 'Harassment and sexual harassment within the meaning of this Directive shall be deemed to be discrimination on the grounds of sex and therefore prohibited.
>
> A person's rejection of, or submission to, such conduct may not be used as a basis for a decision affecting that person.'

This was incorporated into UK law by the Employment Equality (Sex Discrimination) Regulations 2005[26] with effect from 1 October 2005.

So far as other forms of discrimination are concerned, the EU also implemented the principle of equal treatment between persons irrespective of racial or ethnic origin.[27] A directive implementing a general framework for equal treatment in employment and occupation[28] was introduced on 27 November 2000 and established:

---

22 76/207/EEC and 2002/73/EC.
23 Articles 2 and 3(2) of the EC Treaty.
24 2002/73/EC.
25 76/207/EEC.
26 SI 2005/2467.
27 Directive 2000/43/EC.
28 Directive 2000/78/EC.

> '. . . any direct or indirect discrimination based on religion or belief, disability, age or sexual orientation as regards the areas covered by this Directive should be prohibited throughout the Community.'

In the UK these matters are incorporated into domestic law by means of the Sex Discrimination Act 1975, the Race Relations Act 1976, the Disability Discrimination Act 1995, the Employment Equality (Religion or Belief) Regulations 2003,[29] the Employment Equality (Sexual Orientation) Regulations 2003[30] and the Employment Equality (Age) Regulations 2006.[31]

The government proposes to harmonise the provisions of these various anti-discriminatory statutes and statutory instruments by means of the proposed Equality Bill 2008 (previously known as the Single Equality Bill), which is intended to be legislated in 2009. Until then, there are some differences between the various legislative provisions[32] but in general, the various pieces of discrimination legislation should be construed together to try to resolve inconsistencies between them.[33]

The equality legislation outlaws direct discrimination,[34] indirect discrimination,[35] harassment and victimisation.[36] Disability discrimination contains some important differences.[37]

2.3 OTHER STATUTORY DUTIES

2.3.1 Unfair dismissal

The single most important statutory protection for employees is the right not to be unfairly dismissed.[38] A claim for unfair dismissal can be brought to an employment tribunal even where the employee has resigned in circumstances which constitute a repudiatory breach of contract by the employer (which is relatively common in stress claims).[39]

---

29 SI 2003/1660.

30 SI 2003/1661.

31 SI 2006/1031.

32 See generally Chapter 5.

33 *Anyanwu and Another v South Bank Student Union and Another and Commission for Racial Equality* [2001] UKHL 14, [2001] 2 All ER 353, [2001] 1 WLR 638.

34 Discrimination in an employment context against a person for a particular reason provided for by statute. See **5.3.1**.

35 Where an apparently neutral provision, criterion or practice would put persons of one sex, etc at a particular disadvantage compared with persons of a different sex, etc. This is usually of limited application in cases of psychiatric injury.

36 These two concepts are of key importance in stress at work claims. See **5.3.1**.

37 See **5.4** in respect of disability.

38 Employment Rights Act 1996, s 98.

39 See **5.1**.

However, the importance of unfair dismissal as a remedy for employees complaining of psychiatric injury resulting from stress has diminished as a result of the combined effects of the decision in *Dunnachie v Kingston upon Hull City Council*[40] that compensation for non-pecuniary loss cannot be awarded for unfair dismissal[41] and the statutory cap on compensation for unfair dismissal.[42]

2.3.2 Other statutory protections for employees

The Employment Rights Act 1996 further provides protections for employees in respect of:[43]

- whistleblowing;
- trade union related reasons;
- health and safety cases; and
- as employee representatives.

2.3.3 Non-discriminatory harassment

The PFHA 1997 protects employees from non-discriminatory harassment.

Employers will be often be vicariously liable for such harassment in the workplace.[44]

2.4 COMMON LAW DUTIES

The employer owes duties at common law in both tort and contract, which can be summarised as a duty to take reasonable care of the employee's health and safety. This can be expressed either as a duty of care in tort or as an implied term of the contract of employment. For all practical purposes the duty is the same whether expressed in contract or tort, although the language of tort is used in most of the case-law. In *Frost v Chief Constable of South Yorkshire Police*[45] Lord Steyn said that:

> '. . . the rules to be applied when an employee brings an action against his employer for harm suffered at his workplace are the rules of the law of tort. One is therefore thrown back to the ordinary rules of the law of tort which

40 [2004] UKHL 36, [2004] 3 All ER 1011, [2004] 3 WLR 310, [2004] ICR 1052, [2004] IRLR 727, [2005] 1 AC 226.

41 See **6.3.1**.

42 See **7.3.2**.

43 See **5.5**.

44 See **4.3**.

45 [1999] 2 AC 455.

> contain restrictions on the recovery of compensation for psychiatric harm . . . The duty of an employer to safeguard his employees from harm could also be formulated in contract . . . But such a term could not be wider than the duty imposed by the law of tort.'

Although for the purpose of greater ease of understanding and analysis the tort of 'negligence' is split into duty, breach, causation and damage, it is impossible totally to disentangle the concepts, particularly as 'foreseeability' permeates all. It is essential to bear all elements in mind when considering whether liability is likely on particular facts.

From the outset the court has always limited the scope of the duty of care arising under the neighbour principle by a number of different control mechanisms, nowadays usually stated as 'foreseeability', 'proximity' and 'justice and fairness'.[46] In the context of stress at work claims, it has been argued that the principles enunciated in the case-law are 'just a series of filters designed to allow only the claims perceived as meritorious to succeed'.[47]

The control mechanisms are generally used as floodgates where the courts are concerned that there may be a flood of claims on the same or similar issue. It is at the boundaries of personal injury law that this becomes a problem; most cases are, of course, straightforward. However, the principles behind this are difficult to ascertain. In *Gregg v Scott*[48] Lord Nicholls said:

> '"Floodgates" is not a convincing reason for letting injustice stand unremedied. This reason is invariably advanced whenever a development of the law is under consideration.'

And in *St James & Seacroft University Hospital NHS Trust v Parkinson*[49] Brooke LJ traced the course of development of the law of tort over the previous 25 years:

> 'When *Emeh* was decided in July 1984 the law of negligence was quite simple. In *Anns v Merton London Borough Council* [1978] AC 728 Lord Wilberforce had propounded a two stage test. First, the court had to ask whether as between the alleged wrong-doer and the person who had suffered damage there was a sufficient relationship of proximity or neighbourhood such that, in the reasonable contemplation of the former, carelessness on his part might be likely to cause damage to the latter. If the answer was "yes", then the court had to consider whether there were any

---

46 *Caparo Industries plc v Dickman* [1990] 2 AC 605, HL.

47 Andrew Hogarth QC 'Hatton v Sutherland – a stress free guide to stress at work claims?', Proceedings of the Industrial Law Society, 2002 at www.industriallawsociety-.org.uk.

48 [2005] UKHL 2, [2005] 2 AC 176.

49 (2001) 61 BMLR 100, [2001] 2 FLR 401, [2001] 3 All ER 97, [2001] 3 WLR 376, [2001] EWCA Civ 530, [2001] Fam Law 592, [2001] Lloyd's Rep Med 309, [2001] Lloyds Rep Med 309, [2001] PIQR Q12, [2001] PNLR 43, [2002] 2 FCR 65, [2002] QB 266.

considerations which ought to negative, or to reduce or limit, the scope of the duty or the class of person to whom it was owed, or the damages to which a breach of any duty might give rise.

Since 1984 successive decisions of the House of Lords have made the law of negligence much more complicated. The simple approach in *Anns* was eventually abandoned. In different complex factual situations the House of Lords now invented different techniques for identifying situations outside the normal run of cases involving physical injury or physical damage (often coupled with consequential loss) in which the courts might uphold a claim for damages for negligence founded on economic loss.

The researches of counsel have shown that recourse to the principles of distributive justice, familiar as they were to Aristotle, has only recently penetrated this field of English law. Lord Hoffmann drew on recent academic writings on the topic in his speech in *Frost v Chief Constable of South Yorkshire* [1999] 2 AC 455, where he was concerned to resolve the conundrum posed by the decision of the Court of Appeal in that case which had permitted police officers at the scene of the Hillsborough football tragedy to recover compensation for suffering post-traumatic stress disorder when such recovery was denied to relatives of the dead who had suffered in the same way.

Lord Hoffmann took the view that the search for principle in this area of the law had been called off in the earlier Hillsborough case, *Alcock v Chief Constable of South Yorkshire Police* [1992] 1 AC 310. He considered that until there was legislative change the courts had got to live with the control mechanisms stated in the *Alcock* case and that any judicial developments had to take them into account. As a result, the House of Lords was engaged, not in the bold development of principle, but in a practical attempt, under adverse conditions, to preserve the general perception of the law as a system of rules which was fair between one citizen and another.'

The most important of these control mechanisms in stress at work claims is 'foreseeability'.[50]

2.4.1 Health and safety at work

2.4.1.1 Duty to protect health and safety

At common law an employer is under a duty to take reasonable care to provide a safe system of work for the employee. This is a well-established duty in respect of prevention of physical injury. As Lady Justice Hale put it in *Hatton v Sutherland*:[51]

---

50 See **3.4**.

51 *Hatton v Sutherland; Barber v Somerset County Council; Jones v Sandwell Metropolitan Borough Council; Bishop v Baker Refractories Ltd* [2002] EWCA Civ 76, [2002] 2 All ER 1, [2002] ICR 613, [2002] IRLR 263, 68 BMLR 115, [2002] All ER (D) 53 (Feb), CA.

> 'All employers have a duty to take reasonable care for the safety of their employees: to see that reasonable care is taken to provide them with a safe place of work, safe tools and equipment, and a safe system of working: see *Wilsons & Clyde Coal Co Ltd v English* [1938] AC 57.'

This can be framed in a contractual context too. In *Webspe*r *v Thanet District Council*[52] the employee claimed constructive dismissal. He had been off work with work-related stress. The only alternatives offered to him were within the same division, even though the Council had many other divisions in which he could have been deployed. The Employment Appeal Tribunal (EAT) upheld the claim:

> 'It seems to us that since it is common ground that work in the Recovery Section caused ill-health, and since the Applicant was complaining that work anywhere in the Division would cause the same problem, the insistence by the Respondent on looking only for alternative work only within the Division, did not meet his point. In the terms of this case, it did not represent discharge of the contractual term that he would be provided with a safe place to work.'

This duty, whether pleaded in contract or tort or both, is likely to be the core common law duty pleaded in stress claims.

2.4.1.2 *Duty to protect from harassment*

The duty to protect health and safety incorporates a duty of care to protect the employee from bullying and harassment. This can also be expressed as an implied contractual term that the employer will not either directly or through the line manager bully and harass the employee and will protect the employee from harassment by his co-workers.

As long ago as 1965 in *Veness v Dyson Bell & Co*,[53] Widgery J said:

> 'The plaintiff's pleadings told a story of persecution and bullying by office colleagues at various times between 1953 to 1959, when the plaintiff was employed by the defendants, first as a secretary and, subsequently, as a personal clerk to the partner Mr. Liddell . . . his Lordship was not prepared to say that the plaintiff's statement of claim failed to disclose a cause of action for want of an allegation that the plaintiff's injuries were reasonably foreseeable . . . in the end the issue might be one of degree depending on the reasonableness or otherwise of the conduct of the parties and, as such, was not suitable for disposal in the pleadings as a preliminary point of law.'

In *Wigan Borough Council v Davies*[54] Arnold J sitting in the EAT upheld the decision by an Industrial Tribunal that there was an implied term in the applicant's contract of employment that:

---

52 EAT (Judge McMullen QC, R Chapman, DAC Lambert) 30 October 2002.

53 (1965) *The Times*, May 25.

54 [1979] IRLR 127.

> '. . . the employer shall render reasonable support to an employee to ensure that the employee can carry out the duties of his job without harassment and disruption by fellow workers.'

In *Waters v Metropolitan Police Commissioner*[55] the claimant, who was a female police officer, alleged a serious assault by a fellow officer whilst she was off duty in police accommodation. She alleged that she had made numerous prior complaints of similar, although less serious, behaviour and that it had been ignored by superior officers. The House of Lords confirmed that there was an implied contractual term and a common law duty, Lord Hutton stating:

> 'I consider that a person employed under an ordinary contract of employment can have a valid cause of action in negligence against her employer if the employer fails to protect her against victimisation and harassment which causes physical or psychiatric injury. This duty arises both under the contract of employment and under the common law principles of negligence.'

The duty extends to a duty to remedy harassment complaints promptly. In *Blackburn with Darwen Borough Council v Stanley*[56] the employee had raised a grievance about bullying and harassment as early as 1999. Despite various investigations and reports, nothing was done (and recommendations were not implemented) by 2003 when the employee resigned and claimed a constructive dismissal. The EAT held that the failure to investigate and remedy the complaint promptly was a breach of the implied term.

This is the core common law duty likely to be pleaded in bullying claims.

2.4.2 Express contractual terms

2.4.2.1 Statement of principal terms

The principal source of the obligations of the employer towards his employee is the contract of employment. The terms of the contract of employment can be verbal or written and can be contained in one or several documents. A written document stating the main terms of employment must be given by an employer to an employee within 2 months of commencing employment.[57] However, even where this requirement is not breached,[58] the main particulars of employment will rarely state all of the express contractual terms.

It is usually necessary to consider:

---

55 [2000] 4 All ER 934, [2000] 1 WLR 1607, [2000] ICR 1064, HL.
56 EAT (Judge McMullen QC, G Lewis, P Tatlow) 20 January 2005.
57 Employment Rights Act 1996, s 2.
58 The Employment Tribunal may order between 2 and 4 weeks' pay as compensation: Employment Act 2002, s 38.

- the document described as the 'contract of employment' or 'statement of particulars of employment';
- the offer letter (which may contain additional, or different terms);
- job description;
- periodic letters, memos or e-mails containing contractual variations, most often relating to pay, but frequently referring to hours and other conditions of work; and
- disciplinary or grievance procedures expressed to be contractual.

The contractual terms will rarely expressly state that the employer will not subject the employee to stress or bullying. However, in stress at work claims, the hours of work are often important. The express contractual terms should state the normal hours of work and whether overtime is likely or required and whether overtime is paid. In manual or junior office jobs the hours of work are usually clear and overtime paid. In more senior and professional jobs, the contract often provides for normal working hours but requires 'such additional hours as may be necessary for the performance of the duties' without additional remuneration so the old-fashioned distinction between the hourly paid 'blue collar' worker and the salaried 'white collar' worker still remains in practice.

The contract or job description will often set out the main duties of the employee. The stated duties will usually include a catch-all phrase such as 'and such other duties as may be [reasonably] required or assigned to you from time to time'. Even if such a phrase is not included, it is an implied term of the contract that the employer can impose reasonable variations to the job description to meet the needs of the business. However, the job description is a good starting point for an examination of whether the duties imposed on the employee are unreasonable in the light of what the employee was employed to do. The contractual documents should also name the employee's line manager and explain the reporting structure. This is useful in determining to whom the employer has delegated the responsibility for the employee.

Other useful express provisions to consider in the contractual documents include:

- mobility and travel clauses (where unreasonable travelling is causing long hours and stress);
- sick pay; and
- notice periods.

It is of course possible, although unlikely, that the express contractual terms go beyond the implied term to take reasonable steps to protect the health and safety of the employee. If the employee is expected to take unusual risks, the employer might be prepared to accept additional responsibility.

Conversely, it is not lawful for the employer to derogate from his implied common law duty by express contractual terms. The provisions of the Unfair Contract Terms Act 1977 apply so that such a term would be held to be an unlawful exclusion clause.[59]

2.4.2.2 Policies and procedures

It will be a rare case where all terms relevant to a possible claim for occupational stress are incorporated into a single written contract of employment. Ideally, all other written sources of rights and responsibilities will be referred to in the principal written contract. This is rarely the case in practice and it is important in appropriate cases to question the client carefully about any employee benefits and try to ascertain from the nature of such benefits what documents referring to them might exist (which the client may never have personally seen).

In *Christopher Keeley v Fosroc International Ltd*[60] the Court of Appeal examined the extent to which the provisions contained in an employee handbook incorporated by reference into the contract of employment could be held to be enforceable terms of the contract. The court made a useful distinction between parts that are aspirations falling short of a contractual undertaking and contractual provisions. It is necessary to examine closely the words used and the context in each case.

Where the provisions are incorporated as contractual terms, the employer must follow them or risk being in breach of contract. In *Deadman v Bristol City Council*[61] the employee faced allegations of sexual misconduct in the workplace. The Harassment Policy provided for the investigatory panel to consist of three people. Only two people sat on the panel. The Court of Appeal found this to be a breach of contract. However, even if there is a breach of contract, this does not mean that the claim will inevitably succeed. If the breach is relatively minor, the case may well founder on issues of foreseeability or causation anyway[62] as did Mr Deadman's.

Conversely, an employer might be in breach of the implied term of mutual trust and confidence if he insists on following a contractual process to the letter notwithstanding the particular circumstances of the

59 *Brigden v American Express Bank* [2000] IRLR 94.
60 [2006] EWCA Civ 1277.
61 [2007] EWCA Civ 822, [2007] IRLR 888, [2007] All ER (D) 494 (Jul).
62 See Chapters 3 and 6.

employee. In *GMB Trade Union v J Brown*[63] the employer insisted that the employee should submit her grievance to her line manager first in accordance with the policy even though it was her line manager who was the subject of the grievance. She went off sick with stress and depression. The EAT held that the employer had breached the implied term of mutual trust and confidence.

Collective agreements between trade unions and management will usually be incorporated into individual contracts of employment (even for non-union members) but it is unlikely that the client will have all the details easily available. For many public sector jobs, in particular, extensive information relevant to the terms of employment is recorded in collective agreements. The union is an obvious port of call, as is the personnel or human resources department of the employer.

There can also be considerable and important rights incorporated in documents outside the contract of employment. Of key importance is how benefit packages such as income protection benefit, disability benefits, life cover and pensions are treated.[64]

2.4.3 Implied contractual term of mutual trust and confidence

2.4.3.1 Nature of the implied term

It is an implied term of the contract of employment that each party treats the other with trust and confidence. This implied term was examined in depth by the House of Lords in *Mahmud v BCCI; Malik v BCCI.*[65] Two bank workers were made redundant by their employer in each case after more than a decade in employment. Shortly afterwards it became general public knowledge that the bank, the Bank of Credit and Commerce International (BCCI), had operated its business dishonestly. As a result the employees alleged that it was impossible for them to gain employment elsewhere in the banking industry.

The House of Lords confirmed that an implied term of mutual trust and confidence existed. This was of relatively recent origin as a result of the change from the master/servant relationship envisaged by the older case-law to the modern employment relationship. Lord Hoffmann in *Johnson v Unisys*[66] described these developments:

> 'The contribution of the common law to the employment revolution has been by the evolution of implied terms in the contract of employment. The most far reaching is the implied term of trust and confidence.'

---

63 EAT LTL 25 October 2007.
64 See Chapter 10.
65 [1998] AC 20, [1997] 3 All ER 1, [1997] 3 WLR 95, HL.
66 [2001] UKHL 13.

The Lords in *Malik* restated the implied term as follows:

> '. . . without reasonable and proper cause, conduct itself in a manner calculated and likely to destroy or seriously damage the relationship of confidence and trust between employer and employee.'

The Lords point out that:

> '. . . the implied obligation as formulated is apt to cover the great diversity of situations in which a balance has to be struck between an employer's interest in managing his business as he sees fit and the employee's interest in not being unfairly and improperly exploited.'

However, Lord Slynn giving the principal judgment of the court stresses that the conduct has to be unjustified and serious, not trivial:

> '. . . the implied mutual obligation of trust and confidence applies only where there is "no reasonable and proper cause" for the employers conduct, and then only if the conduct is calculated to destroy or seriously damage the relationship of trust and confidence. That circumscribes the potential reach and scope of the implied obligation.'

Lord Nicholls similarly stressed:

> 'The conduct must, of course, impinge on the relationship in the sense that, looked at objectively, it is likely to destroy or seriously damage the degree of trust and confidence the employee is reasonably entitled to have in his employer.'

Finally, the Lords confirmed that whilst a breach of the term is likely to be of such gravity so as to enable the employee to terminate the contract forthwith, the employee does not have to do so and also has a remedy in damages.

There does not have to be a single incident to breach the implied term. In *Lewis v Motorworld Garages Ltd*[67] Glidewell LJ stated:

> 'This breach of this implied obligation of trust and confidence may consist of a series of action on the part of the employer which cumulatively amount to a breach of the term, though each individual incident may not do so. In particular in such a case the last action of the employer which leads to the employee leaving need not itself be a breach of contract; the question is, does the cumulative series of acts taken together amount to a breach of the implied term? (see *Woods v W M Car Services (Peterborough) Ltd* [1981] ICR 666). This is the "last straw" doctrine.'

The test for breach of this implied term is an objective one and the subjective effect on the employee is irrelevant.[68] The 'reasonableness' of

[67] [1986] ICR 157.

[68] *Meikle v Nottinghamshire County Council* [2004] EWCA Civ 859.

an employer is not relevant in assessing breach; the test is whether the breach is so grave that the employee could conclude that by his conduct the employer was repudiating the contract.

The use of this implied term to protect workers from psychiatric injury through excessive stress was recognised by Lord Steyn in the House of Lords in *Johnson v Unisys* where he said:

> '. . . stress-related psychiatric and psychological problems of employees . . . [have] greatly increased . . . These considerations are testimony to the need for implied terms in contracts of employment protecting employees from harsh and unacceptable employment practices . . . Inevitably, the incidence of psychiatric injury due to excessive stress has increased. The need for protection of employees through their contractual rights, express and implied by law, is markedly greater than in the past.'

2.4.3.2 Operation of the implied term of mutual trust and confidence in practice

Horkulak v Cantor Fitzgerald International[69] is an example of the breach of the implied term in a bullying case. Mr Horkulak was an experienced City derivatives trader who had been headhunted by Cantor. As a result of the bullying by his line manager, the judge recorded the following description by his doctor:

> '. . . under threat constantly from his immediate boss of losing his job since December, although he has never been told of any actual thing he has done wrong. He feels he cannot tolerate this any more and broke down yesterday – has been crying and shaking uncontrollably.'

As a result of this breakdown, Mr Horkulak had to give up his City career.

The judge noted that Cantor:

> '(i) admitted Mr Amaitis raised his voice on occasions when he drew the claimant's attention to serious shortcomings in his performance;
> (ii) admitted using words which "might be regarded as extreme in polite conversation but were common currency between Mr Amaitis and the claimant";
> (iii) asserted that "such behaviour" was regarded as acceptable and had a reasonable and proper cause, namely his "frustration at the repeated and serious shortcomings" in the claimant's performance;
> (iv) admitted the occasional banging of the desk in a non-violent and non-intimidatory manner.'

---

69 [2003] EWHC 1918 (QB).

The language was 'foul and abusive', but this was common at Cantor. However, the court found that this was the 'hallmark' of the manager's 'dictatorial style'. As the judge found in respect of one incident:

> 'To threaten "to break" someone "in two" is to adopt the language of criminal intimidators. It was not a criminal threat to harm the claimant but a clear expression of the level of anger and intolerance he harboured for the claimant, which was wholly incompatible with the continuance of a relationship based on mutual trust and confidence.'

The judge found that the employer had breached the implied term of mutual trust and confidence.

Similar findings have arisen in the context of false accusations by the employer,[70] unacceptable abuse by the employer[71] and failure to treat a long-standing employee with dignity.[72]

The implied term of mutual trust and confidence extends to the handling of grievance and disciplinary procedures, although not to the manner of dismissal.[73]

In *Gogay v Herts County Council*[74] a social worker was suspended on full pay following what had wrongly been perceived to be an allegation of child abuse by an 'exceptionally vulnerable child with learning and communication difficulties' 'who had made a series of confusing comments'. The judge found that the defendant had no reasonable grounds for suspension and had failed to carry out a proper investigation. The Court of Appeal upheld the claim for damages for psychiatric injury caused by the breach of the implied term in the way in which the claimant was suspended and investigated.

The duty is to operate grievance and disciplinary procedures in good faith and in accordance with the provisions. In *Deadman* the Court of Appeal rejected the finding of the trial judge that there was an implied term that an investigation would be handled 'sensitively'.

However, it is an implied term that an employer will allow an employee to seek prompt redress for a grievance.[75]

So far as disciplinary procedures are concerned, it is an implied term that these must not be entirely out of proportion to the offence.[76]

---

70 *Robinson v Crompton Parkinson Ltd* (1978) IRLR 61.
71 *Palmanour Ltd v Cedron* [1978] ICR 1008.
72 *Garner v Grange Furnishing* [1977] IRLR 206.
73 See **2.4.3.3**.
74 [2001] 1 FLR 280, [2000] IRLR 703, [2000] Fam Law 883, CA.
75 *Goold (W A) v McConnell* [1995] IRLR 516.
76 *BBC v Beckett* [1983] IRLR 43.

2.4.3.3 *Limitation of application of the implied term (the Addis/Johnson exclusion)*

Claims arising out of a breach of the implied term of mutual trust and confidence can be brought only in respect of psychiatric injury caused during the course of the employment relationship and not as a result of dismissal or the manner of dismissal.

The House of Lords in *Addis v Gramophone Co Ltd*[77] had held that damages for 'injury' caused to the employee by the manner of the dismissal were not recoverable in law. The employer was entitled to bring the contract to an end lawfully by service of proper notice. Even if he did so unlawfully, the employee's claim for compensation was limited to lost benefits during the contractual notice period. As Lord Nicholls put it in *Eastwood and Williams v Magnox*:[78]

> 'In October 1905 Mr Addis was abruptly and ignominiously dismissed as manager of Gramophone Co Ltd in Calcutta. He sued his employer for wrongful dismissal, in proceedings which have cast a long shadow over the common law.'

The court was applying the usual rules that do not normally allow a party in a contract claim to recover compensation for 'distress' or similar injury as a result of breach.

In *Johnson*, the House of Lords had the opportunity to review the *Addis* case and to overrule or distinguish it. To do so would have been in line with the growing trend towards awards for 'non-physical injury' arising out of the employment relationship.

In *Johnson*, the employee had suffered from work-related stress and the employer was aware of his psychological vulnerability. The employer then raised unsubstantiated allegations as to his conduct, called him to a meeting without specific allegations being put to him and he was sacked summarily the same day. He suffered a breakdown.

The House of Lords dismissed the employee's appeal and by a majority affirmed the decision in *Addis*. The fact that Parliament had legislated in respect of unfair dismissal and had capped the employer's potential liability weighed heavily on the majority.

In the conjoined appeals of *Eastwood and Williams v Magnox* and *McCabe v Cornwall County Council* the House of Lords revisited the problem but decided by a majority not to review their decision in *Johnson*.

---

[77] (1909) UKHL 1 (26 July 1909), [1909] AC 488.

[78] [2004] UKHL 35.

Mr Eastwood's supervisor had a grudge against him. A campaign was waged to produce false evidence for disciplinary proceedings. Mr Eastwood was given a final warning for a trivial incident. Mr Eastwood appealed. Mr Williams was told by the supervisor to produce a false statement and when he refused he was himself threatened with investigation when there were no grounds for this. Mr Eastwood's appeal succeeded and the warning was reduced. However, false allegations of sexual harassment were subsequently made against Mr Eastwood and Mr Williams, encouraged by the supervisor. They were very publicly suspended. After unfair proceedings, both men developed a depressive illness. Both were dismissed. They settled claims for unfair dismissal (Mr Williams after establishing liability at a tribunal, but before compensation was assessed and Mr Eastwood before any hearing) and expressly reserved the right to pursue a personal injury claim.

In the conjoined appeal Mr McCabe was a teacher accused of sexual misconduct. He successfully claimed unfair dismissal (although his award was reduced by 20% for contributory conduct). He suffered psychiatric damage and brought a personal injury claim. After the Lords' decision in *Johnson* he sought to limit his claim to pre-dismissal damage as a result of the unfair procedure.

The House of Lords allowed the claims by Eastwood and Williams and dismissed the claim by McCabe. Lord Nicholls said:

> 'As was to be expected, the decision in *Johnson* has given rise to demarcation and other problems. They were bound to arise. Dismissal is normally the culmination of a process. Events leading up to a dismissal decision take place during the subsistence of an employment relationship. If an implied term to act fairly, or a term to that effect, applies to the events leading up to the dismissal, but not to the dismissal itself, unsatisfactory results are inevitable.'

So, as the law currently stands, an employee who is particularly badly treated by his employer in the manner of dismissal (but not otherwise) so as to cause psychiatric injury will have no cause of action, whereas an employee who is badly treated in the disciplinary process (but not in the manner of dismissal) does. The distinction can have interesting implications for causation too. Take, by way of an example, a senior employee who is suffering from stress at work. He is having outpatient psychiatric treatment for this, which is known to his employers. Nothing is done about the stress at work. He makes a serious error at work. He suffers a nervous breakdown and is admitted as an inpatient at a psychiatric hospital. He responds well to treatment. A week later the employers ask him to take a leave of absence from hospital to come into the office, ostensibly to hand over files. During the meeting he is confronted with his mistake, summarily dismissed for gross misconduct and escorted from the building. He suffers a serious relapse and is unable to work again for some years. In bringing the stress at work claim, no damages can be awarded for the injury specifically caused by the manner of his dismissal. It might be hard to separate this from the damage caused by the previous stress which he suffered whilst he was at work. However, the employer might argue that all of the continuing symptoms were in fact caused by the horrific experience of being dragged from a psychiatric hospital to be summarily dismissed. In fact, they might wish to play up the humiliating and inhuman nature of the experience knowing that they are not liable in law for the resulting damage. This would not perhaps be an attractive defence, but one which in principle that would have reasonable prospects of success.

2.4.4 Not to work in excess of the limitations imposed by the Working Time Regulations

It is an implied term of the contract of employment that the employer will not require the employee to work hours in excess of the maximum prescribed by the Working Time Regulations unless the employee has lawfully 'opted out'.[79]

2.4.5 Not to unreasonably deprive of benefits

Ordinarily, an employer has the right to terminate the employment of an employee by giving contractual notice. Such a dismissal is not a breach of contract. Nor will it be unfair if it is for one of the five potentially fair reasons and the employer has acted reasonably in all the circumstances.[80] Even if the dismissal is unfair, unless it is also discriminatory, the compensatory award will be capped at the statutory maximum.[81] However, in certain cases the exercise of this right might lead to severe loss to the employee. In particular, if the employee is in receipt of income protection benefit and the policy requires him to remain employed, consideration needs to be given to whether the employer can lawfully dismiss on the ground of incapacity with the consequent effect of the employee losing the right to benefits from the insurer of the income protection benefit scheme. In *Briscoe v Lubrizol Limited*[82] the Court of Appeal implied a term into the contract of employment that:[83]

> '. . . the employer ought not to terminate the employment as a means to remove the employee's entitlement to benefit but the employer can dismiss for good cause whether that be on the ground of gross misconduct or, more generally, for some repudiatory breach by the employee.'

---

79 Per Gage J QB, *Barber and Others v RJB Mining (UK) Ltd* [1999] ICR 679; [1999] IRLR 308.

80 See **5.2**.

81 See **7.3.2**.

82 *Briscoe v Lubrizol Limited* [2002] EWCA Civ 508, [2002] IRLR 607, [2002] Emp LR 819.

83 This is dealt with in more detail at **9.8**.

Similarly, *First West Yorkshire Ltd t/a First Leeds v Haigh*[84] dealt with lost rights to an ill-health pension because of dismissal. Although the EAT did not need to reach a conclusion they indicated that a similar term might be implied into the contract of employment. And in *Adin v Sedco Forex International Resources Ltd*[85] the court held that employer was not able to lawfully dismiss an employee so as to disentitle him from benefiting under the company sick pay scheme.

2.5 LIABILITY FOR WORKERS OTHER THAN EMPLOYEES

2.5.1 Self-employed workers

The law as to whether a person is an employee or not is beyond the scope of this work, but it requires an analysis of the factual matrix including mutuality of obligation and control.[86] It is important to recognise in this context that the distinction between employed and self-employed is not just the label, it is necessary to look at all surrounding circumstances of each case.

Generally speaking, however, if the claimant is genuinely a self-employed subcontractor the duties of employers to employees set out in this chapter will not apply. The duties in respect of discrimination set out in **2.2.2** relate to employment (and partnership),[87] but the equlaity legislation often provides similar duties with regard to the provision of services which might apply. The PFHA 1997 (discussed at **2.2.3**) is not, of course, restricted to employees. However, vicarious liability is much less likely to be imposed for the acts of non-employees.

2.5.2 Partners

Where a partner in a firm or business is in reality an employee, even though described as and held out to be a partner, then the 'employer' owes the same duties to the 'partner' as he would to an employee. This can be so even if the 'partner' is named on the notepaper of the firm and treated as self-employed for tax purposes. However, if there is an element of participation in management of the business, a contribution of capital, or a sharing of profits or, even more significantly, any losses, then the likelihood is that the partner will be treated as an 'owner' rather than an employee. This will almost certainly be the case for an 'equity partner'.

---

84 UKEAT/0246/07/RN (LTL 20 November 2007).

85 [1997] IRLR 280 OH (Lord Coulsfield) 7 January 1997.

86 See *Ready-Mixed Concrete (South East) Ltd v Minister of Pensions and National Insurance* [1968] 2 QB 497.

87 See **2.5.2**.

This issue can be of particular significance because many City firms (particularly, although not exclusively, in law and accountancy) practise as traditional unlimited partnerships or through limited liability partnerships (LLPs). This is so even in the case of businesses with multi-million pound turnovers and hundreds of partners. Inevitably, with the long hours and high-value transactions there is significant work-related pressure and stress. In a similar environment (eg bank or other financial institution) where the business is conducted through a corporate structure, even senior executives will be employees with their employer subject to the duties set out in this chapter.[88] In many such partnerships, management is entirely devolved to specific partners and whilst he is in law an owner, the individual partner may for all practical purposes be treated as an employee with no management rights (except perhaps by way of voting for appointments to a management body and over key decisions such as mergers).

However, it is important to note that the provisions of the UK equality legislation[89] apply to partners as well as to employees.

For example, the Sex Discrimination Act 1975 provides:

> '11.—(1) It is unlawful for a firm . . . in relation to a position as partner in the firm, to discriminate against a woman—
> (a) in the arrangements they make for the purpose of determining who should be offered that position, or
> (b) in the terms on which they offer her that position, or
> (c) by refusing or deliberately omitting to offer her that position, or
> (d) in a case where the woman already holds that position—
> (i) in the way they afford her access to any benefits, facilities or services, or by refusing or deliberately omitting to afford her access to them, or
> (ii) by expelling her from that position, or subjecting her to any other detriment.'

This was originally limited to partnerships of six or more partners, but was subsequently extended to all partnerships by virtue of s 1(3) of the Sex Discrimination Act 1986.

The prohibition against victimisation[90] and harassment[91] also apply to partners.

88 For example, in *Horkulak v Cantor Fitzgerald International*, Mr Horkulak sought only pure financial loss as a result of the constructive dismissal resulting from bullying. But if he had suffered a recognised psychiatric condition, there is no reason why he could not also have recovered for non-pecuniary loss and associated losses too. And in *Switalski v F&C Asset Management plc* [2008] EAT LTL 9 June 2008 the applicant was described as a 'high-flying City lawyer'.

89 Set out in **2.2.2** and **5.3.1**.

90 Sex Discrimination Act 1975, s 4.

91 Sex Discrimination Act 1975, s 4A.

Similar provisions also apply to partners in respect of all the other equality legislation for employees.

The peculiarity of a partner effectively suing himself (as one of the partners in the defendant firm) was noted, obiter, by Warren J in *Hammonds v Danilunas and Others*,[92] but he held:

> 'It is expressly provided [in the SDA 1975] that 'firm' has the meaning given to it by section 4 Partnership Act 1890. There can be no doubt that, in the context of section 11 [of the SDA 1975], a 'firm' can discriminate against a woman partner notwithstanding that she herself is a partner in the firm; where there is unlawful discrimination within the section, the woman will bring her claim against her partners notwithstanding that those partners are not themselves a firm but only members of a firm of which the woman too is a member.'

Although he was exercised about the position of partners in the firm who were opposed to the discrimination:

> 'It is not clear to me that a partner who is discriminated against in this way would have a claim against dissentient partners who voted against the taking of the unlawful act at least in circumstances where the conduct of the majority to the woman discriminated against was a breach of the duty of good faith owed by the majority to the minority as much as to the woman concerned. In that context one might wonder what the true position is where there is concurrent discrimination against two woman partners. Is each of the two women to be liable (along with all the other partners) to the other woman? Whatever the correct position, which will in any event be dependent on the facts of any particular case, it must at least be arguable that the partners discriminated against could sue all of her partners for discrimination by 'the firm'.'

It seems likely that in practice in most cases the 'firm' will pay the compensation awarded.

The provisions of the PFHA 1997 can also be relied upon by partners in respect of harassment in the workplace in the same way as employees, although the firm will not be vicariously liable for the acts of a partner towards another partner.

The difficulty arises in respect of common law claims. Whereas the existence of a duty of care is usually clear-cut in the workplace, this is not entirely so for a self-employed equity partner who (even in a large partnership) is as a matter of law an owner (or member of an LLP) rather than an employee. There is no clear case-law which establishes that a full equity partner/LLP member can bring a claim for damages against the

[92] [2009] EWHC 216 (Ch).

other partners or the LLP for damages for personal injury. This could be provided for in the Partnership/LLP Members agreement, but this would be unusual.

Indeed, s 10 of the Partnership Act 1890 provides:

> 'Where, by any wrongful act or omission of any partner acting in the ordinary course of the business of the firm, or with the authority of his co-partners, loss or injury is caused to any person *not being a partner in the firm*, or any penalty is incurred, the firm is liable therefor to the same extent as the partner so acting or omitting to act.' (emphasis added)

And this formulation is repeated in s 6(4) of the Limited Liability Partnerships Act 2000:

> 'Where a member of a limited liability partnership is liable to any person *(other than another member of the limited liability partnership)* as a result of a wrongful act or omission of his in the course of the business of the limited liability partnership or with its authority, the limited liability partnership is liable to the same extent as the member.'(emphasis added)

Whether a partner owes a duty of care towards fellow partners is not totally clear as is apparent from the discussion on the subject in the Law Commission's 2003 Report on Partnership Law:

> 'The 1890 Act contains no statement of the duty of care which a partner owes to the partnership. There is uncertainty in both jurisdictions as to the standard of care which is imposed on a partner.
>
> Historically, in English law a partner's duty to the partnership was to act without "culpable" negligence. In the older authorities the nature and extent of the duty owed by one partner to another was not closely explored, and various expressions are found. There are few reported cases of partners attempting to sue each other in negligence.'

The Report concludes that:

> 'As case law contains a number of conflicting formulations of the standard of care, it is not prudent to ignore the uncertainty which has been created. Partners should owe each other duties not to cause personal injury or death or physical damage to a partner's private property through lack of reasonable care.'

It is helpful (although not, of course, determinative) that the Commission concludes that a duty to not cause personal injury to another partner 'should' be owed (although indeed that could be read as implying that at present in the Commission's view it is not owed and so the law should be changed).

There is remarkably little case-law on the subject. In the Scottish case of *Mair v Wood*,[93] one partner brought a claim against the others after being injured on a vessel whilst at sea through the failure of another partner to replace floorboards covering the propeller shaft. This was described by Lord Keith as 'a novel action for which neither party was able to cite any precedent'. In rejecting the claim Lord Keith pointed out:

> 'To take the illustration of a shipwreck, if a partner on board the ship, engaged in trade for the partnership, incurred personal outlay or liability in an attempt to salve ship or cargo, I do not doubt but that he is entitled to be reimbursed by the partnership, and this right of reimbursement might entitle him to recover his expenses in returning himself to the seat of the partnership, including any medical expenses necessary to fit him for the journey. If, however, he lost a leg in the disaster, there is no principle on which the partnership would be bound to compensate him for the permanent loss of a leg. It is a loss incurred while engaged in the partnership affairs, but it is a personal loss compensation for which would have no relation at all to the purposes or objects of the partnership. Illness or incapacity, apart from permanent incapacity, to carry out the partnership contract, does not bring about a dissolution of the partnership nor prevent a partner sharing in its profits. Nor have I ever heard it suggested that a partner is thereby entitled to compensation. If illness or accident gives no right to indemnity from the partnership still less can it give a partner such a right where brought about by the negligence of a fellow-partner.'

However, he concludes:

> 'In such a case the injured partner has a common law remedy against the wrongdoer personally. He has none, in my opinion, against the partnership.'

The only potentially relevant English case-law relates to unincorporated associations such as members' clubs[94] and was surveyed by Warren J in *Hammonds* who accepted that its relevance was limited. This was because he felt that the law had probably moved on since 1950 to impose a duty of care on members of clubs towards other members in some circumstances, and also because the duty of good faith and the principle of agency in the partnership relationship is very different to the relationship between members of clubs.

Warren J was considering an application by the firm to strike out a counter-claim for damages for misrepresentation by former partners, so he was not in a position to finally decide the issue but, in refusing to strike out the counter-claim, said:

> 'It is strongly arguable (I say that simply in order to make clear that I am not deciding anything) that the same approach should apply to any act of a

---

93 [1948] SLT 326.

94 *Prole v Allen* [1950] 1 All ER 476; *Shore v Ministry of Works* [1950] 2 All ER 228; *Robertson v Ridley* [1989] 1 WLR 872 and *Melhuish v Clifford* (unreported) 18 August 1998, per Hooper J.

> partner effected in 'the carrying on in the usual way business of the kind carried on by the firm ...' within the meaning of section 5 [Partnership Act 1890]. There are many aspects of a solicitor's business, not just the giving of advice. Contracting for utility supplies, taking a lease of business premises and hiring staff are as much part of the carrying on of business as preparing a will or drafting a complex commercial document. There will also be tasks of internal administration of the firm which can also be properly described as carrying on in the usual way the business of the partnership, from the trivial such as the changing of a light-bulb in a partner's office to the serious such as preparing management accounts and other financial material or the preparation of strategy documents for the development of the firm. If negligence on the part of the partners carrying out, or responsible for, any particular function causes a particular partner loss and damage, it may well be that the firm as a whole is liable for those damages.
>
> Although every case will be critically fact-dependent, consider the change of the light-bulb. The member of staff employed to carry out this function does so in a thoroughly negligent way: instead of getting a ladder, he props a chair on the partner's desk. He falls off, severely injuring the partner who finds, to his alarm, that another colleague has failed to renew the firm's insurance. It would be entirely unsurprising to my mind that not only the negligent member of staff but also the firm as a whole should be liable for the negligence. Further, assuming that the injured partner would have been covered by the insurance if it had been renewed, it would be unsurprising not only to find the partner responsible for the renewal being held liable for not having done so, but also the firm as a whole.'

However, so far as damages are concerned, the partner bringing proceedings may have to bear his share of the consequent lost profits, but that should not preclude a right of action:

> 'To the extent that there is actionable misrepresentation, the partner who has suffered loss and damage can sue all of his partners; but in the division of profits, this liability will need to be taken into account. For instance, suppose that a partner, in reliance upon the misrepresentation, commits himself to some financial commitment which it transpires he cannot afford, and forfeits a deposit as a result. He may have a claim for the amount of the lost deposit, an amount which would be taken into account in the ascertainment of profits. The partner concerned will him/herself bear part of his/her loss as a result of the reduction in his share of profits. He can no more claim further damages *from the firm* for the reduction in his share of profit any more than any other innocent partner could do so although, I suppose, the partner making the misrepresentation might be so liable.'

In practice, a substantial partnership is likely to stand behind one partner if he is sued personally by another partner for breach of duty which causes work-related stress. This is most likely to occur in the case of a bullying claim where a duty of care is more easily established in respect of an individual. A claim for systemic failing leading to work overload and a breakdown caused by stress would be more difficult to establish against an individual partner, although proceedings against the individual members of the management team might be feasible.

However, even if the right to a cause of action against the firm is denied by the partnership (which for internal 'political' reasons it may well not be), a court may find in the partner's favour on this issue. However, it is also entirely possible that the duty owed to an equity partner (and therefore part-owner of the business) might well be rather lower than would the duty owed as employer to an employee of the partnership.

An alternative route might be a claim by an equity partner against the other partners for damages on an account in a claim for dissolution of the partnership (with the court having the power to order a buy out instead). *Mullins v Laughton & Others*[95] concerned a partnership dispute relating to an insolvency practitioners' practice. A group of partners resolved to remove another partner because of concerns about his performance. This involved summoning him to a meeting to expel him without giving him notice of their intention and changing the locks of the offices in advance. Neuberger J said their behaviour was a breach of the duty of good faith:

> 'I accept that one must avoid the danger of being unrealistic and that one must judge the behaviour of Messrs Laughton, Travers and Clements by reference to the relatively tough and abrasive regime which prevailed at BKR. However, even taking that into account, I consider that the way in which Mr Mullins was "bounced", both into and at the meeting, was outside the comparatively wide range of acceptable behaviour, which accords with the duty of good faith between partners. He was not only set up in terms of attending the meeting without any significant warning, but the conduct of the meeting similarly involved a set up. I think that the meeting was arranged with a view to shocking or surprising Mr Mullins into agreeing to resign (which I accept he got near to doing), and then, while he was still in a state of shock, telling him the financial consequences ... That is not the way partners should behave to each other. Bullying, seeking to trap, and intentionally taking by surprise with a view to shock, in hope of obtaining an advantage for the co-partners and a disadvantage for the partner concerned, must, in my view, amount to a breach of good faith.'

He then concluded that although it would be possible for such conduct to lead to an order for dissolution of the partnership under s 35 of the Partnership Act 1890, that section conferred a discretion and that the court could instead order that the remaining partners buy out the other partner.[96] Most of Mr Mullins claims could be dealt with in that way, but in addition to the usual financial partnership remedies, he claimed damages for 'loss of reputation' 'career disruption' 'as a result of which he

---

95 [2002] EWHC 2761 (Ch) Neuberger J, [2003] 2 WLR 1006, [2003] 4 All ER 94.

96 *Syers v Syers* (1876) 1 App Cas 174 as applied in *Hammond v Brearley* 10 December 1982, Hoffman LJ, CA.

thereby lost the opportunity to maximise his re-employment prospects' relying on *Mahmud v BCCI*.[97] Neuberger J said:

> 'I can see no reason why a former partner who is treated by some or all of his co-partners in a manner which is contrary to an express and/or implied duty of good faith, should not be similarly entitled to recover damages of [that] sort …
>
> In my judgment it would be a most unfortunate state of affairs, and very unfair on a person in the position of Mr Mullins, if the law could afford him no redress in respect of damage which he could establish that he suffered as a result of the way in which he was treated … at least insofar as that treatment was plainly in conflict with the express or implied duty of his partners to act towards him with good faith. I therefore conclude that the account should be carried out taking into account the loss of reputation and other damages, if any, which Mr Mullins can establish that he has suffered as a result of the breach of good faith on the part of his co-partners.'

Although no claim was brought for psychiatric injury, it is submitted that in principle this is no different provided it resulted from a breach of the duty of good faith allowing the court to order a dissolution, but with discretion under s 35 of the Partnership Act 1890 to order an account and a buy out in lieu. This decision in *Mullins* was referred to by Warren J in *Hammonds* without criticism, although he did not expressly rely upon it in reaching his decision.

2.6 LIABILITY OF EMPLOYERS FOR ACTIONS OF THIRD PARTIES

The duty of the employers can in some circumstances extend to a duty owed in respect of the actions of an unconnected third party.

In stress claims this is most likely to arise in the case of liability for discrimination alleged against customers or a contractor engaged by the employer.

In *Burton and Another v De Vere Hotels*[98] the EAT upheld the finding of discrimination by the employer against two black waitresses in respect of racist remarks by the comedian Bernard Manning at a function where they were working. This decision was criticised by the House of Lords in *MacDonald v Advocate General of Scotland*.[99]

However, the Sex Discrimination Act 1975 (Amendment) Regulations 2008,[100] amending the Sex Discrimination Act 1975 (SDA 1975)

---

97 [1998] AC 20.

98 [1997] ICR 1, [1996] IRLR 596, EAT.

99 [2003] UKHL 34, [2004] 1 All ER 339, [2003] ICR 937, [2003] IRLR 512, [2003] ELR 655.

100 SI 2008/656.

with effect from 6 April 2008, have now re-introduced this. The change means that claims can now be made by someone who is not themselves directly subjected to the unwanted conduct but where the effect of the behaviour is to violate their dignity or create an intimidating environment.

It should, however, be noted that the new regulations may not have protected the waitresses in *Burton* because there was no course of conduct on more than one occasion.[101]

[101] See **5.3.1**.

CHAPTER 3

COMMON LAW LIABILITY FOR STRESS AND BULLYING AT WORK

3.1 PRELIMINARY

3.1.1 No special control mechanisms

The general law of tort applies to claims for psychiatric injury arising from stress and bullying at work, without 'special control mechanisms' (*Hatton* Proposition 1):[1]

> '(1) There are no special control mechanisms applying to claims for psychiatric (or physical) illness or injury arising from the stress of doing the work the employee is required to do . . . The ordinary principles of employer's liability apply . . .'

The necessary constituent elements for a claim in tort are:

(1) existence of a 'duty of care';

(2) 'breach' of that duty;

(3) reasonable 'foreseeability' that that breach will cause 'damage' (personal injury); and

(4) 'causation' of that 'damage' by that 'breach'.

In contract, it is necessary to show a breach of an express or implied contractual term, but the courts will still require proof of foreseeability and causation in the same way. In theory, claims in contract may not require the same proof of damage (suggested by the House of Lords in the pleural plaques case, *Johnston v NEI International Combustion Ltd*[2]), but in practice the difference may not be significant.[3]

---

1 *Hatton v Sutherland*; *Barber v Somerset County Council*; *Jones v Sandwell Metropolitan Borough Council*; *Bishop v Baker Refractories Ltd* [2002] EWCA Civ 76, [2002] 2 All ER 1, [2002] ICR 613, [2002] IRLR 263, 68 BMLR 115, [2002] All ER (D) 53 (Feb), CA.

2 [2007] UKHL 39.

3 See **6.2**.

A claim for psychiatric injury at work arising from stress or bullying is a pure psychiatric injury claim. There is rarely an associated physical injury or a single precipitating shocking event. As such, the principles laid down by the House of Lords in the much-criticised decision[4] in *Page v Smith*[5] do not apply. In *Page*, the Lords set down rules for foreseeability for psychiatric injury claims involving a shocking event. Provided that a physical injury was foreseeable, the defendant does not have to be aware of any peculiar vulnerability of the claimant to the psychiatric injury. Any consequent psychiatric injury will be compensateable even though its nature and extent was unknown to, and could not have been known by, the defendant. This is an application of the so-called eggshell-skull principle, often shorthanded to 'eggshell personality'.

In a small number of stress or bullying at work claims there will be psychiatric injury as a result of an event causing the claimant to fear physical injury. This might include a threatened assault. In such cases, the general principles in *Page* will apply, rather than those in *Hatton* described below. In *Donachie v The Chief Constable of the Greater Manchester Police*[6] the claimant was a policeman who suffered psychiatric injury after being assigned to attach a tagging device to the underside of a car in circumstances where he risked serious injury or death if he were caught. In allowing his appeal, the Court of Appeal held:

> '. . . the Judge, in the passages from his judgment that I have set out in paragraph 19 above, wrongly relied on *Sutherland v. Hatton*, a claim for occupational stress induced psychiatric injury that failed because there was no reasonably foreseeable risk of injury of any sort. This case was one in which, as I have said, there was a reasonable foreseeability that the Chief Constable's breach of duty would cause physical injury to Mr Donachie, though not of the kind he actually suffered, and via the unforeseeable psychiatric injury actually caused by his negligence. He was thus a primary victim in respect of whom there was a reasonable foreseeability of physical injury and, in consequence, in respect of whom it was not necessary to prove involvement in an "event" in the form of an assault or otherwise.'

The court went further to emphasise that a single shocking event was not necessarily required:

> 'I should add that, even if it had been necessary to look for an "event" in this case sufficient to enable Mr Donachie to rely as a primary victim on reasonable foreseeability of psychiatric, as distinct from physical injury, I would have had sympathy with Mr Turner's submission that the circumstances in which he had been placed as a police officer, coupled with his fear engendered by those circumstances of physical injury, are indistinguishable in principle from occurrence of such injury. If A puts B in a position which A can reasonably foresee that B would fear physical injury,

4 See, for example, comments of the House of Lords in *Corr v IBC Vehicles Limited* [2008] UKHL 13.

5 [1996] 1 AC 155.

6 [2004] EWCA Civ 405.

> and B, as a result, suffers psychiatric injury and/or physical injury, B is, in my view, a primary victim. If it were necessary to characterise the onset of the fear causative of such injury as "an event", I would do so. There is all the difference in the world between a person like Mr Donachie, put in such a position by the tortfeasor, and someone who happens to learn from afar and/or a significant time afterwards of an event in which he had no involvement, the discovery of which he claims to have caused him psychiatric injury.'

However, in stress at work claims a physical injury is rarely foreseeable, nor often is there any shocking event. The claim usually arises from a continuum in which the stressors are applied over a period of time, even if there is a 'last straw' incident. So, in contrast to *Page*, psychiatric injury at work claims do usually require proof of foreseeability of the damage on the normal tort basis.[7]

As the Court of Appeal in *Pratley v Surrey County Council*[8] put it:

> 'We may further note that in this analysis there is no stark divide between physical and mental injury. A defendant may be liable for mental injury on the basis that he should have taken care to protect the claimant from any injury, of whatever sort, caused by a particular incident. But the case that determined that point, *Page v Smith* [1996] 1 AC 155, involved, like *Jolley*, a foreseeable and direct risk of injury from a specific source, a road traffic collision. It did not, as in our case, involve mental injury from an unforeseeable reaction to a particular circumstance arising at a different time and by a different causal route from that which the defendant had foreseen as potentially hazardous.'

But, beyond this, there are no additional special restrictions imposed on the ability to claim compensation for psychiatric injury at work.

3.1.2 Pre-*Hatton* case-law

The first significant reported claim for compensation for injury caused by stress at work was *Johnstone v Bloomsbury Health Authority*.[9] This claim was in effect a test case brought on behalf of NHS junior doctors who were being asked to work well beyond their contractual 40 hours per week. The claimant was a Senior House Officer. As well as his contractual working hours, he was also required to be on call for an additional 48 hours per week. He alleged that in practice he had often had to work very long hours without sleep; on one occasion, for example, he worked 32 hours over a weekend with 30 minutes sleep. This was well before the implementation of the Working Time Regulations 1998[10] and the revised NHS terms of work for NHS junior doctors. The claimant asserted that

---

7 *Wagon Mound (No 2)* (1967) 1 AC 617 (and see **3.4**).

8 [2003] EWCA Civ 1067, [2004] ICR 159, [2003] IRLR 794.

9 [1991] 2 All ER 293.

10 SI 1998/1833 (as amended).

the defendants had breached their duty to him in contract and in tort to take reasonable care of his health and safety. Although the claimant had pleaded injury and claimed damages, he also sought an injunction. The arguments before the Court of Appeal related to appeals and cross-appeals in respect of applications to strike out parts of the claim. The court affirmed that there was an overlap between tortious and contractual duties[11] and also that, in principle, a claim in damages for breach of the duty to take reasonable safety for the claimant's health and safety could lie; but went no further.

In *Petch v Customs and Excise Commissioners*,[12] Mr Petch had been a high-flying civil servant. He had suffered a breakdown in 1974, returned to the civil service and worked on until he suffered a second breakdown in 1983 which prevented his return to work. He was manic depressive as a result of a genetic condition, but argued that his first breakdown had been triggered by overwork and that the second breakdown was a consequence of the first. He appealed against the judge's conclusion that whilst the employers owed him a duty to take reasonable care of his health and safety, he had not established on the facts that they were, or ought to have been, aware that overwork was potentially going to injure him. Lord Justice Dillon said:

> '. . . unless senior management in the Customs and Excise were aware or ought to have been aware that Mr Petch was showing signs of an impending breakdown, or were aware or ought to have been aware that his workload carried a real risk that he would have a breakdown, then the Customs and Excise were not negligent in failing to avert the breakdown of October 1974.'

There was also some discussion about whether or not the workload had in fact been excessive, but issues of causation were not generally addressed. The crux of the judgment both at first instance and on appeal in dismissing the claim had been that, on the particular facts, foreseeability of injury had not been proved.

However, the case gave rise to some optimism that if foreseeability could be established in an appropriate case, a stress at work claim could succeed. In *Walker v Northumberland County Council*,[13] Mr Walker was able to establish foreseeability of injury in respect of his second breakdown and damages were awarded. The defendant did not appeal the *Walker* decision. The conclusions of the trial judge in *Walker* were affirmed by the Court of Appeal in *Garrett v London Borough of Camden*.[14] This was an appeal by a litigant in person against the dismissal of his claim for damage caused by stress at work at first instance where Tuckey LJ said:

[11] See **2.4**.
[12] [1993] ICR 789.
[13] [1995] 1 All ER 737. See further **3.4.4.2**.
[14] [2001] EWCA Civ 395.

> 'The judge applied the law stated by Colman J in *Walker v Northumberland County Council* [1995] 1 All ER 737, from which he cited extensively in his judgment. The appellant accepts the principles set out in that case between pages 749C and 752C of the report, which I think accurately state the law generally applicable to a case of this kind.'

And in *White and Others v Chief Constable of South Yorkshire and Others*[15] the House of Lords, when looking at the principles of psychiatric injury generally for both primary and secondary victims, reviewed *Walker* and approved the application of the law by the trial judge, Lord Hoffmann stating:

> 'The liability of an employer to his employees for negligence, either direct or vicarious, is not a separate tort with its own rules. It is an aspect of the general law of negligence. The relationship of employer and employee establishes the employee as a person to whom the employer owes a duty of care. But this tells one nothing about the circumstances in which he will be liable for a particular type of injury. For this one must look to the general law concerning the type of injury which has been suffered. It would not be suggested that the employment relationship entitles the employee to recover damages in tort (I put aside contractual liability, which obviously raises different questions) for economic loss which would not ordinarily be recoverable in negligence. The employer is not, for example, under a duty in tort to take reasonable care not to do something which would cause the employee purely financial loss, e.g. by reducing his opportunities to earn bonuses. The same must surely be true of psychiatric injury. There must be a reason why, if the employee would otherwise have been regarded as a secondary victim, the employment relationship should require him to be treated as a primary one. The employee in *Walker v. Northumberland County Council* [1995] 1 All E.R. 737 was in no sense a secondary victim. His mental breakdown was caused by the strain of doing the work which his employer had required him to do.'

So, it is well-established law that an employee suffering from psychiatric injury arising from stress at work is usually a primary victim, not a secondary victim, and that the ordinary rules of recovery in tort apply.

3.2 DIRECT LIABILITY OF EMPLOYER AND VICARIOUS LIABILITY

3.2.1 Direct liability of employer

It is important to distinguish between systemic failures of the employer and the actions of individual managers or fellow employees. Employers will be directly liable for systemic failures; they may also be vicariously liable for individual actions of their employees.

---

[15] [1998] UKHL 45, [1999] 2 AC 455, [1999] 1 All ER 1.

Vicarious liability should not be confused with a direct primary liability of the employer for its own breach, for example, in selecting a particular employee for a particular job (e g an incompetent line manager), or failing to remove or discipline such an employee.

Most claims relating to psychiatric injury caused by stress, such as overwork will normally be as a result of systemic failures rather than the actions of a single individual. By contrast, bullying cases may involve both systemic failures and individual actions.

3.2.2 Vicarious liability of employer

Vicarious liability is the direct liability of a person, even if that person is blameless, for the acts of another. It often features in personal injury claims, usually by way of the liability of an employer for the acts or omissions of its employee. An employer is not usually vicariously liable for the acts of a genuine independent contractor (although it could, for example, be directly liable for negligently choosing the contractor or jointly liable if it ratified or authorised the negligent acts).

The principle of vicarious liability originally developed by way of an extension of the principle of agency. Provided that an employee is working within the scope of the authority given by the employer, vicarious liability will lead directly from the employee's breach of duty.

In the leading case of recent times on vicarious liability, the House of Lords decision in *Lister v Hesley Hall Limited*,[16] Lord Steyn outlined the traditional doctrine:

> 'For nearly a century English judges have adopted Salmond's statement of the applicable test as correct. Salmond said that a wrongful act is deemed to be done by a "servant" in the course of his employment if "it is either (a) a wrongful act authorised by the master, or (b) a wrongful and unauthorised mode of doing some act authorised by the master": *Salmond on Torts*, 1st ed (1907), p 83; and *Salmond and Heuston on Torts*, 21st ed (1996), p 443. Situation (a) causes no problems. The difficulty arises in respect of cases under (b). Salmond did, however, offer an explanation which has sometimes been overlooked. He said (*Salmond on Torts*, 1st ed, pp 83–84) that "a master . . . is liable even for acts which he has not authorised, provided they are so connected with acts which he has authorised, that they may rightly be regarded as modes – although improper modes – of doing them".'

Vicarious liability is common in personal injury litigation, for example the liability of an employer for the negligent driving of its employee in the course of his employment, or for the negligent acts of one employee in the course of employment which cause injury to another employee.

---

[16] [2001] UKHL 22, [2001] 2 WLR 1311, [2001] 2 All ER 769, [2001] ICR 665, [2001] IRLR 472, [2001] 2 FLR 307.

In bullying cases, 'situation (b)' is more likely to apply. For example, in *Green v DB Group Services (UK) Ltd*[17] the bullying claim included a claim that the employer was vicariously liable for the bullies.

It would be unusual for an employer to expressly authorise an employee to behave in a bullying way towards another employee, although it is possible that authorised actions could be construed as bullying (eg aggressive sales target setting and monitoring).

Traditionally, the employer was not vicariously liable if the employee is 'on a frolic of his own'. Many employers might well believe that this would apply to bullying, particularly where this behaviour would, for example, breach the employer's own anti-bullying code. However, recent case-law has drastically narrowed the potential application of this defence. *Lister* itself concerned the liability of an employer for personal injury, the abuse of children by its employees. Obviously, abuse was not in the usual course of employment. The opportunity to abuse arose out of the employment. This might lead to a finding of primary liability on the part of the employer for breach of duty of care in allowing the circumstance to arise. However, the House of Lords held that the employer was vicariously liable for these intentional, unlawful acts by the employee. The principle in *Salmond* set out above was extended, Lord Millett stating in *Lister*:

> 'I would hold the school vicariously liable for the warden's intentional assaults, not (as was suggested in argument) for his failure to perform his duty to take care of the boys. That is an artificial approach . . . The law is mature enough to hold an employer vicariously liable for deliberate, criminal wrongdoing on the part of an employee without indulging in sophistry of this kind. I would also not base liability on the warden's failure to report his own wrongdoing to his employer, an approach which I regard as both artificial and unrealistic.'

Lord Millett returned to vicarious liability in *Dubai Aluminium Co Ltd v Salaam and others,*[18] which was not a personal injury case, but where important principles were elucidated:

> '[It is] no answer to a claim against the employer to say that the employee was guilty of intentional wrongdoing, or that his act was not merely tortious but criminal, or that he was acting exclusively for his own benefit, or that he was acting contrary to express instructions, or that his conduct was the very negation of his employer's duty . . . vicarious liability is not necessarily defeated if the employee acted for his own benefit.'

---

17 [2006] EWHC 1898 (QB), [2006] IRLR 764.

18 [2002] UKHL 48, [2003] 2 AC 366, [2002] 3 WLR 1913, [2003] 1 All ER 97, [2003] 1 Lloyd's Rep 65, [2003] 1 BCLC 32, (2003) 1 CLC 1020, [2003] IRLR 608.

The employer will therefore normally be vicariously liable for bullying by line managers and others within the workplace, even if systemically this is frowned upon by them.

Vicarious liability extends to claims under the Protection from Harassment Act 1997.[19]

3.2.3 Practical implications in stress and bullying claims

It is easy to see how the extension of the principles of vicarious liability can have an important effect on psychiatric injury at work claims, in particular bullying claims. As we shall see,[20] foreseeability by the employer of psychiatric injury to the employee is often an insurmountable hurdle in claims founded on direct liability of the employer for systemic failings. However, where the claimant can point to specific bullying by an individual, for which the employer is vicariously liable, this hurdle may be overcome more easily. The individual employee who is the bully is most likely to be able to see the claimant's reaction to the behaviour, such as distress and other symptoms of psychiatric injury. Where there is a sustained campaign of bullying, it may be difficult for the perpetrator (or the employer as the person vicariously liable for it) to argue that he was not reasonably aware that the consequences may include psychiatric injury.

Establishing vicarious liability is likely to be most straightforward in claims involving allegations of bullying by line managers. However, actions by other fellow employees may also constitute bullying. In *Green*[21] the bullying and harassment included 'silent treatment', exclusion, comments about personal hygiene, hiding administrative post and so on by a group of her co-workers – 'childish and petty' individually, but taken cumulatively 'a relentless campaign of mean and spiteful behaviour designed to cause her distress'. Owen J held:

> 'The question then arises as to whether the defendant is vicariously liable for the conduct of the four women. It is submitted on behalf of the defendant that the women did not work with the claimant, that their behaviour had nothing to do with either their work or hers, and that their employment simply provided the opportunity for them to behave in the way that they did. I do not agree. In my judgment there was a close connection between their employment and the behaviour in issue. It directly affected the working environment within the secretariat department . . .'

On the facts, there was also direct liability:

---

[19] *Majrowski v Guy's & St Thomas's NHS Trust* [2006] ICR 1199, [2006] IRLR 695, [2006] UKHL 34 (see **4.3**).

[20] See **3.4**.

[21] [2006] EWHC 1898 (QB), [2006] IRLR 764.

> 'But in any event I am satisfied that the defendant was in breach of its duty of care to the claimant in failing to take any or any adequate steps to protect her from such behaviour. The line managers knew or ought to have known what was going on. This was a long standing problem. A number of others had been bullied . . . Had the claimant's managers intervened as they ought to have done, there were obvious steps that could have been taken to stop the bullying. It ought to have been made clear that such behaviour was simply unacceptable, and those involved warned that if they persisted, disciplinary action would follow. If necessary they could have been moved to a different location or to a different department. But by whatever means the bullying could and should have been stopped.'

On foreseeability, even without the employer's prior knowledge of her psychiatric history, the judge held:

> 'I am also satisfied that the bullying gave rise to a foreseeable risk of psychiatric injury. Such behaviour when pursued relentlessly on a daily basis has a cumulative effect. It is designed to make the working environment intolerable for the victim. The stress that it creates goes far beyond that normally to be expected in the work place. It is in my judgment plainly foreseeable that some individuals will not be able to withstand such stress and will in consequence suffer some degree of psychiatric injury.'

In *Clark v Chief Constable for Essex*[22] the Chief Constable was vicariously liable for the threat of defamation proceedings made by a senior officer to the claimant:

> 'It is not necessary to be a libel lawyer to appreciate that there is something unrealistic about a police officer being sued for defamation on the basis of a report he makes to his superior officers of allegations that a suspect has made to him in interview about another officer. And the notion that a police officer might be sued for defamation for what he says in evidence to the Crown Court is even more bizarre. Notwithstanding Mr MacInnes's assurances to this effect, none of this could reasonably have been expected to be clear to the Claimant at the time. The fact that senior officers were suggesting some proceedings against him is something that he would be bound to take very seriously indeed.'

The Chief Constable was also vicariously liable for unlawful disciplinary action taken against the claimant:

> 'I find that the Claimant did suffer psychological injury as a result of the events of 11th May 1999, that is by the condemnation by an unlawful disciplinary proceeding and the move which in substance amounted to a demotion by way of punishment.'

22 [2006] EWHC 2290 (QB), [2006] 38 LS Gaz R 32, [2006] All ER (D) 81 (Sep).

The application of vicarious liability in stress cases is less obvious, but it is feasible in cases where a line manager is, for example, directly responsible for allocation of work and can directly see the effect of overwork on the claimant's health.

Vicarious liability still requires proof of foreseeability of the injury. In practice, in many cases it will be easier to prove foreseeability where the claim is founded on vicarious liability than where it is founded on the direct liability of the employer for systemic failures. However, it should be noted that in *Barlow v Broxbourne Borough Council*[23] the judge held:

> 'I should add that, even if I had felt it right to hold that the defendant had through its officers bullied or victimised the claimant, I would still not have held that the claimant had established a right to damages. The reason is that I am unable to accept that the defendant through its officers either knew or ought reasonably to have known or foreseen that the conduct complained of would cause the claimant harm. It was not suggested on behalf of the claimant that any of the officers had actual knowledge that such harm would result. I do not think that those officers ought to have foreseen the harm which in the event occurred.'

3.3 THE APPLICATION OF *HATTON V SUTHERLAND*

The judgment of Hale LJ in *Hatton* is of great importance. The court took six cases together on appeal and laid down 16 propositions which the court felt should be applied to psychiatric injury at work cases. The decision has been widely praised and was generally approved by the House of Lords in *Barber v Somerset*[24] (an appeal by one of the *Hatton* appellants to the Lords). Although the Lords allowed Mr Barber's appeal, this was principally on the ground that the Court of Appeal should not have interfered with the specific findings of fact by the trial judge. The House of Lords did not expressly approve the *Hatton* propositions (except in the dissenting judgment of Lord Scott). However, no real attack was made on the *Hatton* propositions and Lord Walker, giving the main judgment, said:

> 'The Court of Appeal's composite judgment (on the County Council's appeal and the three appeals heard with it) begins with three sections: Introduction; Background Considerations; and the Law. Mr Barber rightly directed hardly any criticism towards these. The exposition and commentary in this part of the judgment is a valuable contribution to the development of the law …'

But, Lord Walker, commenting specifically on para 29 of the *Hatton* Court of Appeal judgment, also said:

---

23 [2003] EWHC 50 (QB).

24 [2004] UKHL 13.

> 'This is, I think, useful practical guidance, but it must be read as that, and not as having anything like statutory force.'

He preferred instead (in contrast to Lord Scott's dissenting judgment) the general formulation of the law in *Stokes v Guest, Keen Nettlefold (Nuts and Bolts) Ltd.*[25] However, the point that *Hatton* is only valuable guidance applies more generally to all of the *Hatton* propositions. In *Hartman v South Essex Mental Health and Community Care NHS Trust*,[26] another series of conjoined stress at work appeals heard by a differently constituted Court of Appeal, Scott Baker LJ said:

> '. . . what was said in *Hatton* was not intended to cover all the infinitely variable facts that are likely to arise in stress at work cases. The general principles are to be found in *Hatton* but we emphasise they need care in their application to the particular facts under consideration.'

This is particularly so in respect of bullying as opposed to stress claims. As Scott Baker LJ pointed out:

> '. . . while each appeal in *Hatton* involved an employee who had suffered ongoing stress in day-to-day work, the case of *Melville*, and to some extent *Hartman*, (see below) involved stress caused by specific traumas.'

And similarly in *Clark v Chief Constable of Essex Police* the judge said:[27]

> 'Mr Waters submitted that this statement was made in the context of a number of appeals arising out of claims for occupational stress, but none of them involved bullying. He submitted that in *Hatton* the stress was not inflicted deliberately: Proposition (3) in *Hatton* includes a reference to normal pressures, namely "An employer is usually entitled to assume that the employee can withstand the normal pressures of the job unless he knows of some particular problem or vulnerability". By contrast, Mr Waters submits that in the present case, while the injury was not inflicted deliberately, the stress was inflicted deliberately. None of the cases to which I have been referred provide any specific guidance on the proper approach in a case where bullying or victimisation is alleged . . .
>
> It seems to me that I can and should be guided by *Hatton*, but that what is foreseeable must depend on the facts of each case. In *Waters* Lord Slynn referred specifically to the need for the injury to be foreseeable, and I see no inconsistency between what he said in that case and what Hale LJ said in *Hatton*. She made the position clear in Proposition (5)(a) and (b), cited above.'

---

25 [1968] 1 WLR 1776, 112 Sol Jo 821, 5 KIR 401.

26 [2005] EWCA Civ 06; [2005] IRLR 293; (2005) PIQR P19; (2005) 85 BMLR 136.

27 [2006] EWHC 2290 (QB), [2006] 38 LS Gaz R 32, [2006] All ER (D) 81 (Sep).

3.4 FORESEEABILITY

Proof of foreseeability of injury as a result of the breach is usually the single most difficult issue in a stress or bullying claim. However egregious the breach of duty, and however severe the consequences, at common law there will be no liability if the wrongdoer did not actually foresee this (or ought reasonably to have done so).

The *Hatton* Propositions 2–7 all consider aspects of this issue. As in the *Hatton* judgment, they are split here for convenience of analysis. But it is essential when seeking to answer the threshold question of foreseeability to look not only at the individual facts by reference to the separate propositions below, but also the facts of the individual case in the round.

3.4.1 The 'threshold question'

Hale LJ described foreseeabilty as the 'threshold question' (*Hatton* Proposition 2):

> '(2) The threshold question is whether this kind of harm to this particular employee was reasonably foreseeable (para 23): this has two components (a) an injury to health (as distinct from occupational stress) which (b) is attributable to stress at work (as distinct from other factors) (para 25).'

The duty applies to the particular employee. It is not an objective standard in respect of employees of 'reasonable fortitude'. The well-known case of *Paris v Stepney Borough Council*[28] applies. In *Paris*, the claimant was blind in his left eye and this was known to his employers. He was therefore particularly vulnerable in respect of any injury to his right eye. They therefore owed him as an individual a particular duty to supply him with safety goggles to protect his right eye from injury, even though it was accepted that there was no general duty in this respect with regard to fully sighted employees. They did not do so and were held negligent when he was left totally blind following an accident at work. So, in stress claims, the employer's knowledge of the employee's particular vulnerability to psychiatric injury has the same effect.

It is, of course, easier to establish knowledge of a particular physical disability than a pre-existing vulnerability to a psychiatric condition (although, even in *Paris*, the evidence was that the employer had not been aware of the disability at the commencement of employment). As Hale LJ said in *Hatton*:

> 'Because of the very nature of psychiatric disorder, as a sufficiently serious departure from normal or average psychological functioning to be labelled a

---

28 [1951] AC 367.

> disorder, it is bound to be harder to foresee than is physical injury . . . But it may be easier to foresee in a known individual than it is in the population at large.'

The second element is to distinguish foreseeability of 'occupational stress' from foreseeability of an injury to health. Earlier in her judgment Hale LJ quoted from guidance from the Health and Safety Executive (HSE):[29]

> 'Stress is not therefore the same as ill-health. But in some cases, particularly where pressures are intense and continue for some time, the effect of stress can be more sustained and far more damaging, leading to longer-term psychological problems and physical ill-health.'

So, foreseeability relates to the foresight of the reasonable employer of the effect of the particular stresses of the particular job on the particular employee. But, in addition, the particular kind of injury must be foreseeable. So, in *Pratley v Surrey County Council*,[30] concern had been raised about heavy workloads which it was acknowledged could lead to stress for employees. The employer had devised a new system of work but before it could be implemented the employee had suffered a breakdown. The Court of Appeal found that the risk of imminent injury had not been foreseeable by the employer. The employer had acted reasonably in identifying a potential long-term injury and in planning to implement a system to deal with it.

In bullying cases, there is often a different perception of the victim and perpetrator as to the nature of the conduct. This must be taken into account in answering the threshold question. In *Hyam v Havering NHS Primary Care Trust*[31] Morland J described the threshold question as it applied to bullying cases in the following terms:

> 'The question is whether [the perpetrators] ought reasonably to have known that their conduct, although not intending to harm, victimize or harass [the victim], might cause him mental illness, having regard to their knowledge of his sensitivity and obsession about his status and the sanctity of his job description, and their knowledge of his potential vulnerability to mental illness . . .'

The test is of course quite different in a case where the bullying is deliberate and intended to harm.[32]

---

29 'Stress at work' (1995).

30 [2003] EWCA Civ 1067, [2004] ICR 159, [2003] IRLR 794.

31 [2004] EWHC 2971.

32 See *Green* (one of the conjoined appeals in *Hartman v South Essex Mental Health and Community Care NHS Trust* [2005] EWCA Civ 06, [2005] ICR 782, [2005] ELR 237, [2005] IRLR 293, (2005) 85 BMLR 136, (2005) *The Times*, 21 January, (2005) PIQR P19, [2005] All ER (D) 141 (Jan) CA).

3.4.2 The employer's knowledge

The issue of foreseeability depends on what the employer knows (or ought reasonably to know) about the individual employee and Hale LJ expanded on this (*Hatton* Proposition 3):

> '(3) Foreseeability depends upon what the employer knows (or ought reasonably to know) about the individual employee. Because of the nature of mental disorder, it is harder to foresee than physical injury, but may be easier to foresee in a known individual than in the population at large (para 23). An employer is usually entitled to assume that the employee can withstand the normal pressures of the job unless he knows of some particular problem or vulnerability (para 29).'

3.4.2.1 More than the normal pressures of the job

The claimant may be able to show that the employer imposed far more than the 'normal pressures of the job'. In *Jones v Sandwell Metropolitan Borough Council*[33] the claimant was a relatively junior grade administrative assistant who had to work:

> ' . . . grossly excessive hours over the 37 per week required by her contract of employment. There was unchallenged evidence that her personnel officer, Mr King, had acknowledged in February 1993 that they knew it was a gamble to expect one person to do the work of two to three.'

The court reached its conclusion on foreseeability 'not without some hesitation' (they would have preferred clearer evidence of the extent of the claimant's complaints), but ultimately felt that she fell into the category described by Lord Slynn in *Waters v Commissioner of Police for the Metropolis*:[34]

> 'If an employer knows that the acts being done by employees during their employment may cause physical or mental harm to a particular fellow employee and he does nothing to supervise or prevent such acts, when it is in his power to do so, it is clearly arguable that he may be in breach of duty to that employee. It seems to me that he may also be in breach of that duty if he can foresee that such acts may happen and, if they do, that physical or mental harm may be caused to an individual . . . Even if this is not necessarily foreseeable at the beginning it may become foreseeable or indeed obvious to those in charge at various levels who are carrying out the [employer's] responsibilities that there is a risk of harm and that some protective steps should be taken.'

But if the employee has control over their workload and the way the work is done, then it will be more difficult to establish that the employer should

---

33 One of the conjoined appeals in *Hatton*.

34 [2000] 4 All ER 934.

have foreseen that overwork might cause psychiatric injury.[35] This difficulty will often apply to senior grade employees where it may be hard to show that the stress was 'employer imposed'. Note also *Hatton* proposition 5.[36]

3.4.2.2 The employee's particular vulnerability

If there is no evidence that the employer imposed far more than the normal pressures of the job, then the claimant will have to show that the particular vulnerability to psychiatric injury was drawn to the employer's attention. Merely having taken time off work in the past with depression will not be enough. In the individual case of *Hatton*, the claimant was a teacher. She had suffered from depression and had had to take time off work after bereavement, an assault in the street and the hospitalisation of one of her sons. However, the court found:

> 'Mrs Hatton's workload was no greater or more burdensome than that of any other teacher in a similar school. Nor had she complained to anyone about it.'

The court concluded that:

> 'Her workload and her pattern of absence taken together could not amount to a sufficiently clear indication that she was likely to suffer from psychiatric injury as a result of stress at work such as to trigger a duty to do more than was in fact done. The school could not reasonably be expected to probe further into the causes of her absence in the summer term 1994 when she herself had attributed it to problems at home which the school knew to be real. Hence the claim must fail at the first threshold of foreseeability.'

Employees are often reluctant to disclose a psychiatric problem or the fact that it is caused or exacerbated by work-related stress for the obvious fear that it might jeopardise their employment or detrimentally affect how they are viewed by their employer. Unfortunately, psychiatric illness still carries a stigma. But if the reasons for absence are concealed or attributed by the employee to a different cause, it will be difficult to establish that the employer could reasonably have been aware of their vulnerability to psychiatric injury from stress at work.

The total number of hours worked by the claimant does not always have to be excessive. In *Wheeldon v HSBC Bank*,[37] the claimant worked 2 or 3 days a week. However, she was diligent and anxious to get on top of her work responsibilities. She found that the pressures of the job made that

---

35 See, for example, the pub manager in *Harding v The Pub Estate Co Ltd* [2005] EWCA Civ 553, dealt with more fully at **3.5.6**.

36 See **3.4.4**.

37 One of the conjoined appeals in *Hartman*.

impossible. Her employers were aware of this and she was assessed by an occupational health doctor who made various recommendations which were ignored:

> 'In our judgment the judge was entitled to conclude that Mr Whigham's failure to take action to reduce the stress on Mrs Wheeldon had the effect that her depression "continued and flourished". The Bank's breach of duty occurred because Mr Whigham failed to sit down and discuss with her the various options such as training her for a different post at Victory Road or taking her away from Alvaston until she was better able to cope with the stresses at that branch. The judge was in our view entitled to find on the basis of the medical evidence that this breach of duty caused Mrs Wheedon to suffer an identifiable psychiatric injury.'

In *Barber* Mr Barber was a teacher and head of mathematics. Following a restructuring, the post of head of department was abolished and he took on additional responsibilities as project manager for public and media relations. He found the new role very stressful. He saw his GP but had no sickness absences until a 3-week absence in the middle of the summer term. The sick certificates had stated 'overstressed/depression' and he had a meeting with the head teacher where he said that he was unable to cope with his workload. Nothing was done. In the middle of the following term he lost control at school and started shaking a pupil. He never returned. The Court of Appeal in *Hatton* allowed his employer's appeal on the ground that the breakdown was not reasonably foreseeable. The Lords, however, allowed Mr Barber's appeal on the basis that they would not interfere with the findings of fact of the trial judge. The Lords felt that the issue of breach was 'close to the borderline', but:

> 'What the Court of Appeal failed to give adequate weight to was the fact that Mr Barber, an experienced and conscientious teacher, had been off work for three weeks (not two weeks, as the Court of Appeal thought at para 160) with no physical ailment or injury. His absence was certified by his doctor to be due to stress and depression. The senior management team should have made inquiries about his problems and seen what they could do to ease them, in consultation with officials at the County Council's Education Department, instead of brushing him off unsympathetically (as Mrs Hayward and Mrs Newton did) or sympathising but simply telling him to prioritise his work (as Mr Gill did).'

But, in *Croft v Broadstairs Town Council*:[38]

> '. . . the claimant was "superficially strong, undoubtedly decisive, methodical, meticulous, to the point of being a perfectionist", but, at the same time, she was, in the words of the medical experts, "psychiatrically vulnerable". She had for many years received specialist treatment by way of drugs and psychiatric counselling for recurrent depression arising from factors in her personal life.'

---

38 [2003] EWCA Civ 676.

The employer was aware that Mrs Croft had been seeing a counsellor, but was unaware of the nature of her psychological problems and on the claimant's own evidence these had largely been related to her personal life and not work. There had been no signs of work-related stress. The court concluded that the employers could not have been expected to foresee psychiatric injury:

> 'That left the council in the position of employers who were entitled to expect ordinary robustness in the claimant in an employment context, including disciplinary matters, in which she had certainly never been involved before. The evidence of the psychiatrist was clear that, in a person of ordinary robustness, which the claimant herself acknowledged was the image she presented to the council, a nervous breakdown would not, medically at least, be a foreseeable result of a reprimand as to her conduct; on the evidence that was the state of play from the council's point of view. In my view, the assertion of the claimant, even if correct, that Mrs Cradduck in a personal capacity was aware that she had had counselling was plainly insufficient to import knowledge on the council's part sufficient to demonstrate the likelihood of feelings of rejection and distress so strong as to trigger a nervous breakdown on receipt of the letter. Such a breakdown was not the reasonably foreseeable product of the conduct concerned, and therefore the council are entitled to succeed in the appeal.'

3.4.3 No intrinsically dangerous occupations

It had been asserted in argument in *Hatton* that some jobs were so intrinsically stressful that foreseeability of the risk of psychiatric injury could be presumed. An example given in argument was that of a traffic policeman who was regularly called upon to witness horrific accident scenes. However, in keeping with her analysis that work-related psychiatric injury resulted from a combination of the stresses of the job and the reaction of the individual to those stresses, Hale LJ rejected this (*Hatton* Proposition 4):

> '(4) The test is the same whatever the employment: there are no occupations which should be regarded as intrinsically dangerous to mental health (para 24).'

In the case of *Hartman*[39] the claimant was employed to look after children with learning difficulties. The Court of Appeal, referring to *Hatton* Proposition 4, commented:

> 'Mr Hogarth, on behalf of the Trust, submitted that there was no basis for concluding, as the judge appears to have done in paragraph 46, that caring for children with serious learning difficulties is a high risk occupation imposing a higher than normal standard of alertness on employers in respect of the risk that employees will sustain psychiatric injury. We agree.'

39 *Hartman v South Essex Mental Health & Community Care NHS Trust* [2005] EWCA Civ 6, (2005) 85 BMLR 136, [2005] ELR 237, [2005] ICR 782, [2005] IRLR 293, [2005] PIQR P19.

However, it should be noted that in *Melville v The Home Office*[40] the claimant was a prison officer whose duties included the recovery of bodies of prisoners who had committed suicide. That these circumstances might be traumatic and cause psychiatric injury had been recognised by the Prison Service, but their guidelines to prevent this had not been implemented by the employer. So, whilst not detracting from the principle that there are no intrinsically dangerous jobs, it is quite likely that in any job where the risk of psychiatric injury was grave, the employer will have foreseen the dangers and put in place guidance to avoid causing injury. Failure to follow such guidance may give rise to a claim with foreseeability being established because the very reason for the guidance was to try to avoid such injury.

3.4.4 Foreseeability: relevant factors

Such is the importance of answering the 'threshold question' of foreseeability, Hale LJ goes on to consider in more detail relevant factors to be taken into account in answering it (*Hatton* Proposition 5). This splits into two parts: (a) the nature and extent of the work done; and (b) the signs of impending harm to health.

3.4.4.1 Nature and extent of the work

> '(a) The nature and extent of the work done by the employee (para 26). Is the workload much more than is normal for the particular job? Is the work particularly intellectually or emotionally demanding for this employee? Are demands being made of this employee unreasonable when compared with the demands made of others in the same or comparable jobs? Or are there signs that others doing this job are suffering harmful levels of stress? Is there an abnormal level of sickness or absenteeism in the same job or the same department?'

With regard to workload being more than normal for the job, we have already seen an example in *Jones v Sandwell Metropolitan Borough Council*.[41] Another example is *Six Continents Retail Ltd v Hone*.[42]

Witness evidence from comparators doing a similar kind of job (but with fewer stresses) is very helpful in establishing this but is often very difficult to obtain as fellow employees may be unwilling to give evidence.

Conversely, everyone within a company or team may be subjected to unreasonable levels of stress. So, for example, where a City law firm required all employed lawyers to opt out of the Working Time Regulations and required them to record in excess of 2,500 billable hours a year (10 billable hours a day for 250 working days a year, plus

40 One of the conjoined appeals in *Hartman*.

41 One of the conjoined appeals with *Hatton*. See **3.4.2.1**.

42 [2005] EWCA Civ 922. See **3.4.6**.

non-billable time), the employer might find it difficult to argue that it was foreseeable that this might cause psychiatric damage to some individuals. However, in *Barber*, Lord Scott, albeit in his dissenting judgment, comments:

> 'The same, I suspect, would apply to many professional employees. Nurses and doctors working in the NHS are an obvious example. Employed lawyers working in busy city firms are probably another. Pressure and stress are part of the system of work under which they carry out their daily duties. But they are all adults. They choose their profession.'

Foreseeability of injury is likely to be more evident in working environments where there are already significant levels of sickness or absenteeism. In her comments, Hale LJ does not expressly describe these absences as being associated with work-related stress. However, unless the employer can point to other reasons for absence, the very fact of them should have put the employer on enquiry as to the reasons.

In *Rowntree v Commissioner of Police for the Metropolis*[43] (albeit a pre-*Hatton* decision) the court held that levels of stress-related sickness put the employer on notice of a high risk of psychiatric injury and the risk was materially higher than that which would ordinarily affect a child protection team worker with a heavy workload.

It may also be the case that although objectively the demands of the job are not excessive, they are for the particular employee. This could occur when an employee is over-promoted beyond their capability. It is particularly difficult to prove foreseeability in such cases. It is rare for there to be clear evidence that the employee demonstrated that the job was too much for him. It might be demonstrated that additional training was requested or promised but not delivered. But in an extreme case, the mistake of over-promotion might only be remedied by demotion.[44]

In *Sayers v Cambridgeshire County Council*[45] the claimant was an Operations Manager. The court found:

> '... the following matters were known to the Council. First, that Mrs Sayers was complaining of being overworked and was working long hours of 50 to 60 hours per week. Secondly, that on certain occasions in 2000, 2001 and 2002 Mrs Sayers had become tearful and upset. Thirdly, that Mrs Sayers had had limited absences from work for illness. Fourthly, Mr Wrycroft had been told once by Mrs Sayers that she was on medication but he did not know what it was but assumed it was due to life stresses. Fifthly, that some other employees had suffered psychiatric illness.'

---

43 QBD (Nelson J) LTL 31 October 2001.

44 As to which see **3.5.5**.

45 [2006] EWHC 2029 (QB), [2007] IRLR 29.

However, the judge held that overwork alone was insufficient to found liability in the absence of evidence that the Council knew about her psychiatric vulnerability:

> 'Mrs Sayers had been working for the Council for some 9 years when she suffered the episode in 2002. She had applied for and obtained promotions during that time without anything being raised by her as to any psychiatric illness. She had a difficult and demanding job which she performed well. In such circumstances, having reviewed all the matters known to the Council and applying the requirement of "positive thought" and taking account of the awareness of stress related illness, I do not consider that it can be said that it should have been plain to the Council that Mrs Sayers was at risk of suffering a psychiatric injury caused by her work. Rather, I consider that the Council was entitled to assume that Mrs Sayers was up to the normal pressures of her job and had no particular reason to apprehend a danger that psychiatric injury would be caused to her.'

3.4.4.2 Signs of impending harm to health

> '(b) Signs from the employee of impending harm to health (paras 27 and 28). Has he a particular problem or vulnerability? Has he already suffered from illness attributable to stress at work? Have there recently been frequent or prolonged absences which are uncharacteristic of him? Is there reason to think that these are attributable to stress at work, for example because of complaints or warnings from him or others?'

Because of the need to show how the stress of the job might affect a particular employee, the signs that there might be psychiatric injury as a result are crucial. The most obvious 'sign' for the employer is a previous incident of work-related stress. In the clearest case, this is a breakdown leading to significant absence which is clearly related, at least in part, to stress at work and which is communicated to the employer. These are the so-called 'second breakdown' cases and are easiest to establish in terms of foreseeability.[46] *Walker v Northumberland County Council* is the paradigm case.

Mr Walker was a middle manager responsible for overseeing the conduct of child abuse cases at Northumberland social services. The volume of work increased steadily; but the number of field social workers did not. Mr Walker had no prior psychiatric history. He suffered a breakdown which the psychiatric evidence attributed to work-related stress. He was off work for 5 months. Before he returned to work, he was assured that he would be given additional support and resources to enable him to cope with the job. In the event, these promises were not kept and he suffered a second nervous breakdown 6 months later.

Mr Walker cogently complained about the problems and the judge found that the service was under-resourced. However, he did not find the

---

[46] But **6.1.3** for a discussion of the consequent difficulties in proving causation of loss.

defendant liable in respect of the first breakdown, because there was no sign evident to the employer that this would cause Mr Walker psychiatric injury:

> 'I am not persuaded that before the first illness Mr Davison ought to have appreciated that Mr Walker was not only dissatisfied and frustrated because his area could not provide the service, but was at materially greater risk of stress-induced mental illness than an area manager with a busy area would normally be.'

However, in respect of the second breakdown, and having found that there were steps a reasonable employer could have taken, the judge found that the risk of injury was foreseeable as after the first breakdown the employer was clearly aware of Mr Walker's vulnerability:

> 'Having regard to the reasonably foreseeable size of the risk of repetition of Mr Walker's illness if his duties were not alleviated by effective additional assistance and to the reasonably foreseeable gravity of the mental breakdown which might result if nothing were done, I have come to the conclusion that the standard of care to be expected of a reasonable local authority required that in March 1987 such additional assistance should be provided if not on a permanent basis, at least until restructuring of the Social Services had been effected and the workload on Mr Walker thereby permanently reduced. That measure of additional assistance ought to have been provided notwithstanding that it could be expected to have some disruptive effect on the Council's provision of services to the public. When Mr Walker returned from his first illness the Council had to decide whether it was prepared to go on employing him in spite of the fact that he had made it sufficiently clear that he must have effective additional help if he was to continue at Blyth Valley. It chose to continue to employ him, but provided no effective help. In so doing it was, in my judgment, acting unreasonably and therefore in breach of its duty of care.'

Similarly, in *Young v Post Office*[47] Mr Young was a vehicle workshop manager for the Post Office. He had no previous psychiatric history. He had been promoted to manager and found it difficult to cope with a new computer system. On one assessment by his employer:

> 'He then wrote on the memorandum in capital letters "I NEED SOME HELP".'

The overwork got too much for him and he had a breakdown. He was off work for 4 months. He returned to work and subsequently suffered a second breakdown. He did not pursue at trial a claim that his first breakdown was foreseeable, but claimed that the second one was. His employers had put in place a flexible working regime to reintroduce him to employment. However, implementation was largely left to Mr Young. May LJ held:

---

47 [2002] EWCA Civ 661, [2002] IRLR 660.

> 'Mr Young had already suffered from psychiatric illness resulting from occupational stress. His employers knew this. After May 1997 it was, in my view, plainly foreseeable that there might be a recurrence if appropriate steps were not taken when he returned to work. The employers owed him a duty to take such steps.'

In other cases there will have been earlier absences which have been related to work-related stress. These might not have been frequent or prolonged. To what extent should that have put the employer on notice of the risk of psychiatric injury if the work-related stress continued? If the absences are not attributed to work-related stress, it will normally be necessary for the employer to have been put on notice by complaints from the employee or by warnings from others.

In *Hiles v South Gloucestershire NHS PCT*[48] R Moxon Browne QC sitting as a deputy High Court judge found the defendant liable in a 'first breakdown' case. Mrs Hiles was a health visitor. Her workload (and that of others) increased and her line manager gave evidence:

> 'Mrs Phillips freely admitted that stress levels were such that it was foreseeable that any one of her Health Visitors might go off sick, and indeed that she herself foresaw just such an eventuality.'

Mrs Hiles had complained about her workload and had on one occasions broken down in tears at a meeting with her line manager. The judge found:

> 'I think this emotional display at an ordinary work interview was a sign not only that Mrs Hiles was under stress, but also, that the stress was in popular language beginning to get to her, and that if it continued or got worse, Mrs Hiles' well being (i.e. her health) might be adversely affected.'

In *Dickins v O2 plc*[49] the claimant had not suffered a previous breakdown. She had, however, taken some limited time off work for irritable bowel syndrome which her GP thought was stress related. This was made known to her employer. She spoke to two managers formally about the stress she was under and requested 6 months off or a 'sabbatical' or a move to a different job. The managers suggested counselling, and a referral to occupational health, but nothing to directly or immediately alleviate the work situation. The judge held that the employer was in breach of duty and that injury was reasonably foreseeable. On appeal, inter alia the employer argued that the judge had misapplied the *Hatton* propositions and that psychiatric injury was not reasonably foreseeable, but the Court of Appeal rejected the appeal, Smith LJ saying:

> 'The judge held, at his paragraph 39, which I have cited at paragraph 19 above, that on or about 23 April, the respondent was "palpably under

48 [2006] EWHC 3418 (QB).

49 [2008] EWCA Civ 1144, [2009] IRLR 58.

extreme stress" and "about to crack up" as she had said. That was or should have been plain to her two managers, Allen and Keith Brown, but they did nothing of substance about it. In my judgment, the evidence was quite strong enough for the judge to conclude, as he did, that the appellant had received a clear indication of impending illness.'

3.4.5 Enquiries by employer

Generally, no specific enquiries by the employer are required (*Hatton* Proposition 6):

> '(6) The employer is generally entitled to take what he is told by his employee at face value, unless he has good reason to think to the contrary. He does not generally have to make searching enquiries of the employee or seek permission to make further enquiries of his medical advisers (para 29).'

However, this formulation of *Hatton* Proposition 6 is controversial. Lord Walker giving the leading judgment allowing the appeal on the House of Lords in *Barber* was expressly referring to this paragraph of the Court of Appeal judgment when he cautioned that it was 'guidance' only and that the law was correctly as stated in *Stokes.*[50] In the Northern Irish case of *Beattie v Ulster Television plc*,[51] Higgins J summarised the position as follows:[52]

> 'The test expounded by Swanwick J in *Stokes*, supra, and accepted by some members of the House of Lords in *Barber* and by the Court of Appeal in *Hartman* is not as restrictive on the issue of foreseeability as that adopted by the Court of Appeal in *Hatton*. It requires a more proactive approach by the employer, than the reactive approach that appears to be have been adopted in Hatton.'

However, if the employee knows that he is particularly vulnerable to psychiatric injury, but does not disclose this to his employer (eg on commencing employment) he will find it particularly difficult to persuade the court that his employer should be liable. In *Garrett v LB Camden*,[53] the applicant (who was in person before the Court of Appeal) was working in conditions which:

> '. . . were chaotic and counterproductive, but this was partly of the appellant's own making. With the benefit of hindsight, more effective management was required to bring the situation under control, but that may have been easier said than done . . .'

However, Simon Brown LJ concluded:

---

50 See **3.3**.

51 [2005] NIQB 36.

52 Cited with approval in *Munkman on Employer's Liability* (Lexis Nexis Butterworths, 14th edn, 2006).

53 [2001] EWCA Civ 395.

'. . . the claimant was "substantially more vulnerable than most to sustaining psychiatric injury" and, second, that when he entered Camden's employment nothing was said or disclosed to put them on notice or enquiry of his mental state . . . The combined effect of those twin findings was that he knew materially more than his employers about his propensity to work-related stress and breakdown, and can hardly, therefore, blame them for not recognising the particular difficulties attendant upon his continued employment.'

Once the employer is aware of the psychiatric vulnerability of an employee, it is not necessary for the employee to raise the fact that further stresses are affecting his condition. In *Young* May LJ said:

'Although, as the case of Sutherland indicates, in many circumstances an employer may not be expected to know that an employee who does not speak up is vulnerable, an employee who is known to be vulnerable is not necessarily to be regarded as responsible for a recurrent psychiatric illness if he fails to tell his employer that his job is again becoming too much for him.'

3.4.6 Plain and obvious signs

In any potential work-related stress claim it will be necessary to analyse foreseeability by going through the various questions posed in *Hatton* Propositions 3–6, outlined above. But, as Hale LJ stressed (*Hatton* Proposition 7):

'(7) To trigger a duty to take steps, the indications of impending harm to health arising from stress at work must be plain enough for any reasonable employer to realise that he should do something about it (para 31).'

It will not be enough to show that there are non-specific complaints or absences. Nor will it be enough simply to show long working hours. The quality of the evidence is critical.[54] Standing back and looking at the facts as a whole: should it have been plain and obvious to a reasonable employer that this individual was at risk of work-related psychiatric injury?

In *Green v Grimsby & Scunthorpe Newspapers*[55] Mr Green had no previous psychiatric history. He did not work particularly long hours, although he was known to be a perfectionist. He sent a memo to his line manager stating that problems over a particular project were beginning to affect his health. The line manager tried to meet him to discuss the memo a week later, but was unable to find him at the start of the day. Half an hour later he spoke to Mr Green and asked him whether it was fine to take a coffee break at 9 am. Mr Green walked out. The Court of Appeal dismissed the appeal:

---

54 See **11.1.5**.

55 One of the conjoined appeals in *Hartman*.

'The suggestion that Mr Green's memo should have put Mr Moore on notice that Mr Green was on a knife-edge from which he could be tipped by an unkind comment about his coffee break is unrealistic. Nor did the evidence suggest that Mr Moore's comment had in fact tipped Mr Green over the edge. This case came nowhere near meeting the requirements identified in *Hatton*.'

Similarly, in *Pakenham-Walsh v Connell Residential*,[56] where the claimant was an estate agent working a 52-hour week, the court dismissed the claim that:

'. . . the work was particularly intellectually or emotionally demanding, though it required dealing with members of the public for many hours. There had been no absences from work and, on the judge's findings, no complaints from the appellant or warnings from others as to stress levels. The present complaints were not made to the Employment Tribunal. Signs of stress must in any event be distinguished from signs of impending harm to health. There was no history of illness attributable to stress at work and there were no contemporaneous medical reports. The circumstances fall far short of establishing a falling below the required standard.'

In *Bonser v RJB Mining (UK) Ltd*[57] the line manager had introduced challenging targets and was forthright in his measurement and criticism of his staff. The claimant had a pre-existing vulnerability to psychiatric injury but this was not known to the employer. At one team meeting, on realising that she would probably have to cancel a holiday that she had been hoping would relieve the pressure, she became tearful and upset. The Court of Appeal found:

'That degree of understandable upset and distress alone does not, however, in my judgment, impose upon a reasonable employer a need to take steps to avert an imminent psychiatric breakdown. I fear the judge fell into error in coming to the conclusion that it was reasonably foreseeable that pressure would cause her to crack. He did not express his conclusion in paragraph 33 as happily as he might have done. There is probably no justification for drawing a distinction between the claimant, a woman with responsibility, and the other male members of the team. More importantly, for my purpose, it is the inference that the judge drew that from that event, viz, that it was reasonably foreseeable that she would crack, which is the error into which the judge fell. That event did not, in my judgment, sufficiently foretell the breakdown that was to occur in February. To the knowledge of her employer she may have become vulnerable to the stress of over-work but not of psychiatric breakdown. There was, in those circumstances, no foresight on the part of the employer which compelled reasonable steps to be taken to avert the threat of that breakdown.'

---

56 [2006] EWCA Civ 90.

57 [2003] EWCA Civ 1296, [2004] IRLR 164.

However, in *Six Continents Retail Ltd v Hone*[58] the claimant was a manager of a pub who was regularly working 90 hours per week over 7 days each week. The Court of Appeal held:

> 'It is that feature of the case, the fact that he was complaining about excessive hours and that he was very tired, together with the fact that he was recording himself as working approximately 90 hours per week on a seven day week basis, which entitled the judge to reach the conclusion he did. The reference to 90 hours in the records is of particular significance because Mr Reynolds' immediate reaction to that claim was that it was "nonsense". But the fact that Mr Hone was making such claims indicated either that he was working hours greatly in excess of anything that could reasonably have been expected of him, week in week out, or that he was making irrational entries and in effect making a cry for help. It was this latter possibility that was suggested by Mr Reynolds in his evidence.'

So, although there was some doubt as to whether quite those number of hours were in fact being worked week in week out, there was no dispute that that what was what the claimant had said to the employer. That alone was enough to fix the employer with knowledge that something was wrong.

3.5 BREACH

Although establishing foreseeability of injury is the 'threshold question', once over the threshold it is still necessary to establish breach. Did the particular breach of duty foreseeably cause the particular injury complained of?

It is essential to identify the specific breaches complained of and address each in terms of the contribution of the breach to the claimant's injury. In the case of a minor breach, the court will be slow to find that steps which could have been taken to avoid the breach would have had the result of preventing the injury in its totality.

In the employment law context, if a breach is serious the employee has the option of treating it as a repudiatory breach, walking out and claiming a constructive dismissal.[59] If the breach led to a breakdown and long-term absence, then a failure to resign as a result of the breach is unlikely to lead to any difficulty. If, however, the employee continued working, there may have been all sorts of good practical reasons why the employee was reluctant to take the irrevocable step of resigning and claiming constructive dismissal. But failing to do so may cause problems if it is later alleged that a breach long beforehand had been serious enough that its remedy would have avoided injury, but the claimant had not at the time treated it as serious enough to claim a constructive dismissal. Of course,

---

58 [2005] EWCA Civ 922.

59 See **5.1**.

in an appropriate case the nature of the claimant's psychiatric condition (which may impair his judgment) might be quite adequate to answer this, but medical evidence on the point will be required.

3.5.1 Reasonable steps

The claimant must establish breach by showing that the employer failed to take reasonable steps to prevent the injury (*Hatton* Proposition 8):

> '(8) The employer is only in breach of duty if he has failed to take the steps which are reasonable in the circumstances, bearing in mind the magnitude of the risk of harm occurring, the gravity of the harm which may occur, the costs and practicability of preventing it, and the justifications for running the risk (para 32).'

The underlying law is well established. In *Stokes v Guest, Keen Nettlefold*,[60] an industrial disease case involving exposure to chemicals which caused cancer, Swanwick J stated the legal principle as follows:

> '. . . the overall test is still the conduct of the reasonable and prudent employer, taking positive thought for the safety of his workers in the light of what he knows or ought to know; where there is a recognised and general practice which has been followed for a substantial period in similar circumstances without mishap, he is entitled to follow it, unless in the light of common sense or newer knowledge it is clearly bad; but, where there is developing knowledge, he must keep reasonably abreast of it and not be too slow to apply it; and where he has in fact greater than average knowledge of the risks, he may be thereby obliged to take more than the average or standard precautions. He must weigh up the risk in terms of the likelihood of injury occurring and the potential consequences if it does; and he must balance against this the probable effectiveness of the precautions that can be taken to meet it and the expense and inconvenience they involve. If he is found to have fallen below the standard to be properly expected of a reasonable and prudent employer in these respects, he is negligent.'

This judgment was quoted with approval by the Lords in *Barber*. This was not a case where the employer was unaware of the risk, nor had he done nothing. The question related to the adequacy of the steps taken, measured against the risks.

In work-related stress claims, the gravity of the harm should easily be established. The effect of psychiatric injury on an individual is devastating. In the modern age, an employer should recognise that a psychological breakdown is as serious as a grave physical injury in terms of the ability to return to work.[61] More difficult will be establishing the magnitude of the risk of harm – most employees will not suffer a psychiatric injury even in obviously stressful circumstances. However, the

---

60 [1968] 1 WLR 1776, 112 Sol Jo 821, 5 KIR 401.

61 Accepted by Colman J in *Walker v Northumberland County Council.*

magnitude of the risk will be increased by the degree of pressure placed on workers or the known vulnerability of a worker. So far as costs and practicability are concerned, the court will not readily find that all pressure can be removed from all workers. Indeed, the court in *Hatton* quoted with approval that part of the HSE publication, *Stress at Work* which stated that pressure can be desirable:

> 'Some pressures can, in fact, be a good thing. It is often the tasks and challenges we face at work that provide the structure to our working days, keep us motivated and are the key to a sense of achievement and job satisfaction.'

The court will expect a common-sense approach to be taken.

Even where an employer is clearly aware of the risk of psychiatric injury to its workforce in general terms, in *Melville v Home Office*[62] the Court of Appeal cautioned:

> 'The mere fact that an employer offers an occupational health service should not lead to the conclusion that the employer has foreseen risk of psychiatric injury due to stress at work to any individual or class of employee. And of course the availability of such a service will mean that the employer is unlikely to be found in breach even if harm is foreseeable (*Hatton* paragraphs 17 and 33). Moreover in a case where a conscientious employer has assessed that there is some potential risk of psychiatric injury, it will still be open to him to argue that it was a mere possibility or so small that it was reasonable for him to neglect it (see *The Wagon Mound No. 2* [1967] AC 617 at 642/3). Nor does it follow that if one employer has foreseen a particular risk, all others in the same field should have done so as well. If there is an issue as to whether a particular employer should have done so, it would fall to be decided in accordance with Swanwick J's statement of general principle in *Stokes v Guest Keen & Nettlefold (Bolts & Nuts) Ltd.*'

Even in 'second breakdown cases', the court will be slow to find an employer negligent where some steps to avoid further injury are considered and are in practice taken. *Vahidi v Fairstead House School Trust Ltd*[63] was another case involving the breakdown of a teacher. The judge held that the employer was not liable for her first breakdown and this finding was not appealed. However, she had returned to work and suffered a second breakdown and had complained that the employer had been negligent in managing her return to work. The judge found that she had received some support from colleagues and distinguished her case from Mr Barber's. The onus is on the claimant to convince the court that the employer should have done something differently:

> 'Mr Hamer criticised the judge's approach in paragraph 79 of his judgment on the basis that he should have asked himself whether the risk of relapse

[62] One of the conjoined appeals in *Hartman.*

[63] [2005] EWCA Civ 765.

was large or small in September or October 1998. He should have concluded that it was by no means a small risk and then have decided that the obligations on the school were substantial and that the school would then be driven to take the steps which Mr Hamer says should have been taken. This criticism of the judge is in my view misconceived. The judge's duty is to decide whether there is a duty of care; if so, whether there has been a breach of it; and, if so, whether that breach of duty has caused loss to the claimant. It is for the claimant to assert what it is the defendant did which it ought not to have done or what it is that a defendant did not do which it ought to have done.'

Employers often need to restructure their businesses for good economic reasons. Such reorganisations may impact on individuals and senior individuals may be opposed to the change. However, if the employee becomes ill as a result, it will not be easy to show that the employer was acting unreasonably in implementing necessary changes, although of course there might be complaint about the way in which this is handled. So in *Foumeny v University of Leeds*[64] university departments were being restructured which would lead to the loss of autonomy of the claimant's department. He was opposed to it. But once the trial judge and the Court of Appeal dismissed the allegation that this was motivated by a desire to damage the claimant, even though after a certain date psychiatric injury was foreseeable, it was impossible to show that the employer had acted unreasonably:

'... liability depended upon foresight of injury to health in which it was necessary to establish not only foresight but the steps which, in all the circumstances, it was reasonable for the employer to take to avoid the injury caused. It was the failure of the applicant to establish every ingredient of that claim which ultimately led to the judge's decision.'

In *Young v Post Office* the employer had put in place a flexible return to work regime after Mr Young's breakdown, but had failed to adhere to it. In the light of the court's finding of foreseeability of vulnerability to psychiatric injury May LJ held:

'There is, in my view, some force in the submission that there was no breach of duty when Mr Young came back to work on an entirely flexible basis under which the amount and type of his work were his own choice. The case is not as strong as that which Colman J considered in Walker, for in Walker no special arrangements were made. On the other hand, the Recorder here was, in my judgment, entitled to hold that the appellants failed to carry through the arrangements which they made. Mr Young's managers did not know what he was doing and agreed in evidence that the course at Ross-on-Wye and the work he did when Mr Legg was away were inappropriate. Seven weeks is quite a short time and the facts supporting the breaches of duty are not extensive. But I have concluded that breaches of duty were established and that the Recorder was entitled so to conclude.'

---

64 [2003] EWCA Civ 557.

Similarly in *MG v North Devon NHS Primary Care Trust*[65] the claimant who was a health visitor had a first breakdown about which no claim was made. However, although a structured return to work was proposed, one of the claimant's colleagues went off sick during this period and she was forced to cover her. She had a second breakdown. The judge held:

> 'True it is that the Defendant had the option of dismissing the Claimant but having made the decision to offer her a return to work programme they cannot thereafter complain if they are held liable having failed to adhere to that programme.'

3.5.2 Size of employer

Often a critical factor in establishing breach in work-related stress claims will be the size of the employer (*Hatton* Proposition 9):

> '(9) The size and scope of the employer's operation, its resources and the demands it faces are relevant in deciding what is reasonable; these include the interests of other employees and the need to treat them fairly, for example, in any redistribution of duties (para 33).'

That is not to say that a small employer cannot ever be liable. However, the court will be slow to find a smaller employer in breach of duty unless the pressures of the job are unreasonable or the vulnerability of the employee is obvious over a reasonably lengthy period which would give an employer the opportunity to come up with a plan for dealing with it.

Conversely, a large employer with both significant resources in terms of other employees or the ability to recruit others and dedicated human resources professionals will find it difficult to escape a breach of duty if action is not taken promptly.

In *Daw v Intel Corp (UK) Ltd*[66] the defendant was a large international company. In a long series of memoranda, the claimant had drawn her superiors' attention to the stress that overwork and confused internal communication lines were causing her. The judge had found:

> 'The real problem was that because of her excessive workload, the demands of those different people [her managers] added to her stress. It was difficult to decide whose demands should be given priority.'

Pill LJ concluded:

> 'That is the essential background against which the respondent's claim must be considered. She was not likely readily to complain of the amount of work she was required to do, or to take time off, or to tackle her problems other than by consulting those who could do something about them. The stress

---

65 [2006] EWHC 850 (QB).
66 [2007] EWCA Civ 70.

> from which she came to suffer was not caused by the volume of work alone. As carefully set out in her memorandum in early March 2001 to Mr Howell, a combination of factors led to the stress becoming intolerable.
>
> In my judgment, the judge was fully entitled to hold that it was a failure of management which created the stresses and led to the breakdown. The judge was entitled to hold that, by early March, injury to the respondent's health was reasonably foreseeable. The indications of impending harm to health were plain enough for the appellants to realise that immediate action was required.'

In *MG v North Devon NHS Primary Care Trust* the complaint was that the employer had failed to put in place cover for another sick member of staff which had led to overwork during a return to work programme for a psychologically vulnerable employee. The judge held:

> 'In my judgment the Defendant was in breach of its duty to the Claimant by failing to take steps to replace Suzanna Carter in June 2002. There were it would appear bank staff available and having regard to the size and scope of the employers organisation it was reasonable to expect that cover would be provided for absent health visitors.'

In *Walker* it was argued that providing support for Mr Walker to prevent the second breakdown would have meant reallocating resources attributed to other statutory functions and that the claimant was therefore trespassing into policy; Morland J gave this argument short shrift:

> 'Whereas the mutual intention to be imputed to the parties to a contract of employment with a public body could be expected to qualify the employer's duty of safety by requiring the employer to do no more than take reasonable steps to procure the employee's safety at work, it is inconceivable that such mutual intention would require the employer to take only such steps for the employee's safety as political expediency from time to time permitted if the exercise of statutory powers were involved.'

It will be no defence for a statutory defendant that meeting the needs of the claimant would be impossible without breaching other statutory duties.

3.5.3 Would those steps have prevented injury?

It is of course no good showing that the employer was in breach of duty by not taking reasonable steps if those steps would not actually have prevented injury (*Hatton* Proposition 10):

> '(10) An employer can only reasonably be expected to take steps which are likely to do some good: the court is likely to need expert evidence on this (para 34).'

In *Best v Staffordshire University*[67] the Court of Appeal pointed out that there was no expert evidence as to what should have been done and whether it would have done any good. The court was particularly concerned about this in a case where it was not disputed that the breakdown was 70% due to non-work related factors.

There is often a failure by employers to carry out any or any appropriate risk assessments. However, courts are slow to find that this alone is a breach which is causative of injury.[68] The employee has to show that the risk assessment would have identified steps that a reasonable employer would have taken and that these would have prevented the injury. Furthermore, in a stress claim the risk assessment will only reveal anything if the employee would have disclosed the stress and the effect it was having. So, for example, in *Sayers v Cambridgeshire County Council* Ramsay J said:

> 'I do not see that a risk assessment would have done anything towards preventing Mrs Sayers' illness in this case. The risk assessment form produced by the Council indicates the matters which might have been assessed. However, the assessment of risk depends on the information available. In this case there is no evidence that Mrs Sayers would have disclosed her previous history of psychiatric illness or any other evidence which would have led to a different conclusion on the foreseeability of a risk than I have found to be the case. The evidence is to the contrary and even Dr Orr was initially unaware of her previous medical history.
>
> The Council had, I find, adequate general strategies for dealing with risks in relation to workplace stress and they employed mentors and coaches to assist employees. Those strategies depend, though, on the needs of Mrs Sayers being assessed and, for the reasons given above, no matter what strategies were implemented, there is no evidence that such strategies or assessment would have led to a different conclusion as to the foreseeability of a risk in this case.'

If the breach relied on is relatively minor, it may be difficult to establish that if there had been no breach there would have been no damage. So, in *Deadman v Bristol City Council*[69] the claimant had suffered a serious psychiatric reaction to a grievance investigation against him. He complained about the way the outcome was notified by way of a letter left on his desk and also that the investigation panel comprised two members instead of three as provided for by a procedure incorporated into his contract. The Court of Appeal were not convinced that the manner of notification was a breach and although the composition of the panel was a breach the court held:

---

67 One of the conjoined appeals in *Hartman*.

68 See **2.2.1**

69 [2007] EWCA Civ 822; [2007] IRLR 888; [2007] All ER (D) 494 (Jul).

'If one had asked either of the parties at that time whether they thought it at all likely that an error of that kind in convening a panel to investigate a complaint of sexual harassment would result in psychiatric harm to one or other of those involved, I think they would have been astonished. If they had thought about it they would probably have said that the investigation might have to be carried out again with a properly constituted panel and that that would add to the stress inevitable in any process of that kind, but I can see no grounds for believing that they would have thought it at all likely to cause either party to suffer psychiatric harm . . . Any damage flowing from the Council's breach of contract in this respect was too remote in law to be recoverable.'

3.5.4 Confidential advice services

Many large employers have established confidential advice services for their employees. Hale LJ said (*Hatton* Proposition 11):

'(11) An employer who offers a confidential advice service, with referral to appropriate counselling or treatment services, is unlikely to be found in breach of duty (paras 17 and 33).'

This was seen by many such employers as a 'get out of jail free card' – set up a confidential advice service and it would not matter what stresses were imposed on employees.

However, although the existence or otherwise of a confidential advice service may be relevant in establishing whether there had been a breach of duty, its relevance to the particular issues for the particular employee must be considered.

In *Best v Staffordshire County Council*,[70] a counselling service was available but the judge at first instance had pointed out that there had been little evidence adduced about it. Although Mr Best's appeal was dismissed on other grounds, the Court of Appeal said:

'We agree that on the facts of this case the availability of a counselling service was not fatal to Mr Best's case. The outcome of Mr Best's claim does not depend on any failure on his part to take up whatever counselling service was available. It is, however, a factor for which the Recorder should have given credit when considering whether the university was in breach of its duty of care.'

However, the court pointed out that there might well have been an argument on foreseeability of psychiatric injury:

'Mr Best was aware of it and had been on counselling courses but he did not use the service. His evidence on cross-examination was that he may have been naïve enough to think he did not need counselling at the time. This

[70] One of the conjoined appeals in *Hartman*.

evidence has relevance to the issue of foreseeability. The university made an obvious point: if Mr Best did not recognise that he needed counselling, how could his employers be in a better position? The Recorder did not deal with this argument.'

Similarly, in *Daw v Intel Corp (UK) Ltd* the Court of Appeal said of the employer's counselling service:

> 'There will be cases in which an employee may be expected to take refuge in counselling services. The problems of this capable and loyal employee could, however, as the judge found, be dealt with only by management reducing her workload.'

And in *Dickins v O2 plc* the claimant's manager had suggested that she take up the employer's counselling service. On appeal, inter alia, the employer argued that the judge had misapplied *Hatton* Proposition 11 and that the suggestion of counselling was enough to avoid a breach of duty. Smith LJ disagreed:

> 'At paragraph 17 of *Hatton*, where the desirability of an advice and counselling service was discussed, it was made plain that the advantage of such a service was because many employees were unwilling to admit to their line managers that they were not coping with their work for fear of damaging their reputations. A confidential service would enable the employee to take advice without making any potentially damaging disclosure direct to the employer. However, in the present case, the respondent was not afraid to tell her line manager (on 23 April) that she was "at the end of her tether". Mr Keith Brown's response included the suggestion that she should seek counselling from the body engaged by the appellant. The respondent did not do so; she was already receiving counselling through her own doctor. Given the situation where the respondent was describing severe symptoms, alleging they were due to stress at work and was warning that she did not know for how long she could carry on, I do not think that a mere suggestion that she seek counselling could be regarded as an adequate response.
>
> In *Daw v Intel Corporation* [2007] ICR 1318, the Court of Appeal observed that the reference to counselling services in Hatton did not make such services a panacea by which employers can discharge their duty of care in all cases. In that case, the judge had been entitled to hold the employer in breach notwithstanding that it provided a counselling service. The employee's problems could only be dealt with by management intervention. The same is true here. Mr Gardiner's reliance on the summary in paragraph 43(11) serves to demonstrate how dangerous it is to apply guidance given by the court as though it were a statutory provision.'

3.5.5 Dismissal or demotion of employee?

In some cases, the employee's stress might in practice only be alleviated by removing him from the post either by dismissal or by demotion. If this is the only practicable solution, the employer is unlikely to be liable (*Hatton* Proposition 12):

> '(12) If the only reasonable and effective step would have been to dismiss or demote the employee, the employer will not be in breach of duty in allowing a willing employee to continue in the job (para 34).'

This principle derives from *Withers v Perry Chain Co Ltd*[71] where an employee had chosen to go on working even though there was a risk that she would develop dermatitis and Devlin LJ said:

> 'In my opinion there is no legal duty upon an employer to prevent an adult employee from doing work which he or she is willing to do. If there is a slight risk, as the judge has found, it is for the employee to weigh it against the desirability, or perhaps the necessity, of employment. The relationship between employer and employee is not that of a schoolmaster and pupil. There is no obligation on an employer to offer alternative safe employment, though no doubt a considerate employer would always try to do so – as the defendants thought they had done here. Nor is there any obligation on an employer to dismiss an employee in such circumstances. It cannot be said that an employer is bound to dismiss an employee rather than allow her to run a small risk. The employee is free to decide for herself what risks she will run.'

In applying this to stress claims in *Barber v Somerset*, although Lord Rodger agreed that the appeal should be allowed, he did point out:

> 'On the judge's findings the school authorities were faced with a situation where Mr Barber was unfit, through no fault of his or theirs, to carry out the duties which he had agreed to perform. In his particular case, one possible way of alleviating the problems might have been for him to give up his position as project manager and concentrate on his work as mathematics co-ordinator. Again, there is nothing in the judge's findings in fact to show whether that step would have relieved the pressure on him sufficiently to allow him to carry on with his duties as mathematics co-ordinator without any risk to his health. Nor is there anything to suggest that Mr Barber ever contemplated taking that step – which would, of course, have meant a reduction in his total salary.
>
> Mr Barber might well have resisted any suggestion that he should give up his work as project manager and take a corresponding reduction in salary. And there must be situations where, just as an adult cannot be required to undergo medical treatment against his will, he is entitled to continue working at high pressure, even though he runs the risk of damaging his health, whether mental or physical. For example, a university teacher

---

[71] [1961] 1 WLR 1314, at 1320.

> employed to do research can surely choose to work all hours of the day and night, at possible or even obvious risk to his health, in the hope of making a breakthrough in deciphering an ancient language or unravelling some secret in genetics. The university authorities can hardly be under any duty to do more than warn of the possible dangers: they cannot be obliged to lock away the photographs of the texts or bar the laboratory doors to prevent him from working into the night. Not only would that be to interfere with his right to carry out his duty of research under his contract: it would risk depriving the world of the benefits of his discovery.'

In *Bishop v Baker Refractories Limited*[72] the employer had been taken over by an American company that had introduced new methods of working. Mr Bishop had been unable to cope. The Court of Appeal concluded:

> 'Mr Bishop knew that his employers had no other work for him, and that his doctor had advised him to change jobs. He chose to go back to work, as he was entitled to do, but there is in our judgment no evidential basis for a finding that the breakdown in his health was reasonably foreseeable, and in any event there was nothing the employers could have done to continue Mr Bishop's employment, if he could not cope with it, because work of the kind he wanted to do was not now available.'

In *Vahidi v Fairstead House School Trust Ltd*[73] the claimant was a reception class teacher who had suffered a breakdown. Despite efforts to arrange a structured return to work by the school (the court found that the school had not been in breach of duty in implementing it), she found it difficult to cope. It was argued that the employer should have sent the claimant home to avoid the stress being caused by the work, but Longmore LJ said:

> 'Courts have to be careful not to conclude that an employer can only perform his duty to his employee by dismissing him or her. The same sort of consideration in my judgment applies to sending a claimant home and effectively prohibiting the claimant from doing the work which she wants to do.'

In *Brookes v North Yorkshire Moors Railway*[74] the employer did canvass changes to the claimant's job, including possible removal of supervisory functions or part-time working. The judge concluded:

> 'I bear in mind that it is clear from the judgment of Hale LJ that it was not for the Defendant to effectively dismiss or demote the Claimant to save him from further injury. That the Claimant wished to retain his pay or something broadly similar is entirely understandable and one should be slow to criticise

72 One of the conjoined appeals in *Hatton*.

73 [2005] EWCA Civ 765.

74 (York) (Mr Recorder Kirtley) LTL 19 December 2005.

any employee for the desire to continue at work; but it is quite another thing to transfer that sympathy to a finding of breach of duty on behalf of his employers.'

However, it should be noted that in *Coxall v Goodyear GB Limited*[75] (which was not a stress at work claim) the Court of Appeal distinguished *Withers*, finding the employer negligent where the employer had blatantly disregarded the advice of its own doctor, line manager and health and safety manager in allowing the employee back to work where his condition deteriorated.

3.5.6 Identify steps employer should have taken

It is not enough to show that injury was foreseeable and that there was a breach, it is also necessary to show how that breach caused the damage. And in answering that question it is essential to consider what could have been done by the employer (*Hatton* Proposition 13):

> '(13) In all cases, therefore, it is necessary to identify the steps which the employer both could and should have taken before finding him in breach of his duty of care (para 33).'

This is especially so when dealing with claims by managers. In *Harding v The Pub Estate Co Ltd*[76] the claimant was a temporary manager of a pub who worked long hours in a difficult environment. He suffered a heart attack which he alleged was the result of stress at work. The courts were obviously concerned about issues of causation, but did not consider these as in their judgment there was no breach of duty:

> 'What should the appellants have done and would it have made any difference? It seems to me these are real difficulties in the respondent's way on this aspect of the case. He was the manager. He accepted he had sufficient staff. What hours he worked was a matter for him. Whatever hours he worked, the content of the job did not change. He never said to the appellants that they must reduce his hours.'

In *Barber v Somerset*, Lord Rodger referred to *Cross v Highlands and Islands Enterprise*:[77]

> 'That was a very sad case of a promising 39-year old executive, employed in a job in which (because of geographical factors) close day-to-day supervision of his work was impossible. He became ill with depressive illness and killed himself. The employer was held not liable because no causative breach of duty was established. After the employee had been off work with depression, his line manager travelled to see him and spent almost the whole day discussing his work and his future with him. He reduced his

[75] [2002] EWCA Civ 1010.
[76] [2005] EWCA Civ 553.
[77] [2001] IRLR 336.

responsibilities and continued to maintain contact with him by telephone (see para 84). Unfortunately the depression continued, but the employer was not liable for the tragedy which ensued because (para 86):

> "... the evidence does not establish that objectively the job was the problem. For all the defenders knew, they were dealing with an employee who, for reasons that were not clear, had become unable to cope with the job that he had previously managed successfully."'

And in *Brookes v North Yorkshire Moors Railway*, in the case of a manager who was unable to cope with his responsibilities, the judge said:

> 'The Claimant identifies a number of things which could have been done. He says that specific guidance could have been had from a specialist occupational health Railway doctor, apparently based in a BUPA hospital, who would have been able potentially to assist. It is contended that the Defendants ought to have thought of a completely different role for the Claimant by way of a carriage inspector or some other task which would have removed his exposure to responsibility, but at the same time would have permitted him to retain the same or roughly the same by way of remuneration ... I bear in mind very much what the Court of Appeal clearly had in mind in the case of Hatton that it would be possible, almost inevitably after the event, to come up with a raft of issues which could perhaps have been tried and undertaken. It is not known at this stage whether those procedures would in fact have done any good. It is very difficult to know without direct evidence as to whether or not such a course of action would really have made any difference. It is not the case that the Defendants simply washed their hands of this Claimant.'

3.6 CONTRIBUTORY FAULT

Pleading contributory fault is not particularly attractive in stress at work cases. However, it was raised by the employer in *Young v Post Office*, who argued that Mr Young was at fault in not drawing the failings in the return to work regime to the attention of his employers. This argument was given short shrift by May LJ:

> 'A finding of contributory negligence in a case of psychiatric illness, although no doubt theoretically possible in other circumstances, does not in my view sit happily with the facts of this case. I know of no case in which a claimant such as Mr Young, vulnerable to psychiatric illness which he successfully holds to his employers, has been held to be contributorily negligent, and counsel was unable to draw our attention to any such case. I would reject this ground of appeal.'

In *Clark v Chief Constable for Essex*[78] contributory negligence was raised, as outlined by the judge as follows:

---

[78] [2006] EWHC 2290 (QB).

> 'The witnesses called for the Defendant also gave evidence of the various avenues of grievance and redress there are for Essex police officers. Superintendant Bottrill lists eight. The first two, and the fifth, speaking to your immediate Line Manager and Supervising Sergeant, and to other officers, were of little relevance in this case. Mr Kreyling was the Line Manager. The Claimant did speak to Mr Bird and CI King. The Claimant also tried the third, the Grievance Procedure but was persuaded by Mr Bird to withdraw it in April 1998. He did not try the fourth, speaking to the Federation Officer. He did try, and did eventually succeed (after he had stopped work) in speaking to Complaints and Discipline. Self-referral to Occupational Health was effectively what he did after 4th October 1999. As noted above, he did refer to the problem at Appraisal in 1998, but he had no opportunity to do so after that.
>
> While I accept that officers in Essex Police did have a number of alternatives open to them to deal with stress at work, in this case the Claimant cannot be criticised for not doing more than he did to address the problems he faced. I reject the plea of contributory negligence.'

However, in *Corr v IBC Vehicles Limited*[79] (where the employer was held liable for losses flowing from the claimant's subsequent suicide after a work-related accident) several of their Lordships indicated that they felt that a finding of contributory negligence would have been appropriate, but it was not applied in that case as it had not been argued.

It is submitted that it will be difficult for an employer to argue contributory fault in a 'second breakdown' case successfully. There may be some prospects of doing so for employers in a first breakdown case, particularly where the employer did try to prevent the employee from overwork, albeit ineffectually.

---

79 [2008] UKHL 13.

CHAPTER 4

NON-DISCRIMINATORY HARASSMENT

4.1 'HARASSMENT' AT COMMON LAW

As we have seen,[1] there is an implied term in the contract of employment that the employer will protect the employee from bullying and harassment during employment. The employer is also under a duty of care to protect the health and safety of employees. Breach of the duty of care or of the implied contractual duty, either directly or because vicariously liable,[2] may lead to a claim in the tort of negligence or in contract, if psychiatric injury is a foreseeable consequence of the breach.[3]

However, such an injury may not be foreseeable; or there may be no direct breach; or the employer may not be vicariously liable for it.[4]

This chapter will mainly look at the use of the Protection from Harassment Act 1997 (PFHA 1997), but it is instructive first to consider other possible torts and whether they might provide a remedy for bullying or harassment.

Other statutory protection against harassment where it constitutes discrimination under the equlaity legislation will be examined in Chapter 5.

4.1.1 Trespass to person

If there is an assault (whether or not combined with physical 'battery'), then there is a potential claim by way of the tort of the trespass to person. Pure psychiatric injury is treated as physical injury for this purpose, provided that the victim suffers from a recognised psychiatric condition.

Assault requires both the intention of the perpetrator and the apprehension of an immediate threat to the person by the victim.[5]

---

1 See **2.4.1.2**.

2 See **3.2.2**.

3 See **3.4**.

4 Note, however, that some of the older case-law pre-dates recent clarification of the law relating to vicarious liability – see **3.2.2**.

5 *Collins v Wilcock* [1984] 1 WLR 1172.

However, as Hale LJ noted in *Wong v Parkside Health and Another*,[6] if a private criminal prosecution has been brought, then the claimant is precluded from subsequently bringing a claim in tort:

> 'Thus the victim of an assault has a choice. If the authorities choose to prosecute, there is no problem. But if they do not, she must choose between bringing a private prosecution or a civil action. The former will destroy her right to bring the latter, irrespective of the outcome. The alleged perpetrator is not to be put in double jeopardy for the same cause. This may be an anomalous approach in today's world, given the differences in the burden of proof and sometimes in the level of compensation awarded by criminal and civil courts. But for as long as s 45 is on the statute book, the effect in a case such as this is clear: the claimant cannot rely upon the assault in any other proceedings. The Recorder was therefore right to exclude it from his consideration.'

It is rare that a stress or bullying at work claim will need to be pleaded in trespass to person. However, a single shocking incident causing serious psychiatric damage might require this as there would be no 'course of conduct' required by the PFHA 1997.

4.1.2 Intentional infliction of harm

However, in few bullying and harassment cases will there be a physical assault or the threat of one. Even if there is, this may be just one incident amid a more general campaign of verbal harassment. If the verbal harassment was negligent then the normal law of negligence applies.[7] If, however, it was 'deliberate', then it might constitute the tort of 'intentional infliction of harm'. In *Wong v Parkside Health NHS Trust and another*[8] Hale LJ surveyed the old case-law:

> 'In *Wilkinson v Downton* [1897] 2 QB 57, the defendant did not intend to cause physical harm to the claimant. He intended to play a particularly nasty practical joke upon her. He told her, knowing that it was not true but meaning her to believe them, that her husband had had an accident returning from the races in a wagonette, had broken both his legs, was lying in a public house in Leytonstone, and wished the claimant to go at once with a cab and some pillows to fetch him home. She suffered a violent shock to her nervous system, producing vomiting and other more serious and permanent physical consequences at one time threatening her reason, and entailing weeks of suffering for her and expense to her husband. Wright J found in her favour . . .
>
> This was approved in the later, and "much stronger" case of *Janvier v Sweeney* [1919] 2 KB 316. In order to persuade the plaintiff to hand over letters belonging to her employer, the second defendant, an employee of the first defendant, pretended to be from Scotland Yard, representing the

6 *Wong v Parkside Health NHS Trust and another* [2001] EWCA Civ 1721, per Hale LJ.
7 See Chapter 3.
8 [2001] EWCA Civ 1721.

military authorities who wanted the plaintiff for corresponding with a German spy. The plaintiff suffered a severe shock, resulting in neurasthenia, shingles and other ailments. Although these cases were concerned with words, the same principle would obviously apply to the intentional infliction of physical harm by other indirect means, such as digging a pit into which it is intended that another should fall.'

Hale LJ continued:

'It follows from Wright J's formulation that, although the tort is commonly labelled "intentional infliction of harm", it is not necessary to prove that the defendant actually wanted to produce such harm. If the conduct complained of was "calculated" to do so, and does so, then that is enough. Much depends, therefore, on what is meant by "calculated".'

Hale LJ explained that Professor Fleming[9] had written:

'Cases will be rare where nervous shock involving physical injury was fully intended (desired). More frequently, the defendant's aim would have been merely to frighten, terrify or alarm his victim. But this is quite sufficient, provided that his conduct was of a kind reasonably capable of terrifying a normal person, or was known or ought to have been known to the defendant to be likely to terrify the plaintiff for reasons special to him. Such conduct could be described as reckless . . .'

But Hale LJ concluded:

'This might be read to mean that the tort is committed if there is deliberate conduct which will foreseeably lead to alarm or distress falling short of the recognised psychiatric illness which is now considered the equivalent of physical harm, provided that such harm is actually suffered. We do not consider that English law has gone so far.'

This reasoning was approved by the House of Lords in *Wainwright v Home Office*.[10]

A claim for the tort of 'intentional infliction of harm' might therefore succeed if a recognised psychiatric injury was caused and the injury was 'calculated', but not otherwise. The burden of establishing that the behaviour was 'calculated' to cause psychiatric injury will be difficult to satisfy, except in the most extreme case.

Theoretically, it might be thought to be preferable for a claimant to frame a claim for harassment at work in the tort of intentional infliction of harm or trespass to person rather than in negligence as, arguably, there is no need to prove foreseeability of psychiatric injury. However, in *Letang v Cooper*[11] the Court of Appeal held that if 'they are simply alternative

---

9 Fleming *The Law of Torts* (Lbc Information Services, 9th edn, 1998).

10 [2003] UKHL 53.

11 [1965] 1 QB 232.

ways of describing the same factual situation', no advantage can be gained from formulating the claim in trespass rather than in negligence.[12]

4.1.3 Harassment at common law?

However, if there was no recognised psychiatric injury, the issue was whether at common law there was a tort of harassment giving rise to potential compensation. In *Wong*, the claimant was a wheelchair administrator who was employed by an NHS Trust and who alleged harassment and bullying in 1995. The Court of Appeal considered the judgment of the House of Lords in *Hunter v Canary Wharf*[13] where Lord Hoffmann had said:

> 'The perceived gap in *Khorasandjian v Bush* was the absence of a tort of intentional harassment causing distress without actual bodily or psychiatric illness. This limitation is thought to arise out of cases like *Wilkinson v Downton* [1897] 2 QB 57 and *Janvier v Sweeney* [1919] 2 KB 316. The law of harassment has now been put on a statutory basis . . . and it is unnecessary to consider how the common law might have developed.'

Hale LJ in *Wong* concluded:

> '. . . Parliament has provided a civil remedy, which includes damages for anxiety, as well as a criminal remedy in the 1997 Act. No doubt the concept of "a course of conduct which amounts to harassment" will be developed in decisions under that Act. Until that Act came into force, there was power to restrain by injunction conduct which might result in the tort of intentional infliction of harm or otherwise threaten the claimant's right of access to the courts, but there was no right to damages for conduct falling short of an actual tort.'

There is therefore no common law tort of harassment separate to the statutory tort, unless the conduct in fact constitutes the torts of 'trespass to person'[14] or 'intentional [ie calculated] infliction of harm [ie recognised psychiatric injury]'.[15]

4.1.4 Defamation and malicious falsehood

If the words spoken (or written) about the claimant were defamatory there may be a separate cause of action for defamation. The law of defamation is beyond the scope of this work, but attention is specifically drawn to the defence of 'qualified privilege' within the employment relationship.[16]

---

12 See *Clerk and Lindsell on Torts* (Sweet & Maxwell, 19th edn, 2007) at 15-08.
13 [1997] AC 655.
14 See **4.1.2**.
15 See **4.1.3**.
16 See, for example, *Clerk and Lindsell on Torts* (Sweet & Maxwell, 19th edn, 2007) ch 23.

In *Adam v Ward*[17] Lord Atkinson defined this as:

> '. . . an occasion where the person who makes the communication has an interest or a duty, legal, social or moral, to make it to the person to who it is made, and the person to whom it is so made has a corresponding interest or duty to receive it . . .'

If qualified privilege applies, then the claimant must show malice in the publication of the material.

In *Crossland v Wilkinson Hardware Stores Ltd*[18] the claimant initiated a grievance, his employment subsequently terminated and a compromise agreement was signed. Notwithstanding this he initially sought to bring employment tribunal proceedings for unfair dismissal. He then brought proceedings for defamation and breach of contract (alleged failure to protect him from harassment) against his employer. The employer sought to strike out the claims. The defamation alleged related to a memorandum concerning his operation of the store and words spoken by other employees in meetings. In striking out the claim, Tugendhat J commented:

> 'The context of this case is one in which it is not at all surprising to find that critical remarks are made of a person in the position of the Claimant. It is not alleged that the publishers have fabricated the complaints against him which gave rise to his grievance. This is a case where it is common ground that there was a complaint against the Claimant, and the Defendant, as a well organised and large scale employer, was bound to investigate. It was also entitled, as an employer, to review the performance of its employees, including the Claimant, whether or not there had been a complaint made. For that matter, if it did want to get rid of the Claimant, as he alleges, there would have been nothing wrong with that in principle, so long as they set about it fairly and lawfully.
>
> This does seem to me to be a case where the Claimant is exaggerating the meanings relied on, and what he alleges to be falsehoods in the statements of which he complains. If the words were understood to mean what he alleges they meant, namely dishonesty or serious wrongdoing, it is hard to explain the outcome of the grievance procedure. The outcome was that no action was taken against him. He was not dismissed. The upshot was that concerns were expressed about how he was carrying out his functions both with regard to his manner towards his staff and on his compliance with company procedures. That is all. The proposal that he leave by agreement arose only in August 2003, after a further note containing a complaint from his staff had been submitted.'

It will be rare that a claimant will be able to establish that statements made about him by fellow employees in the course of employment were actuated by malice.

---

17 [1917] AC 309.

18 [2005] EWHC 481 (QB).

And in considering the extent to which an employer is entitled to make comments about an employee in the course of his business, the judge in *RDF Media Group Plc and Another v Clements*[19] held:

> '... where such allegations and representations are expressed between members of the Board of Directors of a Company which is the employer, it is difficult to conceive of circumstances which can give the employee the right to complain of a breach of the obligation. That is because the Board of Directors is the controlling mind of the Company and representations between individuals on the Board is merely equivalent to the Company thinking aloud to itself. It is not yet the law that an employer is prohibited from thinking even negative and unworthy thoughts about an employee on his payroll.'

And also:

> '... where representations are made between the executive members of a Company (or between managers and personnel officers) about an employment issue affecting an employee, it will usually be the case that the occasion is one where there is 'reasonable and proper cause' for the representation to be made; in such a case the employee, on whom lies the burden of proving the absence of reasonable and proper cause, may well fail to prove this essential element in his case, unless the representations in fact made went well beyond what was reasonable and proper for the occasion.'

So, if an employer has reasonable and proper cause for making the comments which the employee objects to there will be no cause of action.

4.2 STATUTORY LIABILITY FOR HARASSMENT (PROTECTION FROM HARASSMENT ACT 1997)

The PFHA 1997 arose principally out of public concern about 'stalking' whereby individuals could be harassed by an obsessed person who did not assault physically, or cause his victim to suffer a recognised psychiatric condition; but who did alarm or distress the victim. The Act was not directly concerned with workplace harassment, although it should be noted that the Dignity at Work Bill 1997 did contain many similar provisions relating to workplace bullying. This latter was a private members bill introduced by Lord Monkswell which he described as being 'the workplace equivalent of the anti-stalking Bill which the Government are to bring in later this year'.[20] Arguably, the Dignity at Work Bill fell, at least in part, due to assurances given by the government that many of its measures would in effect be introduced through the PFHA 1997. Lord Lucas speaking on behalf of the government in the debate on the Dignity at Work Bill said:[21]

---

19 [2007] EWHC 2892 (QB), [2008] IRLR 207.

20 *Hansard* HL Deb, 4 December 1996, vol 576 cols 754–74.

21 *Hansard* HL Deb, 4 December 1996, vol 576, cols 754–74.

'Under the Government's Protection from Harassment Bill, which we have not yet seen in this House and which is thought of as the "stalking" Bill, it will be an offence to pursue a course of conduct which causes a person to feel harassment or distress. The Bill does not exclude the offence being committed at work. It also contains civil measures enabling a person to seek an injunction preventing further harassment. Breach of an injunction is also an offence.

The Government do not intend to criminalise normal workplace arguments and the Bill includes a defence for conduct which is reasonable in the circumstances. However, that defence will not protect those who use work simply as a pretext to harass someone without reason. When the Bill comes here, I hope that those noble Lords who have spoken this evening will examine it to see whether it would solve a number of problems which they have raised.'

It certainly cannot be said that Parliament was unaware of the possible wider implications of the introduction of a law against stalking.

Section 1 of the PFHA 1997 provides:

'(1) A person must not pursue a course of conduct—
(a) which amounts to harassment of another, and
(b) which he knows or ought to know amounts to harassment of the other.

(2) For the purposes of this section, the person whose course of conduct is in question ought to know that it amounts to harassment of another if a reasonable person in possession of the same information would think the course of conduct amounted to harassment of the other.'

Section 7 of the PFHA 1997 interprets these provisions as follows:

'(2) References to harassing a person include alarming the person or causing the person distress.

(3) A "course of conduct" must involve conduct on at least two occasions.

(4) "Conduct" includes speech.'

Statutory defences to this include: that the conduct was for the purpose of detecting or preventing crime; that the conduct was necessary to comply with another enactment; that the conduct was reasonable in all the circumstances.

Harassment is a criminal offence which carries a sentence of up to 6 months' imprisonment or a maximum fine on scale 5.

Section 3 of the PFHA 1997 provides civil remedies in respect of section 1 of the PFHA 2007 including injunction to prevent a repeat of the conduct and, most relevantly in the context of workplace harassment, compensation. Section 3 of the PFHA 1997 states:

> '(1) An actual or apprehended breach of section 1 may be the subject of a claim in civil proceedings by the person who is or may be the victim of the course of conduct in question.
>
> (2) On such a claim, damages may be awarded for (among other things) any anxiety caused by the harassment and any financial loss resulting from the harassment.'

The civil standard of proof applies to claims brought under s 3 of the PFHA 1997.[22]

In addition to the offence of harassment, s 4 of the PFHA 1997 also provides for a separate criminal offence of 'putting people in fear of violence':

> '(1) A person whose course of conduct causes another to fear, on at least two occasions, that violence will be used against him is guilty of an offence if he knows or ought to know that his course of conduct will cause the other so to fear on each of those occasions.'

The Act does not, however, provide new civil remedies in respect of conduct under s 4 of the PFHA 1997.

4.3 VICARIOUS LIABILITY

Majrowski v Guy's and St Thomas' NHS Trust[23] concerned the issue of whether an employer could in principle be vicariously liable for harassment carried out by its employee contrary to the PFHA 1997. Unless the employer was vicariously liable, potential actions would in practice have been limited as the individual perpetrator may well be a man of straw. In *Majrowski*, the issue of vicarious liability was taken as a preliminary issue. The claimant won 2:1 in the Court of Appeal, but there had been a strong dissenting judgment from Lord Justice Scott Baker.

It is clear from the Lords' judgment that their lordships were also split on the question of whether Parliament had really meant to create vicarious liability for this kind of statutory tort. Baroness Hale, in particular, having spent some considerable time circumscribing the boundaries of actionable stress at work claims,[24] was obviously irritated by what she considered to have been Parliament's rather shorthand approach to

---

22 *Hipgrave v Jones* [2004] EWHC 2901 (QB).

23 [2006] UKHL 34.

24 See the 16 'propositions' in *Sutherland v Hatton* [2002] EWCA Civ 76 discussed in Chapters 3 and 6.

legislation. Lord Nicholls on the other hand could see no reason on policy grounds for denying the claimant relief against an employer on the basis of vicarious liability.

In *Lister v Hesley Hall*[25] and *Dubai Aluminium v Salaam*[26] the House of Lords had made it clear that a wrong closely connected to the acts an employee is authorised to do is regarded as being in the course of employment. So, for example, in *Mattis v Pollock*[27] the nightclub was liable for a doorman who, following an altercation at the nightclub, went home, armed himself with a knife, returned and stabbed a customer in the street. Thus, on this basis, most employers would be liable for harassment carried out by their employees because there is a 'close connection' with the work carried out by the harasser and the harassment itself.[28]

In *Majrowski* the Scottish law lord, Lord Hope, noticed that the part of the Act which related to consequent amendments to rather arcane points of Scottish law on limitation clearly provided for the principle of vicarious liability to apply in Scotland ('that the defender was a person to whose act or omission the injuries were attributable in whole or in part *or the employer or principal of such person*').[29] He persuaded his fellow judges that Parliament could not have intended to create vicarious liability for harassment in one part of the UK, but not in others. The appeal was therefore, somewhat reluctantly, dismissed and the claim against the employer allowed to proceed.

As a deliberate act, rather than a negligent one, there might also be an issue as to whether an employer's compulsory employers' liability insurance covers such claims, although in *Hawley v Luminar*[30] it was held that an assault by a doorman on a member of the public did constitute an accidental injury for the purposes of a public liability policy. In practice, where a harassment claim is brought the defence will usually be conducted by the employer's liability insurers.

4.4 FORESEEABILITY AND INJURY

Claims under the PFHA 1997 in respect of bullying have certain advantages over normal common law claims in contract or tort for workplace stress.

---

25 [2001] UKHL 22.

26 [2002] UKHL 48.

27 [2003] EWCA Civ 887.

28 See **3.2** for a more detailed analysis of vicarious liability generally in this respect.

29 PFHA 1997, s 10, incorporating a new s 18B in the Prescription and Limitation (Scotland) Act 1973, emphasis added.

30 [2006] EWCA Civ 18.

First, foreseeability of injury is not required in order to establish a claim under the PFHA 1997. In stress at work claims arising from a breach of duty in negligence or contract this has become a major problem since *Hatton*.[31]

Harassment is, however, a statutory tort and, as with race and other discrimination, foreseeability is not a necessary ingredient (see *Essa v Laing*[32]).

Insofar as the Court of Appeal, in their rather confused judgment in *Banks v Ablex Ltd*,[33] appeared to require foreseeability of injury as an ingredient under the PFHA 1997 ('proof that the defendants foresaw or ought to have foreseen the particular type of injury suffered by the claimant as a possible consequence of the conduct complained of is a pre-requisite to a finding of liability'), it is submitted that this is wrong. In *Banks* possibly the problem for the court was that the claim had originally been pleaded as a claim in negligence and then in the tort of intentional infliction of harm, harassment being added as an afterthought.

In *Majrowski* Lord Nicholls, in outlining the consequences of a finding of vicarious liability for harassment under the PFHA 1997, acknowledges 'foreseeability of damage is not an essential ingredient' and Baroness Hale confirms:

> 'There is no requirement that harm, or even alarm or distress, be actually foreseeable, although in most cases it would be.'

Secondly, it is not necessary to establish a medically recognised psychiatric condition. 'Alarm and distress' is all that is needed.[34] This can be helpful where perhaps there is an immediate effect, but no long-term depressive illness.

4.5 COURSE OF CONDUCT

The PFHA 1997 stipulates a 'course of conduct'[35] which requires at least two separate incidents.[36]

This requirement was examined more fully in *Banks v Ablex Ltd*. In this case at first instance the findings of the judge were that there was only one incident of harassment and so the claim failed. The claimant appealed.

---

31 See **3.4**.
32 [2004] EWCA Civ 2, [2004] ICR 746, [2004] IRLR 313. Discussed more fully in connection with harassment as statutory discrimination at **6.3.2**.
33 [2005] EWCA Civ 173, [2005] ICR 819, [2005] IRLR 357.
34 PFHA 1997, s 7(2).
35 PFHA 1997, s 1.
36 PFHA 1997, s 7(2).

The Court of Appeal held, first, that the harassment must be targeted at the victim on each occasion:

> 'It also seems to me to be clear beyond argument that the same person must be the victim on each occasion when harassment is alleged to have occurred. That is, in my judgment, clear from the words of the statute and is consistent with the decisions in *Lau v DPP* [2000] 1 FLR 799, *Pratt v DPP* [2001] 165 JP 800 and *Daiichi Pharmaceuticals* [2001] 1 WLR 1503 to which we were referred.'

Secondly, the Court upheld the judge's finding that the alleged earlier conduct of 'loud and aggressive swearing and abuse accompanied by gesticulating and finger pointing' was not harassment particularly as there was 'no evidence that Briggs' outbursts were targeted at the claimant as opposed to anyone else or, indeed, to inanimate tools and equipment'.

Similarly, in *Daniels v Metropolitan Police*[37] McKay J held:

> 'In my view there must be an established case of harassment against at least one employee who is shown on at least two occasions to have pursued a course of conduct amounting to harassment, or by more than one employee each acting on different occasions in furtherance of some joint design. Auld LJ in that paragraph talks of vicarious liability attaching to "harassment in breach of the Act", which to my mind means that an individual or group must as a precondition be shown to have broken the terms of the Act, so as to establish the primary liability for which the employer will be vicariously liable, provided their acts in breach have a sufficiently close connection with the nature of the employment.'

In *Lau v DPP*[38] two incidents 4 months apart were held not to constitute a course of conduct, the court stating that, whilst two incidents are sufficient, the fewer incidents there are and the more widely spread, the less likely it is that a course of conduct will be established. However, the specific circumstances must be considered. In *Pratt v DPP*,[39] two incidents 4 months apart were sufficient as the incidents were sufficiently connected 'in type and context' to justify the conclusion that they were a course of conduct.

4.6 MEANING OF 'HARASSMENT'

In *Thomas v News Group Newspapers Ltd*[40] Lord Phillips of Worth Matravers MR considered the meaning of harassment under the PFHA 1997:

---

[37] [2006] EWHC 1622.
[38] [2000] 1 FLR 799.
[39] [2001] EWHC Admin 483.
[40] [2002] EMLR 78.

> 'The Act does not attempt to define the type of conduct which is capable of constituting harassment. "Harassment" is, however, a word which has a meaning which is generally understood. It describes conduct targeted at an individual which is calculated to produce the consequences described in section 7 and which is oppressive and unreasonable.'

This was not a claim relating to harassment in the workplace. The Court of Appeal in *Majrowski*, in a part of the judgment which was not subject to the appeal to the House of Lords, held (per May LJ):

> 'Thus, in my view, although section 7(2) provides that harassing a person includes causing the person distress, the fact that a person suffers distress is not by itself enough to show that the cause of the distress was harassment. The conduct has also to be calculated, in an objective sense, to cause distress and has to be oppressive and unreasonable. It has to be conduct which the perpetrator knows or ought to know amounts to harassment, and conduct which a reasonable person would think amounted to harassment. What amounts to harassment is, as Lord Phillips said, generally understood. Such general understanding would not lead to a conclusion that all forms of conduct, however reasonable, would amount to harassment simply because they cause distress.'

In *Green v DB Group Services (UK) Ltd*,[41] the judge held that two separate types of behaviour did each constitute harassment under the PFHA 1997. First, there was the 'playground-like' spiteful behaviour of her colleagues in subjecting her to 'silent treatment' and verbal abuse:

> 'She was subjected to a relentless campaign of mean and spiteful behaviour designed to cause her distress . . . I am satisfied that the behaviour amounted to a deliberate and concerted campaign of bullying within the ordinary meaning of that term.'

Secondly, there was the conduct of her line manager. The judge concluded that this also constituted harassment:

> 'I am satisfied that Mr Preston conducted a concerted campaign to advance himself within the department at the expense of the claimant. He was aggressively competitive towards her, a competitiveness that manifested itself in a number of ways. First it is clear that both he and Mr Cummins formed an adverse view of her capabilities, a view for which in my judgment there was little foundation bearing in mind the consistently high level of performance recorded in her regular appraisals . . .
>
> The second and central respect in which Mr Preston's competitiveness and lack of respect for the claimant manifested itself was in his interference with her work. His actions were plainly designed to advance his profile within the company at her expense, and on occasions to give the impression to outside agencies that he was her boss. I have no doubt that he saw her as a rival, and deliberately set out to undermine her. Moreover he persisted in that conduct

[41] [2006] EWHC 1898 (QB), [2006] IRLR 764.

> notwithstanding the attempt by Mr Elliston to control his behaviour (see paragraph 139 above). I have little doubt that Mr Preston saw this as a Darwinian "survival of the fittest".
>
> The question is whether his behaviour amounted to bullying within the ordinary meaning of that term. Bullying can take many forms. As I have already observed, and as was acknowledged by the claimant, the incidents upon which she relies when viewed individually are not of major significance. It is their cumulative effect that is of importance. His behaviour to her was domineering, disrespectful, dismissive, confrontatory, and designed to undermine and belittle her in the view of others. I am satisfied that such a course of conduct pursued over a considerable period amounted to bullying within the ordinary meaning of the term. The claimant was correct to describe it as such in her confrontation with Mr Preston in April 2000. So too was Ms McCall when describing him as a bully in her exit interview in October 2000 (see paragraph 120 above).
>
> Such conduct also amounted to harassment within the meaning of the Protection from Harassment Act 1997. It occurred frequently, was targeted at the claimant, and was calculated to cause distress. In my judgment it was also oppressive and unreasonable.'

However, as the liability falls to be determined under an Act which also provides for criminal sanctions, a high degree of culpable behaviour will be required to found liability. This should not be confused with the standard of proof required which is the ordinary civil standard. In *Green* it seems to have been the sheer weight of evidence of 'bullying' that led the judge to conclude that this constituted 'harassment' under the PFHA 1997. In *Daniels v Metropolitan Police* McKay J dismissed a catalogue of similar complaints by a police officer which were largely unsupported by independent witness evidence.

In the Lords decision in *Majrowski* Lord Nicholls had pointed out:

> '. . . courts will have in mind that irritations, annoyances, even a measure of upset, arise at times in everybody's day-to-day dealings with other people. Courts are well able to recognise the boundary between conduct which is unattractive, even unreasonable, and conduct which is oppressive and unacceptable. To cross the boundary from the regrettable to the unacceptable the gravity of the misconduct must be of an order which would sustain criminal liability under section 2.'

In *Conn v Sunderland*[42] the Court of Appeal raised the bar very high indeed. Mr Conn was a paver who complained of harassment by a foreman. At first instance the judge had found that two instances of harassment had been proved; the first being when the foreman 'threatened to punch out the windows' in front of the claimant and the second when he threatened to give the claimant 'a good hiding'. The court found that

---

42 [2007] EWCA Civ 1492.

the second incident was capable of being harassment. With regard to the first incident, the court held that it was not, saying:

> '. . . this is the sort of bad-tempered conduct which, although unpleasant, comes well below the line of that which justifies a criminal sanction.'

The court said that the nature of the workplace may be relevant:

> '. . . conduct which is oppressive and unacceptable, may well depend on the context in which the conduct occurs. What might not be harassment on the factory floor or in the barrack room might well be harassment in the hospital ward and vice versa.'

But even so:

> 'In my judgment the touchstone for recognizing what is not harassment for the purposes of sections 1 and 3 will be whether the conduct is of such gravity as to justify the sanctions of the criminal law.'

Similarly, in *Hammond v International Network UK Ltd*,[43] in dismissing the claim the judge stressed:

> 'To be actionable under the 1997 Act the conduct in question will be criminal and might even attract a custodial sentence. It must therefore have an element of real seriousness. It must, in Lord Nicholls' words be "oppressive and unacceptable". Thus it has been found to have occurred in cases involving, for example, sustained domestic harassment, including the cutting of a Sikh woman's hair (see the judgment of the learned recorder in Singh v. Bhakar & Others Claim No. 4NGI17900). It has been found not to arise in a case which involved a supervisor ranting and swearing on the factory floor: Banks v. Ablex Limited [2005] EWCA Civ 173, [2005] IRLR 357.'

However, it is submitted that, notwithstanding the decision on the facts in *Conn*, it cannot be right that a threat of physical violence is always required before liability can be established. Section 4 of the PFHA 1997 is entitled 'Putting people in fear of violence' and is a separate and more serious criminal offence than 'harassment' under s 2 of the PFHA 1997. The comments of the court in *Conn* come close to requiring the claimant to establish an offence under s 4 rather than under s 2 of the PFHA 1997.

In *Ferguson v British Gas Trading Ltd*[44] the Court of Appeal revisited this vexed issue. This was not a stress at work claim. The claimant had been subjected to numerous threats for alleged non-payment of bills by British Gas. British Gas acknowledged that these were entirely without foundation as she had lawfully changed suppliers and that the company had done nothing at all to stop the threats continuing. British Gas sought

---

43 [2007] EWHC 2604 (QB).
44 [2009] EWCA Civ 46.

to escape liability inter alia on the ground that their actions could not be construed as harassment as it could not be 'conduct of such gravity as to justify the sanctions of the criminal law', relying on *Conn*. In *Ferguson* the Court of Appeal appear to have rowed back somewhat from *Conn*, finding that the conduct of British Gas could constitute harassment, and Jacob LJ explained:

> 'I accept that a course of conduct must be grave before the offence or tort of harassment is proved. And that, as Mr Porter accepted after some discussion, the only real difference between the crime of s.2 and the tort of s.3 is standard of proof. To prove the civil wrong of harassment it is necessary to prove the case on a balance of probabilities, to prove the crime, the standard is the usual criminal one of beyond a reasonable doubt.
>
> In so accepting I would just add this word of caution: the fact of parallel criminal and civil liability is not generally, outside the particular context of harassment, of significance in considering civil liability. There are a number of other civil wrongs which are also crimes. Perhaps most common would be breaches of the Trade Descriptions Act 1968 as amended. In the field of intellectual property both trade mark and copyright infringement, and the common law tort of passing off (which generally involves deception), may all amount to crimes. It has never been suggested generally that the scope of a civil wrong is restricted because it is also a crime. What makes the wrong of harassment different and special is because, as Lord Nicholls and Lady Hale recognised, in life one has to put up with a certain amount of annoyance: things have got to be fairly severe before the law, civil or criminal, will intervene.'

It may well be that what the Court of Appeal meant to say in *Conn* was simply 'we all know harassment when we see it, and this conduct wasn't harassment' and that the reference to the criminal law was something of a red herring.

Be that as it may, the judicial mood is such that it will require at least two separate serious incidents, probably either involving near violent conduct (as per *Conn*) or alternatively a well-evidenced long and deliberate campaign (as per *Green*) for the claimant to succeed.

Outside the field of employment, the most widespread use of the PFHA 1997 has been with regard to claims brought against anti-vivisection lobbyists. The alleged harassment is often very extreme behaviour involving threats and demonstrations against students and employees that most definitely causes alarm and distress. Much of the civil case-law relates to the grant of injunctions rather than claims for damages.

However, in *Singh v Singh*[45] a Sikh bride had been subjected to a campaign of intimidation and harassment by her mother-in-law. This had included a catalogue of incidents such as forcing her to cut her hair

---

45 *Singh v Singh* (2006) (Nottingham CC) (Timothy Scott QC) 24/7/2006 Lawtel.

(against religious strictures), isolation from her family by refusing to allow her to use the telephone and forcing her to do excessive and pointless housework. The judge said:

> 'In my judgement that is the position here. The course of conduct which I have found on the part of Mrs Bhakar is very serious. I bear in mind the strictures of May LJ [in *Majrowski* in the Court of Appeal], but I have no doubt at all that Mrs Bhakar's conduct is far more than enough to amount to harassment for the purposes of the Act.
>
> This can be tested by taking the hypothetical (but not improbable) case of a young woman who runs away from an arranged marriage. If the husband or members of his family then follow her and make trouble, conduct which is far less serious than I have found in the present case would be enough to found an action for damages and/or injunctive relief. Why should the position be any different when the conduct took place before the breakdown of the marriage? If anything, the situation is more serious in that context.'

And in *Home Office v Wainwright*[46] Buxton LJ said:

> 'Harassment can cover a very wide range of conduct. It may involve actions alone, or words alone (s.7(4)), or both. The actions may be so grave as to amount to criminal offences against public order, or against the person, which cause serious alarm, or they may be little more than boorishness or insensitive behaviour, so long as it is sufficient to cause distress. The words may be, at one extreme, incitements to, or threats of, violence that cause alarm, or at the other, unwelcome text messages sent, for example, to a woman wrongly perceived to be a girlfriend. The conduct may be that of an individual, or of an organisation, including the news media: Thomas v News Group [2001] EWCA Civ 1233; [2002] EMLR 4CA. It may include strip searches (subject to the meaning of "a course of conduct").'

In a criminal appeal on the meaning of 'harassment' under the PFHA 1997 in *Tafurelli v DPP*,[47] Leveson J held that a finding of deliberately inciting dogs to bark was capable of constituting harassment sufficient to form a course of conduct:

> 'The Deputy District Judge found that the appellants had in fact deliberately failed to control their dogs notwithstanding complaint. It may be that they barked if together, or if certain types of noise were made, or if woken in the middle of the night. I am not saying that any one of these activities in fact took place, merely that I can visualise circumstances in which conduct could knowingly provoke a dog to bark. Whereas I accept that a dog owner could not be expected to exercise total control over the barking of his dog or dogs, I am not prepared to say that regular barking in the middle of the night could not be the consequence of deliberate conduct on the part of the owner as part of a campaign to harass. It is that which the District Judge found as a fact. The significance of the conduct described as the deliberate failure to control the dogs is that this evidence goes to establish, along with the

---

46 [2001] EWCA Civ 2081, [2002] 3 WLR 405, [2002] QB 1334, [2003] 3 All ER 943.

47 [2004] EWHC 2791 (Admin).

> different acts of criminal damage of father and son, the course of conduct that is at least two occasions necessary for the finding of harassment.'

In allegations of harassment there can be an interesting conflict between the right to freedom of expression given by the European Convention on Human Rights (ECHR) and the Human Rights Act 1998. The PFHA 1997 should not be interpreted in such a away that it restricts legitimate freedom of expression/freedom of assembly under Arts 10 and 11 of the ECHR.

Article 10 provides as follows:

> '(1) Everyone has the right to freedom of expression. This right shall include freedom to hold opinions and to receive and impart information and ideas without interference by public authority and regardless of frontiers. This Article shall not prevent States from requiring the licensing of broadcasting, television or cinema enterprises.
>
> (2) The exercise of these freedoms, since it carries with it duties and responsibilities, may be subject to such formalities, conditions, restrictions or penalties as are prescribed by law and are necessary in a democratic society, in the interests of national security, territorial integrity or public safety, for the prevention of disorder or crime, for the protection of health or morals, for the protection of the reputation or rights of others, for preventing the disclosure of information received in confidence, or for maintaining the authority and impartiality of the judiciary.'

Section 12 of the Human Rights Act 1998 states:

> '(1) This section applies if a court is considering whether to grant any relief which, if granted, might affect the exercise of the Convention right to freedom of expression.
>
> (2) If the person against whom the application for relief is made ("the respondent") is neither present nor represented, no such relief is to be granted unless the court is satisfied—
>
> (a) that the applicant has taken all practicable steps to notify the respondent; or
>
> (b) that there are compelling reasons why the respondent should not be notified.
>
> (3) No such relief is to be granted so as to restrain publication before trial unless the court is satisfied that the applicant is likely to establish that publication should not be allowed.
>
> (4) The court must have particular regard to the importance of the Convention right to freedom of expression and, where proceedings relate to material which the respondent claims, or which appears to the court, to be journalistic, literary or artistic material (or to conduct connected with such material) to—

(a) the extent to which—
  (i) the material has, or is about to, become available to the public; or
  (ii) it is, or would be, in the public interest for the material to be published;
(b) any relevant privacy code.

(5) In this section . . . "relief" includes any remedy or order (other than in criminal proceedings).'

Section 12(4) applies principally to the case of harassment by publication in the press or by artistic or literary material. Article 10 is clearly wider and will include publishing opinions about an individual or situation. 'Publication' has been given a wide meaning in relation to freedom of expression. It can include making statements to third parties, for example, in *Cray v Hancock*[48] the harasser alleged to a solicitor's partners that he was greedy and incompetent and this was held to be publication.

However, the court will pay more attention to Art 10 rights where the subject matter is publication by the media and public interest is involved than where an individual expresses views about the victim.[49]

In *Crossland v Wilkinson Hardware Stores Ltd*[50] the claimant had been disciplined and dismissed by his employer. He claimed that he had been forced to sign a compromise agreement. Acting in person he subsequently commenced proceedings for defamation, malicious falsehood and for harassment under the PFHA 1997. The harassment alleged largely related to the instigation and conduct of grievance and disciplinary proceedings, but also included an allegation that the failure of the managing director to pass on a message of congratulation amounted to harassment. The judge considered the issue of human rights:

'. . . a broad interpretation of harassment would be capable of seriously interfering with the rights of free speech. It would also be capable of creating serious inroads into the rights of those carrying on business, (and for that matter of employees), to pursue their legitimate aims. It cannot be excluded that the conduct of an employer towards an employee might be harassment. Nor can it be excluded that the conduct of an employee towards an employer, or another employee, might be harassment. But something more is required than the robust pursuit of a person's own interest within what is otherwise recognised as the limits of the law . . .

It does not follow that there is to be imported into the 1997 Act the concept of malice from the law of defamation and malicious falsehood. Nevertheless there must be something alleged by an employee who claims harassment by his employer which is more than that the employer has caused foreseeable distress. Where a claimant invokes Art 10(2) on the basis that his own claim

48 [2005] All ER (D) 66 (Nov).
49 See, eg, *Howlett v Holding* (2006) *The Times*, February 8.
50 [2005] EWHC 481 (QB).

shows an interference with his rights under Art 8, the tension between the competing convention rights is to be addressed in accordance with the guidance given by the House of Lords in *Re S (A Child)(Identification: Restriction on Publication)* [2004] UKHL 47; 3 WLR 1129.'

The House of Lords in *Re S* described this approach as follows:

> 'The interplay between articles 8 and 10 has been illuminated by the opinions in the House of Lords in Campbell v MGN Ltd [2004] 2 WLR 1232. For present purposes the decision of the House on the facts of Campbell and the differences between the majority and the minority are not material. What does, however, emerge clearly from the opinions are four propositions. First, neither article has as such precedence over the other. Secondly, where the values under the two articles are in conflict, an intense focus on the comparative importance of the specific rights being claimed in the individual case is necessary. Thirdly, the justifications for interfering with or restricting each right must be taken into account. Finally, the proportionality test must be applied to each. For convenience I will call this the ultimate balancing test.'

The following are examples where the court has found the conduct to constitute harassment under the PFHA 1997:[51]

- 'abuse, assault and threats;[52]
- alleging more than once without foundation that a neighbour is fraudulently being paid by being at home without good reason during working time;[53]
- threatening letters and phone calls; sending letters maliciously alleging that individuals are paedophiles or sex offenders; causing criminal damage; fire bombings; carrying out intimidating home visits;[54]
- deliberately ignoring a colleague, excluding her from conversations, laughing when she walked past, making crude remarks about her, failing to put through calls and hiding her post;[55]
- assaulting an ex-partner and throwing water over her;[56]
- posting defamatory remarks about a solicitor on a website;[57]
- paying computer hackers £150 to assist in sabotaging an ex-lover's emails (so as to alter emails sent by him or make it appear as if he had sent emails he had not).[58] In the last case a suggestion from the respondent's counsel, apparently accepted by the court, was that

---

51 This list is taken from *Injunctions Against Anti-social or Violent Individuals* (Jordan Publishing, 2008) Chapter 5.

52 For example, *Hipgrave v Jones* [2004] EWHC 2901 (QB), [2005] 2 FLR 174.

53 *Kellett v DPP* [2001] EWHC Admin 107, [2001] All ER (D) 124 (Feb) – the neighbour appeared unaware that the victim was exercising her contractual right to flexi-time.

54 *Daiichi UK Ltd v Stop Huntingdon Animal Cruelty* [2003] EWHC 2337 (QB), [2004] 1 WLR 1503.

55 *Green v DB Group Services (UK) Ltd* [2006] EWHC 1898 (QB), [2006] IRLR 764.

56 *Pratt v DPP* [2001] EWHC Admin 483.

57 *Cray v Hancock* [2005] All ER (D) 66 (Nov).

58 *R v Debnath* [2005] EWCA Crim 3472, [2006] Cr App Rep (S) 169.

> publishing the truth about someone may amount to harassment – for example, the correct address or telephone number of a well-known or infamous individual.'

4.7 OVERLAP WITH COMMON LAW STRESS/BULLYING CLAIMS

Claims for harassment under the PFHA 1997 are often pleaded as an alternative to a claims at common law for breach of duty to protect the health and safety of employees or for breach of the implied contractual term to protect the employee from bullying and harassment.

Prior to *Conn* bullying behaviour was commonly pleaded as harassment under the PFHA 1997 principally to avoid the requirement of foreseeability of psychiatric injury required by *Hatton*.

However, following *Conn*, care should be taken to judge whether the bullying complained of does constitute harassment under the PFHA 1997 and to particularise it carefully.

CHAPTER 5

LIABILITY IN THE EMPLOYMENT TRIBUNAL

5.1 CONSTRUCTIVE UNFAIR DISMISSAL

If the employer is in fundamental breach of his obligations under the contract of employment then the employee has the right to accept the breach by resigning and claiming constructive dismissal. Workplace bullying and harassment (or the failure of the employer to protect the employee from this) may well on the facts constitute a fundamental breach. This point is argued rather less frequently in stress-related claims (e g resulting from overwork), often because the effect is cumulative rather than sudden, but in principle there is no reason why a breach of duty might not similarly be treated as a fundamental breach of contract.

As well as the right to sue in court for damages for breach of contract,[1] the employee can also bring proceedings for unfair dismissal in the employment tribunal. The employee's termination of the contract by resigning is treated as a dismissal that can lead to tribunal proceedings where:[2]

> '... the employee terminates the contract under which he is employed (with or without notice) in circumstances in which he is entitled to terminate it without notice by reason of the employer's conduct.'

As we shall see,[3] it is not possible for the employee to obtain compensation in the tribunal for psychiatric injury in respect of treatment leading to the unfair dismissal, unless the employee also brings a concurrent claim for statutory discrimination or 'detriment'.[4] However, the employee might be determined to leave his employment and obtain statutory compensation for unfair dismissal either instead of or in

---

1 See, for example, *Horkulak v Cantor Fitzgerald* [2003] EWHC 1918 (QB) discussed at **2.4.3.2**. The employment tribunal also has concurrent jurisdiction to hear breach of contract claims up to £25,000 (Employment Extension of Jurisdiction (England & Wales) Order 1994, SI 1994/1623). See further **8.5.2.1** for the problems created by the overlapping jurisdictions.

2 Employment Rights Act 1996, s 95(1)(b).

3 See **6.3.1**.

4 See **6.3.2**.

addition to investigating a civil court claim for psychiatric injury or a concurrent claim in the employment tribunal for discrimination or in respect of a 'detriment'.

The biggest difficulty for the employee is to establish that the breach was fundamental. If he does not, then his actions will be treated as a resignation not as a dismissal. The breach must be:[5]

> '. . . a significant breach going to the root of the contract of employment, or which shows that the employer no longer intends to be bound by one or more of the essential terms of the contract.'

The breach has to be by the employer, but in *Hilton International Hotels v Protopapa*[6] it was established that bullying by a line manager was deemed to be conduct by the employer. The same usually applies to bullying by other fellow employees,[7] but not to bullying by other people who are not fellow employees.[8]

Whether the employer's conduct amounts to a fundamental breach will very much be a question of fact to be determined in the individual case, but examples include:

- foul language and insulting behaviour by a line manager;[9]
- cumulative incidents of poor and unsympathetic management;[10]
- failing to deal adequately or at all with a grievance;[11]
- imposing a disproportionate disciplinary penalty.[12]

It is possible for an employee to resign and claim constructive dismissal following an incident which of itself would not amount to a fundamental breach, but which is the 'last straw' in a series of incidents which together amount to a fundamental breach. In *Omilaju v Waltham Forest London Borough Council* an employment tribunal had accepted the applicant's claims that he had been subjected by his line manager to bullying and abuse amounting to race discrimination over the course of a decade. However, he was absent from work without leave for nearly 2 months attending the tribunal hearing. The employer refused to pay him, arguing

5 *Western Excavating (ECC) Ltd v Sharp* [1978] ICR 221, CA.
6 [1990] IRLR 316, EAT.
7 *Cumbria County Council v Carlisle-Morgan* [2007] IRLR 314.
8 *Yorke v Moonlight* [2007] EAT 0025/06 where the alleged breach was insulting behaviour by the employer's father.
9 *Horkulak v Cantor Fitzgerald*, above.
10 *TSB Bank plc v Harris* EAT [2000] IRLR 157, EAT.
11 *WA Goold (Pearmak) Ltd v McConnell* [1995] IRLR 516, EAT.
12 *Omilaju v Waltham Forest London Borough Council* [2004] EWCA Civ 1493, CA, [2005] ICR 481.

that he had not complied with its policy in respect of such absences. The employee resigned and claimed a constructive dismissal in fresh tribunal proceedings and argued that this failure to pay him was a 'last straw'. The employer said that the refusal to pay was not a breach of contract. In allowing the employee's appeal from the EAT decision and reinstating the finding of the employment tribunal in his favour, Dyson LJ held:

> 'The question specifically raised by this appeal is: what is the necessary quality of a final straw if it is to be successfully relied on by the employee as a repudiation of the contract? When Glidewell LJ said that it need not itself be a breach of contract, he must have had in mind, amongst others, the kind of case mentioned in *Woods* at p 671F–G where Browne-Wilkinson J referred to the employer who, stopping short of a breach of contract, "squeezes out" an employee by making the employee's life so uncomfortable that he resigns. A final straw, not itself a breach of contract, may result in a breach of the implied term of trust and confidence. The quality that the final straw must have is that it should be an act in a series whose cumulative effect is to amount to a breach of the implied term. I do not use the phrase "an act in a series" in a precise or technical sense. The act does not have to be of the same character as the earlier acts. Its essential quality is that, when taken in conjunction with the earlier acts on which the employee relies, it amounts to a breach of the implied term of trust and confidence. It must contribute something to that breach, although what it adds may be relatively insignificant.
>
> I see no need to characterise the final straw as "unreasonable" or "blameworthy" conduct. It may be true that an act which is the last in a series of acts which, taken together, amounts to a breach of the implied term of trust and confidence will usually be unreasonable and, perhaps, even blameworthy. But, viewed in isolation, the final straw may not always be unreasonable, still less blameworthy. Nor do I see any reason why it should be. The only question is whether the final straw is the last in a series of acts or incidents which cumulatively amount to a repudiation of the contract by the employer. The last straw must contribute, however slightly, to the breach of the implied term of trust and confidence. Some unreasonable behaviour may be so unrelated to the obligation of trust and confidence that it lacks the essential quality to which I have referred.'

However, the test is an objective one and Dyson LJ cautions:

> '. . . an entirely innocuous act on the part of the employer cannot be a final straw, even if the employee genuinely, but mistakenly, interprets the act as hurtful and destructive of his trust and confidence in his employer. The test of whether the employee's trust and confidence has been undermined is objective.'

Because the stakes can be so high (win and be compensated for a constructive unfair dismissal; lose and be deemed to have given up all contractual employment rights), employees can be reluctant to take this irrevocable step. This is particularly so where there are benefits such as company sick pay schemes or income protection benefit to which the employee is only entitled whilst his employment continues, even though the employee is unable to attend work as a result of ill-health caused by stress or bullying and harassment.[13] However, if the employee does not act promptly he may be deemed to have affirmed the contract notwithstanding the breach and, in *Omilaju,* Dyson LJ points out:

> 'If the final straw is not capable of contributing to a series of earlier acts which cumulatively amount to a breach of the implied term of trust and confidence, there is no need to examine the earlier history to see whether the alleged final straw does in fact have that effect. Suppose that an employer has committed a series of acts which amount to a breach of the implied term of trust and confidence, but the employee does not resign his employment. Instead, he soldiers on and affirms the contract. He cannot subsequently rely on these acts to justify a constructive dismissal unless he can point to a later act which enables him to do so. If the later act on which he seeks to rely is entirely innocuous, it is not necessary to examine the earlier conduct in order to determine that the later act does not permit the employee to invoke the final straw principle.'

The conduct has to be the cause of the resignation for it to amount to a constructive dismissal. So where there has been an arguable breach, but the employee acknowledges that he has resigned to take a better paid job elsewhere, there will not be a constructive dismissal.[14]

If the employee establishes a constructive dismissal as the result of a fundamental breach of contract by the employer, the tribunal must then go on to establish whether the dismissal was unfair. The usual test of whether there was a potentially fair reason for the dismissal applies.[15] However, as the employee has established the fundamental breach (usually in connection with bullying, or subjecting the employee to unreasonable stress, in breach of duty) it is difficult to imagine how the employer could convince the tribunal that the dismissal had been for a potentially fair reason in practice. In bullying cases, once the constructive dismissal is established, the employee will normally succeed in his claim for unfair dismissal.

5.2 UNFAIR DISMISSAL FOR INCAPACITY

If the employee does not resign and claim constructive dismissal, the employee might still bring a claim for unfair dismissal in the employment tribunal following an actual dismissal by the employer. Although this might be for reasons allegedly entirely unconnected with the stress or

---

[13] See Chapter 9.

[14] As discussed in *Dunnachie* in the Employment Appeals Tribunal decision in *Kingston Upon Hull City Council v Dunnachie* [2003] ICR 1294, [2003] IRLR 384.

[15] Dealt with at **5.2**.

bullying and harassment,[16] the most likely reason which an employer will give for the dismissal will be incapacity, which is a potentially fair reason for dismissal, subject to reasonableness.

The right not to be unfairly dismissed (which only arises after an employee has a year's continuous employment) is set out in s 94(1) of the Employment Rights Act 1996 (ERA 1996) and s 98 of the ERA 1996 provides:

> '(1) In determining for the purposes of this Part whether the dismissal of an employee is fair or unfair, it is for the employer to show—
> (a) the reason (or, if more than one, the principal reason) for the dismissal, and
> (b) that it is either a reason falling within subsection (2) or some other substantial reason of a kind such as to justify the dismissal of an employee holding the position which the employee held.
>
> (2) A reason falls within this subsection if it—
> (a) relates to the capability or qualifications of the employee for performing work of the kind which he was employed by the employer to do . . .
>
> (3) In subsection (2)(a)—
> (a) "capability", in relation to an employee, means his capability assessed by reference to skill, aptitude, health or any other physical or mental quality . . .
>
> (4) Where the employer has fulfilled the requirements of subsection (1), the determination of the question whether the dismissal is fair or unfair (having regard to the reason shown by the employer)—
> (a) depends on whether in the circumstances (including the size and administrative resources of the employer's undertaking) the employer acted reasonably or unreasonably in treating it as a sufficient reason for dismissing the employee, and
> (b) shall be determined in accordance with equity and the substantial merits of the case.'

In stress at work claims, the employee is usually unable to work because of ill-health caused by the stress or bullying. Ill-health absence can constitute incapacity under s 98(2)(a) and is the most likely ground to be given by the employer (rather than inability to do the job, which is also encompassed within the meaning of 'incapacity').

The basic test for incapacity dismissals was neatly summarised by the Court of Appeal in *O'Donoghue v Elmbridge Housing Trust*:[17]

---

16 In which case the employee will have to establish that the stated reason (eg misconduct or redundancy) is not in fact the real reason. If he does so, the dismissal will normally be unfair.

17 [2004] EWCA Civ 939.

> 'The basic test for incapacity arising from ill-health is "whether, in all the circumstances, the employer can be expected to wait any longer and, if so, how much longer." See Spencer v Paragon Wallpapers Ltd [1976] IRLR 373, paragraph 14. The basic question which the Employment Tribunal had to address was whether the Trust's conclusion that there was incapacity, and its decision to dismiss on that ground on 28th June 2001, was within the range of reasonable responses which an employer in the circumstances could adopt.'

It generally makes no difference that the alleged cause of the incapacity is the employer's breach of duty (which is usually alleged in stress and bullying and harassment cases). In *Royal Bank of Scotland plc v Mcadie*[18] the Court of Appeal said:

> 'Mr Over was constrained to accept, in argument, that it was possible on the authorities for an employer who had negligently been responsible for personal injuries suffered by an employee in the course of his employment nonetheless subsequently to dismiss the same employee on the ground of capability without rendering the employer liable to a claim for unfair dismissal. Given that the reason for the dismissal in the instant case – an indefinite incapability on the part of the appellant to do her job – and given that the manner in which the appellant was dismissed was procedurally fair – Mr Over was quite unable to provide a rationale which distinguished the appellant's case from the case of the employee who had been dismissed following an industrial accident which had rendered that employee incapable of continuing in his employment.'

This was particularly so where (as is common in stress and bullying cases) the employee:

> '. . . had made it crystal clear that – no matter what anybody said or did – she was not coming back to work for the Bank – see; (1) the terms of the dismissal letter set out at paragraph 31 above; (2) paragraph 48 of the Tribunal's reasons set out at paragraph 30 above; and (3) the terms of the medical evidence which the Tribunal summarised in paragraphs 63 of its reasons (see paragraph 33 of this judgment). It might have been different if the appellant's case had been that she was willing to try again – but, plainly, she was not. In my judgment, therefore, Mr Over had no answer to the question: "what was the Bank to do in these circumstances?" save to fall back on the mantra that the Bank's behaviour had been so poor, and its responsibility for the appellant's condition so total that there were no circumstances in which it could, fairly, dismiss the appellant. As I have already indicated, that proposition is, in my judgment, simply untenable.'

The employer must follow a fair procedure, but the employee must co-operate. In *O'Donoghue* the claimant failed to co-operate with medical investigations by not returning or unreasonably amending the consent form. The Court of Appeal agreed with the Employment Appeal Tribunal (EAT) that the dismissal was fair, Ward LJ saying:

---

[18] [2007] EWCA Civ 806, [2007] IRLR 895.

'In my judgment it was plain from paragraph 9 of their decision what the reason was. I read one sentence:

> "The Tribunal find that given the particular circumstances of this case namely the lack of consent for any medical records the period of three and a half months from the date the Applicant went off on sick leave to the date of her dismissal was reasonable."

That spells it out quite clearly. She was asked for unequivocal consent on a designated form and she did not give it. That is the reason for it. This was a matter well within the province of the Employment Tribunal to decide. I would have decided it the same way. That does not mean that the Employment Tribunal were right, it simply means that it cannot be said they were so plainly wrong as to have been perverse.'

Between 6 April 2004 and 5 April 2009, the employer and employee were required to follow the provisions of the statutory disciplinary and grievance procedure.[19] An employee could not bring a tribunal claim without first going through the statutory procedure. If the employer failed to follow the procedure the dismissal would automatically be unfair. With effect from 6 April 2009 these provisions are to be abolished by the Employment Act 2008.[20] However, awards may still be increased or reduced by up to 25% if either the employer or the employee unreasonably fails to follow the new ACAS Code of Practice on Disciplinary and Grievance Procedures. Where the dismissal is unfair, but procedural fairness would have made no difference to the outcome, compensation may be reduced by the tribunal.[21]

5.3 DISCRIMINATION CLAIMS

5.3.1 Discrimination on the grounds of race, sex, disability, age, sexual orientation and religion or belief as harassment

The right not to be discriminated against on various grounds is enshrined in statute and can be a useful weapon for lawyers acting for clients who have suffered psychiatric injury as a result of their employment. An employer may not discriminate against an employee on the grounds of race, sex, disability, age, sexual orientation or religion or belief.

This section deals with discrimination insofar as it causes psychiatric injury (eg depression) as the result of the stress it caused. For this reason, indirect discrimination is not discussed here as it is unlikely to give rise to a stress claim. The matters set out here can of necessity only summarise discrimination law and seek to identify possible uses in stress and bullying

---

19 The Employment Act 2002 (Dispute Resolution) Regulations 2004, SI 2004/752.

20 Employment Act 2008, s 1 and the Employment Act 2008 (Commencement No 1, Transitional Provisions and Savings) Order 2008, SI 2008/3232.

21 Reverting to the pre-2004 case-law.

at work claims. Practitioners are referred to specialist texts for more detailed analysis of law and practice.[22]

There is no requirement for a discrimination claim that an applicant has been employed for a minimum period (although tribunals will look sceptically at applicants who appear to be seeking to get round the one-year statutory minimum employment period for unfair dismissal by claiming discrimination).

The test of whether the discrimination is in the course of employment is not the same as the test for vicarious liability under the common law,[23] but is instead governed by the interpretation set out in *Tower Boot Company Ltd v Jones*:[24]

> 'It would be particularly wrong to allow racial harassment on the scale that was suffered by the complainant in this case at the hands of his workmates – treatment that was wounding both emotionally and physically – to slip through the net of employer responsibility by applying to it a common law principle evolved in another area of the law to deal with vicarious responsibility for wrongdoing of a wholly different kind. To do so would seriously undermine the statutory scheme of the Discrimination Acts and flout the purposes which they were passed to achieve.
>
> The tribunals are free, and are indeed bound, to interpret the ordinary, and readily understandable, words "in the course of employment" in the sense in which every layman would understand them. This is not to say that when it comes to applying them to the infinite variety of circumstance which is liable to occur in particular instances – within or without the workplace, in or out of uniform, in or out of rest-breaks – all laymen would necessarily agree as to the result. That is what makes their application so well suited to decision by an industrial jury. The application of the phrase will be a question of fact for each Industrial Tribunal to resolve, in the light of the circumstances presented to it, with a mind unclouded by any parallels sought to be drawn from the law of vicarious liability in tort.'

What constitutes discrimination under the various statutory protections is broadly similar although not at present identical.

Grounds for complaint usually include 'direct' discrimination which is, broadly, less favourable treatment to the applicant's detriment than an (often notional) comparator. This will include insults[25] and unequal

---

22 For example, *Harvey on Industrial Relations and Employment Law* (Lexis Nexis Butterworths, looseleaf) Division L Equal Opportunities.

23 See **3.2.2**, although the two tests are now much closer than they were before the decision in *Lister v Hesley Hall* [2001] UKHL 22, [2001] 2 WLR 1311, [2001] 2 All ER 769, [2001] ICR 665, [2001] IRLR 472, [2001] 2 FLR 307, discussed in that section.

24 [1996] EWCA Civ 1185.

25 As, for example, in the racial abuse in *Essa v Laing Ltd* [2004] EWCA Civ 02. See further **6.3.2**.

treatment of a specific individual by reason of their race, sex (or transgender status), disability, age, sexual orientation or religion or belief.

'Harassment' is now defined by most of the discrimination legislation as 'unwanted conduct' 'which has the purpose or effect of violating the employee's dignity' or 'creating an intimidating, hostile, degrading, humiliating or offensive environment for the employee' and which is 'reasonably considered as having that effect' 'in all the circumstances, including in particular the perception of the [employee]'. This harassment must be in respect of one of the grounds protected by the discrimination legislation (namely, race, sex (or transgender status), disability, age, sexual orientation or religion or belief).

With regard to sex discrimination, the Sex Discrimination Act 1975 (Amendment) Regulations 2008[26] amended the Sex Discrimination Act 1975 (SDA 1975) with effect from 6 April 2008. This was to remedy a defect in the SDA 1975 in that it had been held that the Act did not fully implement the Equal Treatment Framework Directive. The Regulations widened the definition of harassment under the SDA 1975 by replacing the phrase 'on the ground of her sex' with the phrase 'related to her sex or the sex of another person'. The change has the effect that claims can now be made by someone who is not herself directly subjected to the unwanted conduct but where the effect of the behaviour is to violate her dignity or create an intimidating environment. This would allow, for example, a claim for harassment by someone offended by sexist banter in the workplace even though it was not directed at her personally. If employers are not vigilant, offensive cultures of inappropriate personal e-mail use or unpleasant verbal banter may leave them open to claims. To protect themselves, employers will increasingly need to consider implementing and enforcing written policies and procedures and ensure that all personnel with a line management function are properly trained.

In *Showboat Entertainment Centre Ltd v Owens*[27] the EAT upheld a complaint of unlawful racial discrimination brought by a white man who was dismissed by his employers for refusing to obey an instruction to exclude all black customers from the entertainment centre where he worked, holding:

> 'We therefore conclude that section 1(1)(a) covers all cases of discrimination on racial grounds whether the racial characteristics in question are those of the person treated less favourably or of some other person. The only question in each case is whether the unfavourable treatment afforded to the claimant was caused by racial considerations.'

---

26 SI 2008/656.

27 [1983] UKEAT 29 83 2810, [1984] 1 All ER 836, [1984] 1 WLR 384, [1984] IRLR 7.

And in *English v Thomas Sanderson Ltd*,[28] the Court of Appeal by a majority held that the effect of a purposive interpretation of harassment under the relevant legislation was that an employee could successfully claim harassment even though the harassment was offensive homophobic abuse directed at an employee who was not gay and who accepted that the discriminators also knew that he was not in fact gay. The claimant alleged:

> '. . . for a protracted period he had been subjected by four colleagues at work to sexual innuendo suggesting in obvious terms that he was homosexual. Someone had discovered that he had been to a boarding school and lived in Brighton, and these facts seem to have been the genesis of the suggestions. He had to endure names like "faggot", and on two occasions at least, lurid comments in the house magazine. His case was that this cruel and puerile conduct drove him to leave his job.'

Collins LJ held:

> 'It seems to me that, without the benefit of accumulated case-law, that conclusion follows from an objective approach to the characterisation of the conduct. If one were to ask the question whether the repeated and offensive use of the word "faggot" in the circumstances of this case was conduct "on grounds of sexual orientation" the answer should be in the affirmative irrespective of the actual sexual orientation of the claimant or the perception of his sexual orientation by his tormentors.
>
> If the conduct is "on grounds of sexual orientation" it is plainly irrelevant whether the claimant is actually of a particular sexual orientation. In a case of this kind, even if the claimant is homosexual, it is obviously not for the claimant to show that he is homosexual, any more than a claimant in a racial discrimination case must prove that he is Asian or a Jew.
>
> It would follow from the decision of the EAT that if the claimant is actually homosexual, but those who victimise him do not in fact believe him to be so, then Regulation 5(1) would not be engaged. I do not consider that this could have been the intended result of the legislation, and I do not consider that it is its result.
>
> By virtue of section 3A(1) of the Race Relations Act 1976 there will be harassment where a person "on grounds of race or ethnic or national origins" engages in unwanted conduct which has essentially the same purpose or effect as in Regulation 5 of the Employment Equality (Sexual Orientation) Regulations 2003. In my judgment, where an employee is repeatedly and offensively called a Paki or a Jew-boy even when he is not of Asian or Jewish origin, and even when his tormentors do not believe that he is, that conduct can amount to harassment for the purposes of the Race Relations Act 1976.
>
> This is not the same as the example of an able-bodied but clumsy person being called "a spastic" which was mentioned in argument. The Disability Discrimination Act 1995, section 3B, provides that a disabled person is

28 [2008] EWCA Civ 1421.

> subject to harassment where the offensive conduct is engaged in "for a reason which relates to the disabled person's disability". See also sections 28SA, 31AC. Not only does that wording require an actual disability, but also, however unacceptable the word may have become, it does not normally denote actual disability when being used offensively.'

Sedley LJ agreed 'with some reluctance', with Laws LJ dissenting.

Additionally, the changes to the SDA 1975 with effect from 6 April 2008 expressly acknowledge the liability of an employer for harassment of an employee by a third party. There will only be liability if the employer has failed to take such steps as would have been reasonably practicable to prevent the third party from doing so. This provision will only apply if the employer knows that the woman has been subject to harassment in the course of her employment on at least two other occasions by a third party. It can, however, be the same or a different person on each occasion. Employers should therefore consider displaying notices regarding the employer's anti-discrimination policies for third parties, for example customers, to see and imposing appropriate contractual terms on third parties.

With regard to race discrimination, recent case-law suggests that employers can already be held responsible if an employee is racially harassed by a third party. So far as this is concerned, the well-known decision in *Burton v de Vere Hotels Ltd*[29] (the 'Bernard Manning' case where two black waitresses employed by the event organiser were offended by racist jokes made by Mr Manning, an independent contractor) was disapproved of by the House of Lords in *Pearce v The Governing Body of Mayfield School*.[30] However, in *Gravell v London Borough of Bexley*,[31] where the employee housing officer complained of her employer's policy to ignore racial abuse by customers to which she was subjected, the EAT pointed out first:

> '*Burton* was decided before the statutory tort of harassment was inserted into RRA by s3A on 19 July 2003. The black waitresses who were the butt of racist jokes told by Mr Bernard Manning at a private dinner held at their employers' hotel brought claims against the employer of direct race discrimination contrary to s1(1)(a) RRA, coupled with the detriment which they suffered under s4(2)(c).'

Secondly, in respect of *Pearce*, the EAT stated:

> 'In the relevant opinions, their Lordships concentrated on the need for the Claimants to show less favourable treatment on the grounds of sex; see for example Lord Nicholls paras 31–37; Lord Hope, paras 101–103.'

---

[29] [1997] ICR 1.
[30] [2003] ICR 937.
[31] [2007] UKEAT 0587 06 0203.

The EAT concluded:

> 'I have considered whether, as Mr De Silva submits, *Pearce* precludes an Employment Tribunal from finding that an employer has liability for harassment by a third party, here the customer of the Respondent, in the absence of control. In my view it does not. The case which the Claimant wishes to advance is that the Respondent's policy of not challenging racist behaviour by clients is capable of itself of having the effect of creating an offensive environment for her. That, if established on the facts, is capable in my judgment of falling within s3A RRA. In short, the Chairman fell into error in concluding that the opinions of their Lordships in *Pearce*, dealing with a different statutory provision applied in *Burton*, had the effect in law of rendering this part of her claim without reasonable prospect of success.'

And, in any event, although not specifically so defined elsewhere in respect of other statutory discrimination, the Equal Treatment Framework Directive may require other equality legislation to be interpreted purposively in the same way. The government may also review the harassment provisions in other discrimination legislation as part of the consolidation of the law in of the Single Equality Bill 2009.

Recent case-law has also suggested that the Equal Treatment Framework Directive has introduced the concept of 'associative discrimination' (which is discrimination in respect of another person which affects the complainant).

With regard to the Employment Equality (Religion or Belief) Regulations 2003,[32] in *Saini v (1) All Saints Haque Centre (2) Bungay (3) Paul*,[33] the employee was one of two advice workers dismissed by the employer. Both were Hindus. The other employee had established discrimination in the tribunal. Mr Saini had not. However, in allowing his appeal and finding there had been discrimination against him too, the EAT held that:

> 'Thus, if on a proper analysis of the facts, an employee establishes that he has been subjected to paragraph 5(1)(b) conduct because of his employer pursuing a discriminatory policy against the religious beliefs held by another employee that will be enough.'

And in *Coleman v Attridge Law*[34] a secretary employed by the firm required additional time off to care for her disabled son. This was refused and when she complained to the tribunal of disability discrimination it was argued that the protection against discrimination did not apply as she was not herself disabled. The case was referred to Europe. The ECJ held that EC law protects not only disabled employees from direct discrimination and harassment, but also those employees who are

---

32 SI 2003/1660.

33 [2008] UKEAT 0227 08 2410.

34 Case C-303/06.

associated with a disabled person, such as carers. In his opinion for the Court, the Advocate-General indicated that the same principle would apply to religion or belief, age and sexual orientation.

Finally, if the employer takes action against someone who has brought a complaint of discrimination, this amount to victimisation in law and all of the equality legislation provides for remedies for successful complaints of victimisation. Victimisation occurs where the employer penalises an employee for bringing proceedings, giving evidence or information in connection with proceedings or for alleging that someone has contravened the relevant discrimination legislation.

For harassment and victimisation (neither of which depend upon a comparator, unlike direct discrimination), it is necessary to establish that the employer (or fellow employee) behaved in that way 'by reason' of the protected ground. So, if the employer (or fellow employee) is shown to have acted similarly to others irrespective of the protected ground then the claim will fail. For example, in *Chief Constable of West Yorkshire Police v Khan*,[35] where a police officer alleged that he was denied the opportunity of promotion as his chief constable refused to give a reference whilst an earlier claim for discrimination was before an employment tribunal, the House of Lords, in allowing the employer's appeal and remitting the matter back to the tribunal, said (per Lord Nicholls):

> 'Contrary to views sometimes stated, the third ingredient ("by reason that") does not raise a question of causation as that expression is usually understood. Causation is a slippery word, but normally it is used to describe a legal exercise. From the many events leading up to the crucial happening, the court selects one or more of them which the law regards as causative of the happening. Sometimes the court may look for the "operative" cause, or the "effective" cause. Sometimes it may apply a "but for" approach. For the reasons I sought to explain in *Nagarajan v London Regional Transport* [2001] 1 AC 502, 510–512, a causation exercise of this type is not required either by section 1(1)(a) or section 2. The phrases "on racial grounds" and "by reason that" denote a different exercise: why did the alleged discriminator act as he did? What, consciously or unconsciously, was his reason? Unlike causation, this is a subjective test. Causation is a legal conclusion. The reason why a person acted as he did is a question of fact.'

This is a subjective test which requires some examination of the motivation of the discriminator.

---

35 [2001] UKHL 48, [2001] 1 WLR 1947, [2001] 4 All ER 834, [2001] Emp LR 1399, [2001] ICR 1065, [2001] IRLR 830.

5.3.2 Burden of proof

One advantage of discrimination claims in the employment tribunal over court proceedings is that there is a reversal of the burden of proof:[36]

> '(1) This section applies where a complaint is presented under section 54 and the complaint is that the respondent—
> (a) has committed an act of discrimination, on grounds of race or ethnic or national origins, which is unlawful by virtue of any provision referred to in section 1(1B)(a), (e) or (f), or Part IV in its application to those provisions, or
> (b) has committed an act of harassment.
>
> (2) Where, on the hearing of the complaint, the complainant proves facts from which the tribunal could, apart from this section, conclude in the absence of an adequate explanation that the respondent—
> (a) has committed such an act of discrimination or harassment against the complainant, or
> (b) is by virtue of section 32 or 33 to be treated as having committed such an act of discrimination or harassment against the complainant,
>
> the tribunal shall uphold the complaint unless the respondent proves that he did not commit or, as the case may be, is not to be treated as having committed, that act.'

All forms of claims under the equality legislation now allow for the reversal of the burden of proof for most statutory discrimination claims. If the complainant makes out a prima facie case of discrimination, the burden of proof shifts to the employer who must show that it did not discriminate. If it cannot do so, then the tribunal 'must' find for the complainant. Case-law under the sex discrimination legislation following the reversal of the burden of proof has not conclusively shown that the change makes a significant practical difference. However, many sex and race discrimination cases still turn on opposing verbal evidence as to whether discrimination occurred. In the case of disability discrimination complaints the claim is more likely to be founded on arguments that the employer failed to take appropriate action and an absence of records together with the shifting of the burden of proof may well be of great assistance to employees.

However, in *Oyarce v Cheshire County Council*[37] the Court of Appeal held that the reversal of the burden of proof does not apply to victimisation under the Race Relations Act 1976 (RRA 1976):

> 'It does mean that (counter-intuitively) the reverse burden of proof provision does not apply to a case of victimisation in the context of racial

---

[36] For example, Race Relations Act 1976 (RRA 1976), s 54A, inserted by the Race Relations Act 1976 (Amendment) Regulations 2003, SI 2003/1626.

[37] [2008] EWCA Civ 434, [2008] ICR 1179, [2008] IRLR 653.

discrimination although it may well apply to victimisation cases in other discriminatory contexts. That is, no doubt, because in those other context, the draftsman has not found it necessary to confine the concept of the relevant discrimination to discrimination on any specific grounds. In the context of racial discrimination, however, he has found it necessary to confine the grounds of discrimination to which the reverse burden of proof applies because the Directive has itself confined its concept of racial discrimination to certain specific grounds which are more limited than the grounds provided for by our domestic Act.'

5.4 INCAPACITY AND DISABILITY DISCRIMINATION

In stress and bullying at work cases, claims in respect of disability discrimination will often be very important as the employee may well have become disabled as a result of the psychiatric injury which was sustained as a consequence of the stress or bullying. It is essential to consider whether there are grounds for bringing a disability discrimination claim, because such a claim will give the employee additional remedies over and above any common law remedy in respect of the original injury.

5.4.1 Meaning of disability

Section 1 of the Disability Discrimination Act 1995 (DDA 1995) defines disability:

> '1 (1) Subject to the provisions of Schedule 1, a person has a disability for the purposes of this Act if he has a physical or mental impairment which has a substantial and long-term adverse effect on his ability to carry out normal day-to-day activities.'

Long-term adverse effect means a disability that has lasted for at least 12 months or is likely to do so.

Schedule 1 to the DDA 1995 defines mental impairment:

> '1(1) "Mental impairment" includes an impairment resulting from or consisting of a mental illness only if the illness is a clinically well-recognised illness.'

The DDA 1995 as amended prohibits direct discrimination:[38]

> 'A person directly discriminates against a disabled person if, on the ground of the disabled person's disability, he treats the disabled person less favourably than he treats or would treat a person not having that particular disability whose relevant circumstances, including his abilities, are the same as, or not materially different from, those of the disabled person.'

Direct discrimination cannot be 'justified' under the DDA 1995.

---

38 DDA 1995, s 3A(5).

Section 3A(5) of the DDA 1995 introduces a protection against disability related discrimination:

> ' For the purposes of this Part, an employer discriminates against a disabled person if—
> (a) for a reason which relates to the disabled person's disability, he treats him less favourably than he treats or would treat others to whom that reason does not or would not apply; and
> (b) he cannot show that the treatment in question is justified.'

In *Clark v Novocold*[39] the Court of Appeal had held that the focus was on the 'reason' and that it was a different test to that used for direct sex and race discrimination.

However, in *London Borough of Lewisham v Malcolm*[40] the House of Lords doubted this:

> 'Mr Malcolm's schizophrenia is a condition from which he has suffered for some time and for which he has received and needs to continue to receive medication. For a fairly short but, in the event, critical time he omitted to take his prescribed medication. It was during that time that he sub-let the flat that he occupied under a secure tenancy from the appellant Council. The effect of the sub-letting, and his consequent relinquishing of his occupation of the flat, was that his secure tenancy became, pursuant to provisions in the Housing Act 1985, an ordinary contractual tenancy without any security of tenure. It was a term of his tenancy that sub-letting was prohibited (see para.5 of Section B of the Tenancy Agreement). At the time of the sub-letting Mr Malcolm had been actively engaged in pursuing the Right to Buy to which he was entitled under the relevant provisions of the Housing Act 1985. But this statutory right, along with the security of tenure that accompanies a secure tenancy, was lost by the sub-letting and on 6 July 2004 the Council served on him a four weeks notice determining the contractual tenancy. It is not in dispute that, subject to any invalidating effect that the 1995 Act may have had, this was a valid notice. Mr Malcolm did not deliver up possession of the flat and on 25 November 2004 the Council commenced possession proceedings against him and the sub-tenants who were then in occupation. The sub-tenants subsequently vacated the flat, Mr Malcolm moved back into occupation and the possession proceedings have continued against Mr Malcolm alone.'

Malcolm was not an employment case. However, the issue in relation to the interpretation of the DDA 1995 relates to all claims of disability related discrimination:

> 'First, in order for the alleged discriminator's "reason" to "relate to" the disability for section 24(1)(a) purposes, is it necessary for the fact of the disability to have played at least some motivating part in the mind of the alleged discriminator in leading him to subject the disabled person to the

[39] [1999] IRLR 318.
[40] [2008] 3 WLR 194, [2008] IRLR 700, [2008] UKHL 43.

> treatment complained of? And second, who are to be taken to be the comparators, the "others", referred to in section 24(1)(a) and what characteristics should be attributed to them?'

In answering the first question (could there be disability related discrimination where the discriminator was unaware of the disability) the House of Lords held (Baroness Hale dissenting):

> 'My answer to the first question, therefore, would be that if the physical or mental condition that constitutes the disability has played no motivating part in the decision of the alleged discriminator to inflict on the disabled person the treatment complained of, the alleged discriminator's reason for that treatment cannot, for section 24(1)(a) purposes, relate to the disability.'

And in answering the second question (is the comparator a disabled or non-disabled person) the House of Lords held (Baroness Hale dissenting):

> 'I have already referred to *Clark v Novacold.* The case was, in my opinion, wrongly decided. The employers would have dismissed any employee who proposed to be absent from work for up to a year, whatever the cause of the absence. The employers' reason for the dismissal was that the employee's injury was going to keep him off work for a year or so. This was plainly a reason that had been caused by, and, in that sense, related to the employee's disability. The "others", the statutory comparators, "to whom that reason . . . would not apply" would, in my opinion, be employees who would be absent from work for some similar period for a reason unconnected with physical disability. If these others would have been dismissed as Mr Clark was, he would not have been treated less favourably than they. If they, or a significant number of the comparators, would not have been dismissed, discrimination unlawful under the 1995 Act would be shown to have taken place.'

It is submitted that this decision dramatically reduces the protection against disability related discrimination provided by the DDA 1995. As Baroness Hale says in her dissenting judgment:

> 'Is it intended simply to secure that disabled people are treated in the same way as other people who do not have their disability? Or is it intended to secure that they are treated differently from other people in order that they can play as full as possible a part in society whatever their disabilities . . .
>
> In reaching this conclusion I believe that I am faithfully following the intention of Parliament. I am sorry to be disagreeing with your Lordships, but even more sorry that the settled understanding of employment lawyers and tribunals is to be disturbed as a result of your Lordships' disapproval of *Clark v Novacold.* That decision has stood unchallenged for nine years and has not, so far as we are aware, caused difficulty in practice.'

The Employment Appeals Tribunal has now held that the reasoning in *Malcolm* applies equality to employment claims in respect to disability related discrimination.[41]

In practice, unless and until the *Malcolm* decision is reversed by Parliament, disability related discrimination is now unlikely to be of much assistance in stress at work claims. The Government's Office for Disability Issues issued a consultation paper[42] seeking views on their proposal to seek the replacement of 'disability-related' discrimination by 'indirect' discrimination (which is found in other discrimination legislation) in the proposed Single Equality Bill 2009.

5.4.2 Reasonable adjustments

The DDA 1995 imposes obligations on employers which assist disabled people in finding and retaining jobs. In law this public policy aim translates to a duty on employers to make what is referred to in shorthand as 'reasonable adjustments'. Until the DDA 1995 was amended in 2005,[43] the duty to make reasonable adjustments was applied only to 'arrangements made by or on behalf of the employer' which placed the disabled person at a substantial disadvantage. Although this had been given quite a wide interpretation by the higher courts, there were still arguments over the meaning. The amended DDA 1995 now requires employers to consider changes to 'criteria, provisions and practices' as well as arrangements. This should catch selection and interview procedures.

Under s 4A of the amended DDA 1995[44] the Act now requires an employer to make reasonable adjustments:

> 'Where –
> (1)(a) a provision, criterion or practice applied by or on behalf of an employer, or
> (b) any physical feature of premises occupied by the employer,
>
> places the disabled person concerned at a substantial disadvantage in comparison with persons who are not disabled, it is the duty of the employer to take such steps as it is reasonable, in all the circumstances of the case, for him to have to take in order to prevent the provision, criterion or practice, or feature, having that effect.
>
> (2) In subsection (1), "the disabled person concerned" means –

41 *Child Support Agency (Dudley) v Truman* [2009] All ER (D) 105 (Feb), [2009] UKEAT 0293_08_0502.

42 'Improving protection from disability discrimination', November 2008.

43 Disability Discrimination Act 2005.

44 As amended by the Disability Discrimination Act 1995 (Amendment) Regulations 2003, SI 2003/1673.

(a) in the case of a provision, criterion or practice for determining to whom employment should be offered, any disabled person who is, or has notified the employer that he may be, an applicant for that employment;
(b) in any other case, a disabled person who is –
  (i) an applicant for the employment concerned, or
  (ii) an employee of the employer concerned.

(3) Nothing in this section imposes any duty on an employer in relation to a disabled person if the employer does not know, and could not reasonably be expected to know –
(a) in the case of an applicant or potential applicant, that the disabled person concerned is, or may be, an applicant for the employment; or
(b) in any case, that that person has a disability and is likely to be affected in the way mentioned in subsection (1).'

'Justification' is no longer a defence to a claim for failure to make reasonable adjustments.

The Approved Code of Practice produced by the Secretary of State as guidance on the application of the DDA 1995 helpfully sets out matters that can be considered:

'• making adjustments to premises
• allocating some of the disabled person's duties to another person
• transferring the disabled person to fill an existing vacancy
• altering the person's hours of working or training
• assigning the person to a different place of work or training
• allowing the person to be absent during working or training hours for rehabilitation, assessment or treatment
• giving, or arranging for, training or mentoring (whether for the disabled person or any other person)
• acquiring or modifying equipment
• modifying procedures for testing or assessment
• providing a reader or interpreter
• providing supervision or other support
• conducting a proper assessment of what reasonable adjustments may be required
• permitting flexible working
• allowing a disabled employee to take a period of disability leave
• participating in supported employment schemes, such as Workstep
• employing a support worker to assist a disabled employee
• modifying disciplinary or grievance procedures
• adjusting redundancy selection criteria
• modifying performance-related pay arrangements.'

In stress at work claims, the most useful suggested adjustments from this list are likely to be those relating to altering line management, place of work and allowing flexible working, including a graduated return to work after a breakdown. The Approved Code of Practice emphasises that an employer can only be expected to make reasonable adjustments:

'Whether it is reasonable for an employer to make any particular adjustment will depend on a number of things, such as its cost and effectiveness. However, if an adjustment is one which it is reasonable to make, then the employer must do so. Where a disabled person is placed at a substantial disadvantage by a provision, criterion or practice of the employer, or by a physical feature of the premises it occupies, the employer must consider whether any reasonable adjustments can be made to overcome that disadvantage. There is no onus on the disabled person to suggest what adjustments should be made (although it is good practice for employers to ask) but, where the disabled person does so, the employer must consider whether such adjustments would help overcome the disadvantage, and whether they are reasonable.'

In this non-exhaustive list of potential reasonable adjustments, there is reference to transferring a disabled employee to an existing position. In keeping with the non-exhaustive nature of this list, in *Southampton City College v Randall*,[45] the EAT held that the DDA 1995 does not as a matter of law preclude the employer from being required to create an entirely new post for an employee as a reasonable adjustment. This is, however, likely to arise fairly rarely in practice. In this case the employer had failed to consider reasonable adjustments at all and, most significantly, before the dismissal it had gone through a restructuring in the course of which it had a 'blank sheet' for creating new job specifications, so could therefore have easily created one for the employee which took into account the effects of the employee's disability. The EAT held:

'We are mindful that each case is fact specific. In this case, the Appellant did nothing and did not consider reasonable adjustments at all. Further, Section 6(3) does not, *as a matter of law* (our emphasis) preclude the creation of a new post in substitution for an existing post from being a reasonable adjustment. It must depend upon the facts of the case. Paragraphs 51–53 of the Tribunal's judgment show the background to the Tribunal's reasoning in paragraph 56. This case concerned a substantial reorganisation and, as the Tribunal found, Mr Gaynor conceded in evidence that at April 2003, he had "a blank sheet of paper" so far as the job specification was concerned. It followed "it was possible to devise a job which would take account of the effects of his disability (but harnessed the benefits of his long career and successful record), providing that the Claimant would fit in with the new 'ethos' which Mr Gaynor was pursuing". The Respondent did not do so, nor did it make any attempt to apply to the Claimant the pledge in its restructuring plans to consider redeployment and re-training: Judgment paragraph 56. On the facts of this particular case, this was the conclusion to which the Tribunal could come.'

In *Archibald v Fife Council*[46] Mrs Archibald had been a road sweeper for Fife Council. Following a medical procedure she had been unable to return to manual work. She therefore sought redeployment to an office job. It was common ground that she was capable of the work required.

---

45 [2005] UKEAT 0372 05 0711.

46 [2004] UKHL 32.

The employer required Mrs Archibald to undergo competitive interviews and she was unsuccessful, although she had applied for more than 100 posts within the council.

The House of Lords held that the DDA 1995 is different from the other equality legislation because in effect it is more focused on equality of outcome rather than on equality of treatment. The Act therefore requires an element of positive discrimination. Under the Act, by reason of the duty to make reasonable adjustments, the employer is not only permitted, but is obliged, to treat a disabled person more favourably than others. In this case, this meant transferring Mrs Archibald to a vacant office-based position without the need for competitive interview. This was so even though the Local Government and Housing Act 1989 requires all staff engaged by local authorities to be appointed 'on merit'. The House of Lords held:

> 'This means that section 6(7) is subject to the duty to make adjustments in relation to people who are at a substantial disadvantage because they are disabled in comparison with persons who are not disabled: section 6(1). The performance of this duty may require the employer, when making adjustments, to treat a disabled person who is in this position more favourably to remove the disadvantage which is attributable to the disability. Section 7(1) of the Local Government and Housing Act 1989, in its turn, is qualified by section 7(2)(f) of that Act, to which the opening words of section 7(2) make it subject. In terms of section 7(2)(f), section 7(1)(b) is subject to sections 5 and 6 of the 1995 Act. The result is that a disabled person can lawfully be transferred to a post which she is physically able to do without being at risk of dismissal due to her disability, provided the taking of this step is a reasonable thing for the employer to do in all the circumstances.
>
> The tribunal did not consider whether the policy requirement ought to have been adjusted in Mrs Archibald's case to remove the disadvantage which she faced due to the fact that she was at risk of being dismissed because she was no longer able to do her job as a road sweeper. That disadvantage could have been removed by transferring her to a sedentary post for which she was suitable from her previous post as a manual labourer. If that had been done, her disability would no longer have exposed her to the risk of dismissal on the ground that she was not physically able to do the job that she was employed to do.'

Note, however, in *Archibald* it was common ground that she could not return to manual work. If the disabled employee is selected for redundancy for a reason that is not related to his disability, then it might well be reasonable for the employee to have to undergo a selective interview process for alternative employment. In *Marie Difolco v NTL Group Ltd*[47] the Court of Appeal said:

---

47 [2006] EWCA Civ 1508.

> 'I should refer at this point to the decision of their Lordships' House in *Archibald v Fife Council*, referred to by the ET in paragraph 16, as we have seen. That was a case in which, by reason of disability, the employee could no longer meet the requirements of the relevant job description. Neither the nature of the relevant arrangements, nor the substantial disadvantage flowing from them, was as I understand it in the least doubt there. That is a point of departure between this case and that. But *Archibald* is important for another reason: it is material to a submission which is at the heart of Mr Cohen's argument as he developed it this morning. The submission is this: if the respondent had been dismissed for a reason relating to her disability, then it is established, by *Archibald* that the employers would have a duty to redeploy her without competitive selection; but here as I have indicated the EAT have negated (subject to remission to the ET) any link between the dismissal and the disability, and so the *Archibald* duty simply did not arise.'

In *Archibald* it was held that, in the circumstances, the duty to make reasonable adjustments included automatically transferring the disabled road sweeper to an existing administrative post at a higher grade that she was qualified to fill. However, this decision does not mean that a disabled person must automatically be given preferential treatment for all and any vacant posts: whether an employee is qualified for the post is still relevant (though a prudent employer should consider whether it would be reasonable to provide additional training or mentoring where this is not the case). In addition, the House of Lords stressed that this principle would not necessarily apply to more senior positions where it is not only possible, but also important, to make fine judgments about who will be best for the job. Baroness Hale in *Archibald* put in these terms:

> 'We are not talking here of high grade positions where it is not only possible but important to make fine judgments about who will be best for the job. We are talking of positions which a great many people could fill and for which no one candidate may be obviously "the best".'

In *Meikle v Nottinghamshire County Council*[48] Mrs Meikle was a visually impaired teacher. As well as being printed in a font she was unable to read, the timetable required her to move from one end of the school to the other for consecutive lessons. She asked for her lessons to take place in the same classroom or, alternatively, for extra time between lessons. The employer refused. It also admitted to a number of other failures to make reasonable adjustments requested by her and her union (including the printing of a timetable that she could read). As a result of the additional stress she was put under she went on long-term sick leave and eventually left employment and claimed a constructive dismissal. The employer's contractual sick pay policy was full pay for 6 months and then half pay for 6 months.

[48] [2004] EWCA Civ 859, [2004] IRLR 703.

Meikle mainly established that a constructive dismissal amounted to a dismissal for the purposes of the DDA 1995 (the 2003 Regulations[49] amend the 1995 Act to make this clear for dismissals after 1 October 2004). However, the Court of Appeal also held that because the reason for her extended sick leave had been the Council's admitted failures to make reasonable adjustments, she was entitled to full pay rather than half pay for the second 6 months of absence. Contractual sick pay was not excluded by s 6(11) of the Act which relates to pension schemes and the like. The Council was not allowed to plead justification. However, in applying *Meikle,* the EAT in *O'Hanlon v Revenue & Customs Commissioners*[50] made it clear that the failure of the employer to make the adjustments enabling her to return was the crucial point. If they had made the adjustments, she would not have been on sick leave for so long as to suffer the reduced sick pay. It was not the case that the disabled are entitled to receive the higher sums as of right.

Lawyers should be alert to the additional practical remedies the DDA 1995 may give disabled employees. Obviously, it is important to ensure that the client is properly advised as to their employment rights. And if the lawyer acting in a personal injury case is unable to give such advice they should refer the client to a specialist lawyer within the firm or to a specialist at another firm or agency.

If a claim is brought in the employment tribunal for compensation for the failure to make reasonable adjustments, it is important to remember that only losses caused by the failure to make the adjustments can be compensated. Compensation cannot be claimed for the underlying disability itself. So, in *Lewisham London Borough Council v Duberre*[51] the employee suffered an assault at work and became depressed. Following a lengthy period of sick leave, she was dismissed. She succeeded in her claims for disability discrimination and was awarded £130,000 on the basis that she was unlikely to be able to return to employment. The employer argued:

> '. . . there is plainly a very serious issue as to whether the applicant would ever have come to work again even if there had been no breach of the Disability Discrimination Act, and this would affect both future loss and compensation for loss of congenial employment.'

As the tribunal had not given reasons in respect of causation, the EAT remitted it back, saying:

> 'The failure to consider the effect of the applicant's physical injuries is a vital matter which potentially could dramatically affect the level of damages in this case. We have given careful consideration to what the consequences of our findings ought to be. We accept, as Miss Lewis observed, that there may

49 SI 2003/1673.
50 [2006] ICR 1579, [2006] IRLR 840.
51 [2003] UKEAT 19 02 2102.

be an interrelationship between the psychological and physical injuries in a case of this kind, and it is not always easy to disentangle the influence of one upon the other. We also consider that it would be difficult for the same tribunal to consider this argument untainted by its former assessment. In the circumstances, we have concluded that this matter ought to be referred to another tribunal to consider the question of remedies afresh.'

So in a stress or bullying at work claim, the employee may often have an argument that the employer's subsequent treatment of him amounted to failure to make reasonable adjustments (eg a failure to properly enable a graduated return). In a claim under the DDA 1995 in the employment tribunal claim it will only be possible to obtain compensation for the exacerbation of the condition (to the extent that this can be established) by reason of the failure to make reasonable adjustments rather than for the underlying psychiatric condition caused by stress or bullying.

5.4.3 Justification

It should be noted that direct discrimination can never be 'justified' and also that the defence of justification has now been removed from the failure to make reasonable adjustments. 'Justification' is still available as a defence to disability related discrimination.

Section 3A of the DDA 1995[52] provides:

'(3) Treatment is justified for the purposes of subsection (1)(b) [ie disability-related discrimination] if, but only if, the reason for it is both material to the circumstances of the particular case and substantial.

(4) But treatment of a disabled person cannot be justified under subsection (3) if it amounts to direct discrimination falling within subsection (5).

(5) A person directly discriminates against a disabled person if, on the ground of the disabled person's disability, he treats the disabled person less favourably than he treats or would treat a person not having that particular disability whose relevant circumstances, including his abilities, are the same as, or not materially different from, those of the disabled person.

(6) If, in a case falling within subsection (1), a person is under a duty to make reasonable adjustments in relation to a disabled person but fails to comply with that duty, his treatment of that person cannot be justified under subsection (3) unless it would have been justified even if he had complied with that duty.'

In *Jones v The Post Office*,[53] the Court of Appeal held that the focus is on the employer's reason for the less favourable treatment, and whether this is material and substantial. The tribunal will test this by asking if the reason

---

52 As amended by SI 2003/1673.
53 [2001] EWCA Civ 558, [2001] ICR 805, [2001] IRLR 384.

was within the band of reasonable responses that a reasonable employer might have adopted. If the employer's reason passes that test, then the tribunal cannot interfere with the employer's decision merely because the tribunal itself would have reached a different conclusion (per Arden LJ):

> 'A tribunal faced with a claim of justification may well find it helpful to proceed by asking the following questions:–
>
> What was the employee's disability?
>
> What was the discrimination by the employer in respect of the employee's disability?
>
> What was the employer's reason for treating the employee in this way?
>
> Is there a sufficient connection between the employer's reason for discrimination and the circumstances of the particular case (including those of the employer)?
>
> Is that reason on examination a substantial reason?
>
> The first three of those questions involve pure questions of fact. The fourth and fifth questions, however, involve questions of judgement. The latter questions may involve hearing expert evidence but the employment tribunal should not conduct an enquiry into what is the best course of action to take in all the circumstances of the case. Nor are the tribunal required to be persuaded themselves. They are not entitled to find that the employer's reason for the discrimination was not justified simply because they take the view that some conclusion, other than that to which the employer came, would have been preferable. Nor can they conclude that justification has not been shown simply because they entertain doubts as to the correctness of the employer's conclusion. If credible arguments exist to support the employer's decision, the employment tribunal may not hold that the reason for the discrimination is not "substantial". If, however, the employer's reason is outside the band of responses which a reasonable employer might have adopted, the reason would not be substantial. (This test was applied by the Court of Appeal in the different context of unfair dismissal in *Post Office v Foley* [2000] IRLR 827). In short, so far as the second limb of section 5(3) of the 1995 Act is concerned, justification is shown provided that the employer's reason is supportable.'

5.5 'OTHER DETRIMENT'

As well as the protections under the equality legislation considered in section **5.3**, employment legislation also protects various other workers victimised because they have undertaken what are referred to as 'protected acts'. If the victimisation is sufficiently serious to have caused stress and injury (whether or not a recognised psychiatric condition) the employee may bring a claim to the employment tribunal for compensation or other remedy. No minimum period of employment is required to bring a claim and, unlike unfair dismissal, there is no statutory cap on the basic award.

5.5.1 Protected acts

The provisions enabling a claim to an employment tribunal are:

- exercise of trade union rights;[54]
- performance of duties as formal employee representatives;[55]
- performance of duties as pension fund trustees;[56]
- complaints about health and safety at work;[57]
- exercise of maternity or paternity related rights (eg parental leave);[58]
- exercise of rights by shop and betting workers in respect of Sunday working;[59]
- time off work for study where permitted;[60]
- time off work for jury service;[61]
- acting as companion to a worker at a disciplinary or grievance procedure;[62]
- enforcement of rights under the Working Time Regulations 1998;[63]
- enforcement of rights under the national minimum wage rules;[64]
- whistleblowing.[65]

However, although victimisation in respect of any of these matters entitles the employee to bring a claim to a tribunal and might lead to the development of a psychiatric injury, in practice the most frequent in this connection is in respect of whistleblowing.

---

54 Trade Union and Labour Relations (Consolidation) Act 1992 (as amended), s 146.
55 Trade Union and Labour Relations (Consolidation) Act 1992 (as amended), ss 188 and 196.
56 ERA 1996, s 46.
57 ERA 1996, s 46.
58 ERA 1999 (as implemented and amended by regulation from time to time), s 7.
59 ERA 1996, s 101.
60 ERA 1996, ss 63A and 63B, presently restricted to certain 16 and 17-year-olds.
61 ERA 1996, s 98B.
62 Employment Relations Act 1999, s 12.
63 SI 1998/1833, reg 32.
64 ERA 1996, s 104A.
65 ERA 1996, s 43.

5.5.2 Whistleblowers

Where an employee is aware of unlawful activity at his place of work this will inevitably lead to increased stress which might cause psychiatric injury. The Public Interest Disclosure Act 1998 (PIDA 1998) was introduced to give a measure of protection and redress for whistleblowers. The relevant provisions relating to employment are now contained within the amended ERA 1996.

A qualifying disclosure is:[66]

> '... any disclosure of information which, in the reasonable belief of the worker making the disclosure, tends to show one or more of the following—
> (a) that a criminal offence has been committed, is being committed or is likely to be committed,
> (b) that a person has failed, is failing or is likely to fail to comply with any legal obligation to which he is subject,
> (c) that a miscarriage of justice has occurred, is occurring or is likely to occur,
> (d) that the health or safety of any individual has been, is being or is likely to be endangered,
> (e) that the environment has been, is being or is likely to be damaged, or
> (f) that information tending to show any matter falling within any one of the preceding paragraphs has been, is being or is likely to be deliberately concealed.
>
> (2) For the purposes of subsection (1), it is immaterial whether the relevant failure occurred, occurs or would occur in the United Kingdom or elsewhere, and whether the law applying to it is that of the United Kingdom or of any other country or territory.
>
> (3) A disclosure of information is not a qualifying disclosure if the person making the disclosure commits an offence by making it.
>
> (4) A disclosure of information in respect of which a claim to legal professional privilege (or, in Scotland, to confidentiality as between client and professional legal adviser) could be maintained in legal proceedings is not a qualifying disclosure if it is made by a person to whom the information had been disclosed in the course of obtaining legal advice.
>
> (5) In this Part "the relevant failure", in relation to a qualifying disclosure, means the matter falling within paragraphs (a) to (f) of subsection (1).'

A protected disclosure is:[67]

> '... a qualifying disclosure (as defined by section 43B) which is made by a worker in accordance with any of sections 43C to 43H.'

---

66 ERA 1996, s 43B.
67 ERA 1996, s 43A.

However, to become a protected disclosure under the Act, a qualifying disclosure must be made:[68]

> '(1) . . . in good faith—
> (a) to his employer, or
> (b) where the worker reasonably believes that the relevant failure relates solely or mainly to—
> (i) the conduct of a person other than his employer, or
> (ii) any other matter for which a person other than his employer has legal responsibility,
> to that other person.
>
> (2) A worker who, in accordance with a procedure whose use by him is authorised by his employer, makes a qualifying disclosure to a person other than his employer, is to be treated for the purposes of this Part as making the qualifying disclosure to his employer.'

Civil servants may make a protected disclosure in good faith to a Minister of the Crown.[69] Any worker may make a protected disclosure to the 'prescribed person' where such a person has been prescribed by regulation for such purpose.[70]

A worker may also make a protected disclosure to a lawyer in the course of obtaining legal advice.[71]

Where an employee fears making the disclosure to his employer, he can make a protected disclosure to another person:[72]

> '(1) A qualifying disclosure is made in accordance with this section if—
> (a) the worker makes the disclosure in good faith,
> (b) he reasonably believes that the information disclosed, and any allegation contained in it, are substantially true,
> (c) he does not make the disclosure for purposes of personal gain,
> (d) any of the conditions in subsection (2) is met, and
> (e) in all the circumstances of the case, it is reasonable for him to make the disclosure.
>
> (2) The conditions referred to in subsection (1)(d) are—
> (a) that, at the time he makes the disclosure, the worker reasonably believes that he will be subjected to a detriment by his employer if he makes a disclosure to his employer or in accordance with section 43F,
> (b) that, in a case where no person is prescribed for the purposes of section 43F in relation to the relevant failure, the worker reasonably believes that it is likely that evidence relating to the relevant failure will be concealed or destroyed if he makes a disclosure to his employer, or

---

68 ERA 1996, s 43C.
69 ERA 1996, s 43D.
70 ERA 1996, s 43E.
71 ERA 1996, s 43D.
72 ERA 1996, s 43G.

(c) that the worker has previously made a disclosure of substantially the same information—
  (i) to his employer, or
  (ii) in accordance with section 43F.

(3) In determining for the purposes of subsection (1)(e) whether it is reasonable for the worker to make the disclosure, regard shall be had, in particular, to—
(a) the identity of the person to whom the disclosure is made,
(b) the seriousness of the relevant failure,
(c) whether the relevant failure is continuing or is likely to occur in the future,
(d) whether the disclosure is made in breach of a duty of confidentiality owed by the employer to any other person,
(e) in a case falling within subsection (2)(c)(i) or (ii), any action which the employer or the person to whom the previous disclosure in accordance with section 43F was made has taken or might reasonably be expected to have taken as a result of the previous disclosure, and
(f) in a case falling within subsection (2)(c)(i), whether in making the disclosure to the employer the worker complied with any procedure whose use by him was authorised by the employer.

(4) For the purposes of this section a subsequent disclosure may be regarded as a disclosure of substantially the same information as that disclosed by a previous disclosure as mentioned in subsection (2)(c) even though the subsequent disclosure extends to information about action taken or not taken by any person as a result of the previous disclosure.'

In the case of an exceptionally serious failure, the conditions are relaxed:[73]

'(1) A qualifying disclosure is made in accordance with this section if—
(a) the worker makes the disclosure in good faith,
(b) he reasonably believes that the information disclosed, and any allegation contained in it, are substantially true,
(c) he does not make the disclosure for purposes of personal gain,
(d) the relevant failure is of an exceptionally serious nature, and
(e) in all the circumstances of the case, it is reasonable for him to make the disclosure.

(2) In determining for the purposes of subsection (1)(e) whether it is reasonable for the worker to make the disclosure, regard shall be had, in particular, to the identity of the person to whom the disclosure is made.'

Any duties of confidentiality under the contract of employment or in any compromise agreement are overridden by PIDA 1998.[74] There are special provisions relating to the police.[75]

---

73 ERA 1996, s 43H.
74 ERA 1996, s 43H.
75 ERA 1996, s 43KA.

It would seem that reporting bullying and harassment would probably be a protected disclosure. This can constitute a criminal offence under the PFHA 1997. Health and safety issues can constitute a 'failure to comply with a legal obligation'.

It is also possible for an employee who is victimised for making a protected disclosure and suffers stress and psychiatric injury to bring a tribunal claim rather than court proceedings for bullying and harassment. So, in *Virgo Fidelis Senior School v Boyle*[76] the employee was a teacher who:

> '... made a protected disclosure by writing a letter making explicit allegations against various members of the School staff to the Diocese, London Borough of Croydon and the Convent de Notre Dame de Fidelité in France.'

and was subsequently disciplined and dismissed. The EAT upheld the employment tribunal's decision that he had been subjected to a detriment for making a protected disclosure and was unfairly dismissed. He suffered clinical depression. However, although:

> '... the tribunal in referring to Mr Boyle's clinical depression suffered "largely as a result of the respondent's treatment of him" ignored the features set out in the psychiatric report placed before the Tribunal. Mr Boyle had reported an "unbearable" environment before his disclosure was even made and had experienced problems at his new school'

as no claim had been made for psychiatric injury, no separate award was made. However, the EAT made it clear that in an appropriate case compensation for psychiatric injury resulting from the detriment would be made:

> '... to compensate simply for the offence rather than the resulting injury or psychiatric damage would seem to offend against the general principle which was repeated in the Hackney[77] case, that "the aim is to compensate and not to punish" ...
>
> We see no reason for detriment under section 47B to be treated differently; it is another form of discrimination ...
>
> ... section 49(2) refers to any loss which in common with other areas of discrimination would allow Tribunals to make awards for injury to feelings, personal injury, i.e. psychiatric damage, and aggravated damages ...'

---

76 [2004] UKEAT 0644 03 2301, [2004] ICR 1210, [2004] IRLR 268.

77 *London Borough of Hackney v Adams* [2003] IRLR 402 which dealt with similar points arising from detriment suffered as a result of trade union membership.

The awards in detriment cases will, however, follow the guidelines set out in *Vento v Chief Constable of West Yorkshire Police (No 2)*.[78]

[78] [2003] IRLR 102. See **7.6**.

CHAPTER 6

CAUSATION

6.1 CAUSATION AND CLAIMS IN TORT

As with all claims in tort, in claims for compensation for stress at work it is necessary to establish that the alleged breach caused the damage (injury) complained of. This will certainly apply to all claims founded in negligence. Any coterminous claim in contract has slightly different consequences in theory, but the practical difference may be small.[1]

This may sound like an obvious proposition, but prior to *Hatton v Sutherland*[2] judges in stress at work claims commonly fell into error. They often recognised the injury (serious psychiatric damage) and consequent financial loss, found a breach of duty and then went on to find for the claimant in full without considering properly the causal link.

6.1.1 Material contribution by the breach

The claimant must show that the breach of duty (not simply stress) was either the sole cause of the injury or 'materially contributed to it' (*Hatton* Proposition 14):

> 'The claimant must show that that breach of duty has caused or materially contributed to the harm suffered. It is not enough to show that occupational stress has caused the harm (para 35).'

If the claimant has no prior history of psychiatric injury, then the issue of causation of the damage by the employer's breach of duty may well be easier to establish. But, as we have seen,[3] in the absence of any previous psychiatric vulnerability which is known to the employer, it is often difficult to establish foreseeability of injury, so such claims are uncommon. However, in *Jones v Sandwell Metropolitan Borough Council*[4]

---

1 See **6.2**.

2 *Hatton v Sutherland; Barber v Somerset County Council; Jones v Sandwell Metropolitan Borough Council; Bishop v Baker Refractories Ltd* [2002] EWCA Civ 76, [2002] 2 All ER 1, [2002] ICR 613, [2002] IRLR 263, [2002] 68 BMLR 115, [2002] All ER (D) 53 (Feb), CA.

3 See **3.4**.

4 One of the conjoined appeals in *Hatton*.

there had been no previous breakdown and, in upholding the first instance judgment, the Court of Appeal said:

> '... there was evidence before the judge which entitled him to reach the factual conclusions he did, and from those to conclude that the indications of risk to mental health were strong enough for a reasonable employer to think that he should do something about it, not least because senior management did think that there was something they should do. That something was to cease placing unreasonable demands upon the claimant. There was also expert evidence from which the judge was entitled to conclude that it was the failure to take those steps which caused, or at least materially contributed to, the claimant's mental illness.'

If the claimant is not affected by stress other than that arising from his work, causation is easier to establish. But even in these cases it is still essential to link the injury to the breach. So, for example, a court might find that although a job was 'stressful' (or 'pressurised'), this was not the result of a breach of duty by the employer. If there was then a breach which was very small or which occurred very late on in the development of the illness, the claimant may then find it difficult to establish that all of the resultant damage arose as a result of the breach. In *Sparks v HSBC plc*[5] the claimant was an employee of the bank. He was suffering from a depressive illness over a long period of time which the judge held was not caused by work-related stress. There was, however, a breach of duty in his treatment in the last week before he had a breakdown. The judge at first instance held that he had not established causation, saying:

> 'I find that really, although I remind myself of course I am dealing with liability and not quantum, if it is to be taken into account at all, it really does, I am sorry to say for the Claimant, come within the definition of de minimis, if one is entitled to use the Latin expression still.'

This was upheld by the Court of Appeal:

> 'In my view he was entitled on the evidence to reach the conclusion that those very late additions to the medical evidence did not require him to find that the negligence had caused or materially contributed to an appreciable or measurable exacerbation of an illness which, on any view, had been developing for some months and was inevitably going to result in the eventual outcome.'

In *Barber v Somerset*,[6] the breaches of duty found by the judge (which were reversed by the Court of Appeal and reinstated by the House of Lords) came quite late on in the claimant's work history. Although with the majority in allowing Mr Barber's appeal, Lord Rodger pointed out:

---

5 [2002] EWCA Civ 1942.

6 [2004] UKHL 13.

'Here the judge seems to assume that assistance to alleviate Mr Barber's workload would have been provided on a basis that would have meant that, for the rest of his career, Mr Barber would not have been under the same pressures as in 1996.

My Lords, for my part, I find the judge's conclusions on this crucial part of the case very far from satisfactory. Indeed, were it not for the fact that the Council do not really seem to have fought the case on this issue, I would have been disposed to dismiss the appeal on the basis that Mr Barber had failed to prove that, if the Council had taken reasonable care, he would not have developed the illness. But, in the absence of any significant evidence on behalf of the Council dealing with this issue and in the absence of any direct challenge by them, they cannot complain . . .'

It is therefore essential to focus on what it is alleged would have happened if there had been no breach. If the claimant would still probably have developed a serious psychiatric condition anyway, or if the pre-existing psychiatric condition would have led to his employment ending early lawfully in any event, compensation might be very limited.

If there are other stressors operating on the claimant (whether work related but not arising from a breach of duty, or from outside the workplace, such as bereavement or divorce), what then? The claimant does not have to establish that the breach of duty foreseeably was the sole cause of the damage, nor even that it was the major cause. It is sufficient for the claimant to establish that it was a material contribution.

This principle was established as the general rule in tort by *Bonnington Castings v Wardlaw*.[7] The claimant's pneumoconiosis had been contributed to by two sources of dust in the workplace; one was non-negligent as there was nothing at that time which could be done to prevent this and the other was a result of the employer's breach of statutory duty. The court held that provided the claimant could establish a 'material contribution' by the dust resulting from the breach of duty, he would succeed. In considering what was a 'material contribution' the court held (per Lord Reid):

' . . . the source of his disease was the dust from both sources, and the real question is whether the dust from the swing grinders materially contributed to the disease. What is a material contribution must be a question of degree. A contribution which comes within the exception de minimis non curat lex is not material, but I think that any contribution which does not fall within that exception must be material. I do not see how there can be something too large to come within the de minimis principle but yet too small to be material.'

The application of this principle to stress at work claims was acknowledged by Hale LJ in *Hatton*.

---

7 [1956] AC 613.

The claimant does, however, still have to establish that the breach of duty established which is established (not just the 'occupational stress' generally) was one of the causes of the injury. Medically, this may be easier with physical injury like pneumoconiosis than with psychiatric injury. The underlying principle is that the onus is still on the claimant to prove his case and if he cannot show that the breach was a material contribution then he will fail.

This principle was established by the House of Lords in *Wilsher v Essex Area Health Authority*.[8] This was a clinical negligence case where there were six possible causes for the claimant's blindness. Any one of these could have caused the blindness separately and it was impossible to say which one had been responsible. Only one cause was potentially negligent. The claimant was unable to prove causation.

In this context, in *Hatton* Hale LJ drew attention to the Court of Appeal's earlier decision in *Garrett v London Borough of Camden*[9] to show that the claimant may not be able to discharge the burden of proving causation 'where the main cause was a vulnerable personality which the employer knew nothing about'. In *Garrett* the Court of Appeal's main reason for dismissing the appeal was on grounds of foreseeability. However, on causation, in respect of one aspect of the claim for breach of duty that might have been established (alleged detriment as the result of whistleblowing in respect of his employer's activities) the court held (per Tuckey LJ):

> 'It is important to bear in mind that this was not a claim for wrongful or unfair dismissal but a claim for damages which required the appellant to prove that he had negligently been subjected to stress by the conditions in which he was required to work. It was not enough for him simply to say that he had blown the whistle on the MTC affair. He had to show that it was a cause of the stress, the subject of his claim. Relevant contemporaneous documents, all of which I have attempted to summarise earlier in this judgment, suggest that it was not. The appellant was not slow to complain and to put his complaints into writing, and yet he did not complain of stress caused by his concerns about MTC. I think the fact that MTC does not feature at all in the particulars of claim is significant. Furthermore, on his own admission the appellant was not involved at all with MTC until early 1994, yet he traced the cause of his illness back to 1992. Like the judge, it seems to me that the importance of MTC has grown in the appellant's mind as it has become of greater and continuing interest to the outside world. He has retrospectively and incorrectly (although I do not say dishonestly) made the connection between MTC and his illness.'

In cases where there are multiple stressors, the contribution of the individual stressors to the injury is in practice very likely to be held by the

8 [1988] AC 1074.

9 [2001] EWCA Civ 395. See further **3.4.5**.

medical experts to have had a 'cumulative' effect on the claimant's health. In the House of Lords decision of *McGhee v National Coal Board*[10] Lord Simon of Glaisdale said:

> 'But *Bonnington Castings Ltd. v. Wardlaw* [1956] A.C. 613 and *Nicholson v. Atlas Steel Foundry Engineering Co. Ltd.* [1957] 1 W.L.R. 613 establish, in my view, that where an injury is caused by two (or more) factors operating cumulatively, one (or more) of which factors is a breach of duty and one (or more) is not so, in such a way that it is impossible to ascertain the proportion in which the factors were effective in producing the injury or which factor was decisive, the law does not require a pursuer or plaintiff to prove the impossible, but holds that he is entitled to damages for the injury if he proves on a balance of probabilities that the breach or breaches of duty contributed substantially to causing the injury. If such factors so operate cumulatively, it is, in my judgment, immaterial whether they do so concurrently or successively.'

But it is important not to lose sight of the fundamentals. In looking for potential breaches of duty, it is essential to ensure that these actually caused, or materially contributed to, the illness.

Where the injury is a physical one said to be caused by stress (e g a heart attack) the issue of causation may be more difficult to establish medically. In *Harding v The Pub Estate Co Ltd*[11] a pub manager who worked very long hours in a stressful environment suffered a heart attack. The court found that the claimant had not established a breach of duty, so the issue of causation did not strictly arise, but did say (obiter):

> 'What should the appellants have done and would it have made any difference? It seems to me these are real difficulties in the respondent's way on this aspect of the case. He was the manager. He accepted he had sufficient staff. What hours he worked was a matter for him. Whatever hours he worked, the content of the job did not change. He never said to the appellants that they must reduce his hours. The cardiologists' evidence focuses on the environmental side of the job rather than the long hours. How would a reduction in hours or additional help relate to the stressors? In the end I am left in serious doubt whether, even if able to establish a breach of duty, the respondent could show that the breach made a material contribution to his heart attack.'

However, it is submitted that a different conclusion might well be reached in, for example, a bullying case leading to a heart attack if the medical evidence was supportive.

---

10 [1973] 1 WLR 1.

11 [2005] EWCA Civ 553.

6.1.2 Apportionment with other competing causes

If, as is commonly the case, the breach of duty was not the sole cause, but did materially contribute to the injury, what is the practical effect? Controversially, Hale LJ held that the injury needed to be 'apportioned' with the employer paying only for his share of the damage (*Hatton* Proposition 15):

> 'Where the harm suffered has more than one cause, the employer should only pay for that proportion of the harm suffered which is attributable to his wrongdoing, unless the harm is truly indivisible. It is for the defendant to raise the question of apportionment (paras 36 and 39).'

Hale LJ notes that the primary question relating to apportionment is whether the injury suffered is 'divisible' or 'indivisible'.

If the injury is divisible then an apportionment will be made. The most obvious such case was that of industrial deafness where it was possible to measure the deterioration over a period of time.[12] Hale LJ also refers to the more recent House of Lords authority for this proposition in *Holtby v Brigham & Cowan (Hull) Ltd*[13] where the claimant was exposed to asbestos in the course of his employment by different employers, some identified and some not, over a lengthy period.

In *Rahman v Arearose Ltd & University College London NHS Trust*,[14] which was not a stress at work case, the principle was applied to a psychiatric injury claim. In that case the apportionment of the damages was for an indivisible injury between the two wrongdoers (his employer and the NHS Trust who subsequently treated him). This is quite different from the more usual situation in stress at work claims where the injury was caused partly by the employer's breach of duty and partly by factors that do not give rise to any liability.

In *Barber v Somerset*, whilst generally giving implied support for the propositions of Hale LJ in the Court of Appeal, Lord Walker (giving the leading judgment) in connection with *Hatton* Proposition 15 said:

> '. . . your Lordships have heard no argument on the section dealing with apportionment and quantification of damage, and I think it better to express no view on those topics.'

The Court of Appeal revisited this subject in *Dickins v O2 plc*.[15] The employer had appealed a first instance decision in favour of the employee's claim that she had suffered a nervous breakdown caused by overwork. This was a 'first breakdown' case. The Court of Appeal

12 *Thompson v Smiths Ship Repairers (North Shields) Ltd* [1984] QB 405.
13 [2000] PIQR Q293.
14 [2001] QB 351.
15 [2008] EWCA Civ 1144. See further **3.4.4.2**.

rejected the appeal. However, the judge at first instance had allowed only 50% of the claimant's damages by way of apportionment in accordance with *Hatton* Proposition 15 between negligent and non-negligent causes. This finding was not appealed by either side.

In *Dickins*, the non-negligent causes of depression were described as follows:

> 'The judge then considered the various factors which he considered that he would have to take into account on the question of apportionment, if he found breach of duty and causation to be proved. Other factors besides those related to work might have contributed to the respondent's breakdown. The respondent was psychologically vulnerable. He mentioned the respondent's IBS, which her medical advisers seem to have assumed had been stress-related. Dr Gill was of the view that the IBS had been caused by stress but Dr Fahy said that there was no medical consensus as to the cause or causes of IBS and the judge concluded (at paragraph 20) that the cause of the respondent's IBS was "not straightforward". The judge also mentioned the possibility of emotional stress at home; it appears that there had been some difficulties in the respondent's relationship with her partner. However the judge thought that those might have been related to the problems at work. He also mentioned the possible effect of a flood at the respondent's home in 2006 as a result of which the respondent had had to live in an hotel for 9 months. This, he said, might have prolonged her depression.'

Smith LJ referred to a recent decision by the Court of Appeal on the same issue of apportionment in the context of clinical negligence in the case of *Bailey v Ministry of Defence*.[16] The Court in *Dickins* described *Bailey* as follows:

> 'That was a clinical negligence case in which the claimant had suffered brain damage as the result of cardiac arrest following inhalation of vomit. It was common ground that she had inhaled her vomit because she was in a very weakened state. Two causes had contributed to her weakness, one tortious, the other not. The judge below held that the tortious cause had made a material contribution to the weakness and the claimant succeeded in full. This constitution of the Court of Appeal upheld him. It was not possible to say with any confidence whether, without the tortious contribution, the claimant would have been so weak as to inhale her vomit. It was not suggested either in this court or below that the damages should be apportioned.'

So, in *Dickins*:

> 'Was this not a case of an indivisible injury (the respondent's seriously damaged state following her breakdown) with more than one cause? It was not possible to say that, but for the tort, the respondent would probably not have suffered the breakdown but it was possible to say that the tort had

---

16 [2008] EWCA Civ 883.

> made a material contribution to it. If that is a correct analysis, should not the starting point have been that the respondent was entitled to recover in full?'

The Court of Appeal then proceeded, obiter as point was not argued and was not therefore the subject of the appeal, to critique *Hatton* Proposition 15 on apportionment:

> 'It seems to me that, if in one breath the judge holds that all that can be said about the effect of the tort is that it made an unspecified material contribution, it is illogical for him, in the next breath, to attempt to assess the percentage effect of the tort as a basis for apportionment of the whole of the damages.

In the same case Smith LJ revisited the question of whether psychiatric injury is in fact a 'divisible injury' allowing for apportionment:

> 'In my experience, apportionment of the whole of the damages is usually carried out only in cases where the injury is divisible. In such cases the seriousness of the medical condition in question is often related to the degree of exposure to the agent causing it; in other words the condition is 'dose-related'. The true nature of such cases is that the tort has caused only part of the overall injury. The only practicable way of assessing the right sum for the relevant part may be to assess the damages for the whole injury and to apportion them on the basis of an assessment of the tortious and non-tortious exposures. This is possible in cases such as dust exposure, noise-induced deafness and hand/arm vibration syndrome. In other cases, the true nature of the case may be that the tort has aggravated an existing condition or injury and it may be that the only practicable way of assessing the effect of the aggravation is by an across the board apportionment of the total loss. I am doubtful of the applicability of this type of approach to a case of psychiatric injury where there are multiple causes of the breakdown . . . My provisional view (given without the benefit of argument) is that, in a case which has had to be decided on the basis that the tort has made a material contribution but it is not scientifically possible to say how much that contribution is (apart from the assessment that it was more than de minimis) and where the injury to which that has led is indivisible, it will be inappropriate simply to apportion the damages across the board.'

So where does this leave the question of apportionment in psychiatric injury claims? At first sight, it might be thought that *Hatton* Proposition 15 on apportionment would continue to be applied as it forms part of a judgment that has been approved by the House of Lords. However, Smith LJ points out in *Dickens*:

> 'It should be noted however that Hale LJ's remarks were obiter; apportionment did not arise in any of the four appeals under consideration. Moreover, the House of Lords in *Barber* expressly declined to endorse that aspect of Hale LJ's guidance, saying that they had heard no argument on the topic (per Lord Walker of Gestingthorpe at paragraph 63).

I respectfully wish (obiter) to express my doubts as to the correctness of Hale LJ's approach to apportionment.'

So the issue of apportionment has been considered separately by two distinguished Lady Justices of Appeal with great experience in personal injury law. Both comments are obiter and the issue will have to be decided in an appropriate case in the future, possibly in the House of Lords. In the meantime, it would seem that claimants should be wary of accepting arguments on apportionment of injury and should argue for the whole of the injury to be compensated by the employer, subject to 'acceleration' or 'vulnerability' arguments.[17]

6.1.3 Pre-existing disorder or vulnerability

If, prior to the employer's breach of duty, the claimant had a history of psychiatric injury or a pre-existing vulnerability then the court may treat the employer's breach not as the sole cause of the claimant's entire loss, but rather as the trigger which accelerates the onset of an illness that would have developed in any event (*Hatton* Proposition 16):

> 'The assessment of damages will take account of any pre-existing disorder or vulnerability and of the chance that the claimant would have succumbed to a stress related disorder in any event (para 42).'

Dealing with an 'acceleration' of injury is common for personal injury lawyers (e g where a negligent act accelerates back problems which already exist, whether or not they are then symptomatic, through degenerative change). Even this is not entirely straightforward. For example, In *Kenth v Heimdale Hotel Investments Limited*[18] , a back injury case, it was argued in the Court of Appeal that an acceleration approach was not permissible and that the court should instead adopt an all or nothing approach based on the balance of probabilities. However, Laws LJ held:

> 'In my view the judge was entitled here to hold that the Appellant would have suffered largely what she, in fact, suffered in course of time and in consequence of an unrelated supervening event given the pre-existing vulnerability of her back. Indeed, the experts were effectively agreed about that. It is right that there are passages in which they speak of the possibility of such an event as being merely more probable than not, rather than a certainty. Mr de Navarro's submission is that the acceleration approach is only permissible if the proposed future event is a certainty. It seems to me that that is altogether too rigid a position.
>
> Broadly speaking, in the present case, there was a measure of agreement about the onset of a supervening event at some time, but at first at least a measure of difference as to the length of the acceleration that that involved. It might be said that though there are dangers in being over-analytical, that

---

[17] See **6.1.3**.

[18] [2001] EWCA Civ 1283.

the potential future event goes to causation in the case whereas the length of the acceleration goes to quantification. However that may be, the truth is that the judge's approach here gave the Appellant the benefit of five years, assumed to be entirely trouble free, without this accident, and it is to be noted that an appropriate award of loss of earnings of 100 per cent basis was made in respect of the five years. Likewise, of course, the approach assumes it to be a certainty that but for the accident she would have had like troubles after five years.

The position here arrived at might perhaps coarsely be described as a swings and roundabout approach. What one cannot say is that it is, by reference to any principle, in some way less fair or just to the Appellant. Theoretically, indeed, the acceleration approach ought to produce the same result as Mr de Navarro's approach . . .

It is to be noted that the acceleration methodology has been used extremely commonly as cases collected in *Kemp*, referred to by the Respondents, amply demonstrate.'

In the context of psychiatric injury at work Hale LJ goes on to say in *Hatton*:

'Where the tortfeasor's breach of duty has exacerbated a pre-existing disorder or accelerated the effect of pre-existing vulnerability, the award of general damages for pain, suffering and loss of amenity will reflect only the exacerbation or acceleration. Further, the quantification of damages for financial losses must take some account of contingencies. In this context, one of those contingencies may well be the chance that the claimant would have succumbed to a stress-related disorder in any event. As it happens, all of these principles are exemplified by the decision of Otton J at first instance in *Page v Smith* [1993] PIQR Q55 (and not appealed by the claimant: see *Page v Smith* (No 2) [1996] 1 WLR 855). He reduced the multiplier for future loss of earnings (as it happens as a teacher) from 10 to 6 to reflect the many factors making it probable that the claimant would not have had a full and unbroken period of employment in any event and the real possibility that his employers would have terminated his employment because of his absences from work.'

And in *Dickins v O2*, whilst doubting *Hatton* Proposition 15 on apportionment of damages[19] Smith LJ stressed:

'It may well be appropriate to bear in mind that the claimant was psychiatrically vulnerable and might have suffered a breakdown at some time in the future even without the tort. There may then be a reduction in some heads of damage for future risks of non-tortious loss.'

And also:

'That is not to say that it is not important to have in mind in assessing damages the condition of the claimant before any tortious act occurred. In

19 See **6.1.2**.

> particular it might be appropriate, where the judge holds that non-tortious factors have been in play, to discount particular heads of damage, for example, to reflect the risk that the claimant might in any event have suffered a breakdown at some time in the future and would then have suffered some loss of earnings or incurred some expense.'

So on the particular facts of *Dickins v O2*, *Hatton* Proposition 16 might have been applied:

> 'I can see, for example, that it might well have been appropriate for the judge to discount the future losses to some extent on the basis that the respondent might well have suffered a breakdown at some time in the future; alternatively that the flooding of her home in 2006 had prolonged her psychiatric illness so that the appellant was liable only for a reduced period of suffering and absence from work.'

There is therefore a complex interplay between 'apportionment' of different factors contributing to the injury and the assessment of the likelihood that the claimant would have become ill in any event ('acceleration'). It is submitted that Smith LJ's approach is the better one, even though, as she points out:

> '. . . ultimately the result of a different approach might not have been very different.'

In *MG v North Devon NHS Primary Care Trust*,[20] the claimant (who had been misdiagnosed with chronic fatigue syndrome) succeeded in her claim for damages against her employer for mishandling her return to work following a breakdown and a depressive illness. The return to work had not been well handled. The judge said:

> 'Whilst the return to work programmes have been described as generous by Mr Hogarth, I have no doubt they reflected the value placed upon the Claimant as a Health Visitor with an exemplary nursing background whose service with the Defendant went back as far as 1984. True it is that the Defendant had the option of dismissing the Claimant but having made the decision to offer her a return to work programme they cannot thereafter complain if they are held liable having failed to adhere to that programme.'

But:

> 'Both doctors accepted the fact that those who have suffered a mental breakdown are at risk of doing so again … I conclude that an appropriate reduction in Damages to reflect the Claimant's vulnerability following her breakdown in June 2001 to be 20%.'

However, it is not inevitable in the case of a vulnerable employee that the damages will be reduced (whether by apportionment under *Hatton*

---

[20] [2006] EWHC 850 (QB).

Proposition 15 or to reflect 'acceleration' of the injury under *Hatton* Proposition 16). In *Moore v Welwyn Components Limited*[21] the Court said:

> 'The agreed psychiatric evidence was that Mr Moore was a vulnerable individual who was biologically predisposed to suffering from depressive illnesses. He had suffered from periods of significant depressive illnesses in the past triggered by stresses at work and in his domestic life. It was also agreed that the depressive illness which had led to Mr Moore's retirement was "likely to have had more than one causative factor". One factor "would be Mr Moore's constitutional predisposition to depression but it was unlikely that this alone would have brought about an illness without some external stress".'

Mr Moore had suffered earlier breakdowns. However, the bullying giving rise to the claim was described by the judge as 'appalling'. The judge accepted evidence of one of the psychiatrists that if the perpetrator had stopped the bullying Mr Moore would have made a complete recovery.

On the issue of apportionment, the Court of Appeal said:

> 'Once it was shown that the bullying was the cause of the loss of earnings it was for the employer to show that there were other potential causes as well. That could have been established by clear medical evidence, but in this case it was not. The agreed medical evidence was equivocal. The oral evidence was not primarily directed to issues of apportionment or assessment, but to the main issue at trial, which was whether or not Mr Moore had been bullied. Moreover the only non-negligent stressors identified related to Mr Moore's work and were closely connected with the allegations of bullying which had also sensitised Mr Moore to their effect. For these reasons we think the judge was entirely justified in saying that this was not a case for apportionment.'

Nor was there to be any deduction by reason of 'acceleration' of an inevitable psychiatric condition:

> 'Mr Moore's psychiatric history shows that he had always recovered from his illnesses and been able to return to work. He had withstood the sustained bullying for 2½ years before it pushed him to the point where he had to retire. None of his previous illnesses had such an effect or had resulted in any loss of earnings. Mr Moore's entitlement to sick pay would have shielded him from loss of earnings unless sickness caused him to be off work for a period in excess of 6 months. The evidence failed to establish that, but for the bullying, there would have been any likelihood of this. The judge was therefore right to award Mr Moore the full amount of his loss.'

There are few reported cases on the effect of 'self-inflicted' stressors such as alcohol or drugs. However, it is not inevitable that a stress at work

---

[21] One of the conjoined appeals in *Hartman* [2005] EWCA Civ 06, [2005] IRLR 293, [2005] PIQR P19, [2005] 85 BMLR 136.

claim by an alcoholic or drug addict would fail or that damages would be reduced on the grounds of acceleration, particularly where the workplace culture accepted or encouraged this behaviour. The claim of *Horkulak v Cantor Fitzgerald International*[22] did not involve a claim for psychiatric injury even though the claimant alleged a prolonged campaign of bullying. He was content to claim his substantial contractual losses after walking out and claiming constructive dismissal. The employer raised the claimant's use of drugs and alcohol in its defence which contended that they had the right to summarily dismiss him as a result. The judge found:

> 'The evidence does support the conclusion that the claimant was drinking excessively throughout his employment at Cantor, in particular, including during the course of 1999, when he was promoted to senior managing director.'

He was also taking cocaine. However, the judge held:

> 'In 1999 the claimant felt his addiction to alcohol and cocaine was out of hand and he sought help. He went to Dr McGilchrist in July 1999. I regard the fact that he sought medical advice a significant feature of the conflict on this part of the case. I do not accept his evidence that he completely overcame his addiction to cocaine in the time he suggested (by October 1999) but it is likely, and I find, that he had some success in curtailing it. He may have reduced his alcohol intake but he probably continued to drink heavily. The medical evidence does not support the conclusion that in June/July 2000 when he left Cantor he was addicted, but the claim he made to the doctors that he had been free of it for some six months is probably not true.'

The employer's defence was rejected and the claim succeeded. The employment contract had been breached by the bullying and not by the claimant's addictions which did not amount to gross misconduct. However, it should be noted that issues of medical causation did not apply in this case.

In *St George v The Home Office*[23] (which is not a stress at work case) the claimant was a prisoner who had had a seizure as a result of withdrawal from alcohol and drugs to which he had been addicted for many years. He fell from a bunk and suffered a serious head injury. The judge at first instance had made a finding of 15% contributory fault, but the Court of Appeal allowed his appeal on the basis that the addiction was 'not a potent cause' of the injury. In a stress at work claim, it will be important to consider carefully what contribution, if any, a prior addiction made to the breakdown, which will require expert evidence as to whether the addiction is 'a potent cause' or just a 'part of the history'.

---

22 [2003] EWHC 1918 (QB), [2004] ICR 697.

23 [2008] EWCA Civ 1068.

6.2 CAUSATION AND CONTRACT CLAIMS

Although as we have seen,[24] in practice there is very little difference between the duties in contract and tort, the issue of causation is in principle treated differently in contract and tort.

This was expressed in the pleural plaques appeals in the House of Lords in *Johnston v NEI International Combustion Ltd.*[25] The employees in this case had brought claims in negligence against their employer for exposing them to asbestos. The claims failed because, controversially, the court found that they had not suffered any damage as they had developed only symptomless pleural plaques (scarring on the lung) and no other asbestos related disease. The employees had not framed their claims in contract, and Lord Scott pointed out:

> '... a cause of action in tort cannot be based on the presence of asymptomatic pleural plaques, the attendant anxiety about the risk of future illness and the risk itself. It cannot be so based because the gist of the tort of negligence is damage and none of these things, individually or collectively, constitutes the requisite damage. But the conclusion that none of the appellants (leaving out of account for the moment Mr Grieves' damages claim based on his psychiatric illness) has a cause of action against his negligent employer strikes, for me at least, a somewhat discordant note. Each of the appellants was employed under a contract of service. Each of the employers must surely have owed its employees a contractual duty of care, as well as and commensurate with the tortious duty on which the appellants based their claims. It is accepted that the tortious duty was broken by the exposure of the appellants to asbestos dust. I would have thought that it would follow that the employers were in breach also of their contractual duty. Damage is the gist of a negligence action in tort but damage does not have to be shown in order to establish a cause of action for breach of contract. All that is necessary is to prove the breach. The amount of damages recoverable, once the breach of contract has been proved, is subject to well known rules established by the leading cases and, applying these rules, it might be well arguable that the breach of a contractual duty to provide a safe working environment for employees, an environment where reasonable precautions had been taken to avoid their exposure to injurious asbestos dust, would justify an award of contractual damages to compensate the employees for subjecting them to the risk of contracting in the future a life-threatening asbestos related disease. Damages for breach of contract should, in principle, compensate the victim for being deprived of the contractual benefit to which he was entitled.'

And Lord Hope also commented:

> 'The question whether employees might have a remedy against their employers in contract has not been explored in the present context, as my noble and learned friend Lord Scott of Foscote points out. There may be

[24] See **2.4**.

[25] [2007] UKHL 39, [2007] 3 WLR 876, [2007] 4 All ER 1047.

> room for development of the common law in this area. In that connection it is worth noting a recent assessment of the potential for the development of contractual remedies for employees against their employers by Matthew Boyle, "Contractual Remedies of Employees at Common Law: Exploring the Boundaries" [2007] JR 145. But, for the reasons Lord Scott gives, it would not be appropriate to attempt such a difficult and uncertain exercise in these cases.'

If the claimant has in fact suffered a personal injury (in stress at work claims a recognised psychiatric illness) then there seems little point in pursuing the argument that causation is treated differently depending on whether the claim is made in contract or in tort. Where the damage falls short of recognised psychiatric illness, then this point may be worth exploring.

However, it must be doubted whether the difference in law would ultimately lead to a materially different outcome. Damages in contract for anything less than a recognised psychiatric illness may in practice be nominal (and effectively worthless) as 'distress' is not normally recoverable in damages for breach of contract. An exception would be for breach of the implied term of mutual trust and confidence,[26] but quantifying the damage in such a case would not be straightforward.

6.3 CAUSATION IN THE EMPLOYMENT TRIBUNAL

In the tribunal, it is necessary to distinguish causation in unfair dismissal claims from causation in discrimination claims. Particular issues also arise in respect of disability discrimination.

6.3.1 Unfair dismissal

The breach of the right not to be unfairly dismissed is not a tort. As the EAT in *Chagger v Abbey National & Hopkins*[27] said:

> '... the right not to be unfairly dismissed, with which Polkey was concerned, is a sui generis statutory right, the breach of which is not classifiable as a tort. The assessment of compensation for unfair dismissal is governed by s. 123 (1) of the 1996 Act, which reads (so far as relevant) as follows:
>
>> "... the amount of the compensatory award shall be such amount as the tribunal considers just and equitable in all the circumstances having regard to the loss sustained by the complainant in consequence of the dismissal ...".'

[26] *Mahmud v BCCI* [1997] UKHL 23 – see further **2.4.3.1**.
[27] [2009] IRLR 86, [2008] All ER (D) 157 (Oct), [2008] UKEAT 0606_07_1610.

It is important not to introduce the tortious principles from common law claims[28] or indeed from statutory discrimination claims (which, as we shall see, are torts) into claims for unfair dismissal.[29]

If the employee suffers a psychiatric injury as a result of the dismissal we have already seen that he has no claim in contract for this.[30] Can the tribunal award compensation for non-pecuniary loss as part of its 'just and equitable' award under s 23 of the Employment Rights Act 1996 (ERA 1996)? As Lord Steyn put it in *Dunnachie v Kingston Upon Hull City Council*:[31]

> '... the question is whether this provision allows compensation to be awarded for non-economic damage. An employee, who claims to have suffered humiliation, injury to feelings and distress, as a result of a constructive dismissal, argues that properly construed section 123(1) allows for the recovery of non-pecuniary heads of loss. The employer argues that section 123(1) only permits recovery of pecuniary loss. This is the central dispute of statutory construction before the House.'

Very early on after the introduction of the employment protection regime under the Industrial Relations Act 1971 (which in s 116 contained very similar provisions to s 123 of the ERA 1996), the judiciary considered the issue of non-pecuniary loss in *Norton Tool Co Ltd v Tewson*[32] and held (per Lord Donaldson):

> 'In our judgment, the common law rules and authorities on wrongful dismissal are irrelevant. That cause of action is quite unaffected by the Industrial Relations Act 1971 which has created an entirely new cause of action, namely, the 'unfair industrial practice' of unfair dismissal. The measure of compensation for that statutory wrong is itself the creature of statute and is to be found in the Act of 1971 and nowhere else. But we do not consider that Parliament intended the court or tribunal to dispense compensation arbitrarily. On the other hand, the amount has a discretionary element and is not to be assessed by adopting the approach of a conscientious and skilled cost accountant or actuary. Nevertheless, that discretion is to be exercised judicially and upon the basis of principle.
>
> The court or tribunal is enjoined to assess compensation in an amount which is just and equitable in all the circumstances, and there is neither justice nor equity in a failure to act in accordance with principle. The principles to be adopted emerge from section 116 of the Act of 1971. First, the object is to compensate, and compensate fully, but not to award a bonus, save possibly in the special case of a refusal by an employer to make an offer of employment in accordance with the recommendation of the court or a tribunal. Secondly, the amount to be awarded is that which is just and

---

28 See **6.1**.

29 See **6.3.2**.

30 See **2.4.3.3**.

31 [2004] UKHL 36, [2004] 3 All ER 1011, [2004] 3 WLR 310, [2004] ICR 1052.

32 [1972] ICR 501.

> equitable in all the circumstances, having regard to the loss sustained by the complainant. "Loss" in the context of section 116 does not include injury to pride or feelings.'

And as Lord Steyn notes in *Dunnachie*:

> 'There was no appeal. The decision in *Norton Tool* was generally assumed to reflect the correct legal position until it was called into question in the judgment of Lord Hoffmann in *Johnson v Unisys Ltd* [2003] 1 AC 518.'

We have seen that in *Johnson* the House of Lords declined to overrule *Addis v Gramophone*[33] and held that there was no claim at common law for non-pecuniary loss arising out of the manner of the dismissal.[34] As Lord Steyn said, the ratio of the decision was:

> '. . . under Part X of the Employment Rights Act 1996 Parliament had provided the employee with a limited remedy for the conduct of which he complained; that, although it was possible to conceive of an implied term which the common law could develop to allow an employee to recover damages for loss arising from the manner of his dismissal, it would be an improper exercise of the judicial function for the House to take such a step in the light of the evident intention of Parliament that such claims should be heard by specialist tribunals and the remedy restricted in application and extent.'

Lord Hoffman, however, had indicated in *Johnson* that he thought that there might be a remedy in the employment tribunal:

> 'In my opinion, all the matters of which Mr Johnson complains in these proceedings were within the jurisdiction of the industrial tribunal. His most substantial complaint is of financial loss flowing from his psychiatric injury which he says was a consequence of the unfair manner of his dismissal. Such loss is a consequence of the dismissal which may form the subject matter of a compensatory award. The only doubtful question is whether it would have been open to the tribunal to include a sum by way of compensation for his distress, damage to family life and similar matters. As the award, even reduced by 25%, exceeded the statutory maximum and had to be reduced to £11,000, the point would have been academic. But perhaps I may be allowed a comment all the same. I know that in the early days of the National Industrial Relations Court it was laid down that only financial loss could be compensated: see *Norton Tool Co Ltd v Tewson* [1973] 1 WLR 45; *Wellman Alloys Ltd v Russell* [1973] ICR 616. It was said that the word "loss" can only mean financial loss. But I think that is too narrow a construction. The emphasis is upon the tribunal awarding such compensation as it thinks just and equitable. So I see no reason why in an appropriate case it should not include compensation for distress, humiliation, damage to reputation in the community or to family life.'

---

[33] [1909] AC 488, [1909] UKHL 1.

[34] See **4.3.3**.

There followed a series of cases which sought to overturn *Norton Tools* leading to the House of Lords decision in *Dunnachie*. The Lords (including Lord Hoffmann) scotched this attempt holding:

> '. . . the plain meaning of the word loss in section 123(1) excludes non-economic loss.
>
> . . . Given the hypothesis that the legislature expressly provided for the recovery of economic loss, it fails to explain why the legislature did not also expressly provide for compensation for injury to feelings. It also fails to take full account of the context.'

In a stress at work case which gives rise to a claim for unfair dismissal in the employment tribunal, there can therefore be no claim for psychiatric injury or injury to feelings.

6.3.2 Discrimination claims

Section 56(1)(b) of the Race Relations Act 1976 (RRA 1976) provides that in a case of race discrimination brought in the employment tribunal any award of compensation should:

> '. . . [correspond] to any damages [the employer] could have been ordered by a county court . . . to pay to the complainant if the complaint had fallen to be dealt with under section 57.'

Under s 57(1) of the RRA 1976 a race discrimination claim may be brought in the county court:

> '. . . in like manner as any other claim in tort ...'

The effect of those two provisions is that a race discrimination claim should be treated for causation purposes as a claim in tort.

The RRA 1976 and the Sex Discrimination Act 1975 (SDA 1975) should be interpreted consistently[35]. The same principle applies to all the equality legislation.

The equality legislation does add one further head of loss to those available in common law torts. Section 66(4) of the SDA 1975, s 57(4) of the RRA 1976 and s 8(4) of the DDA 1995 all provide that:

> '. . . for the avoidance of doubt it is hereby declared that damages in respect of an unlawful act/compensation in respect of discrimination in a way which is unlawful may include compensation for injury to feelings whether or not they/it includes compensation under any other head.'

[35] *Rhys-Harper v Relaxion Group plc* [2003] UKHL 33, [2003] ICR 867.

In *Sheriff v Klyne Tugs (Lowestoft) Ltd*[36] Stuart Smith LJ said:

> '. . . section 57(4) [of the RRA 1976] adds a head of injury for which compensation is payable since at common law a claimant cannot as a rule recover damages for injuries for feelings, save in defamation and false imprisonment.'

Similar principles also apply to other specific 'detriment' claims in the tribunal where, unlike unfair dismissal, non-pecuniary loss is not excluded. So, for example, ss 146–149 of the Trade Union and Labour Relations (Consolidation) Act 1992 (TULRA) relate to action short of dismissal on grounds related to union membership or activity and s 149(2) states:

> 'The amount of the compensation awarded shall be such as the tribunal considers just and equitable in all the circumstances having regard to the infringement complained of and to any loss sustained by the complainant which is attributable to the [act or failure] which infringed his right.'

In *Cleveland Ambulance NHS Trust v Blane*[37] the EAT upheld an award by a tribunal which included compensation for injury to feelings as well as for pecuniary loss, contrasting the position with that relating to compensation for unfair dismissal:

> 'It is nothing to the point that an award for injury to feelings cannot be recovered in a wrongful dismissal or unfair dismissal claim. They are different claims, compensated in different ways. We do not accept that a complaint under section 146(1) of the Act of 1992 can simply be categorised as less serious and therefore cannot allow of a head of compensation not provided for in claims of unfair dismissal or wrongful dismissal. Apart from the different wording of the section, the intention behind it is clear; an employee who is unfairly dismissed would normally suffer pecuniary loss, and that, Parliament has decided, will adequately compensate him for the wrong. In a case of action short of dismissal it may very well be that he can point to no pecuniary loss; nevertheless, Parliament has decided that he should be able to recover financial compensation "having regard to the infringement complained of". That must, in our judgment, include injury to his feelings occasioned by the unlawful act.'

Similarly, s 49 of the ERA 1996 relates to detriment in respect of claims relating to health and safety, Sunday working and time off for reasons dealt with in the ERA 1996 and s 49(2) of the ERA 1996 provides that:

> 'The amount of the compensation awarded shall be such as the Tribunal considers just and equitable in all the circumstances having regard to—
> (a) the infringement to which the complaint relates, and
> (b) any loss which is attributable to the act, or failure to act, which infringed the complainant's right.'

---

36 [1999] ICR 1170.
37 [1997] ICR 851.

Compensation can therefore be awarded for non-pecuniary loss, even if there is no economic loss suffered by the employee.

Essa v Laing[38] was a discrimination claim brought by a black Welshman who had been singled out from the other workers on the Millennium Stadium by the foreman who called him a 'black cunt'. The Employment Tribunal at first instance described the effect on him:

> 'Mr Essa gave evidence as to the effect Mr Pritchard's remark had on him. He said that he came from a decent family where obscenities were never used. He had heard bad language on sites but had never been spoken to in the way Mr Pritchard had spoken to him. He said the incident of 28 July so affected his health that he had been treated by his doctor for depression. He has stopped looking for work because he will always be wondering if his boss is thinking of him in the terms expressed by Mr Pritchard. It also affected his boxing. He was picked to carry the Welsh flag before boxing for Wales against Scotland but became upset whilst carrying it, asking himself what right he had to be representing Wales. He was overcome with similar feeling during the fight. He says why cannot people see him for what he is and not for the colour of his skin. He says it was "the way he spoke to me, it was the way he treated me, I'll take it to my grave . . . The only thing I'd done was to be black and to go to work . . . I am Welsh and no one can take that away from me". His sense of rejection as a Welshman has so distressed him that he intends to leave Wales and to take up professional boxing in England.'

A key issue in this case was whether foreseeability was a necessary component of the statutory tort of discrimination. If the claim had been brought at common law Mr Essa having no previous psychiatric history known to his employers would almost certainly have lost his case for failing to establish foreseeability under *Hatton*.[39] However, the Court of Appeal in *Essa* held (per Pill LJ):

> 'I see no need to superimpose the requirement or pre-requisite of reasonable foreseeability upon the statutory tort in order to achieve the balance of interests which the law of tort requires. It is sufficient if the damage flows directly and naturally from the wrong. While there is force in the submission that, to prevent multiplicity of claims and frivolous claims, a control mechanism beyond that of causation is needed, reliance upon the good sense of employment tribunals in finding the facts and reaching conclusions on them is a sufficient control mechanism, in my view. As a mechanism for protecting a defendant against damages which, on policy grounds, may appear too remote, a further control by way of a reasonable foreseeability test is neither appropriate nor necessary in present circumstances.'

Clarke LJ agreed with Pill LJ, adding:

---

38 [2004] ICR 746.

39 See **3.4**.

> 'In all the circumstances I agree with Pill LJ that there is no need to add a further requirement of reasonable foreseeability and that the robust good sense of employment tribunals can be relied upon to ensure that compensation is awarded only where there really is a causal link between the act of discrimination and the injury alleged. No such compensation will of course be payable where there has been a break in the chain of causation or where the claimant has failed to take reasonable steps to mitigate his loss.'

Rix LJ dissented. Although Clark LJ had sympathy with Rix LJ's view, he (Clark LJ) ultimately agreed with Pill LJ and said:

> '... it seems to me that that balance is best achieved by affording compensation for injury caused by the act of discrimination. Such an approach affords justice to the claimant who has been unlawfully discriminated against and is not unjust to the perpetrator because he deliberately made the racist remark. Like Rix LJ, I am intrigued by the just and equitable phraseology found in section 56 of the 1976 Act. Although no-one placed reliance upon it in the course of the argument, it seems to me that for the reasons already given, in the particular circumstances of this statutory tort, justice and equity are best served by holding that a simple test of causation is sufficient. The position might be different if there were a real risk that, without a further requirement of reasonable foreseeability, the floodgates of unmeritorious claims might be opened. I adhere to my view that there is no such real risk.'

However, in considering causation in discrimination claims, it is necessary to examine the effect the specific discrimination had and whether that is what caused the loss. If the loss would have been incurred in any event the whole of the employee's loss may not be recovered. In *Chagger v Abbey National & Hopkins* the EAT (Underhill J) pointed out:

> 'What therefore is required is the comparison of the Claimant's current position with what would have been his position if the wrong had not been done. The first step must be to define the wrong in question. The provision of the 1976 Act on which this part of the Claimant's claim was based must be s. 4(2)(c), which renders it unlawful to discriminate against an employee "by dismissing him or subjecting him to any other detriment": that is nowhere spelt out, but it is self-evident and is reflected in the Tribunal's identification of dismissal as the relevant detriment (see para. 40 above). It might therefore be contended that the relevant question was, straightforwardly, what would have happened if the Claimant had not been dismissed, which would at least arguably exclude consideration of whether he might have undergone the same dismissal but on different grounds. But in our view that is an inadequate formulation. Dismissal is not itself a wrong: what renders it unlawful in a case under s. 4 is the discriminatory grounds on which it occurs. It is the discrimination which is the essence of the wrong. If that is the right characterisation, then the correct question is what would have happened if the Claimant had not been discriminatorily dismissed: that formulation plainly requires consideration of whether the same dismissal might have occurred but on legitimate grounds. Accordingly, we believe that the Tribunal was wrong not to consider that question.'

And if the employer might have dismissed the employee lawfully:

> 'We believe that the reliance placed by Ms. Heal and the Tribunal on "material contribution" is, with respect to them, misconceived. In order to establish liability in the case of common law torts where damage is a necessary part of the cause of action, a claimant only has to show that the alleged tortfeasor materially contributed to the damage in respect of which he claims, and not that his wrongful act was the only or main cause. There is of course a similar rule in cases of discrimination, though the label "material contribution" is not generally used. But that rule is not relevant to the different issue which arises here – namely whether in assessing compensation it is relevant to take into account the chance that the respondent might have caused the same damage lawfully if he had not done so on discriminatory grounds.
>
> It might seem unattractive that a discriminator can reduce, and perhaps in some cases extinguish altogether, the compensation which he would otherwise have to pay by taking credit for potential legitimate grounds for his action when ex hypothesi his actual grounds were illegitimate. But the same objection might be taken to the rule in unfair dismissal cases: the answer in both cases is the same, namely that an award on ordinary compensatory principles requires the Polkey question to be asked. It will only assist the respondent if he is able to show that the victim would or might have been dismissed anyway – which will only be an available argument in a fairly limited class of cases (of which discriminatory selection for redundancy may be the most obvious example). In such cases it could equally be said to be unattractive that a claimant should make a "windfall" 100% recovery in circumstances where he was likely to be dismissed in any event, simply because his employer had – it may be subconsciously and only to a small extent – allowed himself to be influenced by discriminatory considerations. There is nothing in the statute to suggest that discrimination is to be treated as a specially heinous wrong to which special rules of compensation should apply.'

Although the EAT seeks to minimise the impact, this is an important decision which potentially creates difficulties for applicants in many discrimination claims relating to dismissal. It will not be enough to establish the discrimination but it will also be necessary to establish that the employee would not have been dismissed anyway. In stress at work discrimination claims, mainly resulting from harassment, the practical impact may be limited.

In *Chagger v Abbey National & Hopkins* the employee also sought to argue that his marketability had been damaged by his discriminatory dismissal. This was not a 'stigma damages' claim like *Malik*[40] where the stigma related to association with the employer, but related to alleged ongoing stigma in the job market of making a claim for the unlawful discrimination:

---

[40] See **2.4.3.1**.

'In our view the risk that future potential employers may decline to employ the Claimant because of the claim which he has brought against the Appellants is not a matter which can be reflected in his compensation. It is well recognised that wrongdoers cannot be saddled with every consequence of their actions.

Nevertheless in this particular context the fact that the loss in question arises only indirectly, and that the immediate cause is the unlawful conduct of third parties, does seem to us a powerful reason for holding it to be too remote.

The natural scope of liability for a discriminatory dismissal does not seem to us to extend beyond the injury inherent in the loss of the employment in question.

We note, though this is not central to our reasoning, that if such a claim were admissible in principle it would be available in the case of every claim for dismissal in breach of the employment protection or anti-discrimination legislation. It is not without significance that no such claim has, so far as we are aware, ever been upheld (or indeed advanced). If such claims were admitted, the difficulties of proof and evaluation would be formidable, since it would be necessary to make judgments about the conduct of other employers which would be of their nature speculative and unquantifiable.'

In principle, the legal rules which govern causation at common law (including material contribution, acceleration and, arguably, apportionment) also apply to discrimination claims in the tribunal.[41] However, employment tribunals, although they will have a legally qualified chair, do not have the same experience of determining causation of personal injury as the court's. The vast majority of claims they deal with have no issues of medical causation at all because they are unfair dismissal claims[42] or because they are discrimination claims where there is a claim for injury to feelings, but there is no claim for psychiatric illness. Employment lawyers may also be less comfortable with dealing with medical conditions. As the EAT put it in their decision in *Dunnachie*:[43]

'But it is not simply a question of Employment Tribunals having to gain more expertise, or to acquire similar expertise to that of the common law courts, or to expand their task from the realm of discrimination into unfair dismissal. In practice, notwithstanding the suggestion of Stuart Smith LJ in *Sheriff* at paragraph 21 that in discrimination cases, where a claim included or might include injury to health as well as injury to feelings "a complainant and his advisers may wish in those circumstances to heed the advice of the editors of Harvey . . . to obtain a medical report", medical reports have been rare in discrimination cases.'

---

41 See **6.1**.

42 See **6.3.1**.

43 [2003] UKEAT 0726 02 2205.

Issues relating to causation are inevitably dealt with in a rather rough and ready way. In *Salmon v HM Prison Service*[44] the employee had been subjected to very serious sexual harassment and discrimination. The tribunal had awarded £15,000 for psychiatric injury and a further £15,000 for injury to feelings. The awards were then discounted by 25% on the twin grounds (1) that the psychiatrists were agreed that she was a 'vulnerable' personality and (2) that some of the actions of her employer which contributed to her illness could not be said to be unlawful sexual discrimination.

Underhill J dismissed the employer's appeals and said with regard to the approach to causation in the tribunal:

> 'Miss Downing argues that the reduction of 25% was wholly inadequate and that on the evidence before it the Tribunal was obliged to discount the "100% figure" by at least a half. Before dealing with that contention, we should observe that there may be some room for argument about whether the approach adopted by the Tribunal was correct in principle. Conventionally, a claimant is entitled to recover damages on a 100% basis where the tortfeasor's act has made a material contribution to his suffering the injury in question, even though there may have been other (or even more) material contributory causes. On that basis, the fact that a victim has a pre-existing vulnerability to injury, or that the injury was only part of a complex of causes, is no ground – as such – for reducing his or her damages. That is not to say that it is wholly irrelevant. To the extent that the court concludes that by reason of that vulnerability the injury in question might well have occurred in any event, that factor would be reflected in the overall quantification of damages: that may produce a similar result to what would have been achieved by an apportionment of causation, but the reasoning is different and it will certainly not always do so. These principles have been applied to cases of psychiatric injury in such cases as *Page v. Smith (No 2)* [1996] 1 WLR 855 and *Vernon v. Bosley* (No 1) [1997] 1 All ER 577. However, the law as regards material contribution and apportionment of causation has recently been considered again by the Court of Appeal in *Holtby v. Brigham & Cowan (Hull) Ltd* [2000] 3 All ER 420 (and see now, decided since the argument in this case, *Allen v. British Rail Engineering Ltd* [2001] EWCA Civ 242); and the conventional view summarised above may be in doubt. Neither party, understandably, was anxious on this appeal to enter into these treacherous waters. Specifically, there was no cross-appeal by Mr Fairweather on behalf of Mrs Salmon claiming that no discount should have been made at all. Pragmatically, that was no doubt a sensible approach, since even if we had acceded to such a submission this might well have been one of those cases where a similar result would have been reached by discounting for the likelihood that Mrs Salmon would or might have suffered a serious psychiatric illness in any event.
>
> We proceed therefore to consider the exercise which the Tribunal performed of seeking to assess the extent of the contribution which the unlawful conduct by the Prison Service made to the causation of Mrs Salmon's illness. Such an exercise cannot, of its nature, be performed with any precision.

44 [2001] UKEAT 21_00_2404.

> Having given careful consideration to the expert evidence, it was for the Tribunal to make what was inevitably a very broad assessment. We are not prepared to say that its assessment was wrong in principle. No doubt Mrs Salmon was a vulnerable personality, and there were various threats to her psychiatric well-being which were not the result of sex discrimination by the Prison Service. But there was ample evidence on which the Tribunal was entitled to reach the view that it was the matters which it held to constitute sex discrimination – mainly, but not only, the dock book incident – which constituted the main cause of the serious depression into which she fell. Another tribunal on the same evidence might equally reasonably have made a larger discount; but we see no basis for saying that 25% was wrong in law.'

So although the tribunal has to have regard to these issues, precise calculation is not expected and the tribunal will only be able to make a 'broad assessment'. Some might say that in effect that is also what happens in the courts.

In *Prison Service v Beart*[45] the Court of Appeal held that a subsequent unfair dismissal did not break the chain of causation in respect of damages for discrimination. Mrs Beart suffered from depression and had been unable to work. The Court said:

> 'In September 1997, however, Mrs Beart went off work suffering from depression, and never returned to work. A subsequent joint medical report made in September 2003 in the course of these proceedings diagnosed a pre-existing vulnerability to minor depressive illness. But it had never before materially interfered with her work. What triggered a severer depression on this occasion was an altercation with her immediate superior, Mrs Tetley, who misunderstood her inquiry about the possibility of working part-time (to assist with collecting children from school) as an intention to resign her job as temporary executive officer. She was therefore reassigned a part-time job as an administrative officer (a lower rank with a substantial pay cut) which did not in any event meet her child care problem. When Mrs Beart tried to get her old job back, she was told that the advertisement for it could not be withdrawn, which was not true.'

Medical advice sent to the employer was that she should be redeployed and that this would probably allow her to return to work. This was ignored. Mrs Beart also owned a shop and a party clothes business. This was known to her employer. Whilst she was off sick from work the employer engaged private detectives with a view to trying to establish that Mrs Beart was working on her own account whilst still employed. She was disciplined and dismissed. Her claims for disability discrimination and unfair dismissal were eventually upheld by the Court of Appeal. The claims were then remitted to the tribunal for compensation to be assessed but this issue also ended up in the Court of Appeal. The employer contended that because of the unfair dismissal the statutory cap[46] applied to limit her compensatory award, notwithstanding the finding of

---

45 [2005] EWCA Civ 467.

46 See **7.3.2**.

discrimination. In effect, the employer argued that the unfair dismissal broke the chain of causation. The Court of Appeal applied *Coudert Brothers v Normans Bay Ltd*,[47] where it was held that a defendant cannot rely on his own wrong to break the chain of causation and dismissed the employer's appeal:

> 'The issue of unfair dismissal having been properly raised and established, albeit by Mrs Beart the claimant, the Prison Service as respondent then sought to rely on its own wrongful act, its dismissal of Mrs Beart from her employment, as limiting the damages which would otherwise flow from the separate tort of disability discrimination which it had previously committed. It is true in one sense that the Prison Service does not seek to rely on the fact that it had acted unfairly, as distinct from the fact of dismissal itself. But it cannot take the one without the other. As stated above, if the dismissal had been justified, then Mrs Beart's claim would have been affected, albeit for quite different reasons and in different ways than those advanced by Mr Underwood. As it is, the dismissal was unfair and if the Prison Service is to rely on it as breaking the chain of causation that it must take it with all its qualities. Indeed, that is just what the Prison Service is seeking to do by relying on the statutory cap of £12,000 as explaining why, unusually, in this case it benefits a wrongdoer to rely on its own wrong.'

6.3.3 Special factors relating to causation under the Disability Discrimination Act 1995

The points set out in **6.3.2** relating to causation in discrimination claims equally apply to claims made under the DDA 1995.

However, there is a further practical issue that must be considered. In a stress at work claim the cause of action under the DDA 1995 is most likely to relate to the treatment of the employee after he has suffered a breakdown. For example, there may be a claim for failure to make reasonable adjustments in relation to a proposed return to work or a claim for harassment.[48]

However, as the claimant has already suffered a psychiatric injury which has led to the disability, the psychiatric injury itself has not been caused by the discrimination. Compensation may therefore be low. A substantial claim might still be framed:

- if disability discrimination can be established by showing that the employer failed to make reasonable adjustments to enable the employee to return to work;

- if adjustments had been made, the employee would have been able to return to work, and he would have earned the same (or maybe less,

---

47 [2003] EWCA Civ 215.

48 See **5.4.2**.

but still significant, for part-time work) which would probably have continued for the medium term; and

- if his residual earning capacity on the open labour market is much lower than the likely earnings on a return to work at the previous employer.

CHAPTER 7

REMEDIES

7.1 DAMAGES FOR NEGLIGENCE OR BREACH OF STATUTORY DUTY

A claim for compensation for stress at work founded in tort or for breach of statutory duty requires the claimant to show damage; namely a recognised psychiatric condition (not just anxiety or distress).[1]

Provided that the claimant can establish a recognised psychiatric condition compensation will, in the usual way, consist of 'general damages' for pain, suffering and loss of amenity and also an award for the past and future loss and expense suffered as a result of developing the condition.

It is not always easy to separate normal reactions such as grief, anger or distress from a psychiatric condition. It is important for the psychiatric expert to refer the claimant's symptoms to the two principal diagnostic tools, the ICD-10 or the DSM IVR. Further, it is essential for the psychiatrist to consider not only the existence of the symptoms but also their severity.

7.1.1 General damages

The claimant will be entitled to 'general damages' for pain, suffering and loss of amenity. The quantum of general damages will depend upon the individual circumstances of the case. However, The Judicial Studies Board's *Guidelines for the Assessment of General Damages in Personal Injury Cases* ('the JSB Guidelines')[2] will usually set the parameters for the award of general damages to be made by the judge. These do not provide a fixed tariff. But, as Lord Donaldson said in the foreword to the first edition in 1992:

> '. . . whilst no two cases are ever precisely the same, justice requires that there be consistency between awards.'

---

1 *McLoughlin v O'Brian* [1983] 1 AC 410, 418.

2 JSB Guidelines, 9th edn, September 2008.

And the JSB Guidelines are now almost invariably adopted as the starting point in assessing general damages.

So far as psychiatric injury at work claims are concerned, general damages will almost always fall within the scope of section 3 of the JSB Guidelines, 'Psychiatric Damage'. The section opens with some general points about the assessment of general damages for psychiatric injury:[3]

> 'The factors to be taken into account in valuing claims of this nature are as follows:
> (i) the injured person's ability to cope with life and work;
> (ii) the effect on the injured person's relationships with family, friends and those with whom he or she comes into contact;
> (iii) the extent to which treatment would be successful;
> (iv) future vulnerability;
> (v) prognosis;
> (vi) whether medical help has been sought;
>
> (vii) (a) whether the injury results from sexual and/or physical abuse and/or breach of trust;
>
> (b) if so, the nature of the relationship between victim and abuser, the nature of the abuse, its duration and the symptoms caused by it.'

These are all important factors to be borne in mind when preparing the witness statement of the claimant. In stress at work claims it is easy to fall into the trap of focussing on the liability issues and neglecting the quantum aspect of the claim. The use of the above paragraph as a checklist should minimise that risk.

It should be noted that general damages awards made by judges will normally, for comparison purposes, be uprated by inflation measured in accordance with the Retail Prices Index in order to reach a present day value of the award. Similarly, new editions of the JSB Guidelines, with current values of awards uprated for inflation, are published regularly.

The JSB Guidelines set out four categories of psychiatric injury and the appropriate band of awards for each.

7.1.1.1 Severe psychiatric injury

The first category in the JSB Guidelines relates to what is described as 'severe' psychiatric injury:

> '(a) Severe: £35,000 to £74,000
>
> In these cases the injured person will have marked problems with respect to factors (i) to (iv) above and the prognosis will be very poor.'

---

3 Section 3(A) of the JSB Guidelines.

Only a few psychiatric injury at work claims will come into this category. However, in *Green v DB Group Services (UK) Ltd*[4] Owen J summarised the claimant's condition (she was aged 33 at the date of her breakdown in 2003) as follows:

> '... the claimant stands to be compensated for two major episodes of depressive disorder followed by a period of four years in which she has not been well enough to return to work and in which her capacity to enjoy life to the full has been seriously disrupted in particular by the relapse in her condition in 2004. She is also entitled to be compensated for the degree to which her vulnerability to depressive disorder has been increased.'

He held that:

> '... the case is at the bottom end of the category of severe psychiatric injury. In my judgment the appropriate award for general damages is £35,000 in the Guidelines for the assessment of General Damages in Personal Injury Cases published by the Judicial Studies Board.'

7.1.1.2 Moderately severe psychiatric injury

The second category in the JSB Guidelines relates to what is described as 'moderately severe' psychiatric injury:

> '(b) Moderately Severe: £12,250 to £35,000
>
> In these cases there will be significant problems associated with factors (i) to (iv) above but the prognosis will be much more optimistic than in (a) above. While there are awards which support both extremes of this bracket, the majority are somewhere near the middle of the bracket. Cases of work-related stress resulting in a permanent or long-standing disability preventing a return to comparable employment would appear to come within this category.'

The middle of the bracket is about £23,500 and the JSB Guidelines therefore suggest that this will be a 'normal' award for stress claims where there is no return to work.

In *MG v North Devon NHS Primary Care Trust*[5] the claimant was a health visitor (aged 53 at trial) who had suffered stress-related illness leading to absence from work. She suffered a breakdown during a return to work which was not properly supported and was subsequently unable to return to that job. The judge awarded £17,500 for general damages, which was at that time the midpoint in the 'moderately severe' bracket of the JSB Guidelines on a full liability basis, but ordered that damages be reduced by 20% to take account of her prior vulnerability to psychiatric injury.

---

4 [2006] EWHC 1898 (QB), [2006] IRLR 764.

5 [2006] EWHC 850 (QB).

In *Daw v Intel Corp (UK) Ltd*[6] the claimant was an analyst (she was aged 32 at the date of her breakdown) earning £33,000 per annum in 2001. She suffered a nervous breakdown and attempted suicide. She was suffering from chronic depression at the time of the trial. She was awarded £16,000 in general damages (in arriving at that sum general damages of £20,000 had apparently been subject to a 25% deduction 'for the possibility of mental illness without a breach of duty by the appellants') and this award was not the subject of appeal.

In *Jones v Sandwell Metropolitan Borough Council*,[7] Mrs Jones was an administrative assistant who was aged 42 when she went on sick leave with anxiety and depression. The Court of Appeal recorded that:

> 'In February 1996 her treating psychiatrist diagnosed "an acute anxiety state 12 months ago which has developed into a generalised anxiety state with agoraphobia accompanied by mild depression and obsessive compulsive symptoms of which the anxiety symptoms seem the most troublesome".'

She was awarded general damages of £22,500 which was not the subject of appeal.

In *Young v Post Office*[8] the Court of Appeal dismissed the employer's appeal against the trial judge's finding in the claimant's favour on liability. The first instance decision on quantum was not appealed and is not therefore referred to in the Court of Appeal. The judge at first instance commented on the claimant's state of health as follows:[9]

> 'The claimant's health was substantially improved by the date of the hearing but "he was not the man he was"; he did not like driving on motorways or in towns and could not cope with telephones. Further improvement was anticipated.'

The claimant was aged 50 at the date of injury, 54 at the date of trial, and he was expected to return to employment within one year of the trial. The judge awarded general damages of £16,000.

In *Garrod v North Devon NHS Primary Care Trust*[10] the claimant was a health visitor who was aged 49 at the date of the incidents complained of and 53 at the date of the trial. She suffered from moderately severe depression and was likely to remain on anti-depressants for the foreseeable future. Her condition was improving and was likely to

---

6 [2007] EWCA Civ 70.

7 One of the conjoined appeals in *Hatton v Sutherland* [2002] EWCA Civ 76.

8 *Young v Post Office* reported in *Kemp & Kemp: The Quantum of Damages* at C1-013.

9 Barnsley County Court, 4 July 2001 reported in *Kemp & Kemp: the Quantum of Damages* at C1-013.

10 *Garrod v North Devon NHS Primary Care Trust* (28 April 2006, Henriques J QBD (Administrative Court) reported in *Kemp & Kemp: the Quantum of Damages* at C1-019.1).

continue to do so and she was expected to return to employment within a year of the trial. She was awarded general damages of £14,000.

In *Lancaster v Birmingham City Council*,[11] the claimant was a housing officer aged 39 at the date of her breakdown and 44 at the date of trial. Her depression was expected to largely resolve within 5 years. The judge awarded her general damages of £12,000.

In *Barber v Somerset*[12] the claimant, a teacher with 40 years' experience, was close to retirement. He suffered a breakdown in November 1996 and took early retirement 6 months later. The judge found that he would have been fit to return to work in March 1998 (a year later) and there was no challenge to the award of general damages of £10,000 for 'a moderately severe psychiatric illness'.

In *Hartman v South Essex Mental Health & Community Care NHS Trust*,[13] the claimant had a troubled psychiatric history. The court described it thus:

> 'Mrs Hartman has a history of sociological problems. She was sixty at the time of trial in 2002. She had an unhappy childhood and was sexually abused by her stepfather. In 1965 she lost her 17 month old son who died from meningitis. She had an unhappy marriage to her first husband who subjected her to domestic violence. In 1976 she consulted a psychiatrist and was prescribed anti-depressants and tranquillisers. She remained on these drugs for the next ten years. During the 1980s she regularly consulted her GP complaining of depression, irritability, anxiety, headaches, sleep disturbance, stress, high blood pressure, low moods and lassitude.'

It was agreed that at the time of the trial she suffered from a 'mood disorder of moderate severity characterised by depression and anxiety', and the judge accepted the claimant's expert evidence that 'but for the accident and pressures at work, her condition would not have become chronic or lasted so long'. The judge awarded Mrs Hartman £7,500 for pain, suffering and loss of amenity 'having discounted the figure by 25% to take account of her pre-existing vulnerability'.

It should be noted that, even where the injury is found to be 'severe', if the judge finds that it would have occurred for non-negligent reasons in any event, the award might be reduced to reflect the limited period of time for which the claimant would, in the court's view, have enjoyed good health. The damages awarded will then be akin to those awarded for a moderately severe injury rather than for a severe injury. In *Cowley v Mersey Regional*

---

11 *Lancaster v Birmingham City Council* (Birmingham County Court, 25 June 1999, Assistant Recorder Kirkham, reported in *Kemp & Kemp: The Quantum of Damages* at C1-019).

12 A conjoined appeal in *Hatton v Sutherland* [2002] EWCA Civ 76.

13 [2005] EWCA Civ 6; (2005) 85 BMLR 136; [2005] ELR 237; [2005] ICR 782; [2005] IRLR 293; [2005] PIQR P19.

Ambulance Service NHS Trust[14] the claimant suffered from severe reactive depression. At the time of the trial he had not returned to employment and the prognosis was uncertain. However, the judge found that he would have succumbed to severe depression within 6 years in any event and awarded general damages (and loss of earnings) for the 6-year period only. The judge awarded general damages of £15,000.

7.1.1.3 Moderate psychiatric injury

The third category in the JSB Guidelines relates to what is described as 'moderate' psychiatric injury:

> '(c) Moderate £3,750 to £12,250
>
> While there may have been the sort of problems associated with factors (i) to (iv) above there will have been marked improvement by trial and the prognosis will be good.'

This is likely to be the appropriate category for stress at work claims where the claimant has largely recovered by trial. Where a claim falls within the band will depend on the severity of the injury, taking into account the seven factors set out in **7.1.1**.

In *Hiles v South Gloucestershire NHS PCT*[15] the claimant was a health visitor (aged 42 at trial) who had suffered chronic depression as a result of work-related stress in 2002. She had not been able to return to work by the date of the trial in 2006, but the prognosis for her return to some form of employment after the trial was reasonably good. The judge held:

> 'In my view the severity of the Claimant's breakdown in health, and the persistence of her symptoms, puts this case either at the very top end of the JSB Guideline bracket A(c), or perhaps at the bottom of the bracket A(b). I assess general damages at £12,500. This figure is intended to include something for the fact that Mrs Hiles has been unable to work in a job she says she loved since the date of her breakdown, i.e. in effect, for loss of congenial employment; but I bear in mind that she may soon be back to her chosen work. I do not think it appropriate to make a separate award in respect of loss of congenial employment in a case like this.'

In *Hatton v Sutherland*[16] the claimant was a French teacher employed by the school from 1980. She had taken a term off with a depressive illness in 1994. She suffered a breakdown in 1995 and retired on health grounds in 1996. The judge had found that she had an 'obsessive personality' and that an assault on her and the illness of her son had contributed to her depression. She was able to return to work within 2 years of her

---

[14] Liverpool County Court, 1 February 2001, HH Judge Douglas Brown, reported in *Kemp & Kemp: The Quantum of Damages* C1-015.

[15] [2006] EWHC 3418 (QB).

[16] [2002] EWCA Civ 76.

breakdown. The award of general damages of £6,000, subject to liability, was not challenged by the employer on appeal.

In *Bishop v Baker Refractories Ltd*,[17] Mr Bishop suffered a breakdown which included a suicide attempt. He was awarded £7,000 in general damages. The Court of Appeal allowed the employer's appeal on liability and made no comment on the assessment of damages by the trial judge.

In *Wheeldon v HSBC Bank Ltd*[18] Mrs Wheeldon had suffered panic attacks and was off work with stress and depression for periods from the summer of 1999. She went off on long-term sick leave in October 2000, but it was accepted that she had been fit enough to return 2 years later. She was awarded general damages of £3,500 and neither side appealed on this issue.

7.1.1.4 Minor psychiatric injury

The final category in the JSB Guidelines relates to what is described as 'minor' psychiatric injury:

> '(d) Minor £1,000 to £3,750
>
> The level of the award will take into consideration the length of the period of disability and the extent to which daily activities and sleep were affected. Awards have been made below this bracket in cases of temporary "anxiety".'

It is very unlikely that this category will be applicable to a stress at work claim unless the psychiatric injury has been very limited.

7.1.1.5 Physical injury caused by stress

If the claimant can establish a causal link between a physical injury and the stress (eg a heart attack, as in the case of *Harding v The Pub Estate Co Ltd*[19] which failed because breach of duty was not established), then regard should also be had to the relevant JSB Guidelines and case-law. As well as heart attacks, other conditions caused or affected by stress might include ulcers and neurological conditions such as multiple sclerosis.

7.1.2 Loss of earnings

Usually in a stress at work case, almost by definition, the claimant will have stopped working at least for a period of time (his contract of

---

17 One of the conjoined appeal in *Hatton v Sutherland* [2002] EWCA Civ 76.

18 A conjoined appeal in *Hartman v South Essex Mental Health & Community Care NHS Trust* [2005] EWCA Civ 6, (2005) 85 BMLR 136, [2005] ELR 237, [2005] ICR 782, [2005] IRLR 293, [2005] PIQR P19.

19 [2005] EWCA Civ 553.

employment may or may not have come to an end) and will have a loss of earnings claim. Unless the case has taken an exceptionally long time to be concluded, the claimant has made a good recovery and therefore failure to mitigate is being argued, the claim for past loss of earnings to trial is likely to be uncontroversial.

However, calculation of future loss of earnings in a stress at work claim is rarely straightforward. In *Ronan v Sainsbury's plc*[20] (which was not itself a stress at work claim) the Court of Appeal helpfully clarified the approach the judge should take particularly where the past earnings history or the future prospects are sketchy. The Court of Appeal stressed that the three methods of calculating loss – an award for specific future financial loss, a *Blamire*[21] award or a *Smith v Manchester*[22] award – were all very different.

Where the amounts and periods of loss are reasonably clear, the court should use a conventional approach of multiplier and multiplicand, using the Ogden Tables.[23] The Ogden Tables enable the lawyer to work out the appropriate actuarially calculated figure subject to adjustment for contingencies as provided in the Tables (the 'multiplier') to apply to the present day value of the annual earnings after tax (the 'multiplicand'). The resulting lump sum will give the present day value of future loss after taking into account accelerated receipt, anticipated return on the investment of the lump sum after inflation, the risk of mortality and, where appropriate, discounts for other contingencies.

And in 'loss of a chance' promotions the principles for calculation of the loss of future earnings in cases are as set out in *Doyle v Wallace*[24] where:

> '. . . it was argued that failing qualifications as a teacher she would have obtained clerical or administrative work. On behalf of the plaintiff it was contended that her chances of becoming a teacher were not less than 50%, that her past loss should be assessed on the basis of allowing the plaintiff a 50% chance of becoming a teacher and her loss assessed on the basis of taking a middle figure between earnings as a teacher and earnings in a clerical capacity.'

so in respect of the future loss calculation the court said:

> 'However, I have come to the conclusion that the learned Judge fell into error by his application of the 16 year multiplier to both the clerical and the dancer earnings. I regard it as not unreasonable to apply to a female aged 27 with a retirement age of 60 a multiplier of 16 in respect of the clerical

20 [2006] EWCA Civ 1074.

21 *Blamire v South Cumbria HA* [1993] PIQR Q1; [1993] CLY 1403.

22 *Smith v Manchester Corporation* (1974) 17 KIR 1.

23 'Actuarial Tables with explanatory notes for use in Personal Injury and Fatal Accident cases' prepared by an inter-disciplinary working party of actuaries, lawyers, accountants and other interested parties, produced by the Government Actuary's Department and published by The Stationery Office, 6th edn, 2007.

24 [1998] EWCA Civ 1030.

earnings. However, the assumption that the plaintiff would have continued as a full-time drama teacher throughout the whole of her working life is not justified by the evidence. Moreover, the Judge considered that nearly everybody would have been able to claim rather more than the plaintiff had to offer in this field. Thus she would have been at a disadvantage in the labour market against a better qualified and younger teacher. This must lead inexorably to a lower multiplier under this head. I would discount the multiplier to 14. Thus 16 years would be applied to 50% of £8,909 net clerical earnings mid career (£71,272) and a 14 year multiplier would be applied to 50% of £12,545 net drama teacher earnings mid career (£87,815). The remaining 2 points of the multiplier would be at 50% of the clerical earnings figure (£8,909). That gives a total future loss of earnings figure of £167,996.'

A rather more complicated 'career model' approach was approved by the Court of Appeal in *Langford v Hebran*[25] (the 'kick boxer' case). In that case the claimant was a builder who was also a successful amateur kick boxer who had the potential to turn professional and possibly even become world champion. There was a small chance that he had lost very high earnings, a larger chance that he had lost significant earnings and an even greater chance that he had lost quite low earnings. The Court of Appeal agreed that it was correct to calculate the loss of the chance by applying the probability of each eventuality to the net earnings claimed for it.

If the conventional multiplier and multiplicand approach is impossible, then a lump sum may be awarded instead (a '*Blamire*' award). The Court of Appeal in *Ronan* said:

> 'The [*Blamire* award] is appropriate where the evidence shows that there is a continuing loss of earnings, but there are too many uncertainties to adopt the conventional multiplier and multiplicand approach to its quantification.'

and

> 'The [*Smith v Manchester* award] is nothing to do with a continuing loss. It is an award for a contingent future loss, in the event of the claimant losing his current job, where, as a result of the accident, he would then be at a handicap on the labour market at which he would not have been but for the accident.'

In stress at work cases, the claimant should where possible seek to quantify the claim on a conventional basis, including any 'loss of chance' career models where appropriate. However, in many cases where the prognosis is unclear, but it is quite likely on the medical evidence that the claimant will eventually return to some work, then a *Blamire* lump sum award may well be made.

---

25 [2001] EWCA Civ 361.

On top of this a *Smith v Manchester* award for handicap on the labour market may well also be appropriate, subject to the comments about this in respect of the use of the sixth edition of the Ogden Tables.[26]

The three types of award are considered in more detail below.

7.1.2.1 Conventional multiplier/multiplicand approach (with appropriate discount)

The conventional multiplier/multiplicand approach is particularly likely to be followed where there is no real likelihood of a return to work. This is so even if the full multiplier is discounted to reflect the likelihood of the claimant developing a career ending stress-related illness as the result of non-negligent causes in any event.

In *Moore v Welwyn Components Ltd*[27] the claimant was an accountant who had retired on ill-health grounds at the age of 55 following a long period of bullying by the employer's finance director. The employer appealed to the Court of Appeal on both liability and quantum, particularly the award of approximately £150,000 for further loss of earnings. The Court of Appeal noted:

> 'The judge found that the illness which resulted in Mr. Moore's retirement was caused by the fact that he had been subjected to sustained bullying from the end of 1995 to August 1998 by the employer's finance director, Mr. Watson. The employer was liable in negligence for what Mr. Watson did. The judge described his conduct as appalling. It would have exposed any employee of reasonable fortitude to the risk of psychiatric illness.'

Mr Moore was not an employee 'of reasonable fortitude'. The court found that he was a vulnerable individual with a history of psychiatric illness. The experts had agreed that he was 'a vulnerable individual who was biologically predisposed to suffering from depressive illnesses'. However, although the judge had apportioned the general damages for the contribution of non-negligent stressors, he had declined to make such an apportionment for future loss of earnings. The Court of Appeal agreed with the trial judge upholding the full award for loss of future earnings and finding that this was not a suitable case for apportionment.

In *Daw v Intel Corp (UK) Ltd*[28] the claimant had not returned to work and was suffering from chronic depression at the date of trial. The total award was £134,545.18, including interest and general damages of £16,000, but gross of the sum of £19,780.30 deductible by the Compensation Recovery Unit (CRU). The loss of earnings element of the

---

26 See **7.1.2.4**.

27 A conjoined appeal in *Hartman v South Essex Mental Health & Community Care NHS Trust* [2005] EWCA Civ 6, (2005) 85 BMLR 136, [2005] ELR 237, [2005] ICR 782, [2005] IRLR 293, [2005] PIQR P19.

28 [2007] EWCA Civ 70.

award was appealed by the employer. The multiplicand was agreed at a net loss of £12,500 per annum (after taking into account receipt of £13,000 per annum from the employer's ill-health income protection scheme). A full multiplier to retirement age would have been 18.41. The judge held that a multiplier of six should be applied. The judge had found that there was a 50% chance of a severe breakdown in any event by 2006, 5 years after the claimant had actually had her breakdown as a result of the work-related stress. The employer contended that future loss of earnings should be cut off at this point and that the multiplier of six for future loss from the date of the trial (which took place in 2006) was therefore excessive. The Court of Appeal disagreed:

> 'The judge had to consider what would have happened had there been no illness caused by the breach of duty. There would have been "episodes" of psychiatric illness but their intensity was difficult to predict. They would not necessarily have been as disabling or as prolonged as the current illness caused by the breach of duty. The judge was entitled to conclude that there would probably have been periods of employment after 2006. He was not required to conclude that an episode or episodes would be as severe as that sustained in 2001. On that basis, the multiplier cannot be criticised.'

In *Barber v Somerset*,[29] Mr Barber was close to retirement. The parties had agreed before trial that, subject to arguments about discount, the appropriate full multiplier for future loss of earnings was four to take into account different possible arguments about retirement age. The judge did not discount the full multiplier to reflect the chance that Mr Barber, arguably a vulnerable individual, might have developed a psychiatric illness before retirement anyway. The judge pointed out that until the incidents complained of he had never suffered any psychiatric illness and rarely visited his GP. The Court of Appeal rejected the claimant's argument that the future loss should be calculated on the basis of 'balance of probability' and confirmed that this was a 'loss of a chance' case, referring to the first instance decision in *Page v Smith*.[30] The court reduced the multiplier from four to one, saying:

> 'In our judgment the judge was wrong not to reduce the multiplier for future loss to cover the chance that if Mr Barber had continued with a similar teaching job, his health might nevertheless have broken down in the same way. He was a man, after all, who had showed himself on the evidence unable to adopt the alleviating measures that were necessary if he was to manage his not unreasonable workload successfully. There was evidence that he had disliked the changes the school had felt obliged to introduce, and on the hypothesis (which the judge adopted) that he would have opted to soldier on as a teacher until his normal retirement age, we consider that there was a significant chance, which the judge should have taken into account when

---

[29] One of the conjoined appeals in *Hatton v Sutherland* [2002] EWCA Civ 76.

[30] [1992] PIQR Q55, 75–76.

computing damages, that he would have found it altogether too much for him, to the extent that his health would have been detrimentally affected in the same way.'

Although Mr Barber succeeded in overturning the Court of Appeal's decision on liability in the House of Lords,[31] the quantum decision of the Court of Appeal was not appealed.

In *Jones v Sandwell Metropolitan Borough Council*, the findings of the trial judge on the issue of quantum were not appealed by the employer. The Court of Appeal found in the claimant's favour on the issue of liability and so her damages award stood. The Court of Appeal explained how the award had been calculated:

> 'Judgment was entered in her favour for £157,541, made up of £22,500 general damages, together with interest of £1,300, past loss of earnings, medical expenses and travelling expense totalling £32,499, together with interest of £6,422, and future loss of earnings, pension and medical and prescription costs totalling £94,820.'

In *Hartman v South Essex Mental Health & Community Care NHS Trust*,[32] Mrs Hartman was 58 at the time of her breakdown and would have retired at the age of 60. The trial judge awarded her £34,319.33 for loss of earnings with no discount for the chance that she might have not reached retirement age without a similar breakdown as the result of non-negligent causes. He did, however, discount general damages by 25%. There was no appeal on quantum so the findings were not disturbed, although the employer's liability was upheld. But the Court of Appeal commented:

> 'We cannot reconcile the judge's discount of general damages with his failure to make any discount for contingencies that might have prevented her from continuing to work. It is true that the court was concerned with a relatively short period; Mrs Hartman had her breakdown in the spring of 1998 and was 60 in December 2001. But on the facts of this case there plainly should have been a discount (Mrs Hartman's counsel did not suggest otherwise at the trial) and it is difficult to see why the discount should be other than the same as was applied to the general damages i.e. 25%. However, as in our judgment the appeal on liability succeeds, the judgment must be set aside and the discount on damages is a matter of academic interest only.'

It should be noted that the discounts applied by the courts to future loss of earnings by courts often rely on findings of apportionment between negligent and non-negligent stressors. The Court of Appeal in *Dickins v*

---

[31] *Barber v Somerset* [2004] UKHL 13, (2004) 77 BMLR 219, [2004] 1 WLR 1089, [2004] 2 All ER 385, [2004] ELR 199, [2004] ICR 457, [2004] IRLR 475, [2004] PIQR P31.

[32] [2005] EWCA Civ 6, (2005) 85 BMLR 136, [2005] ELR 237, [2005] ICR 782, [2005] IRLR 293, [2005] PIQR P19.

O2[33] have doubted that this is the right approach to causation. However, such discounts might be reframed as an 'acceleration' of injury. It is submitted that discounts in future may be little different in practice from those in the past, albeit for different reasons.

In *Young v Post Office*, Mr Young was likely to return to work within a year but with a reduced residual earning capacity. The trial judge found:

> 'From May 1998 the claimant had worked part-time on a pig farm and, despite medical evidence that the claimant may have been able to return to full-time work before the trial, the judge rejected the contention that he had failed to mitigate his losses on the grounds that the claimant would have had difficulty finding alternative employment and was lucky to have found a sympathetic employer. However the judge found that, with the case behind him, the claimant could obtain full-time employment in about a year. Future loss of earnings was calculated, therefore, at GBP8,385 for one year with a further seven-and-a-half years at GBP3,744: a total of GBP36,465.'

7.1.2.2 Lump sum award

A *Blamire* lump sum award is made where the court feels the future is simply too uncertain to predict and so the precision inherent in the conventional multiplier/multiplicand approach is inappropriate.

In *Hatton v Sutherland*, Mrs Hatton would have been well enough to be re-employed as a teacher in June 1998, 2 years after her breakdown, and it was reasonable to assume that she could have found employment within 6 months of this date. She was awarded £46,876.14 (gross of CRU, which was £18,866.31) for past loss of earnings. This award was not challenged, subject to liability. The trial judge awarded her £53,560 in respect of future loss of earnings using a complex calculation based on a gradual return to work in the private sector initially on a part-time basis. The future loss multiplier applied was six. The employer had argued that she had not looked for public sector teaching jobs because she would have lost her rights to her ill-health pension. The Court of Appeal allowed the employer's appeal on liability but commented on the award for future loss of earnings as follows :

> 'If we had upheld this judgment on liability, we would have awarded her a sum of £10,000 in respect of her loss of earning capacity for the period from 1st December 1998 onwards. The idea that she might have been able to go on teaching at any comprehensive school and avoided stress-related illness appears to us to be a little far-fetched, and Mrs Hatton clearly made no attempt to find any public sector teaching, part-time or otherwise, for fear of losing her pension. We consider that there is considerable force in the defendant's contentions, and that justice demands that we should approach the question of compensation for the period in the broad-brush way we have indicated.'

33 [2008] EWCA Civ 1144. See further **6.1.2**.

In *Wheeldon v HSBC Bank Ltd*,[34] the trial judge awarded Mrs Wheeldon £18,861.71 (including £3,500 for general damages). The sum awarded amounted to 2 years' loss of earnings. The Court of Appeal said:

> 'The judge at paragraph 48 of his judgment pointed out that at the date of the trial in the autumn of 2003 Mrs Wheeldon had still not returned to work but that she had limited her claim for loss of earnings to 2 years. This was on the basis of the time she would have needed (i) to make a full physical recovery and (ii) to appreciate she was better and then to find another job. The judge observed that such a transition, had she chosen to make it, would have been quite difficult. He said he had initially thought 12 months was the appropriate period for loss of earnings but on reflection revised his view upwards.'

The Court of Appeal agreed with the trial judge's broad-brush approach.

In *Lancaster v Birmingham City Council*[35] the claimant was a housing officer whom the court felt would return to employment shortly after trial, but in a lower paid job. The trial judge said:

> 'The medical prognosis was that the claimant would eventually be able to undertake part-time and then full time work of a relatively straightforward and undemanding nature. The judge found that the claimant's work capability would increase but had regard to her difficulties in finding work. An award for future wage loss and vulnerability on the labour market and pension loss was based on a five year multiplier, following the approach in *Blamire v South Cumbria HA* [1993] P.I.Q.R. Q1; [1993] C.L.Y. 1403 in relation to the uncertainties as to the future.'

7.1.2.3 Handicap on the labour market

A psychiatric injury normally renders the claimant vulnerable to recurrences, so a *Smith v Manchester* award is often appropriate in addition to any specific award for future loss of earnings.

In *MG v North Devon NHS Primary Care Trust*,[36] the judge awarded the claimant £12,500 for 'handicap on the labour market' as at the date of trial she was fit to return to work, but not as a health visitor.

In *Green v DB Group Services (UK) Ltd*[37] the claimant had been employed in the Company Secretariat division of DB, earning £45,000 per annum plus bonuses. Following her breakdown she had not been able to

---

[34] One of the conjoined appeals in *Hartman v South Essex Mental Health & Community Care NHS Trust* [2005] EWCA Civ 6, (2005) 85 BMLR 136, [2005] ELR 237, [2005] ICR 782, [2005] IRLR 293, [2005] PIQR P19.

[35] Birmingham County Court, 25 June 1999, Mr Assistant Recorder Kirkham, reported in *Kemp & Kemp: The Quantum of Damages* at C1-019.

[36] [2006] EWHC 850 (QB).

[37] EWHC 1898 (QB), [2006] IRLR 764.

return to that work and had decided to undertake a Phd with a view to working as a college lecturer. The trial judge held:

> 'I accept that that is likely to take of the order of five years during which she will have little if any earning capacity. Furthermore I am satisfied that her decision to embark upon such a career change, once this litigation is at an end, is entirely reasonable'

He also found that she was entitled to claim £3,100 per annum for the cost of retraining. The detail of the future loss of earnings calculation was then left to the parties to calculate and does not appear in the judgment. The trial judge also made a *Smith v Manchester* award:

> 'I have little doubt that given the ability and determination that she has demonstrated in the past, this is an ambition that she will achieve. But it is equally clear that she will inevitably be at some disadvantage in the labour market as a consequence of having been unable to work for many years as a result of her psychiatric illness, and of the fact that she is at a markedly increased risk of further psychiatric disorder. She has sensibly chosen now to pursue a career that should not impose the stresses to be encountered in a competitive commercial working environment, a factor which of course reduces the risk of further episodes of further depressive disorder; but it is nevertheless a factor which has to be taken into account in assessing damages under this head.
>
> I have come to the conclusion that the appropriate award under the Smith and Manchester head is the sum of £25,000 representing, in round terms, one year's net loss of earnings as a lecturer.'

In *Garrod v North Devon NHS Primary Care Trust* the trial judge said:[38]

> 'The prognosis was for G's illness largely to resolve within six to twelve months of the completion of litigation. She would never be able to under take a stressful occupation or one of management responsibility but should be able to return to some form of alternative work within two years of the end of litigation.'

The judge made a *Smith v Manchester* award of £10,000.

In *Hiles v South Gloucestershire NHS PCT*[39] the medical evidence was that the claimant was likely to return to her employment as a health visitor following cognitive behavioural therapy within 6 months of trial. The trial judge awarded her only £6,000 for future loss of earnings (although her past loss was allowed in full). He also made a *Smith v Manchester* award, saying:

---

38 28 April 2006, Henriques J QBD (Admin Ct), reported in *Kemp & Kemp: The Quantum of Damages* at C1-019.1.

39 [2006] EWHC 3418 (QB).

> 'Having suffered depression as a result of the Defendant's breach of duty, the Claimant is at some risk of a recurrence, which could of course affect her ability to earn. See Dr O'Connell's Report paragraph 13.4 (1/99). However such a recurrence is by no means inevitable or even probable; and if there is a recurrence its severity and persistence are matters of uncertainty. I award the sum of £5,000 to protect the Claimant against the risk of the recurrence of illness. This figure is intended to reflect the uncertainties which I take to surround this issue.'

In *Young v Post Office* the judge made a *Smith v Manchester* award of £4,000.

7.1.2.4 Possible impact of Ogden Six

In all of the cases reported to date courts have made awards either by using the conventional approach of multiplier/multiplicand in accordance with the fifth edition of the Ogden Tables or by arriving at a lump sum figure for a *Blamire*. Either type of award is often supplemented by a *Smith v Manchester* award.

However, the sixth edition of the Ogden Tables, published in April 2007, sets out an entirely new approach. It draws on new research on estimating working life expectancy by Butt, Haberman, Verrall and Wass.[40] The guidance notes accompanying the new edition state:

> '. . . new research ... demonstrated that the key issues affecting a person's future working life are employment status, disability status and educational attainment.'

And whilst occupation, industrial sector and geographical regions were also analysed:

> '. . . the researchers concluded that the most significant consideration was the highest level of education achieved by the claimant and that, if this was allowed for, the effect of the other factors was relatively small. As a result, the Working Party decided to propose adjustment factors which allow for employment status [i.e. employed or not employed], disability status and educational attainment only.'

So far as disability status is concerned, the sixth edition of the Ogden Tables follows a similar approach to the Disability Discrimination Act 1995, so long as the disability affects either the kind or the amount of paid work a disabled person can do. Unfortunately, an error has crept into the definition of 'disability' in that it was limited to 'illness' but

---

40 Verrall, Butt, Haberman and Wass 'Calculating compensation for loss of future earnings: Estimating and using work life expectancy, with discussion' (2008) *Journal of the Royal Statistical Society: Series A (Statistics in Society)* 171(4), 763–805.

correspondence in *PI Focus* (March 2008) clarified this definition was meant to read 'disability or illness which must have lasted for at least a year'.

The key factor influencing working life expectancy for both disabled and non-disabled employees is educational achievement. Different reduction factors are proposed for claimants with respectively degree or equivalent, GCSE A–C grades/A Levels and GCSEs at lower grades/no qualifications.

As the authors accept, the research and the reduction factors derived from it in the sixth edition of the tables are not the last word, but:

> '... provide a more accurate starting point within the established broadbrush framework that is used by the courts. The intention is that the courts may deviate from this starting point subject to the particular characteristics and circumstances of individual cases.'

The intention is to reduce the number of *Smith v Manchester* and *Blamire* awards and replace them with awards calculated on the basis of multiplier and multiplicand using the Ogden Tables. Earlier research by Lewis et al[41] had showed that this led to widespread inaccuracy in compensation, most claimants being 'under-compensated' (especially young men with residual earning capacity) but with a quarter of claimants being 'over-compensated'. Whilst calculating compensation will never be an exact science, such discrepancies were of great concern.

In theory, the sixth edition of the Ogden Tables, combined with the judicial disapproval of overall deductions by reason of apportionment,[42] should lead to a move away from the broad-brush approach to future loss outlined in the reported cases. However, it seems likely that in the field of stress at work litigation, the courts will remain reluctant to follow the Ogden Tables strictly rather than sticking to the more traditional methods of calculating future loss.

7.1.3 Other heads of loss

Set out below are some examples of other types of loss that have been successfully claimed for in the reported cases. There may of course be others.

41 Lewis, McNabb, Robinson and Wass 'Court Awards of Damages for Loss of Future Earnings: An Empirical Study and an Alternative Method of Calculation' (2002) *Journal of Law and Society* 29, 406–435.

42 *Dickins v O2 plc* [2008] EWCA Civ 1144, see **6.1.2**.

7.1.3.1 Loss of congenial employment

In *MG v North Devon NHS Primary Care Trust*, although the claimant was fit to return to work she could not return to work as a health visitor, and the trial judge awarded £5,000 for loss of congenial employment. He also awarded £4,000 in respect of past care and domestic assistance. In *Hiles v South Gloucestershire NHS PCT*[43] the claimant was also a health visitor, but the trial judge said that his award of £12,500 for general damages included an element in respect of loss of congenial employment. In *Hiles*, unlike *MG*, it was, however, expected that the claimant would return to similar work.

7.1.3.2 Therapies

If the medical experts are positive in respect of prognosis, it is very likely that a course of cognitive behavioural therapy (CBT) will be recommended. It is often suggested that this should take place after the conclusion of the litigation, to ensure that the stressors associated with bringing the claim have been removed. In *Hiles* the judge awarded £2,900 (plus associated travel costs of £80) for CBT.

7.1.3.3 Care

In any case where there has been a breakdown or prolonged severe depression it is likely that some award for past care and assistance, usually gratuitous 'family care', will be allowed. However, a study of the reported cases suggests that awards for future care are difficult to obtain in stress at work claims. If the claimant nevertheless wishes to contend for an award for future care it is essential to gather strong medical and witness evidence supporting this and to set out the claim for such an award fully in the particulars of claim or schedule of loss.

In *Young v Post Office* the claimant was awarded £5,361 in respect of past care. No award was made for the future.

7.1.3.4 Pension loss

If there is a career long earnings loss, there may also be a claim for the loss of pension rights. There is a key distinction between final salary/defined benefit schemes and money purchase/defined contribution schemes.

Final salary/defined benefit schemes give the employee the right to a pension which is usually dependent upon multiplying the final salary earned in the job by the years served subject to a factor established in the scheme rules (eg £30,000 x 20 x 1/80 = pension of £7,500 per annum

---

43 [2006] EWHC 3418 (QB).

gross). The pension does not depend upon the performance of the pension fund. That risk has been assumed by the employer who will have to top up the fund if the fund has not performed as expected. Final salary schemes are increasingly rare and are now most often found in the public sector. The most valuable are schemes operated by employers such as the army or the police where full pensions can be drawn at a relatively early age after a certain number of years service have been completed. When calculating the loss of pension rights the sums used should be those applying at the date of trial (ie at the present day value) rather than at date of retirement. So the claimant's multiplicand for loss of earnings net of tax (adjusted for the vagaries of 'pensionable pay') will be the starting point for the lost pension calculation. If the claimant has already retired then the actual net pension receipt will be set against this. If the claimant has not yet retired, the pension fund trustees will provide a calculation of the present day value of the claimant's accrued pension rights. This must be calculated net of tax. The potential lump sum has to be discounted for early receipt at trial. Part of any actual lump sum received or to be paid must be credited. A discount for other contingencies will be then applied.[44]

Money purchase/defined contribution schemes give the employee the right to a pension the amount of which depends upon the investment performance of the fund made up of the contributions invested. No sum is guaranteed. This type of scheme includes many occupational pension schemes where the employer contributes, or where he matches employee contributions, and many personal pension plans and stakeholder pensions. (Many Additional Voluntary Contribution (AVC) add-ons to a final salary scheme are also in effect money purchase add-ons.) The problem in calculating loss is that the pension which will be payable is uncertain and depends entirely upon investment returns. The future contributions are speculative investments; they are unlikely to be a recoverable loss, just as one would not expect to recover the lost chance of speculative gains from anticipated investment on the stock exchange. A loss of pension claim in respect of a money purchase/defined contribution scheme is in effect a claim for the loss of the opportunity to invest tax-free sums (paid by the claimant or his employer) in a pension fund over future years until retirement. However, with the introduction of stakeholder pensions allowing for contributions to be made even if the person is not in employment the claimant is now entitled to use his damages to make a similar investment into pensions if he wishes. But pension loss can still be claimed for. Any employer contributions (at past or reasonably anticipated future amounts, including increases following likely promotions) can be added back to the multiplicand to enhance the future loss of earnings claim.

---

[44] *Auty v National Coal Board* [1985] 1 WLR 784 is still the leading case, notwithstanding the criticisms of the court's approach, most notably in the introduction to the Ogden Tables, and see also *Longden v British Coal Corporation* [1997] UKHL 52.

Finally, there is a state basic pension and also an earnings related additional state pension (full entitlement to which depends upon national insurance contribution record). Potential loss is usually small and complex to calculate.

Practitioners must also consider carefully what the appropriate retirement age is for the loss of future earnings claim. Few claimants will retire at 55 or even at 60 in the future. The state retirement age is rising to 67. Practitioners should take careful instructions from their client on how long he intends to continue working and on what basis. It may also be necessary to obtain information from potential comparators in order to justify the retirement age used for the purposes of the loss of earnings claim.

7.2 DAMAGE ARISING FROM NON-DISCRIMINATORY HARASSMENT

In claims under the Protection from Harassment Act 1997 (PFHA 1997) there is no need for the claimant to prove that the harassment caused a recognised psychiatric condition; 'distress' is sufficient.

In practice, in stress at work claims the claimant will normally have suffered a psychiatric injury, so the same principles relating to the award of general damages for pain, suffering and loss or amenity will apply as outlined in **7.1** in respect of claims for negligence.

In *Singh v Singh*[45](which was not work-related harassment claim) the trial judge awarded the sum of £35,000 in damages, the judge commenting on the award as follows:

> '. . . there are three important differences between damages for personal injuries resulting from a single trauma and damages under the Act:–
>
> (i) In a personal injury action there is rarely any significant element to reflect the trauma of the accident itself. The focus is very much on compensating the claimant for the consequences of the accident. Here I must take account not only of the period after 2/3/03, but of the four months of hell which I find Gina lived through while the conduct was continuing.
>
> (ii) Secondly the course of conduct towards Gina was not merely negligent or even reckless but deliberate. While avoiding any punitive element, I believe that I can and should take into account that for Gina it must have been much worse to know that she was the target of malevolent behaviour than if she had suffered through someone's carelessness. She is entitled to an element of compensation for having been deliberately targeted.
>
> (iii) Thirdly there is the element of quasi-aggravated damages which I have dealt with.

45 Nottingham County Court, 24 July 2006, Timothy Scott QC (see **4.5**).

> In my judgement the first and second of these matters alone, taken in conjunction with the evidence as a whole (including the evidence of Dr Stocking Korzen) would be sufficient to take Gina close to the top of the agreed bracket. She was utterly miserable and wretched during those four months, and was suffering from what was for her an incomprehensible personal attack. On this basis alone I would have awarded general damages of £27,500. Taking into account the way in which the defence case has been conducted (though not, I emphasise, by Mr Anderson), the overall award should be £35,000.'

If there is no psychiatric injury, merely distress, the awards are likely to be low – perhaps akin to the lowest *Vento* bracket.[46]

7.3 COMPENSATION FOR (CONSTRUCTIVE) UNFAIR DISMISSAL

An employee suffering from stress at work may leave employment in circumstances in which he has a potential claim for unfair dismissal. This might arise by way of an alleged constructive dismissal where the employee has accepted the employer's repudiatory breach of contract by resigning.[47] This resignation is treated as a dismissal. Alternatively, the employer might dismiss the employee, for example on the ground of incapacity because of longstanding absence from work. If the employee believes that this is unfair,[48] he may bring a claim of unfair dismissal in the employment tribunal in the usual way.

If the tribunal finds that the dismissal is unfair then the compensation payable is determined by s 118 of the Employment Rights Act 1996 (ERA 1996) (Chapter 18 as amended). This provides:

> '(1) Where a tribunal makes an award of compensation for unfair dismissal under section 112(4) or 117(3)(a) the award shall consist of—
> (a) a basic award (calculated in accordance with sections 119 to 122 and 126), and
> (b) a compensatory award (calculated in accordance with sections 123,124, 126 and 127).'

7.3.1 Basic award

The tribunal will make a 'basic award' in all unfair dismissal cases which is calculated as follows:[49]

> **'119.** – (1) Subject to the provisions of this section, sections 120 to 122 and section 126, the amount of the basic award shall be calculated by—

46 See **7.4.1**.
47 See **5.1**.
48 See **5.2**.
49 ERA 1996, s 119.

(a) determining the period, ending with the effective date of termination, during which the employee has been continuously employed,
(b) reckoning backwards from the end of that period the number of years of employment falling within that period, and
(c) allowing the appropriate amount for each of those years of employment.

(2) In subsection (1)(c) "the appropriate amount" means—
(a) one and a half weeks' pay for a year of employment in which the employee was not below the age of forty-one,
(b) one week's pay for a year of employment (not within paragraph (a)) in which he was not below the age of twenty-two, and
(c) half a week's pay for a year of employment not within paragraph (a) or (b).

(3) Where twenty years of employment have been reckoned under subsection (1), no account shall be taken under that subsection of any year of employment earlier than those twenty years.'

There are some special exceptions in the Act where a minimum basic award is provided[50] or where the Act specifies a basic award of two week's pay.[51]

The week's pay is capped as follows:[52]

'**227.** – (1) For the purpose of calculating—
(a) a basic award of compensation for unfair dismissal . . .

the amount of a week's pay shall not exceed £350 [with effect from 1st February 2009].'

The amount of the cap is indexed linked (up or down) by reference to the Retail Prices Index for September in each year.[53]

The basic award may be reduced where the tribunal considers it to be 'just and equitable' if the employee has unreasonably refused reinstatement or by reason of the employee's conduct.[54]

In unfair dismissal cases the tribunal may not make an award for injury to feelings.[55]

50 ERA 1996, s 120.
51 ERA 1996, s 121.
52 ERA 1996, s 227.
53 ERA 1999, s 34(1)(e).
54 ERA 1996, s 122.
55 *Dunnachie v Kingston-Upon-Hull City Council* [2004] UKHL 36, see **6.3.1**.

7.3.2 Compensatory award

The tribunal may also make a 'compensatory award':[56]

> '(1) Subject to the provisions of this section and section 124, the amount of the compensatory award shall be such amount as the tribunal considers just and equitable in all the circumstances having regard to the loss sustained by the complainant in consequence of the dismissal in so far as that loss is attributable to action taken by the employer.'

It should be noted that the award is what is 'just and equitable'. This is different from how compensation at common law, or indeed for discrimination in the employment tribunal,[57] is calculated.

ERA 1996, s 123 goes on to set out the matters that may be included in the loss:

> '(2) The loss referred to in subsection (1) shall be taken to include—
> (a) any expenses reasonably incurred by the complainant in consequence of the dismissal, and
> (b) subject to subsection (3), loss of any benefit which he might reasonably be expected to have had but for the dismissal.'

If the employee also receives a redundancy payment then this must be set against the basic award.[58] The employee is under a duty to mitigate his losses.[59] If the employee has a claim for unfair dismissal and discrimination the employee can only claim once in respect of each head of loss.[60]

If the tribunal considers that the employee has been guilty of 'contributory fault', it may reduce the award. So, for example, in *Jumard v Clwyd Leisure Centre*[61] the award in respect of unfair dismissal (but not for discrimination) was reduced by 20% because the tribunal had found the employee to be aggressive. The EAT commented:

> 'The finding of 20 per cent contributory fault was manifestly justified given the finding of fact that the Claimant himself was aggressive. This was correctly applied to unfair dismissal only. It was not applied to the discrimination claims. There was evidence justifying the Tribunal to reach that conclusion, and accordingly no point of law arose. Reliance was placed on the case of *Maris v Rotherham Corporation* [1974] ICR 435 in which the National Industrial Relations Court (Sir Hugh Griffiths presiding) emphasised that when considering contributory fault a tribunal should have

---

56 ERA 1996, s 123.
57 See **7.4**.
58 ERA 1996, s 123(3).
59 ERA 1996, s 123(4).
60 ERA 1996, s 126.
61 *Jumard v Clywyd Leisure Centre* [2008] IRLR 345, [2008] UKEAT 0334_07_2101.

regard to all the circumstances surrounding the dismissal and not just factors which contribute to the unfairness.'

In unfair dismissal cases the compensatory award is subject to the statutory cap:[62]

'(1) The amount of—

...

(b) a compensatory award to a person calculated in accordance with section 123,

shall not exceed £66,200 [with effect from 1 February 2009].'

The cap on the compensatory award can have a very significant effect on stress at work claims in the employment tribunal based on an unfair dismissal (whether constructive or not) as opposed to discrimination. Not only is there no award for injury to feelings or for personal injury, but there is also no realistic prospect of a career-long loss claim because of the statutory cap.

In stress at work claims, there is also the issue that the tribunal can only make a compensatory award in respect of the effect of the unfair dismissal and not incapacity caused by the stress prior to dismissal. This would otherwise enable an employee to bring a stress at work claim in the employment tribunal by the back door. The back door was firmly shut by the Court of Appeal in *Triggs v GAB Robins (UK) Limited*.[63] In this case, Mrs Triggs, who had been overworked and bullied, resigned and brought a claim for unfair constructive dismissal in the employment tribunal. The Court of Appeal found:

'She was a conscientious and loyal employee, who shouldered an excessive workload and put in long hours without extra pay in order to provide the necessary support to the two investigators. From about April 2001 Mr Carter raised with his manager, Mr Baldock, the problem of her workload. On 6 August 2003 Mrs Triggs collapsed at home, following which she was signed off work for a week with stress. Although the two investigators continued to raise the matter of her workload with Mr Baldock, she remained overworked. In addition, she found Mr Baldock's treatment of her such as to amount to bullying (the ET gave an example at [22] and [23] of their judgment).

On 30 September 2004 Mrs Triggs returned to work after two days' sick leave and had to suffer Mr Baldock shouting at her down the telephone. She decided she had had enough. She left the office that morning, never to return. Her doctor signed her off sick with stress and depression, later diagnosed as anxiety and depression. No-one from senior management contacted her. She became frightened to go out alone and spent time at home sobbing uncontrollably and sleeping for long periods.'

62 ERA 1996, s 124.
63 [2008] EWCA Civ 17.

The employment tribunal had correctly determined that there could be no injury to feelings award and neither could they award anything for her loss of earnings during a period of sickness caused by stress prior to her resignation.

However, with regard to the future, the tribunal held that:

> 'Having resigned in response to the Respondent's conduct which was no longer capable of resolution under the terms of the contract of employment, [Mrs Triggs's] loss thereafter flows from the dismissal. The Tribunal has found that [Mrs Triggs] became ill as a result of the Respondent's conduct and in those circumstances it matters not that by the time of the dismissal [Mrs Triggs] was in receipt of only statutory sick pay from her employer. She is entitled to recover the loss of her salary flowing from her dismissal at the full rate for such period as the Tribunal determines at the adjourned hearing with the Tribunal taking account of such payments [Mrs Triggs] has received since that time it considers it is required to do. In deciding what is a reasonable period for [Mrs Triggs] to recover compensation for, the Tribunal will have to have regard to what period of [Mrs Triggs's] ill-health is attributable to the Respondent's conduct.'

The tribunal awarded her a compensatory award of £58,000. The decision was upheld by the EAT.

However, despite 'instinctive sympathy' for Mrs Triggs, the Court of Appeal disagreed. They said:

> 'To the question whether Mrs Triggs's reduced earning capacity by reason of her illness was a loss suffered by her "in consequence of the dismissal" (section 123), the answer is no. It is correct that the dismissal was a constructive one, that is that it was the result of, and followed upon, her acceptance of the employer's antecedent breaches of the implied term of trust and confidence that had caused her illness and, in turn, her reduced earning capacity. But it is fallacious to regard those antecedent breaches as constituting the dismissal. The dismissal was effected purely and simply by her decision in February 2005 that she wished to discontinue her employment. On a claim for unfair dismissal, that entitled her to compensation for whatever loss flowed from that dismissal. But that loss did not include loss (including future loss) flowing from wrongs *already* inflicted upon her by the employer's prior conduct: those losses (including any future lost income) were not caused by the dismissal. They were caused by the antecedent breaches of the implied term as to trust and confidence and Mrs Triggs had an already accrued right to sue for damages in respect of them before the dismissal. The ET's error in concluding that it was suffered in consequence of the dismissal was to treat the unfair dismissal claim as, in effect, a claim for damages for the employer's fundamental breach and repudiation of the employment contract that Mrs Triggs had accepted by her decision to leave. But her claim was not such a claim. It was simply a statutory claim for unfair dismissal.'

The compensatory award was overturned. The employee would have to pursue compensation for future loss of earnings in the courts via a 'stress at work' claim under the common law.

In addition, there is always the risk of a *Polkey*[64] reduction. In *C&A Pumps Ltd v Thompson*[65] the employee had a history of psychiatric reaction to workplace stress. In breach of contract the employer changed his company car. He suffered a relapse and subsequently resigned and claimed a constructive dismissal. It was established that he had been unfairly dismissed. However, the employment tribunal had failed to consider any *Polkey* reduction to reflect the possibility that he might well have been fairly dismissed in any event shortly afterwards. The employee argued that the only reason he might be dismissed would be on the grounds of ill health caused by the employer's own conduct in subjecting him to stress. However, in remitting the issue of compensation back to the tribunal, the EAT held:

> 'It is possible however, that it may be relevant in the context of *a Polkey* defence as to what the causation of the medical condition was.'

7.4 COMPENSATION FOR DISCRIMINATION

In discrimination claims the tribunal is entitled to award compensation for 'injury to feelings'. For example, under s 56 of the Race Relations Act 1976 (RRA 1976) the employment tribunal is empowered as follows:

> '(1) Where an [employment tribunal] finds that a complaint presented to it under section 54 is well-founded, the tribunal shall make such of the following as it considers just and equitable—
>
> . . .
>
> (b) an order requiring the respondent to pay to the complainant compensation of an amount corresponding to any damages he could have been ordered by a county court or by a sheriff court to pay to the complainant if the complaint had fallen to be dealt with under section 57 . . .'

Section 57 of the RRA 1976 provides:

> '(4) For the avoidance of doubt it is hereby declared that damages in respect of an unlawful act of discrimination may include compensation for injury to feelings whether or not they include compensation under any other head.'

Other equality legislation contains similar provisions which fall to be construed in a similar manner.[66]

---

64 See **7.3.2**.

65 [2006] UKEAT 0218_06_2610 (Burton J, C Baelz, D Bleiman) 26 October 2006.

66 *Anyanwu and Another v South Bank Student Union and Another and Commission For Racial Equality* [2001] UKHL 14, [2001] 2 All ER 353, [2001] 1 WLR 638.

There are no statutory rules as to the quantum of an award for injury to feelings, but in *Vento v Chief Constable of West Yorkshire*[67] the Court of Appeal set out guidance for tribunals considering making such awards.

There is sometimes an overlap with a personal injury award, but if there is a recognised psychiatric injury supported by medical evidence then separate awards may be made for the personal injury and for injury to feelings.

7.4.1 Injury to feelings awards: principles

In *Vento* the Court of Appeal pointed out that valuation of 'injury to feelings' was like valuing general damages for pain, suffering and loss of amenity, a difficult and somewhat unreal exercise:

> 'It is self evident that the assessment of compensation for an injury or loss, which is neither physical nor financial, presents special problems for the judicial process, which aims to produce results objectively justified by evidence, reason and precedent. Subjective feelings of upset, frustration, worry, anxiety, mental distress, fear, grief, anguish, humiliation, unhappiness, stress, depression and so on and the degree of their intensity are incapable of objective proof or of measurement in monetary terms. Translating hurt feelings into hard currency is bound to be an artificial exercise.'

However, the tribunal had to do their best:

> 'Although they are incapable of objective proof or measurement in monetary terms, hurt feelings are none the less real in human terms. The courts and tribunals have to do the best they can on the available material to make a sensible assessment, accepting that it is impossible to justify or explain a particular sum with the same kind of solid evidential foundation and persuasive practical reasoning available in the calculation of financial loss or compensation for bodily injury.'

Furthermore, in the EAT decision in *Armitage, Marsden and HM Prison Service v Johnson*[68] quoted and adopted in *Vento*, Smith J giving judgment on behalf of the Employment Appeal Tribunal said:

> '(i) Awards for injury to feelings are compensatory. They should be just to both parties. They should compensate fully without punishing the tortfeasor. Feelings of indignation at the tortfeasor's conduct should not be allowed to inflate the award. (ii) Awards should not be too low, as that would diminish respect for the policy of the anti-discrimination legislation. Society has condemned discrimination and awards must ensure that it is seen to be wrong. On the other hand, awards should be restrained, as excessive awards could, to use the phrase of Sir Thomas Bingham MR, be seen as the way to "untaxed riches". (iii) Awards should bear some broad general

67 [2002] EWCA Civ 1871.

68 [1997] IRLR 162.

similarity to the range of awards in personal injury cases. We do not think that this should be done by reference to any particular type of personal injury award, rather to the whole range of such awards. (iv) In exercising that discretion in assessing a sum, tribunals should remind themselves of the value in everyday life of the sum they have in mind. This may be done by reference to purchasing power or by reference to earnings. (v) Finally, tribunals should bear in mind Sir Thomas Bingham's reference for the need for public respect for the level of awards made.'

In the particular case of *Vento,* the Court of Appeal said:

> 'In our judgment, taking account of the level of awards undisturbed on recent appeals to the Appeal Tribunal and of the JSB Guidelines, the fair, reasonable and just award in this case for non-pecuniary loss is a total of £32,000, made up as to £18,000 for injury to feelings, £5,000 aggravated damages and £9,000 for psychiatric damage, which took the form of clinical depression and adjustment disorder lasting for 3 years (and against which there was no appeal). We also bear in mind that there was no finding by the Employment Tribunal that the injury to Ms Vento's feelings would continue after the psychiatric disorder had passed. During the period of psychiatric disorder there must have been a significant degree of overlap with the injury to her feelings.

In respect of injury to feelings the Court of Appeal therefore reduced the award of £50,000 made by the employment tribunal (which had already been reduced by the EAT to £25,000) to £18,000. The separate award of £9,000 for psychiatric injury was upheld by the EAT and the Court of Appeal. The Court of Appeal explained their reasoning as follows:

> 'It should be understood that the reduction in the amount of compensation is made solely to bring the global award more into line with conventional wisdom on levels of compensation for non-pecuniary loss generally. The reduction does not mean that this Court takes a less serious view than the Employment Tribunal did of the persistent unlawful discrimination suffered by Ms Vento at the hands of her colleagues in the Police Service, which is expected to set an example of abiding by the law, including the law governing all forms of discrimination.'

And in *Johnson* an award of £21,000 for injury to feelings was made to a black prison officer who, for a period of just under 2 years, was ostracised by his colleagues after objecting to the manhandling of a black prisoner by prison officers and subjected to racist remarks, false accusations, together with other acts of discrimination which the tribunal had described as a campaign of appalling treatment.

In *Jiad v Byford*[69] while determining a striking out application in respect of a victimisation claim described by the court as 'weak', the Court of Appeal considered the overlap between injury to feelings and personal injury:

---

[69] [2003] EWCA Civ 135.

'Transitory hurt feelings may not (depending on the facts) suffice, but enduring physical or psychological injury could (again depending on the circumstances) be capable of constituting detriment in the sense that a reasonable worker would regard it as a disadvantage. With some hesitation, I conclude that Dr Jiad's case here crosses the line of possibility and is not bound to fail for want of a sufficient allegation of detriment. It may be tenuous, but that is not enough in the sense in which I read paragraph 19 of the Tribunal's decision. He claims to have suffered psychological and physical stress. He consulted his general practitioner twice. On the first occasion the general practitioner prescribed medication.'

7.4.2 The *Vento* guidelines

The Court of Appeal in *Vento* went on to lay down guidelines on injury to feelings awards:

'Employment Tribunals and those who practise in them might find it helpful if this Court were to identify three broad bands of compensation for injury to feelings, as distinct from compensation for psychiatric or similar personal injury.

(i) The top band should normally be between £15,000 and £25,000. Sums in this range should be awarded in the most serious cases, such as where there has been a lengthy campaign of discriminatory harassment on the ground of sex or race. This case falls within that band. Only in the most exceptional case should an award of compensation for injury to feelings exceed £25,000.

(ii) The middle band of between £5,000 and £15,000 should be used for serious cases, which do not merit an award in the highest band.

(iii) Awards of between £500 and £5,000 are appropriate for less serious cases, such as where the act of discrimination is an isolated or one off occurrence. In general, awards of less than £500 are to be avoided altogether, as they risk being regarded as so low as not to be a proper recognition of injury to feelings.

There is, of course, within each band considerable flexibility, allowing tribunals to fix what is considered to be fair, reasonable and just compensation in the particular circumstances of the case.'

Aggravated damages might be awarded in addition:

'The decision whether or not to award aggravated damages and, if so, in what amount must depend on the particular circumstances of the discrimination and on the way in which the complaint of discrimination has been handled.'

However, awards for injury to feelings and other non-pecuniary loss are never simply cumulative:

'Common sense requires that regard should also be had to the overall magnitude of the sum total of the awards of compensation for non-pecuniary loss made under the various headings of injury to feelings, psychiatric damage and aggravated damage. In particular, double recovery should be avoided by taking appropriate account of the overlap between the individual heads of damage. The extent of overlap will depend on the facts of each particular case.'

Similar issues can arise where there are several distinct discrimination claims. In *Jumard v Clwyd Leisure Centre*[70] the employee was a disabled Iraqi who was the manager of the employer leisure centre. The tribunal specifically found that there had been acts of direct disability discrimination and direct race discrimination. The tribunal awarded the employee £13,000 for injury to feelings, which was at the top end of the middle *Vento* band. They separately awarded £5,000 in respect of personal injury (pain, suffering and loss of amenity) caused by the failure to make reasonable adjustments. They also made an award of £1,500 aggravated damages in respect of the employer's conduct (which had, for example, included subjecting him to surveillance). The EAT held that the tribunal had adopted 'too broad brush an approach' to the injury to feelings award. They held that where different types of discrimination arose out of different incidents, separate awards for each should be calculated. The tribunal should then go on to consider the total figure arrived at in the round to ensure it was proportionate and that there had been no double counting. They said:

> 'However, where, as in this case, certain acts of discrimination fall only into one category or another, then the injury to feelings should be considered separately with respect to those acts. Each is a separate wrong for which damages should be provided. Apart from that, it will help focus the Tribunal's mind on the compensatory nature of the award. We would suggest for example, that it would not at all follow that the level of awards should be the same for different forms of discrimination. The offence, humiliation or upset resulting from a deliberate act of race discrimination may quite understandably cause greater injury to feelings than, say, a thoughtless failure to make an adjustment under the Disability Discrimination Act.
>
> . . . Similarly, we think that the Tribunal was obliged to have regard to the victimisation claim and to consider whether it justified any separate head of loss. Since the Tribunal found that this act constituted race and disability discrimination in any event, it might properly come to the view that any further injury to feelings would be nominal. But in our view the issue needed to be addressed.
>
> We do not think, however, that it was necessary or in this case desirable to fix a separate sum for the injury to feelings flowing from acts of direct disability discrimination and the failure to make reasonable adjustments respectively, although it would not necessarily be wrong for a tribunal to do that in an appropriate case It is, however, important that the tribunal keeps firmly in mind that there are the different forms of disability discrimination, and they may contribute in different measure to any injury to feelings

[70] UKEAT/0334/07/LA.

because, as we have said, the extent to which feelings are injured is not necessarily the same for each category of discriminatory act.

. . . Notwithstanding the errors in the approach which we have identified, we do not say that the figure overall was necessarily or obviously wrong, and we certainly do not think that each of the two claims of race and disability discrimination should, considered separately, inevitably to have been located in the higher bracket, as the Claimant argues. As we have emphasised, in any event a tribunal has to stand back and look at the global figure and simply adding the compensation for each might well result in a disproportionate sum or involve double counting.'

This judgment also confirmed that there should be no *Polkey* reduction[71] for contributory fault in respect of the discrimination claims. It should only apply to the unfair dismissal award.

7.4.3 Examples of injury to feelings awards in stress and bullying claims

In *Miles v Gilbank*,[72] a sex discrimination claim, the Court of Appeal upheld an award of £25,000 for injury to feelings which was at the very top of the *Vento* top band for the most serious cases. The court quoted from the tribunal's judgment as to the nature of the discrimination:

'The Claimant was clear about her feelings on this matter. She used the terms "very shocked and embarrassed" at the First Respondents reaction to her pregnancy. She was made to feel that she had "done something wrong" and "was being pushed out of the salon" which she had believed was her security and future. She was made to feel that though she was her unborn child's only source of food and well being she would not be able to give her that while she was at work. She was in fear of the loss of her job in making any complaints. She was "distraught" when sent back to work though bleeding, she was very "hurt" by comments on the part of the First Respondent and was made to feel she was risking colleagues futures. She felt degraded. She was forced to protest about unfair pressure and stress. Her requests to be left alone were ignore and that she was reduced to tears. She was publicly reprimanded and "felt demoralized and severely distressed". She was made to feel "undervalued" and felt that the First Respondent did not care for "her or her unborn child". She felt reluctant in climbing the cupboard to retrieve the paper work. She was "disheartened upset" and was caused "a lot of distress". She was distraught "at the end of each day" (which was confirmed very clearly by her witness Miss Nibre Walker, who told the Tribunal how the Claimant would go straight to her after work most night[s] in a distraught state because of things that had been said to her in the salon each day). She was made to feel "I was being demoted and that I had no future in the salon all because of my pregnancy". She was "embarrassed and left the team room distraught". She was told by Shenel "you aren't right" and as "upset distressed and anxious to the point I could

71 See **7.3**.

72 [2006] EWCA Civ 543.

not stand". She suffered "undue anxiety stress and bullying". She felt she was being "laughed at". She was very upset "about being snubbed" and so "upset" so that an employee tried to intervene on her behalf (see above).

All in all, there was a catalogue of behaviour towards her on the part of the First Respondent and the other Managers named above which goes beyond malicious and amounts to downright vicious. It was an inhumane and sustained campaign of bullying and discrimination which could not, in the circumstances on the facts found as above, be reasonably seen to have been accidental or merely insensitive. It was targeted, deliberate, repeated and consciously inflicted. It not only demonstrated to the Claimant a total lack of concern for the welfare of the Claimant herself, but a callous disregard or concern for the life of her unborn child.'

The Court of Appeal held:

'In the *Vento* case, this court contemplated that there would be cases where the amount of the award could exceed even its guidelines. So, although this award is at the top end of the highest bracket, it does not mean that the Employment Appeal Tribunal and the tribunal did not consider that a more serious case could not occur. There clearly are more serious cases. However, in this case there were repeated acts of discrimination, and the conduct of Ms Miles was found to be deliberate and very hurtful and distressing (see para. 24 of the tribunal's decision set out above). Moreover, it also involved the well-being of Ms Gilbank's unborn child. That gives this case added seriousness and must have imposed an additional level of stress on Ms Gilbank as an expectant mother.'

In *Reid v BT plc*[73] the employee had been overlooked for promotion and subjected to unwarranted disciplinary proceedings. The tribunal summarised the complaint as follows:

'The applicant had a very unpleasant time after the 5 November incident and had to suffer the indignity of a disciplinary investigation, which was totally unjustified. His health suffered and he had to have a considerable time off work. He went back to work on 17 April 2001 at St Albans and was transferred to Bletchley on 29 May 2001. He found this stressful and became sick on 8 October 2001 with stress. He was transferred to Mondial House on 30 October 2001. The grievance investigation by Mr Godsafe was not finalised until 11 December 2001 and the appeal by Ms Corby was not finalised until 12 February 2002. The applicant therefore had some 14 months while he was waiting for his grievance to be dealt with.'

The employee was awarded £6,000 for injury to feelings with no separate award for personal injuries. The employer appealed on the grounds that the award was too high. The award was upheld by both the EAT and the Court of Appeal.

---

73 [2003] EWCA Civ 1675.

7.4.4 Compensatory awards in discrimination claims

As we have seen, the equality legislation provides for compensation for discrimination in the employment tribunal to be analogous to that the damages which could be awarded in the county court.[74]

However, until 22 November 1993 the statutory cap on the compensatory awards in the tribunal applied to discrimination claims, as it still does for unfair dismissal claims.[75] Until it was removed there was little opportunity for substantial 'career loss' damages to be awarded (at the time of its removal the cap had been £11,000). The cap was removed following a challenge to its legality which was referred by the House of Lords to the European Court of Justice (ECJ) for determination. The ECJ[76] held that:

> 'Where financial compensation is the measure adopted . . . it must be adequate, in that it enables loss and damage actually sustained as a result of the discriminatory dismissal to be made good in full in accordance with the applicable national rules.'

The cap was subsequently removed by parliament for all claims for discrimination (not just for 'discriminatory dismissal').

In *Ministry of Defence v Cannock*[77] the EAT reviewed seven appeals by servicewomen in sex discrimination claims and laid down general guidelines for the assessment of compensation. Morrison J in the EAT held:

> 'It seems to us quite clear that the correct measure of damage is based on the principle that, as best as money can do it, the applicant must be put into the position she would have been in but for the unlawful conduct . . .'

and rejected the MOD's argument that the contractual measure of damages was appropriate instead of the measure appropriate for a statutory tort. So far as future loss was concerned, whilst pointing out that the specific calculation in individual cases might differ from that used in personal injury claims, the EAT said:

> '[Employment] Tribunals should calculate the loss of earnings up to the date of the hearing (the past loss) and should normally calculate damages for future loss of earnings, having regard to the matters to which we have referred, by using the usual multiplicand and multiplier method adopted by the courts.'

---

74 See **7.4**.

75 See **7.3.2**.

76 *Marshall v Southampton and South West Hampshire Health Authority (No 2)* (Case C-271/91) [1993] 4 All ER 586.

77 [1995] 2 All ER 449, [1994] ICR 918, [1994] IRLR 509.

In *Vento* the employer had also challenged the compensatory award and the Court of Appeal summarised the issue as follows:

> 'The question is: what were the chances, if Ms Vento had not been discriminated against and dismissed, of her remaining in the police force until the age of retirement at 55?'
>
> 'It has to be answered on the basis of the best assessment that can be made on the relevant material available to the court. That includes statistical material, such as that produced to the tribunal showing the percentage of women who have in the past continued to serve in the police force until the age of retirement.'

In *Vento* the tribunal had calculated the award for future loss of earnings on the basis that she had a 75% chance of remaining in the police force until retirement at the age of 55. They awarded her £165,829. The Chief Constable appealed and his appeal was upheld by the EAT, inter alia on the grounds that Ms Vento had only been employed for 2 years, that she had suffered from a depressive illness in the past and that statistics showed that only 49% of men and 9% of women worked until police service retirement age. However, Ms Vento appealed to the Court of Appeal. She argued that she was unable to have further children and adduced evidence of her life-long desire to join the police service. She also pointed out that the police service also introduced more 'family friendly' policies with a view to redressing the statistical imbalance between men and women. In upholding the tribunal's decision (and allowing Ms Vento's appeal from the EAT on this issue) the Court of Appeal said:

> 'In our judgment, the Employment Tribunal did not apply any wrong principle of law or reach a perverse decision in the difficult and imprecise exercise of assessing the relative future chances. There was material on which its evaluation could be justified. It explained its conclusion sufficiently to comply with its duty to give sufficient reasons for its decision. The parties were able to tell in broad terms why they had won or lost on that issue. It is difficult to see what further reasons or explanation could reasonably be expected of the tribunal on a point such as this. It referred to the statistics on which the police relied. It also referred to the factors casting doubt on the applicability of past statistics to the future prospects of this particular police officer.'

So, in substantial 'career loss' discrimination claims, the tribunal is supposed to assess damages in a similar way to a court, using the multiplier/multiplicand approach. Are the Ogden Tables to be used? This has caused some controversy. Personal injury practitioners may be surprised that there is any argument about this, but until 1993 there was little point in looking at the Ogden Tables in the employment tribunal because of the statutory cap on compensation. And even now employment tribunals more often encounter unfair dismissal claims where the compensation is capped and is subject to the 'just and equitable' test,[78] rather than an assessment of future loss in accordance with the principles applied to tortious claims in the courts. In the employment tribunal it is common for future loss of earnings to be assessed in a more 'rough and ready' way by awarding compensation in full for the period during which the tribunal believes the employee is likely to be out of work. (For example, if an employee is earning £20,000 and the tribunal thinks he will be out of work for a further 6 months, the award is likely to be £10,000). This approach does not take into account the risk of mortality, accelerated receipt and investment of the lump sum awarded. This is unlikely to be significant in respect of a short period of loss. Nor for a longer period of loss where the tribunal is awarding compensation for the difference in earnings from his previous and likely future employment (e g the employee earned £20,000 per annum with his old employer, and is likely to get another job at £18,000 per annum and the shortfall of £2,000 is likely to continue for 3 years, making a loss of £6,000). However, in a 'career loss' claim the rough and ready approach is less likely to be an appropriate method of calculation because of the risk of mortality, accelerated receipt, inflation and the anticipated return on investment of the lump sum, all of which are taken into account by the Ogden Tables.

In *Chagger v Abbey National & Hopkins*[79] the EAT considered the use of the Ogden Tables in the tribunal in detail. The employee was 40 years old and earning about £100,000 per annum as a trader for Abbey National. He suffered race discrimination in selection for redundancy and put forward a 'career loss' claim with a multiplier of 16. The tribunal made a compensatory award of £2.8m. The employer appealed. Underhill J pointed out:

> 'It should be noted that the situation here is not the same as that in the well-known "career-loss" cases of *Ministry of Defence v. Cannock* [1994] ICR 918 and *Vento v. Chief Constable of West Yorkshire Police (no. 2)* [2003] ICR 318. In those cases the claimants were employed in occupations in which they would (or very probably would) remain with a single employer – the armed forces or a particular police force – for the whole of their careers. The cases were not concerned with a field of employment where job mobility was common.'

The EAT then turned to the use of the Ogden Tables. Firstly, it was pointed out that in most dismissal cases, unlike most personal injury claims where the disability is lifelong, the loss is not usually to retirement age:

> 'There is of course nothing unusual in an employment tribunal using a multiplier/multiplicand approach when assessing future loss of earnings in a dismissal case: it will indeed almost inevitably do so when the loss extends much over a year. It is, in our experience, much less usual for it to use the

78 See **7.3.2**.

79 [2009] IRLR 86, [2008] All ER (D) 157 (Oct), [2008] UKEAT 0606_07_1610.

> Ogden Tables. These are Tables published by the Government Actuary as an aid to the calculation of damages in personal injury cases. Tables 3–14 in the current (6th) edition identify multipliers (for men and women separately) from any given age up to retirement age (with alternatives at five-yearly intervals from ages 50 to 75). These Multipliers take account of – only – (a) accelerated receipt and (b) mortality risk. In most dismissal cases the tribunal will not normally be concerned with a loss continuing to retirement date, and tables 3–14 will accordingly be of no assistance: it will have to choose a multiplier which it judges best balances all the contingencies affecting the duration of the loss (and, unless this is insignificant, accelerated receipt).'

The EAT had found that the loss was not in fact career long. However:

> 'But if, contrary to our decision, the Tribunal here had indeed been concerned with loss extending for the entirety of the Claimant's career there could be no objection to it using the appropriate Ogden table – though only, as explained at para. 114 below, as a starting-point . . .
>
> 114. Even in a case where it is appropriate to use the Ogden Tables, it will never be right to use the multiplier taken from the main tables without considering the contingencies which those tables do not reflect. For a claimant to be compensated in full (subject to accelerated receipt) for his assumed annual loss for every year and month of the rest of his career involves treating as a certainty the assumption that he would have continued for the rest of his career to receive his predismissal earnings. But that cannot be a certainty. On the contrary, it is subject to a number of contingencies: he might have died or become too ill to work, or his employer might have gone out of business, or he might have been dismissed for some other good cause or have left voluntarily for any one of a number of reasons. The only one of those contingencies taken into account in the main Ogden tables is the possibility of death (and even that may be inadequately represented if there is reason to believe that the claimant's risks are substantially worse than those of the general population from which the Ogden figures derive). Those other contingencies must be properly reflected in the ultimate multiplier used. There may be cases where a tribunal believes the contingencies in question are balanced by "upside" contingencies not reflected in the multiplicand (e.g. promotion); but otherwise the multiplier will fall to be reduced.'

The EAT pointed out how the tribunal had fallen into error and stressed with regard to deduction for contingencies:

> ' . . . we doubt whether it is right to assess contingencies in a given case, at least in the employment field, only on the basis of discounting factors of the kind used in section B of the Ogden Tables. These are based on general population figures, and they will in any event contain no allowance for the possibility of the claimant leaving his employment voluntarily. An employment tribunal should normally be in a position to make a case-specific assessment for contingencies applicable to the claimant's own case.'

And concluded:

> 'We do not wish by these observations to discourage tribunals from using the Ogden Tables in cases where sophisticated calculations of long-term future loss are required. But if they are used they must be used with care and with a proper understanding of their limitations.'

So, the Ogden Tables will rarely be relevant in unfair dismissal cases (because of the statutory cap) or in discrimination claims where the effect of the discrimination is not career long. If the loss will last for a short period, the tribunal will usually accept a rough and ready calculation. In fact, discrimination-related stress may well lead to long-lasting psychiatric injury resulting in 'career loss'. In such cases, the Ogden Tables should be used, but with caution, particularly with regard to the deduction for contingencies.

With regard to loss of pension, the tribunal will not use the Ogden Tables, but will instead follow the principles of calculation set out in 'Compensation for Loss of Pension Rights'.[80]

7.4.5 Aggravated damages

In some exceptional cases the employer's response to complaints of discrimination by the employee might lead to an award of aggravated damages.

Exemplary damages must be distinguished from aggravated damages. They are only available in actions against an emanation of the state. In *Boyle v Virgo Fidelis Senior School*[81] the EAT held exemplary damages could not be awarded. They commented:

> 'It seems to us that there were here factors which entitled the tribunal to make an award of aggravated damages. In particular they identified the third appellants' conduct of the investigation of the complaints of race discrimination. The tribunal described this as a travesty of what it should have been. Instead of providing the respondent with a remedy for the wrongs which he had suffered, the third appellants added to his injury by attributing all his problems to his own defects of personality. We think that this was a true case of aggravation: a case where the appellant's actions rubbed salt in the respondent's wounds.'

And in *Reid v BT plc*[82] the Court of Appeal upheld the tribunal's award of £2,000 by way of aggravated damages.

---

80 D Sneath 'Compensation for loss of pension rights: employment tribunals' (The Stationery Office, 3rd edn, reprinted February 2005).

81 [2004] ICR 1210, [2004] IRLR 268, (2004) *The Times*, 26 February, [2004] UKEAT 0644_03_2301.

82 [2003] EWCA Civ 1675.

7.4.6 Exemplary damages

For example, in *Boyle v Virgo Fidelis Senior School*[83] the EAT upheld an award of aggravated damages of £7,500 'although we would have awarded somewhat less', commenting:

> 'Whilst we have not found this an easy issue, we conclude that the School in exercising their disciplinary powers were not acting as servants or agents of the executive, even at a local level. Further, whilst the actions of the School in dealing with Mr Boyle were criticised quite properly by the Tribunal, there was in our view not sufficient before them to enable them to say that this was oppressive, arbitrary or unconstitutional action.'

7.5 OTHER TRIBUNAL REMEDIES

The employment tribunal also has the power to order reinstatement or re-engagement. Neither will be appropriate in most stress at work claims. Either the employee will not be fit to return to work, or the stress of the job which he left will render it impracticable.

Under s 114 of the ERA 1996:

> '(1) An order for reinstatement is an order that the employer shall treat the complainant in all respects as if he had not been dismissed.
>
> (2) On making an order for reinstatement the tribunal shall specify—
> (a) any amount payable by the employer in respect of any benefit which the complainant might reasonably be expected to have had but for the dismissal (including arrears of pay) for the period between the date of termination of employment and the date of reinstatement,
> (b) any rights and privileges (including seniority and pension rights) which must be restored to the employee, and
> (c) the date by which the order must be complied with.
>
> (3) If the complainant would have benefited from an improvement in his terms and conditions of employment had he not been dismissed, an order for reinstatement shall require him to be treated as if he had benefited from that improvement from the date on which he would have done so but for being dismissed.
>
> (4) In calculating for the purposes of subsection (2)(a) any amount payable by the employer, the tribunal shall take into account, so as to reduce the employer's liability, any sums received by the complainant in respect of the period between the date of termination of employment and the date of reinstatement by way of—
> (a) wages in lieu of notice or ex gratia payments paid by the employer, or
> (b) remuneration paid in respect of employment with another employer,

---

83 [2004] ICR 1210, [2004] IRLR 268, (2004) *The Times*, 26 February, [2004] UKEAT 0644_03_2301.

and such other benefits as the tribunal thinks appropriate in the circumstances.'

As the employee will be reinstated in the same job where the stress was caused, this will rarely apply to a discrimination claim resulting from stress at work.

If the employer is very large, it may be appropriate for an employee to be re-engaged (in a different role or part of the organisation). Section 115 of the ERA 1996 provides:

> '(1) An order for re-engagement is an order, on such terms as the tribunal may decide, that the complainant be engaged by the employer, or by a successor of the employer or by an associated employer, in employment comparable to that from which he was dismissed or other suitable employment.
>
> (2) On making an order for re-engagement the tribunal shall specify the terms on which re-engagement is to take place, including—
> (a) the identity of the employer,
> (b) the nature of the employment,
> (c) the remuneration for the employment,
> (d) any amount payable by the employer in respect of any benefit which the complainant might reasonably be expected to have had but for the dismissal (including arrears of pay) for the period between the date of termination of employment and the date of re-engagement,
> (e) any rights and privileges (including seniority and pension rights) which must be restored to the employee, and
> (f) the date by which the order must be complied with.
>
> (3) In calculating for the purposes of subsection (2)(d) any amount payable by the employer, the tribunal shall take into account, so as to reduce the employer's liability, any sums received by the complainant in respect of the period between the date of termination of employment and the date of re-engagement by way of—
> (a) wages in lieu of notice or ex gratia payments paid by the employer, or
> (b) remuneration paid in respect of employment with another employer,
>
> and such other benefits as the tribunal thinks appropriate in the circumstances.'

Section 116 of the ERA 1996 sets out the grounds on which the tribunal will exercise its discretion:

> '(1) In exercising its discretion under section 113 the tribunal shall first consider whether to make an order for reinstatement and in so doing shall take into account—
> (a) whether the complainant wishes to be reinstated,
> (b) whether it is practicable for the employer to comply with an order for reinstatement, and

(c) where the complainant caused or contributed to some extent to the dismissal, whether it would be just to order his reinstatement.

(2) If the tribunal decides not to make an order for reinstatement it shall then consider whether to make an order for re-engagement and, if so, on what terms.

(3) In so doing the tribunal shall take into account—
(a) any wish expressed by the complainant as to the nature of the order to be made,
(b) whether it is practicable for the employer (or a successor or an associated employer) to comply with an order for re-engagement, and
(c) where the complainant caused or contributed to some extent to the dismissal, whether it would be just to order his re-engagement and (if so) on what terms.

(4) Except in a case where the tribunal takes into account contributory fault under subsection (3)(c) it shall, if it orders re-engagement, do so on terms which are, so far as is reasonably practicable, as favourable as an order for reinstatement.

(5) Where in any case an employer has engaged a permanent replacement for a dismissed employee, the tribunal shall not take that fact into account in determining, for the purposes of subsection (1)(b) or (3)(b), whether it is practicable to comply with an order for reinstatement or re-engagement.

(6) Subsection (5) does not apply where the employer shows—
(a) that it was not practicable for him to arrange for the dismissed employee's work to be done without engaging a permanent replacement, or
(b) that—
   (i) he engaged the replacement after the lapse of a reasonable period, without having heard from the dismissed employee that he wished to be reinstated or re-engaged, and
   (ii) when the employer engaged the replacement it was no longer reasonable for him to arrange for the dismissed employee's work to be done except by a permanent replacement.'

In practice, however, neither remedy will be practicable in most cases where there has been discrimination leading to significant stress at work.

7.6 OTHER DETRIMENT CASES

The prohibition on injury to feelings awards in the tribunal[84] applies to unfair dismissal claims, but not to other claims in the employment tribunal where the employee claims that he has been subjected to a 'detriment'.[85]

---

[84] See **6.3.1**.

[85] See **5.5**.

In *Boyle v Virgo Fidelis Senior School* the EAT held that the *Vento* guidelines applied to other detriment cases (such as whistleblowers). Mr Boyle had been concerned about certain aspects of his school and had reported them to the school governors and to the local authority. Disciplinary proceedings were commenced against him and he was dismissed. The EAT said:

> 'We are firmly of the view that the Tribunal were in error in not having regard to the Vento guidelines, albeit that detriment suffered by "whistle-blowers" should normally be regarded by Tribunals as a very serious breach of discrimination legislation.
>
> . . . there was a prolonged course of conduct over many months calculated to make Mr Boyle's position untenable and to avoid in any way acknowledging the legitimate concerns that he had raised which were of a very serious nature. For example, a music teacher had fallen to her death from the School roof and another teacher had resigned after an incident relating to sexual harassment.'
>
> It is also clear that the extract from his GP records presented to the Tribunal made it abundantly clear that there was a deterioration in his health within a few weeks of his July letter which had continued throughout the next few months. By November 2001 the GP's notes record that Mr Boyle appeared to be experiencing a major depressive episode, reactive in nature.
>
> We would therefore propose to make an award for injury to feelings of £25,000. There being no separate head of claim for psychiatric damage, we make no separate award under this head.'

In *Cleveland Ambulance NHS Trust v Blane*,[86] in respect of a claim under s 146(1) of the Trade Union and Labour Relations (Consolidation) Act 1992, the EAT concluded that the tribunal had power under s 149(2) to award compensation for injury to feelings:

> 'Section 149(2) adds the words: "having regard to the infringement complained of and . . ." It seems to us that those words grant the industrial tribunal a power to award compensation over and above the pure pecuniary loss suffered by the applicant. Given the scope for awards to complainants who have suffered by way of sex or race discrimination to reflect injury to feelings, we see no reason in principle why the words of the section cannot extend to such award. Put another way, what do the words add to the normal formulation of available pecuniary loss claims for unfair dismissal, if not to include an award for non-pecuniary loss including injury to feelings? (3) It is not fatal to our construction that the Sex Discrimination Act 1975 and the Race Relations Act 1976 contain specific references to awards for injury to feelings, and section 149(2) of the Act of 1992 does not. Those provisions are inserted "for the avoidance of doubt", not to create an otherwise otiose head of claim.'

86 *Cleveland Ambulance NHS Trust v Blane* [1997] UKEAT 1046_96_1902.

In *London Borough of Hackney v Adams*[87] the EAT applied the *Vento* guidelines to trade union discrimination cases:

> 'Again, although the tribunal made no express reference to any specific award in personal injury cases, the reference to the Tchoula case in paragraph 39.3 of their decision indicates that they had well in mind that their award should have "a broad general similarity" to the range of awards in such cases.'

The EAT went onto consider the quantum of injury to feelings awards in other detriment cases:

> 'That is not to say, however, that it will in all cases be just as easy to establish injury to feelings in relation to one form of discrimination as another. We doubt whether that can be right. Sometimes such injury will be the almost inevitable concomitant of the discrimination having occurred. For example, it can readily be assumed where someone has suffered an act of race or sex discrimination that will by its very nature have caused injury to feelings: it is demeaning to the individual and offensive to his or her dignity to be so treated. A tribunal will readily infer some injury to feelings from the simple fact of the discrimination having occurred. Such injury may of course be compounded by the particular manner in which the discriminatory conduct itself is made manifest. For example, harassment over a lengthy period will plainly result in more considerable distress than a single act of discrimination and should be compensated for accordingly. There will, however, have to be evidence of the nature of the discriminatory conduct.
>
> By contrast, other forms of discrimination may leave the victim relatively, if not wholly, unscathed from any real distress. For example, it is unlawful to discriminate against someone on the grounds that he or she is a non-unionist. It seems to us that it is far from self evident that, for example, someone refused employment on those grounds will necessarily suffer any injury to feelings at all. The status of not being a trade union member is not likely, at least in most cases, to be an essential part of an individual's make up, or to be a characteristic which is central to a person's sense of self respect and self esteem. Making good the financial loss actually suffered may in such a case be adequate compensation. Even if there is any injury to feelings, the distress is likely to be less severe than with forms of discrimination which engage the core of a person's being. Of course, that is not to say that there may not be particular cases where such injury cannot be established, such as a non-unionist who for that reason suffers harassment in a trade union shop. But it ought not readily to be assumed that injury to feelings inevitably flows from each and every unlawful act of discrimination. In each case it is a question of considering the facts carefully to determine whether the loss has been sustained. Some persons discriminated against on trade union grounds may feel deeply hurt by that affront, particularly where union membership is an important feature of their lives; other more robust characters may consider it a matter of little consequence and suffer little, if any, distress. Since the aim is to compensate and not to punish, the compensation to be awarded ought not to be the same in each case.'

87 [2003] IRLR 402, [2003] UKEAT 1318_01_0602.

They then went on to consider the case before them in the light of the *Vento* guidelines and approved the tribunal's award of £5,000 for injury to feelings whilst stating that 'it was on the high side'.

CHAPTER 8

LIMITATION PERIODS AND OVERLAPPING CLAIMS

8.1 LIMITATION PERIOD: CLAIMS FOR PERSONAL INJURY IN COURT

The usual 3-year personal injury limitation period will apply.

It can, however, still sometimes prove a problem to ascertain the date of expiry of the limitation period because in many cases there will be a series of events stretching over a period of time. If the claimant is to recover compensation for damage caused by the earliest incidents, 'date of knowledge' and Limitation Act 1980, s 33 discretion arguments may need to be employed.

8.1.1 Three years

Section 11 of the Limitation Act 1980 (LA 1980) provides:

> '(1) This section applies to any action for damages for negligence, nuisance or breach of duty (whether the duty exists by virtue of a contract or of provision made by or under a statute or independently of any contract or any such provision) where the damages claimed by the plaintiff for the negligence, nuisance or breach of duty consist of or include damages in respect of personal injuries to the plaintiff or any other person.'

Instead of the usual 6-year limitation period for claims in contract or tort, s 11(4) provides:

> '(4) [except in the case of fatal accident claims], the period applicable is three years from—
> (a) the date on which the cause of action accrued; or
> (b) the date of knowledge (if later) of the person injured.'

Unlike accident claims, claims for stress at work rarely relate to a single incident but rather to a continuum. Also in many cases the claimant will not be immediately aware of the psychological effect of the stress and bullying. The provisions of s 11(4)(b) will therefore often be relevant.

8.1.2 Date of knowledge

Under s 14(1) of the LA 1980, 'date of knowledge' is defined as:

> '. . . in sections 11 and 12 of this Act references to a person's date of knowledge are references to the date on which he first had knowledge of the following facts—
> (a) that the injury in question was significant; and
> (b) that the injury was attributable in whole or in part to the act or omission which is alleged to constitute negligence, nuisance or breach of duty; and
> (c) the identity of the defendant; and
> (d) if it is alleged that the act or omission was that of a person other than the defendant, the identity of that person and the additional facts supporting the bringing of an action against the defendant;
>
> and knowledge that any acts or omissions did or did not, as a matter of law, involve negligence, nuisance or breach of duty is irrelevant.'

So far as 'significant' is concerned, s 14(2) of the LA 1980 provides:

> '(2) For the purposes of this section an injury is significant if the person whose date of knowledge is in question would reasonably have considered it sufficiently serious to justify his instituting proceedings for damages against a defendant who did not dispute liability and was able to satisfy a judgment.'

And as regards 'knowledge', s 14(3) of the LA 1980 provides:

> '(3) For the purposes of this section a person's knowledge includes knowledge which he might reasonably have been expected to acquire—
> (a) from facts observable or ascertainable by him; or
> (b) from facts ascertainable by him with the help of medical or other appropriate expert advice which it is reasonable for him to seek;
>
> but a person shall not be fixed under this subsection with knowledge of a fact ascertainable only with the help of expert advice so long as he has taken all reasonable steps to obtain (and, where appropriate, to act on) that advice.'

In *A v Hoare*[1] the House of Lords revisited the question of the appropriate limitation period in claims involving sexual assault and overturned their previous decision in *Stubbings v Webb*[2] that the limitation period was 6 years. As well as deciding that the appropriate limitation period was 3 years in all personal injury cases, the Lords also examined the meaning of 'date of knowledge' under s 14 of the LA 1980 and their comments are of relevance to all personal injury claims and not just sexual abuse cases.

---

1 [2008] UKHL 6, [2008] 2 WLR 311.
2 [1993] AC 498, 506.

The Lords put an end to arguments that the test of knowledge is entirely subjective, Lord Hoffmann saying:

> 'It follows that I cannot accept that one must consider whether someone "with [the] plaintiff's intelligence" would have been reasonable if he did not regard the injury as sufficiently serious. That seems to me to destroy the effect of the word "reasonably". Judges should not have to grapple with the notion of the reasonable unintelligent person. Once you have ascertained what the claimant knew and what he should be treated as having known, the actual claimant drops out of the picture. Section 14(2) is, after all, simply a standard of the seriousness of the injury and nothing more. Standards are in their nature impersonal and do not vary with the person to whom they are applied.'

And Lord Carswell agreed:

> 'It is in my opinion incorrect to import the circumstances, character or intelligence of the claimant into the determination of reasonableness under section 14(2). It is irrelevant whether the claimant is intelligent or unintelligent or whether his personal characteristics or his circumstances may influence his decision not to sue at that time. Some people are more robust than others and would shrug off the possibility of suing for the injury (a possibility more likely in the case of minor conditions than in the example I have given). Others may be temperamentally averse to making the effort to institute proceedings, or to appearing in court, or may be unable or unwilling to risk incurring the costs. Some may feel too ill to contemplate litigation. What is material in determining if the injury is significant within the meaning of subsection (2) is whether a reasonable person, possessed of the facts known or available to the claimant, would consider the injury sufficiently serious to justify instituting proceedings for damages, assuming that the defendant will not dispute liability and is able to satisfy a judgment. Under this construction of section 14 some claimants with merit on their side will undoubtedly fail, but those characteristics or circumstances to which I have referred can and should be taken into account in the exercise of the discretion under section 33 to disapply the limitation provisions, as I shall explain in more detail below.'

If the allegations are serious (as they usually will be, particularly in a bullying case), it will be difficult to persuade a court that the claimant did not have knowledge:

> 'The description of the assaults and indignities which the claimant says he suffered seem to me to put the matter beyond doubt ... On the true construction of section 14(2), I do not think that a later date can be justified.'

And the following alternative argument:

> '. . . that, even if the test which section 14(2) applied to the injury as known to the claimant was entirely impersonal, the claimant in this case could not be said to have had knowledge of his injury. This was because, according to

the evidence of the claimant, supported by an expert witness, he had "blocked out his memory", or, in another metaphor which he used in evidence, put his memories "in a box with a tightly sealed lid in the attic". He was, he said, "in denial" about the psychological injuries which he had suffered'

was also rejected:

> 'I do not doubt the value of these explanations of the claimant's mental processes when it comes to an assessment of whether he could reasonably have been expected to commence proceedings. But they are difficult enough concepts to apply in that context and I do not think that section 14(2) was intended to convert them into even more difficult questions of epistemology. If one asked an expert psychologist whether the claimant "really" knew about his injuries, I expect he would say that it depends on what you mean by "know". And he might go on to say that if the question was whether he "knew" for the purposes of the Limitation Act, it would be better to ask a lawyer. In my opinion the subsection assumes a practical and relatively unsophisticated approach to the question of knowledge and there seems to me to have been much sense in Lord Griffiths' observation in *Stubbings v Webb* [1993] AC 498, 506 that he had "the greatest difficulty in accepting that a woman who knows that she has been raped does not know that she has suffered a significant injury".'

However, in an appropriate case the court still has discretion to consider the circumstances of the individual claimant:

> 'This does not mean that the law regards as irrelevant the question of whether the actual claimant, taking into account his psychological state in consequence of the injury, could reasonably have been expected to institute proceedings. But it deals with that question under section 33, which specifically says in subsection (3)(a) that one of the matters to be taken into account in the exercise of the discretion is "the reasons for … the delay on the part of the plaintiff".
>
> In my opinion that is the right place in which to consider it. Section 33 enables the judge to look at the matter broadly and not have to decide the highly artificial question of whether knowledge which the claimant has in some sense suppressed counts as knowledge for the purposes of the Act. Furthermore, dealing with the matter under section 14(2) means that the epistemological question determines whether the claimant is entitled to sue as of right, without regard at any injustice which this might cause to the defendant. In my view it is far too brittle an instrument for this purpose.'

The issue of 'date of knowledge' in the context of a bullying at work case was considered in *Parchment v Secretary of State for Defence*[3] (albeit well prior to the decision in *Hoare*).

In *Parchment* the claimant was a soldier of mixed race with a black father and white mother. He absconded from his unit without leave. He was not

---

[3] (1998) QBD (J Griffiths Williams QC) LTL 23 February 98.

apprehended until 5 years later. He launched employment tribunal proceedings alleging extreme racist abuse and violence against him by other soldiers, but this was withdrawn because he was out of time.

Originally he was diagnosed as suffering from an adjustment disorder, but after his arrest and imprisonment he developed a major depressive illness with features of post-traumatic stress disorder. He then brought civil proceedings arguing that he only knew that he had suffered significant injury after his arrest, not 5 years earlier when he absconded as a result of the racist conduct.

However, in striking out his claim, the judge noted that between 1989 and 1994 he consulted various solicitors with a view to bringing proceedings and held that he must have been aware that he had suffered a significant injury as a result of the acts or omissions of the defendant.

8.1.3 Discretion

As a result of *Hoare*, the impact of the residual discretion of the court in personal injury cases becomes increasingly important. Section 33 of the LA 1980 provides:

> '(1) If it appears to the court that it would be equitable to allow an action to proceed having regard to the degree to which—
> (a) the provisions of section 11 ... of this Act prejudice the plaintiff or any person whom he represents; and
> (b) any decision of the court under this subsection would prejudice the defendant or any person whom he represents;
>
> the court may direct that those provisions shall not apply to the action, or shall not apply to any specified cause of action to which the action relates.'

And in s 33(3):

> '(3) In acting under this section the court shall have regard to all the circumstances of the case and in particular to—
> (a) the length of, and the reasons for, the delay on the part of the plaintiff;
> (b) the extent to which, having regard to the delay, the evidence adduced or likely to be adduced by the plaintiff or the defendant is or is likely to be less cogent than if the action had been brought within the time allowed by section 11 [F4, by section 11A] or (as the case may be) by section 12;
> (c) the conduct of the defendant after the cause of action arose, including the extent (if any) to which he responded to requests reasonably made by the plaintiff for information or inspection for the purpose of ascertaining facts which were or might be relevant to the plaintiff's cause of action against the defendant;
> (d) the duration of any disability of the plaintiff arising after the date of the accrual of the cause of action;

(e) the extent to which the plaintiff acted promptly and reasonably once he knew whether or not the act or omission of the defendant, to which the injury was attributable, might be capable at that time of giving rise to an action for damages;
(f) the steps, if any, taken by the plaintiff to obtain medical, legal or other expert advice and the nature of any such advice he may have received.'

Following the House of Lords decision in *Hoare,* the exercise of the discretion under s 33 has had to be reconsidered judicially. In *Hoare,* after the Lords judgment the case was remitted back to the High Court for consideration of the application of s 33 discretion. Coulson J held:[4]

> 'The parties before me are agreed that section 33 provides the court with a wide and unfettered discretion. In Nash v Eli Lilly and Co [1993] 1 WLR 782, at 802, the Court of Appeal said that "subject to acting judicially, the discretion of the court is entirely unfettered. The specific matters set out in sub-section (3) are exemplary and not definitive".'

He quoted from the House of Lords in *Horton v Sadler*:[5]

> 'In resolving an application under section 33, the court must make a decision of which the inevitable effect is either to deprive the defendant of an accrued statute-bar defence or to stifle the claimant's action against the tortfeasor who caused his personal injuries. In choosing between those outcomes the court must be guided by what appears to it to be equitable, which I take to mean no more (but also no less) than fair, and it must have regard to all the circumstances of the case and in particular the six matters listed in sub-section (3) . . .'

Coulson J pointed out that:

> 'It has been stressed that the court must take into account all of the circumstances specified in section 33(3), and indeed all the circumstances of the case relevant to its decision, and should conduct a balancing exercise in respect of them. A decision should not be reached on the strength of just one of the relevant circumstances: see Long v Tolchard and Sons Limited [2001] PIQR P18, 26, per Roch LJ.'

But the burden is on the claimant:

> 'The authorities make plain that the burden of showing that it would be equitable to disapply the limitation period rests with the claimant and that it is a heavy burden. In Thompson v Brown above, Lord Diplock pointed out that an order under section 33 was an exception to a general rule and that the onus of showing that, in the particular circumstances of the case, it would be equitable to make such an exception, lay upon the claimant. He reiterated, however, that, subject to this, the court's discretion to make or refuse an order if it considered it equitable to do so was unfettered'.

---

4 *A v H* [2008] EWHC 1573 (QB).
5 [2006] UKHL 27, [2007] 1 AC 307.

So far as length of delay is concerned:

> 'Depending on the issues in the action, and the evidence going to them, the longer the delay then the more likely, and the greater, the prejudice to the defendant: see Auld LJ in Bryn Alyn. Furthermore, in determining whether the primary limitation period should be disapplied, any delay on the part of the claimant, both before and after the expiration of the limitation period, must be considered: per Lord Oliver of Aylemerton in Donovan v Gwentoys [1990] 1 WLR 472, at 479D–480B.'

With regard to the reasons for the delay, the test is subjective. If the claimant has earlier decided not to proceed and has later simply changed his mind it will be difficult to persuade the court to exercise discretion.

In *Parchment v Secretary of State for Defence*[6] the claimant sought the exercise of the s 33 discretion and argued that he was effectively disbarred from bringing proceedings because he was a 'fugitive from the services' but the judge unsurprisingly said: 'I am unimpressed by that submission.'

8.1.4 Disability

If the claimant is a patient by reason of mental incapacity, s 28(1) of the LA 1980 provides that a period of limitation is suspended during the period of disability.

This will rarely apply in a stress or bullying case where even in the most extreme case the breakdown rarely leads to loss of mental capacity. However, it may be of use in a limited number of claims.

8.2 LIMITATION PERIOD: TRESPASS AND HARASSMENT UNDER THE PROTECTION FROM HARASSMENT ACT 1997 (PFHA 1997)

8.2.1 Trespass to person

In *A v Hoare*[7] the House of Lords overturned *Stubbings* and as Lord Hoffmann said:

> 'I therefore think that it would be right to depart from *Stubbings* and reaffirm the law laid down by the Court of Appeal in *Letang v Cooper* [1965] 1 QB 232.'

Lord Brown of Eaton-Under-Heywood expanded on the court's reasoning:

---

6 See **8.1.3**.

7 [2008] UKHL 6, [2008] 2 WLR 311.

> 'It was consistently held (initially in *Letang v Cooper* [1965] 1 QB 232, a case of accidental trespass to the person, then later in *Long v Hepworth* [1968] 1 WLR 1299, a case of intentional assault) that all such cases fell within the definition: all were actions for "breach of duty". The claims, therefore, having been brought outside the unextendable three-year period, were all statute-barred. That then was the position when Phase Three was introduced by the 1975 Act, only now, of course, that line of authority was ordinarily to the advantage of those claiming damages for assault because the shortened three-year time limit was extendable.
>
> And this continued to be everyone's understanding of the position until the House's decision in *Stubbings v Webb* [1993] AC 498 (28 years after *Letang v Cooper* and 18 years after the introduction of Phase Three) when for the first time it was held that an action for damages for personal injuries for an intentional trespass to the person fell, after all, outside the statutory definition.
>
> As to whether the House should now depart from its decision in *Stubbings v Webb*, I fully share Lord Hoffmann's view that it should . . .'

So, any claim for personal injury arising from stress or bullying at work and brought in respect of assault, trespass, intentional infliction of injury or otherwise (other than under the PFHA 1997) will as a result of *Hoare* now be subject to the 3-year limitation period as outlined in **8.1**.

8.2.2 Harassment under the PFHA 1997

However, if the claim is for personal injuries arising from harassment under the PFHA 1997 then *Hoare* does not apply as s 11(1A) of the LA 1980 expressly provides:

> '(1A) This section does not apply to any action brought for damages under section 3 of the Protection from Harassment Act 1997'

so that the 3-year period provided by s 11 does not apply. The limitation period is therefore 6 years, but there is no discretion to extend it under s 33 of the LA 1980.

8.3 TIME LIMIT FOR CLAIMS: UNFAIR DISMISSAL CLAIMS IN THE EMPLOYMENT TRIBUNAL

To establish the time limit for an unfair dismissal claim in the employment tribunal, it is first necessary to establish the 'effective date of termination'. Section 97(1) of the Employment Rights Act 1996 (ERA 1996) provides:

> '"the effective date of termination"—
>
> (a) in relation to an employee whose contract of employment is terminated by notice, whether given by his employer or by the employee, means the date on which the notice expires,

(b) in relation to an employee whose contract of employment is terminated without notice, means the date on which the termination takes effect, and
(c) in relation to an employee who is employed under a contract for a fixed term which expires without being renewed under the same contract, means the date on which the term expires.'

However, s 97(2) provides that if the contract is terminated by the employer on less notice than the employee is entitled to under statute,[8] then the effective date of termination is the expiry of the statutory notice period.

Section 111(2) of the ERA 1996 provides that:

'(2) . . . an employment tribunal shall not consider a complaint under this section unless it is presented to the tribunal—
(a) before the end of the period of three months beginning with the effective date of termination, or
(b) within such further period as the tribunal considers reasonable in a case where it is satisfied that it was not reasonably practicable for the complaint to be presented before the end of that period of three months.'

It is very difficult for the employee to establish that 'it was not reasonably practicable' to bring a claim within 3 months.[9]

Under the provisions of Employment Act 2002 (Dispute Resolution) Regulations 2004,[10] the claimant was required to commence a grievance procedure prior to issue of proceedings in the employment tribunal. However, such provisions were confusing and much criticised and are to be abolished with effect from 6 April 2009.

8.4 TIME LIMITS FOR CLAIMS: STATUTORY DISCRIMINATION CLAIMS IN THE EMPLOYMENT TRIBUNAL

The provisions relating to time limits are different for discrimination claims. Section 76(1) of the Sex Discrimination Act 1975, for example, provides:

'(1) An [employment tribunal] shall not consider a complaint under section 63 unless it is presented to the tribunal before the end of —
(a) the period of three months beginning when the act complained of was done . . .

---

8 ERA 1996, s 86(1) provides that an employee is entitled to one week's notice for each completed year of continuous employment up to a maximum of 12 weeks.

9 See *Harvey on Industrial Relations and Employment Law* (Lexis Nexis Butterworths, 1996) Division T.

10 SI 2004/752.

(5) A court or tribunal may nevertheless consider any such complaint, claim or application which is out of time if, in all the circumstances of the case, it considers that it is just and equitable to do so.

(6) For the purposes of this section—
(a) where the inclusion of any term in a contract renders the making of the contract an unlawful act that act shall be treated as extending throughout the duration of the contract, and
(b) any act extending over a period shall be treated as done at the end of that period, and
(c) a deliberate omission shall be treated as done when the person in question decided upon it,

and in the absence of evidence establishing the contrary a person shall be taken for the purposes of this section to decide upon an omission when he does an act inconsistent with doing the omitted act or, if he has done no such inconsistent act, when the period expires within which he might reasonably have been expected to do the omitted act if it was to be done.'

So, in the case of discrimination claims, the tribunal has the discretion to allow applications received after 3 months if it is 'just and equitable' to do so, rather than the 'reasonable practicability' test required for unfair dismissal claims.[11]

However, the application of this test in practice, particularly in the case of a series of acts of discrimination with reliance on a 'last straw', is often complex.[12]

8.5 OVERLAPPING CLAIMS

At first sight, having several potential causes of action might appear to be good news for the claimant. However, in practice the lawyer has to make a quick decision as to whether to advise the client to pursue a claim for psychiatric injury in the court or in the employment tribunal. An inappropriate decision can lead to a potential cause of action being permanently lost.

The main issues to consider are:

- where there are identical causes of action (eg breach of contract);
- where there are overlapping causes of action (eg discrimination and common law claims for bullying and harassment);
- the extent of the *Johnson* exclusion zone (especially in constructive dismissal cases);

[11] See **8.3**.
[12] See *Harvey on Industrial Relations and Employment Law* (Lexis Nexis Butterworths, 1996) Division T.

- when the principle of res judicata applies;
- whether multiple claims arising from the same facts is an abuse of process; and
- whether claims can be effectively withdrawn from one forum for litigation in another.

8.5.1 Discrimination and personal injury claims

There is an overlap between the awards for injury to feelings in discrimination claims and damages for psychiatric injury. In a case involving harassment it is important to consider whether or not tribunal proceedings for sex/race discrimination should be brought instead of a personal injury claim.

In *Sheriff v Klyne Tugs (Lowestoft) Ltd*[13] the claimant suffered race discrimination. He was a Muslim who suffered from extreme racial abuse from his work colleagues, including being forced to eat pork. He suffered a nervous breakdown. He was dismissed. He brought a claim for unfair dismissal and race discrimination (including a claim for compensation for 'injuries to feelings') in the employment tribunal. He settled 'all claims which he has or may have against the respondent arising out of his employment or the termination thereof being claims in respect of which an Industrial tribunal has jurisdiction' using the standard COT3 procedure. He then sought to bring a personal injury claim in the county court for psychiatric injury caused by the racial abuse during his employment. The county court judge struck out the claim as an abuse of process.

The Court of Appeal dismissed Mr Sheriff's appeal. They ruled that the compensation for injuries to feelings in a discrimination claim in the employment tribunal included within it the claim for psychiatric injury:

> 'Although the Act creates a statutory tort, it is one that can only be enforced in accordance with the provisions of the Act (1976 Act s.53 (1)). Thus complaints under Part II in relation to employment must be presented to the Employment Tribunal (s.54(1)). It is an exclusive jurisdiction. Complaints under Part III must be brought in designated county courts. This is provided by s.57 of the Act . . .
>
> In my judgment both the Employment Tribunal under s56 and the County Court under s57 have jurisdiction to award damages for the tort of racial discrimination including damages for personal injury caused by the tort. The question, which may be a difficult one, is one of causation. It follows that care needs to be taken in any complaint to an Employment Tribunal under this head where the claim includes, or might include, injury to health as well

13 [1999] ICR 1170, [1999] IRLR 481, (1999) 143 SJLB 189, CA.

as injury to feelings. A complainant and his advisers may well wish in those circumstances to heed the advice of the editors of Harvey, just referred to, to obtain a medical report. This has particular relevance as the time within which to make a complaint is only 3 or 6 months and, unless an adjournment is obtained, an adjudication may follow quite shortly.'

The compromise of a race discrimination case in respect of 'all matters capable of being brought before the Tribunal' meant that a subsequent personal injury case for psychiatric injury caused by bullying must be struck out as an abuse of process as the client had been fully compensated by the sum paid to settle the tribunal claim. Having decided to commence employment tribunal proceedings, he had to bring all his claims before the employment tribunal and, having settled them, he was precluded from pursuing his psychiatric injury claim in the county court.

The Court of Appeal stated:

> 'I do not think this is a case of res judicata in the strict sense, because the cause of action is not the same in both proceedings. However, the principle applies to matters which could have been raised in previous proceedings, but were not. In *Henderson v Henderson* (1843) 3 Hare 100 Wigram V-C at p114–115 said:
>
> > "In trying this question, I believe I state the rule of the court correctly, when I say, that where a given matter becomes the subject of litigation in, and of adjudication by, a court of competent jurisdiction, the court requires the parties to that litigation to bring forward their whole case, and will not (except under special circumstances) permit the same parties to open the same subject of litigation in respect of matter which might have been brought forward as part of the subject in contest, but which was not brought forward, only because they have, from negligence, inadvertence, or even accident, omitted part of their case. The plea of res judicata applies, except in special cases, not only to points upon which the court was actually required by the parties to form an opinion and pronounce a judgment, but to every point which properly belonged to the subject of litigation, and which the parties, exercising reasonable diligence, might have brought forward at the time."
>
> This principle was applied in the case of *Talbot v Berkshire County Council* [1994] QB 290. After citing it, I said at p296D:
>
> > "The rule is thus in two parts. The first relates to those points which were actually decided by the court; this is res judicata in the strict sense. Secondly, those which might have been brought forward at the time, but were not. The second is not a true case of res judicata but rather is founded on the principle of public policy in preventing multiplicity of actions, it being in the public interest that there should be an end to litigation; the court will stay or strike out the subsequent action as an abuse of process: per Lord Wilberforce in *Brisbane City Council v Attorney-General for Queensland* [1979] AC 411, 425G.

> . . . In my judgment there is no reason why the rule in Henderson's case should not apply in personal injury actions. Indeed there is every reason why it should. It is a salutary rule. It avoids unnecessary proceedings involving expense to the parties and waste of court time which could be available to others, it prevents stale claims being brought long after the event, which is the bane of this type of litigation; it enables the defendant to know the extent of his potential liability in respect of any one event; this is important for insurance companies who have to make provision for claims and it may also affect their conduct of negotiations, their defence and any question of appeal."'

The court concluded:

> 'The principle applies in this case. The same issue of the conduct of the master of the Respondent's vessel lies at the heart of both the proceedings in the Employment Tribunal and the County Court action, although in the latter the Appellant assumes the additional burden of proving negligence. For the reasons I have already given, the Appellant could have brought forward his whole claim for compensation in the Tribunal. He did not do so.'

And the Court of Appeal did not think that the claimant could establish 'special circumstances' to avoid the rule in *Henderson's* case. The claimant argued that these included:

> '(a) the different limitation period and in particular the very short period in the Employment Tribunal.
> (b) different cost provisions; an applicant in the Employment Tribunal is not usually awarded costs. This may be a disadvantage to a claimant with a heavy claim.
> (c) the procedure in the court is more suitable for trying a complex personal injury claim.
> (d) there is no facility for interim payments or provisional damages in the Employment Tribunal.
> (e) the expertise of the Employment Tribunal does not lie in the field of adjudication on perhaps difficult questions of psychiatric injury.'

However, the court was not persuaded and concluded:

> 'The principle of public policy is that claims that have been or could have been litigated in one tribunal, should not be allowed to be litigated in another.'

The Court of Appeal did concede that:

> 'What might be a special reason would be if the claimant's condition had not come to light at the time the earlier proceedings were concluded. That is not the position here. Although the Appellant's condition may not have been formally diagnosed as post traumatic stress disorder by October 1995, it is

clear that he was complaining of anxiety and depression from February 1995 and continuing. This was not mere injury to feelings, but was the essence of his psychiatric injury.'

In *Johnson v Awe plc*,[14] however, the EAT held that the settlement of a personal injury action did not give rise to issue estoppel in respect of a claim in the employment tribunal for disability discrimination and a failure to make reasonable adjustments. The claimant had suffered from ankylosing spondylitis. He had been injured in an accident at work which exacerbated the condition. After the accident his employer had terminated his employment on the grounds of ill health 2 years before his retirement age. He brought a personal injury claim which was settled by a normal form of consent order. He also brought a claim for disability discrimination in the employment tribunal alleging that if his employer had made reasonable adjustments to his job, he could have continued to work until retirement age. The employment tribunal struck out the disability discrimination claim on the grounds of issue estoppel. The EAT disagreed. The effect of the consent order had been to discharge the employer from further liability in respect of negligence connected with the accident and breach of statutory duties under health and safety legislation. The claim was sent back to a new employment tribunal to consider whether the employer had failed to make reasonable adjustments, but not to allow double compensation if it considered that the claimant had already received compensation for those items in the personal injury claim or if those heads of loss were themselves subject to issue estoppel.

8.5.2 Non-discrimination tribunal claims and personal injury

8.5.2.1 Breach of contract and personal injury

There is a concurrent jurisdiction between the employment tribunal and the court for breach of contract claims. However, the jurisdiction of the employment tribunal is limited to claims up to £25,000. This can cause a problem in stress and bullying cases where the employee has initiated such a claim in the employment tribunal and then realises that he seeks more substantial compensation.

It is possible to 'withdraw' employment tribunal proceedings. However, such a request will probably bring about the standard employment tribunal order 'claim dismissed upon the application of the Applicant'. This is potentially disastrous for the claimant, because the claims for compensation for psychiatric injury will have been technically 'decided' by the employment tribunal and dismissed for no compensation, preventing the claims from being litigated in the county court. To avoid this, it must be made clear that this is a withdrawal, not a request for a decision. If an

---

[14] EAT (Bean J) LTL 27 June 2008.

order to dismiss is still made, the employee should immediately apply to the employment tribunal chairman for a review.

In *Sajid v Sussex Muslim Society*,[15] Dr Sajid was dismissed and brought a claim for unfair dismissal and breach of contract in the employment tribunal. However, Dr Sajid withdrew the breach of contract claim from the tribunal because it might exceed the £25,000 maximum that could be awarded in the tribunal (he was claiming £72,053.12). On the ET1 form Dr Sajid added:

> 'This claim is made recognising that the Industrial Tribunal has jurisdiction up to a claim of £25,000 in relation to breach of contract claims and I, therefore, reserve the right to rely upon the findings of the Tribunal as res judicata in proceedings in another Court to recover the balance.'

The following week Dr Sajid issued a claim for breach of contract in the High Court and shortly afterwards the employment tribunal issued a decision:

> 'The breach of contract claim is dismissed on withdrawal by the applicant.'

Some months later the claims of Dr Sajid in the employment tribunal were settled on terms recorded in a unanimous decision signed by the chairman whereby the employer agreed to pay a sum of £6,500 to Dr Sajid in full and final settlement of all the claims and matters before the employment tribunal. Dr Sajid then sought to pursue his contractual claims in the High Court, but was faced with an application to strike out on the grounds of abuse of process and/or res judicata. The Court of Appeal allowed Dr Sajid's claim to proceed:

> 'The Employment Tribunal is a creature of statute exercising exclusive jurisdiction over causes of action, such as unfair dismissal and sex, race and disability discrimination. It has only recently acquired a limited jurisdiction over common law claims, such as breach of contract or wrongful dismissal brought by an employee against a former employer. Claims in excess of the limit of £25,000 in the Employment Tribunal must still be brought in the ordinary courts. There is, so far as counsel have been able to ascertain, no procedure in the Civil Procedure Rules or the Employment Tribunal Regulations providing for the transfer of claims from the Employment Tribunal to the ordinary courts or vice versa. There is no option but to start a fresh case or to make a fresh application in order to ensure that proceedings are brought for determination in the appropriate forum. The order of 5th May 1999 was made in this context.
>
> It would not expose the society to any injustice but it would inflict injustice on Dr Sajid, because it would prevent him having his claim determined on its merits, which it had not been in the Employment Tribunal. The consequence of this appeal succeeding would be that Dr Sajid could not

15 [2001] EWCA Civ 1684, [2001] IRLR 113.

> pursue his claim in the Employment Tribunal, because of the order of 6th May 1999, and he could not pursue his claim in the High Court or the County Court because – Mr Rogers says – of the effect of the order made on 6th May. So by a neat, technical swipe the society would have eliminated a substantial claim without any tribunal or court having heard any evidence or argument about it. That seems to be a decision to which this court is not driven by any principle of cause of action estoppel.'

However, the withdrawal of the contractual claim from the employment tribunal must be clear and unequivocal. In *Sivanandan v Enfield London Borough Council*[16] the employee had brought proceedings in the employment tribunal for race discrimination and victimisation under the Race Relations Act 1976, unfair dismissal, breach of contract and sex discrimination under the Sex Discrimination Act 1975. These claims were struck out after the employee had not attended the employment tribunal hearing on the grounds of ill health, but the tribunal had refused to allow her further postponements.

In this case there had never been a formal order for withdrawal of the breach of contract claim. The employee had said that she had withdrawn it orally at an employment tribunal hearing and sought to rely on her own notes, but the Court of Appeal held:

> 'In the light of these authorities, I have come to the clear conclusion that on the facts of this case Ms Sivanandan's claim for breach of contract was not withdrawn from the Employment Tribunal. It was therefore struck out with the remainder of her claims on 6 September 2000. It is, accordingly, res judicata and cannot be revived.
>
> It is, of course, the case that the Employment Tribunal never adjudicated on the merits of Ms Sivanandan's breach of contract claim, nor did it adjudicate on the extent to which it would permit her to pursue it. However, it had held on 23 January 1998 that it had jurisdiction to entertain the claim. That decision was not appealed and remained extant on 5 September 2000. In my judgment, therefore, the breach of contract claim was never withdrawn and was dismissed by the Employment Tribunal on 6 September 2000.'

The Court stressed:

> '. . . if a claim is to be withdrawn from the Employment Tribunal on the basis that it is to be pursued elsewhere, as in Sajid, the position must be made clear, and it would be desirable for the Employment Tribunal to adjudicate by making an order dismissing the claim on withdrawal. That would mean that either on the face of the order itself, or in the record kept by the Employment Tribunal, there would be unambiguous evidence of the circumstances in which, and the reasons for which, the application was withdrawn. In my judgment, expressions of intent are insufficient. It is of the utmost importance that the issues on which an Employment Tribunal is

[16] [2005] EWCA Civ 10, [2005] All ER (D) 169 (Jan), (2005) *The Times*, 25 January.

being asked to adjudicate are clearly defined, and good practice requires that if a claim is to be withdrawn, both the fact that it is being withdrawn and the reasons for its withdrawal should be clear.'

So far as abuse of process was concerned, the Court of Appeal also distinguished *Sivanandan* from *Sajid*:

> 'In my judgment, the two critical distinctions between the instant case and Sajid (apart from the fact that in Sajid there was a formal order dismissing the breach of contract claim on withdrawal) are, in the abuse context, (1) that the facts underlying Ms Sivanandan's claim for racial discrimination and victimisation were the same as those underlying any claim for damages based on breaches of her contract of employment; and (2) that the Employment Tribunal had jurisdiction on her claims under RRA 1976 to award Ms Sivanandan unlimited damages. In my judgment, it was immaterial that in the Employment Tribunal Ms Sivanandan could not claim unfair dismissal. If the Employment Tribunal had found that she had been racially discriminated against, or that the racial victimisation had taken the form of improperly suspending and dismissing her, any damages for either breach of contract or unfair dismissal based on a breach of a statutory obligation would have been subsumed under the claim under RRA 1976.
>
> For these reasons, the instant case to my mind is closer to Sheriff than Sajid. If Ms Sivanandan's claim in the Employment Tribunal had proceeded to a hearing, and had Ms Sivanandan established race discrimination and victimisation in the manner of her treatment and dismissal by Enfield, those claims would have embraced the claims relating to breach of contract, and she would have recovered appropriate, and unlimited, damages.'

8.5.2.2 Unfair dismissal and personal injury

In *McCabe v (1) Cornwall County Council (2) Governing Body of Mounts Bay School*[17] the Court of Appeal described the issue which they had to determine:

> 'This is an appeal by Mr. Robert Jocelyn McCabe against an order of His Hon. Judge Overend on 31st May 2002, sitting as a High Court Judge in Exeter, refusing him permission to amend his statement of claim by substitution of a new claim and striking out his claim as disclosing no cause of action. The proceedings arise out of an original claim by Mr. McCabe, a teacher employed by the Respondents, for damages for psychiatric injury in respect of events leading up to and arising out of their dismissal of him. By his proposed amendment, Mr. McCabe sought to substitute and limit his claim to damages for breach of an implied contractual duty of mutual trust and confidence and/or in negligence in respect of their suspension and manner of investigation of his conduct prior to dismissal.'

---

17 [2002] EWCA Civ 1887, [2003] ICR 501, [2003] IRLR 87, [2003] PIQR P19.

In early May 1993 a number of girl pupils made complaints against the employee of inappropriate sexual conduct. He was suspended a few days later and was interviewed a week later. In the interview the head teacher gave him no details of the allegations, but suggested a formal written warning, which the employee declined to accept. He remained suspended but nearly 4 months elapsed before he learned of the allegations made against him and he began to suffer from a psychiatric illness. Three disciplinary hearings took place over the following 3 years. He applied to the employment tribunal:

> 'Three months later, in November 1996, an industrial tribunal heard Mr. McCabe's complaint of unfair dismissal, and, in December 1996, upheld it. It did so because the manner of dismissal was in breach of the Respondents' disciplinary procedures in that a senior member of the School's staff had not promptly investigated the matter and that all but one of the written statements attributed to the complainants were unsigned. The tribunal deferred a decision as to contributory fault and as to the amount of compensation to be awarded in order to give the parties an opportunity to settle the matter. At an adjourned hearing in April 1997 the tribunal ordered payment to Mr. McCabe of compensation of £11,000, the then maximum sum awardable under the statutory scheme, but found him to be contributorily at fault to the extent of 20%. On appeal by both parties to the Employment Appeal Tribunal, the Tribunal upheld the finding of unfair dismissal but quashed the finding of contributory negligence.'

In the meantime the employer had commenced these proceedings in the High Court seeking damages for psychiatric illness in contract caused by the employer's conduct of the disciplinary procedure leading up to his dismissal and in tort caused by such procedure and by the dismissal itself. This claim was subsequently amended to delete claims relating to the dismissal as a result of *Johnson*.[18] The Court of Appeal allowed the High Court claim to continue:

> 'As to the suggested similarity of the claims before the industrial tribunal and that now sought to be made in these proceedings, I should caution against such comparisons of the "substance" of the claim in the two jurisdictions. There may be sound policy and conceptual reasons for looking for a certain and "tidy" outcome, that is, of avoidance of overlap between compensation for unfair dismissal and common law damages for breach of duty associated with and prior to it. I have in mind the concerns expressed by Lord Hoffmann in Johnson at paragraphs 47-50 of his speech as to difficulties of attribution in causation and to the open-ended nature of a common law liability in this context. I also have in mind the problems for the claimant in having to separate his claims, that is, to bring his statutory claim first, within the three months time limit permitted for it, and the common law claim second, albeit with the greater latitude of the three years limit for personal injury claims, for additional loss not flowing from his dismissal but from his employer's unlawful conduct prior and leading to it. However, the other side of the coin may be that the tribunal may not award all the

[18] *Johnson v Unisys Ltd* [2001] UKHL 13, [2003] 1 AC 518 – see **2.4.3.3**.

compensation claimed before it because it does not regard it as a consequence of the "dismissal" and/or its possible maximum award under the legislation may not, in any event, be sufficient to cover the seriousness of the loss caused by such conduct. In such a circumstance, unless there is some scope for appropriately separate treatment of the two forms of claim, a claimant could be left without adequate remedy in either jurisdiction for loss attributable to prior unlawful conduct which, but for the supervening dismissal, would have been available to him at common law.

I should add, that to identify any offending overlap or exclusion of liability by reference to how the case was put before a tribunal or as to the basis of the tribunal's award is not, in my view, a logical or permissible way in which to determine whether a common law claim survives the fact of termination of employment. The facts on which the common law claim turns are for the court to decide, not a tribunal. And the existence of a common law entitlement does not, or should not, depend on whether the claimant has in fact made a claim to a tribunal for compensation for unfair dismissal, or, if he has, how he framed the claim or how the tribunal characterised it and dealt with it. Such matters may be relevant to an assessment of the credibility or other reliability of his evidence in the common law claim, but that is all – and rarely, if at all, at the strike-out stage. It may be – and I express no view on this – that if he has succeeded in obtaining a compensatory award from a tribunal, the extent and make-up of the award could have some bearing on the amount of damages, if any, which he could recover in a common law claim, if only to prevent inadvertent double recovery. But that is a different question from the survival of a separate and discrete common law remedy notwithstanding recovery for unfair dismissal before a tribunal. I do not understand Peter Gibson LJ's reference to such matters in paragraphs 24 and 25 of his judgment in Eastwood and Williams (see para. 14 above) in support of the view of the judge below to be part of the ratio of his decision.

In any event, there is a wider point of principle that the existence of a common law claim in any given case should not depend on the chance that an employer chooses not to terminate the contract by dismissal or that an employee chooses not to treat his employer's improper conduct as amounting to constructive dismissal. In the latter circumstance, the extent of the common law right would leave the employee with a dilemma that surely the legislature cannot have contemplated – still less have intended – of requiring him to choose early in the piece between accepting constructive dismissal and losing his common law claim or retaining his common law claim and losing his statutory entitlement for unfair dismissal. Such a dilemma could produce great injustice in cases where there has been a malicious attempt by an employer to force constructive dismissal. Mr. Mawhinney, in argument, recognised such a dilemma sub silentio when acknowledging that, if there had been no dismissal in the present case, there might well have been a claim actionable at common law.

For all those reasons, I am of the view that the Judge wrongly struck out this claim as disclosing no cause of action and that he should have allowed the matter to proceed on the proposed amended statement of case, leaving it to

> the trial judge to determine the matter in accordance with the law as indicated, so far, by the authorities and on the particular facts of the case. I would accordingly allow the appeal.'

The employer appealed to the House of Lords in an appeal that was conjoined with that of *Eastwood & Williams v Magnox Electric plc.*[19] The Lords dismissed the employer's appeal as the claim fell outside the Johnson exclusion zone, Lord Nicholls saying:

> 'It follows from what is set out above that I would dismiss the appeal in Mr McCabe's case and allow the appeals of Mr Eastwood and Mr Williams. In the case of all three men the assumed facts constitute causes of action which accrued before the dismissals. They disclose reasonable causes of action which should proceed to trial.'

However, in *Jones v Caerphilly County Borough Council*[20] the court held that a finding of fact in the employment tribunal with regard to whether there had been a breach of the implied term of mutual confidence was binding on the court by way of issue estoppel. The employee had brought a grievance alleging bullying at work. She had been suspended and whilst suspended someone else had been appointed to her job. She resigned and claimed constructive dismissal. The employment tribunal held that she had been unfairly dismissed and awarded her the statutory maximum in compensation. She then issued county court proceedings for damages for breach of the implied term of trust and confidence. The employer said that she was arguing the same conduct to show breaches of the implied term of trust and confidence that she had relied upon before the tribunal as cumulatively amounting to a fundamental breach of contract leading to her resignation and claim for constructive dismissal for which she had been compensated in the employment tribunal.

The county court judge struck out the claim, holding that the claim fell within the *Johnson* exclusion zone as the extent of this had been determined by the employment tribunal:

> 'As a jurisdictional matter it would have been possible for Mrs Jones to have chosen the courts as opposed to an employment tribunal, to have adjudicated upon the scope of the Johnson exclusion zone in her case. Although the time for bringing a claim in the tribunal is short, it was open to her to have commenced proceedings in both and then sought a stay of the tribunal proceedings pending determination of the relevant issues in this court. In those circumstances, the findings of this court as to scope of that zone would have been binding on the tribunal. That course would have maintained her claim for unfair dismissal, insofar as this court might have found that there was compensatable pre-dismissal conduct. However, she

19 [2004] UKHL 35. See further **2.4.3.3**.

20 (Unreported) 7 April 2006, Cardiff County Court, HHJ Hickinbottom LTL, 30 August 2006.

> chose an employment tribunal to determine the scope of the zone and, it having done so, she cannot now ask this court to revisit the findings of the tribunal.'

However, as a first instance county court judgment, this case is not binding and might perhaps be doubted as its reasoning is inconsistent with the principle set out by the Court of Appeal in *McCabe* which was affirmed by the House of Lords in dismissing the employer's appeal from that decision. It should be recognised, however, that determining the extent of the *Johnson* 'exclusion zone' is never easy.

8.5.3 Jurisdiction

If the claim is brought against an employer who is immune from suit, such as an embassy, the concurrent jurisdiction of employment tribunal and the court for psychiatric injury caused by discriminatory bullying and harassment can be useful in providing a remedy.

In *Kuwait v Caramba-Coker*[21] the employee was able to pursue a claim for personal injuries in either the court or tribunal. The employer as an embassy was exempt from the jurisdiction of the tribunal for wrongful dismissal or unfair dismissal claims through immunity from suit under the State Immunity Act 1978. However, claims for personal injury are excluded from the immunity under the provisions of the Act. The EAT held that an award for injury to feelings would fall within the state immunity, but not an award for personal injury caused by the discrimination.

[21] EAT LTL 10 April 2003.

CHAPTER 9

SICK PAY AND INCOME PROTECTION BENEFIT

9.1 CONTRACTUAL SICK PAY

In most stress at work cases the claimant will have to take time off work through ill-health. This is frequently protracted prior to dismissal or resignation. This absence will usually lead to a loss of income before any legal proceedings are brought or contemplated. It is therefore essential to ascertain the claimant's right to sick pay.

The starting point is the claimant's contract of employment. There is no obligation on an employer to provide under the contract of employment for payment of sick pay[1] at all. However, many employers will do so, but it is important to read the contractual provisions carefully to ascertain the employee's rights.

In some cases the right to sick pay for a certain period of absence is set out in the contract – typically this will be a period (perhaps 6 months) at full pay followed by a further period at reduced (often half) pay before the contractual entitlement ceases. This is nowadays a generous entitlement and is rarely found outside the public and 'not for profit' sectors.

In the private sector, the entitlement might sometimes dovetail with an income protection benefit scheme provided by a third party insurer (which typically pays out after 3 or, more usually, 6 months absence from work through ill-health). There is sometimes a contractual right to full sick pay up to the date on which income protection benefit is payable to provide continuity of income.

More commonly (whether or not there is also an income protection benefit policy), the contract will provide for a shorter period of paid sick leave as a contractual entitlement with payment beyond that time being made at the discretion of the employer. The employer must exercise the discretion rationally, in good faith[2] and on non-discriminatory grounds. However, subject to those caveats, discretionary contractual sick pay is

---

1 But see **9.2** for a discussion of the right to statutory sick pay.

2 *Cantor Fitzgerald International v Horkulak* [2004] EWCA Civ 1287.

discretionary and the employee's remedies are limited if the employer chooses not to exercise its discretion.

If the employer has wrongfully withheld contractual sick pay the simplest remedy is a complaint to the employment tribunal in respect of unlawful deduction from wages.[3] Similarly, if the employee believes that the employer has wrongfully exercised his discretion so as not to pay, then this route can also be employed.

Normally, an employer is required to take a medical certificate at face value. In *Merseyrail Electrics 2002 Ltd v Taylor*[4] the Employment Appeal Tribunal (EAT) upheld the employee's complaint of unlawful deduction from her wages. The contractual term in this case stated:

> 'Payment [of sick pay] may also be withheld if there is any doubt that the absence is due to reasons other than health or personal accident which prevents the employee from undertaking any duty for which they are competent to perform.'

The EAT held that in the light of the medical certificate and in the context of the express contractual term, the employer was not entitled to substitute its own judgment that the employee was not really ill. The EAT considered:

> '. . . the court of appeal decision in *Teinaz v London Borough of Wandsworth* [2002] IRLR 721. That is, as Mr Pitt-Payne points out, a different case on its facts. The question there was whether an employment tribunal had erred, in refusing an adjournment to a party who did not attend the tribunal on the date fixed for the hearing, but instead put in a medical note advising him not to work nor attend court for the relevant period.
>
> The Court of Appeal made observations on the significance of a medical certificate, but in the absence of any contradictory medical evidence, the thrust of the decision is that in that case a tribunal should not go behind what appears on the face of the medical certificate. In my view, that principle applies equally in construing this contractual terms. It was not open, once that medical certificate had come in, for the Respondent to maintain any doubt as to the reason for absence in the absence of any contradictory medical evidence. Accordingly, for these reasons, I shall dismiss this appeal.'

However, where there has been bullying and harassment and the employee has been off on long-term sick leave, the employee is not entitled to require the employer to move his place of employment or place other unreasonable demands and expect to continue to be paid.[5] In *Luke v Stoke on Trent City Council*:[6]

---

3 ERA 1996, s 13.

4 *Merseyrail Electrics 2002 Ltd v Taylor* [2007] UKEAT 0162_07_1805.

5 But note the right to request reasonable adjustments under the DDA 1995 – see **5.4.2**.

6 [2007] EWCA Civ 761, [2007] ICR 1678, [2007] IRLR 777.

> 'Mrs Luke said that she was the victim of bullying and harassment involving her Head Teacher, Mrs Chambers, who had raised a number of potential disciplinary issues against Mrs Luke. Mrs Luke was off sick with stress between October 2002 and April 2003. It was agreed that she would not return to the ACE Centre until her allegations had been investigated.'

The council commissioned an independent report and made certain changes as a result, but the employee refused to return to work. The Court of Appeal commented:

> 'The Council did all that it reasonably could to investigate the allegations, utilising the services of an external investigator, Mrs Carol Chadwick. It deferred the disciplinary procedure issues until after the investigation. Mrs Chadwick delivered her report on 23 April 2003 (the Chadwick Report). She upheld one of Mrs Luke's complaints and dismissed the remaining 32. The Chadwick Report contained "an Action Plan" involving the use of a mediator designed to get Mrs Luke back into work at the ACE Centre.
>
> The Council was willing to implement the Action Plan consistent with its duties to Mrs Luke and her colleagues. Over the next 10 months the Council, through its officials Mr Penny and Mr Cartlidge (Assistant Director of Support Services), tried to find a solution. The problem was that, although Mrs Luke said that she was willing to follow the Action Plan, she also said that she was not willing to accept the substance of the Chadwick Report, which she felt undermined her in a number of respects.'

The EAT had sought to imply a term into the contract of employment that the employee would act reasonably in this respect. Whilst dismissing the employee's appeal, Mummery LJ said that this implied term was unnecessary:

> 'This was a straightforward case of "no work, no pay": no work at the ACE Centre, no pay under the ACE Contract. It was not necessary for the employment tribunal or for the EAT to imply a further term into the ACE Contract to cover this situation. The ACE Contract covered the situation at the ACE Centre. It did not cease to cover the situation by reason of the Council's efforts to find her work outside the ACE Centre, while she was not teaching there.
>
> To sum up, whether a term should be implied along the lines favoured by the employment tribunal or along the lines preferred by the EAT was irrelevant in this case. It was apparent from the findings of the employment tribunal that, without the implication of any term, the Council was not obliged to continue to pay Mrs Luke for not working at the ACE Centre. She was not performing any work for the Council under the ACE Contract. Contrary to the reasonable stance taken by the Council she would not accept the Chadwick Report. Had she chosen to comply with the Council's reasonable position she could have returned to the ACE Centre and the Action Plan could have been implemented. She would have been back at work and there has never been any dispute that she would then have been entitled to be paid for her work.'

9.2 STATUTORY SICK PAY

An employer is obliged to pay statutory sick pay (SSP) for a maximum of 28 weeks over a period of 3 years to an employee who is absent from work as the result of sickness.[7]

Until 1994 the employer recouped most of the cost from the state and therefore merely acted as the state's agent in the payment of benefit. After 1994 the liability to pay SSP is that of the employer. If the employer has promised to pay more than the SSP under contractual arrangements with the employee, then the employer will top up the SSP to reach the contractual sum.

There is no entitlement to SSP for the first 3 days of absence. Thereafter the employer is obliged to pay the prescribed amount.[8]

The employee is required to notify the employer that he is unfit for work, this is usually by means of a medical certificate for a period exceeding 7 days. The employer is entitled to require medical evidence for period of sickness exceeding 7 days, but not for less unless expressly provided for in the contract of employment.

9.3 ON PAYROLL WITHOUT PAY

An employee can remain as an employee 'on the payroll' but receive no pay. Indeed this is commonly the case with an employee in receipt of income protection benefit where it is usually a policy requirement that the employee remains employed.

However, the doctrine of frustration should not be overlooked. If an employee remains unable to perform the job because of ill health and neither party brings the contract to an end, the contract might be discharged by the contractual doctrine of frustration, although as is stated in *Chitty on Contracts*:[9]

> 'It may be that permanent incapacity alone will not suffice to frustrate the contract of employment, on the basis that the contract may itself, exceptionally, envisage the possibility that the employee will continue to be employed notwithstanding the fact that he or she is suffering a permanent incapacity.'

---

7 By various statutory provisions which are now largely consolidated in the Social Security and Benefits Act 1992.

8 £75.40 per week until 5 April 2009.

9 *Chitty on Contracts* (Thomson Reuters Legal Limited, 30th edn, 2008) Chapter 23-038, footnote 171.

9.4 NOTICE

At the time his employment terminates, the employee in a stress at work case is commonly on sick leave and may be receiving a reduced salary or no salary at all. The amount that is due in respect of the notice period depends upon an interaction between contractual terms and the statutory provisions for periods of notice.

Section 88 of the Employment Rights Act 1996 (ERA 1996) provides for minimum periods of notice (one week's notice for each completed year of service, up to a maximum of 12 weeks) to be incorporated into contracts of employment. Section 87 of the ERA 1996 provides:

> '(1) If an employer gives notice to terminate the contract of employment of a person who has been continuously employed for one month or more, the provisions of sections 88 to 91 have effect as respects the liability of the employer for the period of notice required by section 86(1).
>
> (2) If an employee who has been continuously employed for one month or more gives notice to terminate his contract of employment, the provisions of sections 88 to 91 have effect as respects the liability of the employer for the period of notice required by section 86(2).
>
> (3) In sections 88 to 91 "period of notice" means—
> (a) where notice is given by an employer, the period of notice required by section 86(1), and
> (b) where notice is given by an employee, the period of notice required by section 86(2).'

And by virtue of s 88 of the ERA 1996:

> '(1) If an employee has normal working hours under the contract of employment in force during the period of notice and during any part of those normal working hours—
> (a) the employee is ready and willing to work but no work is provided for him by his employer,
> (b) the employee is incapable of work because of sickness or injury,
> (c) the employee is absent from work wholly or partly because of pregnancy or childbirth, or
> (d) the employee is absent from work in accordance with the terms of his employment relating to holidays,
>
> the employer is liable to pay the employee for the part of normal working hours covered by any of paragraphs (a), (b), (c) and (d) a sum not less than the amount of remuneration for that part of normal working hours calculated at the average hourly rate of remuneration produced by dividing a week's pay by the number of normal working hours.'

Similar provisions apply under s 89 of the ERA 1996 in respect of employees without normal working hours.

So, if the implied statutory notice period applies (either because there is no agreed contractual notice or the contractual notice is less than the statutory minimum) then the employee is entitled to be paid usual remuneration for the notice period. This is notwithstanding the fact that he is sick, unable to work and would otherwise only receive contractual sick pay, statutory sick pay or indeed no pay at all (if contractual and statutory sick pay has been exhausted). The employee does have to give full credit for any other receipts (eg SSP).[10]

However, under s 87(4) of the ERA 1996:

> '(4) This section does not apply in relation to a notice given by the employer or the employee if the notice to be given by the employer to terminate the contract must be at least one week more than the notice required by section 86(1).'

Therefore, if the employer has provided under the contract for at least one week more than the statutory minimum, the statutory provisions do not apply. The position is governed by contract so that if the contractual sick pay provisions have been exhausted the employee may receive no pay for the notice period.

This seems to produce a rather anomalous result and was challenged in *Burlo v Langley and Carter*.[11] The employers gave notice to their nanny. Her notice period was longer than the minimum required by s 86 of the ERA 1996. A couple of days later the nanny was injured in a car accident and was unable to work out her notice. She had no right to contractual sick pay and was entitled only to SSP. The employers refused to pay her more than this and the nanny brought tribunal proceedings in which this was one issue. It was argued that *Norton Tool Co Ltd v Tewson*[12] was authority for the proposition that full pay should be paid during the notice period – the 'narrow' *Norton Tool* principle:

> '*Norton Tool* was authority for the proposition that it was good employment practice for an employer who has dismissed an employee without notice to make a payment in lieu of notice and that, in assessing compensation for dismissal, this payment should not be subject to any deduction for sums earned in other employment during the notice period.'

However, Smith LJ pointed out that *Norton Tool* related to a payment in lieu of notice which was not worked, so was not entirely on point. She concluded:

> 'However, the Court of Appeal in *Babcock* has in my view made clear that there is in *Norton Tool* no wider principle by which newly formulated precepts of good industrial or employment practice can be applied to the

10 ERA 1996, s 88(2).

11 [2006] EWCA Civ 1778, [2007] 2 All ER 462, [2007] ICR 390, [2007] IRLR 145.

12 [1973] 1 WLR 45.

assessment of compensation under section 123 of ERA 1996 if the result of such application would be an award greater than the loss caused to the employee as a consequence of the dismissal.

Accepting therefore, for the moment, that the EAT was right to say that good industrial practice requires that an employee who is summarily dismissed while unfit for work through sickness should receive pay in lieu of notice at the normal rate of pay, the decision in Babcock makes it plain that that precept cannot be prayed in aid in the assessment of compensation in the instant case. If Ms Burlo had not been dismissed, she would have received SSP during her period of absence. Therefore SSP is the correct measure of her weekly loss during the notice period.

That disposes of this appeal in favour of the respondent employers. I would add, however, that I am not convinced that it is or should be a precept of good industrial practice, as the EAT held in this case, that an employer should pay wages in lieu of notice at the full weekly rate to an employee who is unfit through sickness, in cases which fall outside section 88 of ERA. It seems to me that Parliament has laid down the extent to which the obligation exists to provide pay in lieu of notice at the full rate when the employee is unfit for work. Nor, more generally, am I convinced that the concept of "good industrial practice" should be used to create new bases upon which loss can be claimed. However, those points do not arise for decision for reasons which should by now be clear.'

Whilst agreeing, Mummery LJ added:

> 'I appreciate that uncertainty about an everyday legal point like this is not satisfactory for tribunals, practitioners, employers or employees. The sooner that the House of Lords can settle the law one way or the other the better, dealing also, if possible, with a related controversy on the duty to mitigate under section 123(4), another point which has not arisen for decision in this case: (see, for example, the decisions of the EAT in *Hardy v Polk (Leeds) Ltd* [2005] ICR 557 and *Morgans v Alpha Plus Security Ltd* [2005] ICR 525; cf *Voith Turbo v Stowe* [2005] ICR 543).'

The latter point relates to a related discrepancy under employment law as to whether an employee is under a duty to mitigate loss and account for any pay received from other employment during an implied statutory period of notice. However, unless or until the House of Lords are asked to deal with the point and rule, the position as to payment for notice depends upon the length of notice period set out in the employment contract.

9.5 HOLIDAY PAY ENTITLEMENT DURING SICK LEAVE

For an employee who has been absent though ill health as the result of stress or bullying, a similar question can arise as to payment for holidays accrued but not taken during the period of sickness. Unfortunately, once again the position is complex.

Under the Working Time Regulations 1999 (as amended) every employee has the right to holiday and for payment in respect of accrued holiday not taken at the end of the employment. The entitlement (which can include public and bank holidays) was originally 4 weeks, and this increased to 4.8 weeks with effect from 1 October 2007 and to 5.6 weeks with effect from 1 April 2009.

If the employee is on sick leave with no entitlement to pay, or a reduced entitlement to pay, is the accrued holiday to be paid on termination at the normal rate of pay or the reduced rate of pay? This is the question that the House of Lords referred to the European Court of Justice (ECJ) in *Inland Revenue Commissioners v Stringer*:[13]

> **'Questions referred**
>
> (1) Does Article 7(1) of Directive 2003/88/EC mean that a worker on indefinite sick leave is entitled (i) to designate a future period as paid annual leave and (ii) to take paid annual leave, in either case during a period that would otherwise be sick leave?
>
> (2) If a Member State exercises its discretion to replace the minimum period of paid annual leave with an allowance in lieu on termination of employment under Article 7(2) of Directive 2003/88/EC, in circumstances in which a worker has been absent on sick leave for all or part of the leave year in which the employment relationship is terminated, does Article 7(2) impose any requirements or lay down any criteria as to whether the allowance is to be paid or how it is to be calculated?'

In its judgment in January 2009[14] the ECJ said:

> 'It follows that, with regard to a worker who has not been able, for reasons beyond his control, to exercise his right to paid annual leave before termination of the employment relationship, the allowance in lieu to which he is entitled must be calculated so that the worker is put in a position comparable to that he would have been in had he exercised that right during his employment relationship. It follows that the worker's normal remuneration, which is that which must be maintained during the rest period corresponding to the paid annual leave, is also decisive as regards the calculation of the allowance in lieu of annual leave not taken by the end of the employment relationship.'

Although it was permissible not to require a payment in lieu of the holiday entitlement to be made during the sickness absence, the employee must be given the right to carry the untaken paid holiday forward or to be paid for it on termination of employment. The ECJ determined that:

---

13 HL (Lord Nicholls of Birkenhead, Lord Hoffmann, Lord Hope of Craighead, Lord Walker of Gestingthorpe, Lord Brown of Eaton-under-Heywood) LTL 13 December 2006.

14 *Stringer and Others v HMRC* (C-520/06).

'1. Article 7(1) of Directive 2003/88/EC of the European Parliament and of the Council of 4 November 2003 concerning certain aspects of the organisation of working time must be interpreted as not precluding national legislation or practices according to which a worker on sick leave is not entitled to take paid annual leave during that sick leave.

2. Article 7(1) of Directive 2003/88 must be interpreted as precluding national legislation or practices which provide that the right to paid annual leave is extinguished at the end of the leave year and/or of a carry-over period laid down by national law even where the worker has been on sick leave for the whole or part of the leave year and where his incapacity to work has persisted until the end of his employment relationship, which was the reason why he could not exercise his right to paid annual leave.

3. Article 7(2) of Directive 2003/88 must be interpreted as precluding national legislation or practices which provide that, on termination of the employment relationship, no allowance in lieu of paid annual leave not taken is to be paid to a worker who has been on sick leave for the whole or part of the leave year and/or of a carry-over period, which was the reason why he could not exercise his right to paid annual leave. For the calculation of the allowance in lieu, the worker's normal remuneration, which is that which must be maintained during the rest period corresponding to the paid annual leave, is also decisive.'

The matter has now returned to the House of Lords and their final decision is awaited. However, it seems likely that it will be that employees on long-term absence through sickness will be entitled to payment of their usual salary in lieu of holiday accruing during the sickness absence. This will apply to the minimum holiday periods required by the Working Time Regulations 1999, but probably not strictly to any additional contractual holiday entitlement over and above that minimum.

9.6 THE DISABILITY DISCRIMINATION ACT 1995 (DDA 1995) AND SICK PAY

In *O'Hanlon v HMRC*[15] the employee had suffered from depression since 1998. It was accepted that she suffered from a disability under the DDA 1995.[16] From 2001 she began to take substantial amounts of time off work through sickness:

'In total, in the four years prior to the 15 October 2002, Mrs O'Hanlon had a total absence of 365 days of sickness, which comprised 320 relating to her disability and 45 of unrelated days of sickness absence.'

[15] [2007] EWCA Civ 283.

[16] See **5.4**.

The employer argued that she tended to return when her contractual full sick pay was exhausted. The employee argued that she remained sick, but had no alternative than to return to work as she was unable to cope financially.

The employee claimed that by reducing her pay for prolonged absence through sickness related to her disability the employer was discriminating against her contrary to the DDA 1995. She argued that she should continue to receive full pay whilst she was absent for a disability related sickness. The Court of Appeal disagreed:

> 'It is relevant that the aspect of the scheme with which we are concerned is not a term of a kind which every contract of employment has to contain. An employee who is absent for 6 months or more because of chronic illness, whether or not it amounts in law to a disability, might well find that at common law the contract has been frustrated by illness and that a consequent dismissal is held to be fair. A scheme which preserves the contractual relationship in such circumstances and assures first full pay and then half pay for extended periods of time therefore goes well beyond anything required by law. This is not of course to say that it is permissible, much less justified, to construct or administer such a scheme so that it operates arbitrarily to the disadvantage of the disabled. But any unplanned discriminatory impact may well be justified on the ground that such exceptions as can fairly be made in favour of disabled employees are already programmed into the scheme.
>
> That, in my judgment, is this case. Both tribunals below were understandably concerned at the impact on staff relations of extending full pay indefinitely to those whose sick absence was caused by disability, which was the principal way the case was put to them. But the same concern, in kind if not in degree, arises from any enlargement of the entitlement to full pay and then to half pay based on the nature of the employee's illness. The respondent's scheme, even so, permits a measure of enlargement in individual cases, and that is all that Ms Williams, in her more discreet argument, contended for. It is not for us to say which cases these should be, and for the reasons explained by Hooper LJ Mrs O'Hanlon's was not necessarily one.'

So, disability discrimination will rarely provide a remedy for reduction in pay by reason of sickness.

9.7 COMPENSATION AND SICKNESS

If the employer has caused the injury by reason of a breach of duty or discrimination, the compensation will inevitably include a claim for lost earnings.[17]

---

[17] See Chapter 7 for the principles of compensation in such claims.

However, in *Sheffield Forgemasters International Ltd v A M Fox; Telindus Ltd v C Brading*[18] the EAT held that, in an unfair dismissal claim, the fact that an employee is in receipt of incapacity benefit does not preclude a compensatory award being made.

The EAT noted that the tests for incapacity benefit are specific to entitlement to the benefit rather than a finding that the employee is incapable of work. It is possible that an employee might receive incapacity benefit, but still be capable of work but for the unfair dismissal or discrimination. The tribunal needs to consider the totality of the evidence before making a finding.

9.8 INCOME PROTECTION BENEFIT

Income protection benefit (otherwise known as permanent health insurance (PHI)) is a common benefit in the private sector, particularly for senior employees and professional businesses. As we shall see, schemes can vary considerably and it is essential to consider the specific scheme rules for the particular employee.

9.8.1 Policy terms

Most schemes involve a contractual benefit whereby the employer promises to insure the employee with an insurer to provide the employee with a proportion of their usual earnings (commonly 50% or 66% or 75%) whilst they remain unable to work through ill-health. The benefit is usually deferred and requires a prior period of absence through illness (usually 3 months or 6 months) before the employee is eligible for the benefit. Some schemes will continue to pay whilst the employee is unable to fulfil any occupation, others whilst he is unable to fulfil his usual occupation. Some schemes provide payment of the benefit to normal retirement age, others time-limit it (perhaps for 2 years). Some schemes exclude or limit the benefit payable in the case of certain illnesses (e g psychiatric conditions). Most schemes require the employee to remain employed with the employer (although not working), unless the insurer consents. The insurer will invariably have the right to insist that the employee submits to regular medical examinations.

The arrangement usually provides that the policyholder is the employer. The benefit is therefore paid to the employer and the employer passes it on to the employee through the payroll. From the employer's perspective, it is essential that the provisions in the contract dovetail precisely with the provisions of the income protection policy. Otherwise the employer might find itself promising more under the contract than it has insured for.

[18] EAT (Silber J, DG Smith, P Tatlow) LTL 13 November 2008.

In the case of any dispute the scheme rules will need to be obtained. It is quite possible that the contractual promise made in the contract of employment may not have in fact been reflected in the scheme rules themselves. In such cases, unless the employer has expressly reserved the right to vary, or a contractual variation has been expressly agreed or agreed by conduct following notice of the change (eg by agreeing the variation after notice of change through conduct such as working on without protest), there may be a separate cause of action for breach of contract against the employer for not supplying the benefits contracted for.

Usually there is no contractual nexus between the claimant and the permanent health insurer, so the claimant may well have no direct right of action if there is a complaint. The claimant's rights will usually be against his employer.

Sometimes it can be difficult to reconcile the inconsistencies and make any sense of the facts. As Ward LJ put it in *Briscoe v Lubrizol Ltd*:[19]

> 'Trying to pick up the scheme in this case is like trying to pick up a ball of mercury. In other words, it is nigh on impossible.'

In *Villella v MFI Furniture Centres Ltd*[20] the EAT made it clear that any restrictions on the policy should be drawn to the attention of the employee. Similarly, in *Jowitt v Pioneer Technology (UK) Ltd*,[21] a provision in the insurance contract that, after 2 years, benefits would only be paid if the employee was incapable of following any occupation (as opposed to his usual occupation) was not reflected in the handbook. The EAT held that the employer could not rely on the clause and was obliged to continue payment notwithstanding their inability to claim under the insurance policy.

The usual implied terms as to construction of insurance policies will apply.

An insurance contract is a contract of 'uberrima fides' (utmost good faith). This obligation applies not only to inception of the policy (eg a duty to disclose material facts), but is a continuing one.

The construction of the terms of the contract will usually be 'against the insurer' as the insurer will be the person who has put forward the relevant term.

---

[19] [2002] EWCA Civ 508, [2002] IRLR 607, [2002] Emp LR 819.

[20] [1999] IRLR 468, QBD.

[21] [2002] IRLR 790, EAT.

The provisions of the Unfair Terms in Consumer Contracts Regulations 1999[22] will apply:

> **'5. Unfair Terms**
>
> (1) A contractual term which has not been individually negotiated shall be regarded as unfair if, contrary to the requirement of good faith, it causes a significant imbalance in the parties' rights and obligations arising under the contract, to the detriment of the consumer…
>
> **6 Assessment of unfair terms**
>
> (1) Without prejudice to regulation 12, the unfairness of a contractual term shall be assessed, taking into account the nature of the goods or services for which the contract was concluded and by referring, at the time of conclusion of the contract, to all the circumstances attending the conclusion of the contract and to all the other terms of the contract or of another contract on which it is dependent…
>
> **7 Written contracts**
>
> (1) A seller or supplier shall ensure that any written term of a contract is expressed in plain, intelligible language.
>
> (2) If there is doubt about the meaning of a written term, the interpretation which is most favourable to the consumer shall prevail…
>
> **8 Effect of unfair term**
>
> (1) An unfair term in a contract concluded with a consumer by a seller or supplier shall not be binding on the consumer.
>
> (2) The contract shall continue to bind the parties if it is capable of continuing in existence without the unfair term.'

The provisions of the Consumer Protection from Unfair Trading Regulations 2008[23] may also apply to contracts made after 26 May 2008.

These two sets of regulations can be particularly useful if the insurer seeks to prevent an employee claiming a benefit under the policy by an exclusion that was not clearly drawn to the attention of the employee on inception.

If the employee seeks to dispute the terms of either policy with the insurer, he has to seek to rely on s 1(1)(b) of the Contracts (Rights of Third Parties) Act 1999 which confers upon a third party the right to enforce a term of a contract if the term purports to confer a benefit upon him. However, the employee cannot rely on this provision if it appears that on a proper construction of the contract, the parties did not intend

22 SI 1999/2083.

23 SI 2008/1277.

the term to be enforceable by a third party.[24] This will be evident from the wording of the policy. In any event, if the employee is restricted to a claim against the employer, it is very likely that the employer will join the insurer into proceedings for an indemnity by way of a claim under Part 20 of the Civil Procedure Rules 1999.

On 9 January 2008, the Association of British Insurers (ABI) published guidance on the fair treatment of claims for UK life, critical illness, income protection and other long-term protection insurance contracts. This sets out guidelines as to how insurers should treat alleged non-disclosure and the obtaining of medical evidence.

9.8.2 Usual occupation

There are also often issues as to the meaning of 'usual' or 'normal' occupation and 'any' occupation. In *Walton v Air Tours (1) Sun Life (2)*[25] the claimant was a pilot who suffered from chronic fatigue syndrome. He sued his employer for wrongful termination of employment after he was dismissed when the provider refused to pay benefits because they believed him capable of following an occupation, although not his previous employment as a pilot. The employer joined in the insurer as a Part 20 defendant for an indemnity. The Court of Appeal held:

> '"To follow ANY occupation" naturally connotes to be engaged in regular work, not temporarily but for a substantial or indefinite period. "To follow ANY occupation" also, to my mind, plainly implies an element of continuity. Further, given that the purpose behind the relevant provision of the manual is to provide an entitlement to income to an ex-employee who cannot earn income by working, it makes little commercial sense to treat the condition for the payment of benefit as not being satisfied if the person in question can only start a job for a few days but thereafter cannot continue to earn income. It is scarcely conceivable that such an unfair and insensitively harsh term in respect of an employee who has suffered from serious illness, as is suggested by Mr Bellamy, would form part of any modern contract of employment.
>
> The crucial finding is not that Mr Walton was medically fit to undertake light sedentary work on a part-time basis, the adverb "medically" showing that the judge was treating such fitness as only qualifying. It is the finding in the remainder of the sentence which I have already cited that, in order that the claimant should be able to follow an occupation involving such work, it would be necessary that he should have a programme of rehabilitation, including psychiatric support and the help of his employer. The judge, thus, was finding that Mr Walton could not follow an occupation at all without such support. But the judge had immediately before that set out the medical evidence which led him to that conclusion, and it included Professor Neary's view, agreed by Professor Wesseley, that any work would have to be

24 Contracts (Rights of Third Parties) Act 1999, s 1(2).
25 [2002] EWCA Civ 1659, [2003] IRLR 161, [2004] Lloyd's Rep IR 69.

> introduced – and I stress introduced – in a structured way and Dr Bowden's view that any attempt to return to work should be preceded by rehabilitation and accompanied by a programme of support.'

It is certainly arguable that any failure by the employer to allow for a structured return to work might be a failure to make a 'reasonable adjustment' under the DDA 1995. If the employer failed to make available the opportunity for a structured return, and the permanent health insurer ceased paying out because it felt that the claimant would be capable of some work, there could be a substantial DDA 1995 claim against the employer. However, adjustments can be a particular problem in stress claims where the workplace is usually the issue.

In *Marlow v East Thames Housing Group Limited*[26] the court made it clear that where the employer was to pay the employee and receive an indemnity from the PHI provider, the employer was under an implied duty to pursue the PHI provider on behalf of the employee for payment of benefits if they are wrongly ceased by the provider.

9.8.3 Remaining employed

Some benefits require the beneficiary to remain in employment with the employer (even though he is not working). In *Briscoe v Lubrizol Ltd* the Court of Appeal considered earlier lower court decisions (such as *Aspden v Webbs Poultry*[27] and *Villella v MFI*) and held that there is an implied term that the contract cannot be lawfully terminated other than for good cause if this would deprive the employee of benefits under a PHI scheme. An employer who dismisses an injured employee and who thereby deprives the employee of their right to payments under a contractual PHI scheme could themselves be sued by the employee for damages for breach of contract equivalent to the lost benefits under the PHI scheme. In the case of income protection schemes providing salary to retirement, such claims would be substantial and an uninsured liability of the employer. Small employers might even go under as a result and not be able to pay.

In *First West Yorkshire Ltd t/a First Leeds v Haigh*[28] the EAT expressly applied this principle to a case where a bus driver with 30 years' service was dismissed on grounds of capability and hence deprived of potential entitlement to an ill-health pension.

However, in *Briscoe v Lubrizol Ltd* the Court of Appeal held (by two to one) that the employer can dismiss for good cause whether that be on the ground of gross misconduct or more generally for some repudiatory breach by the employee. The employee must therefore co-operate with his employer and with the scheme provider (eg in reporting on his condition

26 [2002] IRLR 798, [2002] All ER (D) 393 (May).
27 [1996] IRLR 521, QBD.
28 UKEAT/0246/07/RN 20 November 2007.

and attending medical reviews). Whether a genuine redundancy situation could be used to this effect is still unclear (although *Hill v General Accident Fire and Life Assurance Co plc*[29] suggests it can be). However, it is submitted that in most cases where the employer is no longer paying the employee from his own resources dismissal for redundancy would seem to be an unnecessary course and one which would fundamentally and adversely affect the employee's rights to receive payment under the PHI scheme. This might be different if the employer closes down business entirely and all workers are laid off.

It is also unclear as to what the attitude of the court would be to a claim where the contract expressly reserves a right for the employer to terminate, even if this would lead to a loss of benefits under the PHI scheme. Although it is submitted that the court would be sympathetic to the employee, it is difficult to see how an implied term (of mutual trust and confidence) could override an express contractual term. In *Reda v Flag Ltd*[30] (in the employment context of a dismissal which deprived the employee of stock options) it was held that it did not, although clearly the employer would risk its reputation by acting so callously.

Resignation (often the uninformed choice of the employee) would be disastrous as the employee would lose the benefits under the PHI scheme. There is often a good case to be made for clients, subject to limitation issues, to sit tight (perhaps having reserved their positions regarding any possible constructive dismissal) until the PHI insurers have accepted the claim and started paying out (usually after 6 months). In *Crossley v Faithful & Gould Holdings Ltd*[31] the Court of Appeal dismissed a claim that the employer owed a duty to the employee to notify him that resignation would operate to deprive him of benefits under the PHI scheme. However, the court did stress the seniority of the employee and his access to insurance broking advice. The position might be different for a more junior employee.

9.8.4 Overlap with personal injury claims

In *Marlow v East Thames Housing Group Ltd* the employer had not made a contractual promise to allow the employee to enter into the PHI scheme and argued that this was an ex gratia scheme that entitled it to benefit employees in its discretion. After the claimant fell ill the employer wrote to the claimant in terms that entitled her to benefit. The employer also obtained her signature to a 'waiver' letter that provided that if she became well again the PHI benefits would cease, her employment would thereupon come to an end and she would have no further claim against the employer. Here the court held that there was consideration for this waiver because she was accepted into the scheme late. There might be

29 [1998] IRLR 641, 1998 SCLR 1031, Court of Session (OH).
30 [2002] UKPC 38, [2002] IRLR 747.
31 [2004] EWCA Civ 293, [2004] 4 All ER 447, [2004] ICR 1615, [2004] IRLR 377.

consideration difficulties for an employer otherwise seeking to impose such a term. How this might be permissible given the strict provisions of the ERA 1996 relating to compromise agreements and indeed her rights under DDA 1995 were not discussed.

In *Vincent v Servite Homes Ltd*[32] Mrs Vincent had brought a personal injury claim against her employer after an accident at work and subsequent dismissal. The claim settled for £10,000. All parties seemed to have forgotten about the PHI policy. Some years later she brought a separate action against her employer for breach of contract in terminating her employment and depriving her of her right to payments under the PHI scheme. The Court of Appeal pointed out that if she had been entitled to PHI payments this should have been deducted from her loss of earnings claim in the personal injury claim, but no reference had been made to it in her schedule or elsewhere. The Court of Appeal did not allow the claim on the ground that she had ceased employment and the benefits were therefore no longer due. They pointed out that no claim had been made in respect of any alleged breach of an implied term that employment would continue. They rejected an estoppel argument on the facts. This appears to be a pragmatic decision by the court determined to avoid giving Mrs Vincent what they considered to be an undeserved windfall.

Cases involving obvious bodily injury rarely lead to a problem with PHI schemes. The employer will notify the scheme provider and benefits will be paid. Some issues may arise in the future if the scheme provider requires the injured person to return to some sort of work and the employer is reluctant to have them back, but this is usually resolvable, particularly with the assistance of employee's rights under the DDA 1995. However, with psychiatric injury cases, especially where the tortious claim is debatable, there can be a complex three-way negotiation between client (who may not want to return), employer (who may not want the client back) and provider (who does not want to pay out until retirement).

It is becoming increasingly common for providers to try to bring matters to a head by insisting on medical examinations which might suggest that at some time in the near future the claimant will be fit for work and seeking to buy off the annuity payments with a one-off lump sum. These are often attractively large capital payments, but nothing like the value of income protection to retirement if recovery is not made or maintained. It can be a difficult decision for the client to decide whether to accept this lump sum and risk their future well-being (which is particularly dangerous in stress cases as a first breakdown is surely going to leave the client vulnerable to non-negligently caused future injury). The decision-making in the light of a difficult tortious or employment claim and an unclear medical prognosis is hard, especially for a psychologically vulnerable client.

---

32 [2002] EWCA Civ 852.

9.8.5 Financial Services Ombudsman

The employee might bring proceedings for breach of contract against the employer if there is a dispute as to his entitlement to income protection benefit. However, such proceedings will be expensive and if they do not succeed the employee risks a costs order. Also, although the legal fiction is that the employee claims against his employer for failing to provide a contractual benefit, it will rarely be the case that the issue relates to the employer's failure rather than to the insurer's refusal to carry on paying the benefit.

The employee may also have the remedy of a complaint to the Financial Services Ombudsman (FSO). The FSO will usually find it has jurisdiction in respect of complaints by an employee under a group scheme set up by an employer:[33]

> 'Our jurisdiction is a broad one – but not quite as broad as some consumers believe. We do sometimes have to explain that we are unable to deal with a particular complaint – often because the firm concerned is not regulated. When we are unable to deal with an insurance case, it can sometimes be because the consumer bringing the complaint to us is not the beneficiary of the insurance contract that is the subject of the dispute . . .
>
> We see plenty of cases relating to group Permanent Health Insurance (PHI) and similar policies, where the employer has taken out the policy for the benefit of its employees and one of those employees refers a complaint to us. Some insurance firms have tried to argue that we cannot investigate cases that involve group policies (even where the policy was taken out for the benefit of an employee) if the policyholder is a large company with an annual turnover of £1million or more.
>
> Under our rules (DISP 2.4), an eligible complainant (someone who is able to bring their complaint to the ombudsman service) includes "a person for whose benefit a contract of insurance was taken out or was intended to be taken out".
>
> To decide whether a case is one we can look into, we need to assess whether the policy was taken out for the benefit of the individual who has complained to us. We do this by looking at the policy wording and the employment contract. If it is clear that any payments made by the insurer go directly to the employee, then we will probably conclude that the complaint is within our jurisdiction.
>
> But where we find the employer is effectively reinsuring its own clear contractual liability to pay sickness benefits, or is merely protecting the business – for example, with a 'key man'-type policy – then we might conclude that the complaint was not taken out for the employee's benefit and is not one we are able to deal with.

---

[33] *Ombudsman News* issue 32, October 2003.

The fact that individuals other than the person who complains to us might also benefit under the policy does not automatically exclude the complaint. We look carefully to see if there is a direct or indirect link between the payments made by the insurer and the payments the employer makes to the employee. If we are satisfied that the employer is contractually obliged to make payments to the employee only if the insurer accepts the claim – then we are likely to conclude that the complaint is within our jurisdiction. In such circumstances the policy was clearly taken out for the benefit of the employee.

Of course, if the employer has a turnover of less than £1million and is well-disposed towards its employee, it may bring the complaint to us in its own right as the firm's customer.'

And an FSO decision sets out the factors that often mean that an employee beneficiary of a group policy can complain to the FSO:[34]

'Mr H worked at GJ Ltd, a large supermarket that offered private health insurance to its staff. After a period of ill health, Mr H put in a claim to the insurance firm. When the firm refused to pay, Mr H referred his complaint to us.

Complaint within our jurisdiction

The firm argued that the complaint was not one we could deal with because neither GJ Ltd nor Mr H were eligible complainants; GJ Ltd because it was a commercial customer with an annual turnover of over £1million, and Mr H because the policyholder was GJ Ltd, not him.

We found that the complaint was within our jurisdiction. It was true that, because of its size, GJ Ltd was not an eligible complainant. However, Mr H was. Under the rules (DISP 2.4.12R), we were able to look at this complaint because " . . . the complainant [was] a person for whose benefit a contract of insurance was taken out or was intended to be taken out".

It was clear that the policy was taken out for the benefit of GJ Ltd's employees, including Mr H. For the complaint to be within our jurisdiction, it was not necessary for Mr H to be the only person to benefit from the policy. The fact that the employer also benefited was immaterial.'

The FSO has wide-ranging powers to order remedies against the insurer, including compensation limited to £100,000, but perhaps more importantly declarations as to the meaning of policy wording which may require the insurer to honour the policy. In the case of an income protection policy which potentially pays out until retirement age, a finding by the FSO that the insurer must honour the policy may be a very

[34] FSO Decision 32/10.

valuable remedy. That said, as the FSO is an industry funded body, many employees are sceptical about its independence. The FSO describes its role:[35]

- 'It's our job to settle individual complaints between consumers and businesses providing financial services. If we uphold a complaint, we can order matters to be put right.
- We were set up by parliament to do this – as independent experts – and our service is free to consumers.
- We can look at complaints about a wide range of financial matters – from insurance and mortgages to investments and credit. Each year we deal with over a million enquiries and settle around 100,000 disputes.
- We're completely independent and impartial – just as a judge would be if the consumer went to court instead.
- We are not a regulator ("watchdog") or a trade body or a consumer champion. Our role is to settle disputes, without taking sides. So when we look at a complaint, we give both sides a fair hearing.
- If a business isn't able to resolve a customer's complaint on its own, we'll see if we can help settle the dispute. But the business must first have the chance to sort things out itself.
- We can often resolve disputes informally, but some cases are more complex and take more time. We aim to settle most disputes within six to nine months.
- Consumers don't have to accept any decision we make. They are always free to go to court instead. But if they do accept an ombudsman's decision, it is binding both on them and on the business.
- Our service is confidential – we do not publish the names of businesses or consumers whose complaints we handle.'

The process is as follows:

> 'If you'd like us to look into your complaint, we will need you to fill in our complaint form. This will help us understand what exactly your complaint is about. We can help you fill in the form over the phone (call us on 0845 080 1800). Or you can download the form below.
>
> When you have completed our complain form – please send it back to us by post. Your handwritten signature is important to show us that you understand and agree to the declaration at the end of the form. You will also probably have other documents that you need to post to us with your completed form.'

The FSO issues decisions in respect of its findings relating to issues which often recur. Disputes in respect of income protection benefit are common complaints to the FSO. Issue 52 of *Ombudsman News* (11 April 2006) is mainly dedicated to income protection benefit policies.

Commonly, there is a query as to the amount of benefit payable. This is usually relatively straightforward. However, the FSO will also:

[35] See www.financial-ombudsman.org.uk/about/index.html.

'. . . examine the advice the firm gave at the time it sold the policy. We do not assume that simply because the insurance does not currently meet the policyholder's needs, it must have been mis-sold originally.'

A difficult issue often relates to 'own occupation' policies. The FSO has a wide jurisdiction in respect of remedies it can offer:

'Own occupation policies often have clauses allowing the firm to pay a reduced benefit if, after a period of total disability, the policyholder returns to work in a reduced capacity or a different occupation – and can demonstrate a reduction in their earnings.

In general, however, if a policyholder does not return to work, no proportional or rehabilitation benefit is payable. The requirement to return to work can be onerous for policyholders if:

- the failure of their business prevents them from performing their occupation part-time; and
- their disability makes them unfit for any similar occupation.

In our view, it may not be an appropriate response for the firm to either:

- make no benefit payments; or
- continue with full benefit.

So depending on the terms of the policy, we will consider whether good industry practice suggests the best solution would be for the firm to make some part-payment of benefit.'

An example of this appears in one of the FSO case studies[36] (albeit for a self-employed policy-holder):

'Mr G, a self-employed butcher, developed disabling back pain and claimed under his income protection insurance policy. In December 1990, the firm accepted his claim and started paying him benefits.

By 1996, Mr G was still unable to work. The firm offered to make final settlement of the claim by paying him a lump sum of £167,376. Mr G did not accept the offer and he continued to receive monthly payments.

In 1999, the firm required Mr G to attend a 'functional capacity' examination by a physiotherapist. She concluded that Mr G had not been exerting himself in the tests to his full ability, and that it was impossible to determine whether he was physically capable of returning to his former occupation. The firm had also obtained video evidence. On the basis of this and the test results, it stopped paying Mr G's benefits.

Complaint upheld in part

We appointed an independent consultant orthopaedic surgeon to examine Mr G and to consider the video evidence. This showed Mr G playing golf,

36 FSO 24/02.

driving and gardening. The consultant concluded that Mr G was not fit to carry out the work of a butcher and was unemployable in that capacity. However he might be able to undertake some part-time work in a butcher's shop if it only involved – for example – serving customers and handling cash.

The policy definition of "disability" was very strict. Taken literally, it might mean that a policyholder's ability to carry out a minor administrative element of an otherwise physically demanding job would justify a firm's rejection of a claim. However, it is accepted market practice to treat someone as "disabled" if they are unable to perform the "material and substantial" duties of their ordinary occupation.

As a butcher, Mr G's main duties involved heavy physical work, with much bending and carrying. He spent most of the day on his feet. As well as preparing food, he had to lift heavy carcasses and to spend a considerable time standing behind the counter, serving customers.

When he first applied for the policy, Mr G had described his normal day's work as being split equally between "jointing" and "selling/serving" and the firm had insured him on this basis. The type of part-time work that the consultant had suggested he might be able to do was markedly different from this. Any difficulty Mr G might encounter in finding such work was not relevant to an assessment of his disability.

We accepted that Mr G was capable of performing some part-time work, but only in a limited and lower-skilled role. The duties involved would be materially different from his original occupation and less remunerative.

The policy did not deal clearly with this type of situation, but it did provide for the payment of a reduced benefit. We concluded that the firm should reinstate Mr G's claim and pay him benefits calculated at 66% of the full rate. It should also make him backdated payments at this reduced rate, plus interest, from the time when it had stopped his benefits.'

There can sometimes be disputes as to whether the condition which has led to the claim was a pre-existing condition that should have been notified to the insurer (some schemes require prior notification, some do not). The FSO state:

'We continue to face difficult decisions on how insurers have applied exclusions for pre-existing medical conditions. And in considering these cases, we continue to adopt the approach suggested by our predecessors following the House of Lords' decision in *Cook v Financial Insurance Company Ltd* [1998] 1 Weekly Law Reports 1765.

Briefly, "condition" – in the context of these exclusions – should mean a medical condition recognised as such by doctors (not simply some generalised symptoms). When we consider individual cases we will look at the position when the policy was taken out. In particular, we will review the customer's medical history, including:

- the intensity of symptoms
- the seriousness with which they are regarded
- the diagnosis that has been made; and
- the treatment given.

We will also consider the significance of the difference between the customer's symptoms up to the point when the policy was taken out, and the medical condition that gave rise to the claim, when it was finally diagnosed. The more remote the connection, the less likely we are to accept that the "condition" existed at the time the policy was taken out. Finally, we try to ascertain what the customer knew about their condition when entering into the policy.

Since the *Cook* case, some insurers appear to have altered their policy wording, in an attempt to extend the exclusion for pre-existing conditions to conditions that are related to symptoms that were apparent before the start of the policy. Case 13/03 provides an example of this, albeit in the rather specialist context of a moratorium exclusion in medical expenses insurance. A moratorium of this type excludes, for a specified period, a medical condition that existed when the insurance was issued. The specified period (frequently two years) must then have passed without the policyholder having received any further treatment or advice for this condition before it is covered by the insurance. The use of moratorium exclusions means that the insurer does not require details of the policyholder's health before it issues the policy. Instead, it relies on the exclusion to reject any claim made for existing conditions during the specified period.

Our approach in this area is developing and we will need to consider further, in the light of a wider range of cases, how such exclusions should be interpreted. In particular, we need to consider if it is reasonable:
- to describe a person with a common condition – such as high blood pressure – as having a 'related condition'; and then
- to apply the exclusion when the person subsequently suffers from a more serious condition, such as a stroke, where the original condition is known to be a contributory or risk factor.

Our initial view is that such exclusions have the potential to be onerous. Whatever the case, we are more likely to uphold insurers' preferred interpretation of such exclusions if their wide potential scope was fully and clearly explained to customers before they took out the policy.'

In stress claims, the working environment might itself mean that it is difficult to return without exacerbating the illness. This can lead to a dispute as to whether the employee remains incapable of undertaking his usual occupation:[37]

'On holiday in France, Mr N had a transient ischaemic attack. He was subsequently diagnosed as suffering from heart disease and he gave up work. He claimed benefits under his permanent health insurance on the ground that his state of health totally prevented him from working. The insurer

[37] FSO 13/04.

made medical enquiries and found that although Mr N's GP and his consultant neurologist had both recommended he should give up work, they agreed that he was physically fit to resume work. His occupation, as managing director of the company he had started many years before, was highly stressful. The insurer maintained that there was no physical reason why Mr N should not return to work.

The medical evidence was inconclusive. So we arranged for Mr N to undergo an independent examination. The independent consultant considered there was no medical reason why Mr N could not return to work, but that he should not do so because of the risk to his health. The consultant felt that Mr N's occupation involved such a degree of stress that the risks of further disability would be increased if he went back to work, and there would be a very real risk of his illness recurring.

Complaint upheld

This was an unusual case. Generally, a person with a stable medical condition who is fearful that returning to work may aggravate their condition – perhaps through stress – will have difficulty demonstrating they are not able to work. Here, however, the medical evidence pointed strongly to a worsening of the policyholder's condition being not just a worry but a foreseeable result of returning to work. So although Mr N's position had clearly stabilised after he gave up work, that was not sufficient justification for rejecting his claim. The medical evidence made it clear that he was only well so long as he did not work. Returning to work would put his health at risk, so it was not right to conclude that he was not "disabled".

We required the insurer to meet Mr N's claim from the end of the deferred period of six months, and to add interest to the back payments.'

There can often be difficulties which arise as a result of discrepancies between the employee's own medical advisers and independent medical examiners appointed by the insurer. These disputes are, of course, fact sensitive, but the FSO comments:

'It is not part of our role to diagnose the policyholder's condition. We look at all the evidence before reaching an opinion on their probable circumstances – and how these relate to the insurance policy.'

The FSO will, however, have to weigh up the evidence from various medical practitioners, giving more weight to specialists and taking into account knowledge of the claimant's condition. There is sometimes a difference between the insurer's view of the employee's condition and that of medical practitioners:

'Firms sometimes argue that a doctor has been too ready to "sign-off" a policyholder as "unfit" for work. Firms also consider that some doctors – when asked whether a policyholder is capable of continuing to work – place undue weight on whether suitable work is available, or on the policyholder's social and economic circumstances, rather than reporting against the specific requirements of the policy.

Conversely, we find that some doctors make over-ambitious estimates of what the policyholder can reasonably be expected to achieve. This may result from a misunderstanding about what the person's occupation entails, or perhaps from comparison with an apparently similar patient who may have been more than normally well-motivated, or have had very different circumstances to contend with.'

They are particularly wary of 'functional evaluation' and similar tests that purport to show exaggeration or malingering:

'Firms sometimes conclude that policyholders must have been exaggerating the effect of their physical symptoms if they appear not to have exerted maximum effort during a test. Substantial exaggeration is, of course, likely to raise questions about the validity of the claim. But there may be a perfectly innocent explanation for a policyholder's appearing to "hold back" when undertaking test activities. Someone already in considerable pain, for example, may understandably be wary of any movement that might make matters worse.

As in litigation, video evidence is often obtained by insurers, but is not always unequivocal:

'Firms often ask us to take into account evidence obtained by surveillance – usually by video. Inconsistencies between what a video shows a policyholder doing – and what the policyholder has told their doctor and the firm that they can manage – will not necessarily lead to the failure of the complaint. However, serious inconsistencies are likely to weaken the policyholder's case and to reduce the weight we would normally place on the relevant medical reports.

Someone who claims to be too ill to continue in work, for example, but who is then filmed carrying out a similar occupation, is unlikely to succeed with their claim.

More often, however, video evidence is ambivalent. First, it may show activity over a limited period, so it does not prove that the person can perform the activity consistently over the longer term. Second, videos seldom show activity that is of direct relevance to the dispute. So it should not automatically be assumed that the ability to perform one sort of activity indicates the ability to carry out another.

What, for example, does a trip to the supermarket demonstrate, in relation to the ability to carry out a full-time occupation? The definition of "disability" in most policies does not require a person to be housebound. So video evidence of someone shopping, hanging out washing on the line, or making a trip to the pub with friends is unlikely to be proof that the person fails to comply with the policy definition of "disability".

> In assessing video evidence of a policyholder's capabilities, we exercise caution before reaching any conclusions that conflict with the medical evidence. Normally, we favour medical evidence over video evidence unless an independent medical assessment suggests that the activity shown in the video is inconsistent with previous medical reports. So where appropriate, for example, we may ask the doctor who carried out the independent medical examination, to comment on the apparent inconsistency.'

The FSO can therefore be an important additional route for redress in an appropriate case.

CHAPTER 10

COSTS AND FUNDING

10.1 INITIAL INSTRUCTIONS AND FUNDING

10.1.1 The retainer

In a stress at work claim success is uncertain. If the case fails, the solicitor needs to know whether or not he is to be paid and, if so, how much and by whom. If he is not to be paid at all, the solicitor should be compensated for taking this risk by a success fee under a conditional fee agreement (CFA) or, in tribunal cases, a contingency fee (the costs being a sum equal to a percentage of the compensation recovered).

If the claim is brought in the employment tribunal it is unlikely that costs will be recovered from the opponent.

If, however, the claim is brought in the courts then, if the case succeeds, it is usual under the English 'loser pays' rule for the defendant to be liable for the claimant's costs on top of the damages. The order for costs in the claimant's favour is by way of an indemnity for the costs the claimant has incurred ('the indemnity principle'). If the claimant has incurred no legal liability for costs to the solicitor, then there is nothing to indemnify and the costs order is worthless.

10.1.2 Pre-screening work

Stress and bullying at work claims have a notoriously high overall turn-down rate. Many potential clients who telephone a solicitor with an enquiry have no legal case for compensation. The client may have a serious psychiatric condition, but it may not be the result of work-related stress. There may have been a breach of duty, but psychiatric damage was not foreseeable.

Commonly, such claims produce voluminous paperwork which has to be reviewed. It is essential to obtain and review the full personnel file and medical records before advising on merits.

That said practitioners should be slow to advise there is no case or indeed decline to investigate further on inadequate evidence. It is often a fine balance. If instructions are declined without full investigation, it is often safer from a professional indemnity insurance perspective to advise in general terms on limitation and stress that the firm is simply declining instructions, rather than giving a view on the merits, even an informal one.

10.1.3 Preliminary investigations

If there does appear to be a prima facie case to investigate, then the question of the retainer for this work needs to be addressed.

If the client is eligible for public funding and the firm has a contract for controlled work in employment, then subject to the terms of that contract it may be possible to screen the case under Legal Help (broadly, the old Green Form scheme). However, public funding is not available for personal injury claims, nor is it available for tribunal representation.

If the firm does not have a controlled work contract, but the client is likely to be eligible for public funding on financial grounds for Legal Help, then care should be taken to record the reasons for any private client retainer for payment.

The firm might:

- investigate pro bono (and never seek costs for this work); or
- sign a CFA immediately; or
- sign a contingency fee agreement immediately; or
- seek to recover costs prior to the date of the CFA retrospectively; or
- enter into a 'pre-litigation costs agreement'; or
- enter into a full or partial (eg disbursements only) retainer.

Pro bono investigation is simple, but expensive to the firm. A limit on time to be spent and money expended should be set.

A private retainer for the investigation might be a full retainer or one that provides for disbursements and maybe a fixed fee. If so, only costs which the client is liable to pay can be recovered as costs from the defendant at the end of the case. In addition, the client's potential liability both for the immediate costs and some explanation as to what might happen at the end of the investigation must be given at the outset. The Solicitors Regulation Authority Guidance states:

> 'When a potential client contacts you with a view to giving you instructions you should always, when asked, try to be helpful in providing information on the likely costs of their matter.'

It is possible to enter into a 'pre-litigation agreement' (which provides for normal costs if the case is won and nothing if the case is abandoned after investigation, or lost) following the Court of Appeal's decision in *Gaynor v Central West London Buses Ltd.*[1] But care should be taken as this applied only to 'modest pre-litigation services' and is a somewhat peculiar decision perhaps rather on its own facts rather than for general application. The line of cases leading to *Geraghty & Co v Awwad*[2] remains good law that such an agreement will normally be an unenforceable contingency fee if it relates to court proceedings (but not if it relates solely to tribunal proceedings).

An immediate CFA is relatively simple. If the ultimate funding mechanism is likely to be a CFA this can be a sensible step as it is not absolutely certain that a CFA can operate retrospectively at all, or that a success fee can be claimed retrospectively. (There is no definitive higher court authority to this effect, although it is likely that it can be).[3] It is important to make it clear on the face of the CFA that it is dated when signed and operates retrospectively (and not actually to 'backdate' it by implying that the CFA was signed at an earlier time than it in fact was).[4] It is important to amend the Law Society's model conditional agreement to provide for the agreement to operate from an earlier date rather from 'the date of this agreement'. The model agreement should also be amended to make it a contentious business agreement, as s 59(1) of the Solicitors Act 1974 expressly allows for a contentious business agreement to be in respect of work 'done or to be done'.

Similarly, it might be possible to enter into a contingency fee agreement immediately. However, care should be taken as it is only lawful in respect of employment tribunal claims. If it is decided to pursue a court claim instead then the agreement will be treated as an unlawful contingency fee agreement and no costs could be enforced.

10.2 SOLICITORS CODE OF CONDUCT 2007

The Solicitors' Code of Conduct ('the Code') came into force on 1 July 2007. It replaces the old Practice Rule 15 and the Solicitors' Costs Information and Client Care Code 1999. Rule 2.03, 'Information about the cost', is the key provision.

---

1 [2006] EWCA Civ 1120.

2 [2000] 3 WLR 1041, [2000] 1 All ER 608.

3 Christopher Clarke J in *Forde v Birmingham City Council* [2009] EWHC 12 (QB) held that it could, but permission to appeal to the Court of Appeal has been sought.

4 See *Holmes v McAlpine* [2006] EWHC 110 (QB).

The importance of considering all funding options and of costs estimates is stressed. The use of the mandatory 'must' rather than the exhortatory 'should' (which is repeated throughout the new rule) is significant.

> **'2.03 Information about the cost**
>
> (1) You must give your client the best information possible about the likely overall cost of a matter both at the outset and, when appropriate, as the matter progresses. In particular you must:
>
> (a) advise the client of the basis and terms of your charges;
> (b) advise the client if charging rates are to be increased;
> (c) advise the client of likely payments which you or your client may need to make to others;
> (d) discuss with the client how the client will pay, in particular:
> (i) whether the client may be eligible and should apply for public funding; and
> (ii) whether the client's own costs are covered by insurance or may be paid by someone else such as an employer or trade union;
> (e) advise the client that there are circumstances where you may be entitled to exercise a lien for unpaid costs;
> (f) advise the client of their potential liability for any other party's costs; and
> (g) discuss with the client whether their liability for another party's costs may be covered by existing insurance or whether specially purchased insurance may be obtained.'

The Solicitors Regulation Authority Guidance to the Code of Conduct advises that:

> 'It is often impossible to tell at the outset what the overall cost will be. Sub-rule 2.03 allows for this and requires that you provide the client with as much information as possible at the start and that you keep the client updated. If a precise figure cannot be given at the outset, you should explain the reason to the client and agree a ceiling figure or review dates.'

Likely disbursements should be included in estimates.[5]

With regard to CFAs, as well as the matters outlined above, the solicitor must also explain:

> **'2.03 (2) . . .**
>
> (a) the circumstances in which your client may be liable for your costs and whether you will seek payment of these from the client, if entitled to do so;
> (b) if you intend to seek payment of any or all of your costs from your client, you must advise your client of their right to an assessment of those costs . . .'

The Solicitors Regulation Authority Guidance advises that:

5 Solicitors Regulation Authority Guidance, note 39.

> 'Different cost options may have different implications for the client – for example, where the choice is between a conditional fee agreement and an application for public funding. In those circumstances clients should be made aware of the implications of each option.'

Rule 2.03(5) specifies that 'Any information about the cost must be clear and confirmed in writing'. Rule 2.03 emphasises the importance of risk and cost/benefit analysis for all cases (and not just in conditional fees cases where the lawyer is risking his own fees). Rule 2.03(7) accepts that it might be appropriate in certain circumstances not to fully comply; but this should be exceptional and the reasons should be fully recorded.

The Solicitors Regulation Authority Guidance stresses that the rule is not exhaustive, but subject to the basic principle that the solicitor must: 'act in the client's best interests' and 'must not abuse or exploit the relationship by taking advantage of a client's age, inexperience, ill health, lack of education or business experience, or emotional or other vulnerability'.

The Solicitors Regulation Authority Guidance states that:

> 'It is not envisaged or intended that a breach of 2.02, 2.03 or 2.05 should invariably render a retainer unenforceable . . . the rule will be enforced in a manner which is proportionate to the seriousness of the breach.'

This is intended inter alia to prevent paying parties from arguing that any breach of the Solicitors Practice Rules renders the retainer unenforceable and thus by way of the indemnity principle escape liability to pay costs.

Solicitors usually pay particular attention to costs and funding issues at the outset (backed by their firm's precedents and procedures). But the duties are ongoing and must be particularly borne in mind near settlement (particularly with regard to any likely deductions from the damages).

10.3 PRIVATE PAYING RETAINER

10.3.1 Full hourly rates plus expenses (the private paying client)

Traditionally, the private paying client has paid for work as it is done. The solicitor agrees to take on the case for the client and will deliver bills for the work done on the basis of an hourly rate for the solicitor's fees and by passing on to the client out-of-pocket expenses at cost.

For reasons of regulation, enforceability against the client and recovery of costs by the client from the opponent, the terms of the private retainer should be written down expressly and clearly. It may seem obvious common sense that a solicitor should ensure that his agreement with the client is in writing and clearly expressed. However, until recent years many cases were dealt with on the basis that the solicitor would do the work and afterwards (or on an interim basis) render a bill. The solicitor would expect the client to pay without question, and/or would anticipate recovering the costs or a proportion of them from the other side if and when the case was won. Doing so, without agreeing with the client in advance the basis of the charges, was of course unacceptable and poor practice. The profession has got its act together with increasing detailed guidance in respect of costs information to be given to clients.

Almost all hourly rates are now expressed to be inclusive of any 'mark-up'. Traditionally, solicitors often presented their charging structures to clients on the basis of 'expense' and 'mark-up'. This was on the basis of a standard mark-up on expense of 50% (but with a higher mark-up in the case of more complex cases). This reflected the old method of recovery of costs 'between the parties' whereby a full bill for detailed assessment would include the expense rate (the 'A' rate) and the mark-up for care and conduct (the 'B' rate). The standard 50% mark-up reflected the assumed mix of a solicitor's costs reflecting one-third salary, one-third other expenses and one-third profit. In the modern world, a variable element for care and conduct as between solicitor and client (to be determined at the end of the case) is subject to criticism (and possible striking out as an unfair contract term).[6] It is impossible for the client to know at the outset the rate for the work that the solicitor is doing if the retainer letter is expressed in this fashion. If, however, the mark-up is fixed (whether at 50% or otherwise), what is the point of splitting the rate rather than calculating the total rate inclusive of mark-up?

Most solicitors therefore now express their agreement with the client in the retainer letter on the basis of an hourly rate inclusive of mark-up for care and conduct. This practice is now the preferred course in the Code. It has also been recognised by the courts in respect of assessment of costs 'between the parties'. Bills under the Civil Procedure Rules (CPR) are expected to include a single rate for each grade of fee-earner rather than an 'A' (expense) rate and a 'B' (care and conduct) rate as previously used. Thus it is essential that solicitors consider at the outset what is the right rate for that job. This rate must include any additional element of mark-up for care and conduct that the solicitor would have been seeking to charge under the old regime. It follows that a solicitor's charges for routine litigation may, for example, be £150 per hour plus VAT and expenses, reflecting an old 'A' rate of £100 per hour and a 'B' rate for care and conduct of 50%. If the case will require exceptional speed or is of exceptional complexity, then this rate might be increased by the solicitor to, say, £200 per hour, reflecting an old 'A' rate of £100 per hour with a 100% mark-up for care and conduct for an exceptional case. If 'A' and 'B' rates disappear, it is essential that the initial hourly charge-out rate does

---

6 See the Unfair Contract Terms Act 1977 and the Unfair Terms in Consumer Contracts Regulations 1994, SI 1994/3159 and the Consumer Protection from Unfair Trading Regulations 2008, SI 2008/1277.

reflect the complexity of the case. As a matter of good practice this has to be clear and agreed up-front with the client.

Stress and bullying at work claims are usually complex cases for vulnerable clients and under the old regime would have normally justified a 'B' rate well in excess of 50% and perhaps as high as 100%.

Consideration can be given to entering into a formal contentious business agreement under the Solicitors Act 1974 where the client's right to challenge hourly rates on assessment are severely curtailed. This may not be appropriate for unsophisticated private clients and this is why the Law Society's model CFA expressly states that it is not a contentious business agreement.

The Code specifically requires solicitors acting for privately paying clients to focus on explaining to clients their primary liability for their own legal fees and exposure to adverse costs orders. Solicitors should ensure clients understand that, even if they win, their opponent may be unable to pay their costs, although if the claim is against an employer for work-related stress then they are in practice likely to be met by the employer's liability insurers.

The client's own credit-worthiness must be considered: can or will the client actually pay? Solicitors can and, it is recommended, should ask for money on account of costs, both at the outset and throughout the different stages of the case. It will limit exposure to bad debts and guard against the situation where a deadline is imminent but no funds are in place. If solicitors are willing to give a client credit, it is recommended that this is only after credit checks have been undertaken unless the firm is willing to take the risk for commercial reasons. It is possible to secure fees against property (as is not untypical in a family law context) and, in common with other businesses, there is no reason why solicitors should not request charges or guarantees from third parties. However, care should be taken where security is given over shared assets, such as a matrimonial home, that the co-owner receives independent advice before entering into the security or charge. Otherwise, as illustrated by *Barclays Bank plc v O'Brien*[7] the security may not be enforceable against the co-owner. Guarantees must be in writing to be enforceable.

Few solicitors can afford to wait until the outcome of a case to be paid. Interim bills should be rendered at regular intervals. Interim bills also benefit the client by keeping them informed of costs and assisting them to budget for litigation. The Code provides that solicitors should keep clients informed of costs by rendering interim bills at agreed intervals.

Solicitors need to be careful to distinguish between interim bills on account and interim statute bills and it is recommended that they confirm

---

7 [1994] 1 AC 180.

the position in writing in the letter of retainer. Interim bills on account have the advantage of flexibility since they do not represent final quantification for the relevant period. Statute bills are a final costing for the period in question and the solicitor cannot reassess such bills to reflect a successful outcome.

The disadvantage of interim bills on account is that solicitors cannot sue on such bills; equally clients cannot apply to have such bills assessed.

A solicitor cannot assume that the client's agreement of hourly rates enables them to charge for whatever time they have spent; see above regarding the Code and the comments below about the court rules governing recoverability of costs.

If solicitors seek to bill sums which vary substantially from any estimates, including revised estimates, then there must be a risk that such sums will be disallowed by the Legal Complaints Service (LCS) as misleading or inaccurate in breach of paragraph 3(a) of the Code. A substantial variance may also be indicative of negligence or overcharging.

Stress and bullying at work claims are likely to involve very significant costs. Only very wealthy individuals are likely to be able to afford the risk of paying both sides costs up to a full trial (the costs and disbursements of both sides in a High Court case could well exceed £250,000). Although lawyers may be wary of risking taking such claims under a CFA, great care in explaining the costs and potential liability must be taken before accepting instructions on a private paying basis.

10.3.2 Fixed/capped fees agreed with the client

The agreement of fixed fees (perhaps for each stage of the case) entitles a solicitor to charge a set amount for work done, irrespective of how much time has been spent on the matter. Capped fees preclude the solicitor from charging fees in excess of the cap. Fees within the cap will be charged by reference to hourly rates. However, solicitors have always been wary of agreeing fixed or capped fees in litigation. There are two reasons for this. One is practical and the other is obscurely technical.

The practical reason is that litigation is inherently uncertain with regard to size, length and complexity, so a promise to take a case for a fixed fee can carry dangers for the solicitor.

The other reason why solicitors have been reluctant in litigation matters to agree fixed fees with their clients is the technical point of the 'indemnity principle'. A solicitor is not able to recover from the other side more than he has agreed with his client that he should be paid for the work. If, therefore, the solicitor had agreed a fixed fee with his client, he would not be able to recover a full hourly rate from the other side.

However, as will be seen, it is possible to combine private fee paying agreements, discounted rates or fixed fees with a CFA. This will have the effect of allowing a solicitor to agree with a client a fixed fee in the case of a loss, but a full hourly rate if the case succeeds.

10.4 CASES FUNDED WITH LEGAL EXPENSES INSURANCE

10.4.1 Fundamental terms

Before the event (BTE) insurance polices are legal expense insurance policies which have been taken out prior and unrelated to the event which requires legal assistance. They can be stand alone, but are more typically an add-on to motor or contents or other insurance policies. BTE policies are contracts as between the insurer and the insured client. Insurance contracts which are subject to the principles of insurance law such as, for example, the concepts of utmost good faith and subrogation. In theory, at least, it is a contract of indemnity so that the insurer's obligation is to make good the insured's loss (ie legal expenses) for which the insured has primary liability. However, because the legal expenses insurer is paying the bills, there is a third party in the solicitor-client relationship. Indeed, that third party often seeks to influence that relationship such as by directing the client to its own panel of solicitors and refusing to indemnify full hourly rates (or sometimes at all) in cases where there is no costs recovery from the defendant.

The solicitor should first check that the policy is valid and advise about the risk of avoidance (eg for the failure to disclose known claims on inception or on renewal which may entitle the insurer to avoid the policy).

BTE cover is rarely retrospective and written confirmation of cover is required before cover is granted. This usually requires the solicitor to certify reasonable prospects of success. Where BTE insurers require solicitors to report on the merits, solicitors need to consider and agree with the client the initial basis of charging for advising on the scope of the policy, the investigatory work in connection with the claim itself and the report to the insurers.

10.4.2 Scope of policy

It is essential for the solicitor to check the policy document including the schedule and all the terms and conditions relating to legal expense insurance. Typically, the main insurer for motor or home contents will have subcontracted the legal expenses element to a specialist legal expenses insurer.

It is first essential to check that a stress at work claim is within the scope of the cover. In respect of most add-ons to motor insurance, cover is limited to personal injury arising out of the use of the vehicle so would not cover a stress at work claim. The scope of stand alone BTE and add–ons to household contents and other policies vary widely. The wording of exclusions can often be quite opaque. Often psychiatric injury at work claims are expressly excluded (although discrimination claims would normally be covered). It is also common for 'progressive' or 'disease' claims to be excluded. Most stress claims would fall into this exclusion as there is no single event which has caused damage.

Then it is necessary to consider the amount of the indemnity. With a BTE policy, this is for both sides costs. It can range for £5,000 to £100,000. A policy with £25,000 cover both sides costs is, for example, unlikely to cover the costs of both sides taking a stress at work claim to trial.

The limit of indemnity is very likely to be inadequate. However, the BTE policy may be useful for initial investigation. It is then necessary to consider how to top it up (eg use it as insurance against for other side's costs only and sign a CFA for own costs; or use it to purchase after the event insurance (ATE)) at the outset and get the consent of the BTE provider (and any top up ATE insurer). All this must be clearly explained to the client and documented to ensure compliance with the Code.

10.4.3 Retainer

The solicitor's retainer should provide that the client is primarily liable for their fees even if they have BTE insurance. The insurer may object to paying some part of the solicitors' fees on the basis that the client has been unreasonable. Alternatively, it may transpire that the insurer is entitled to avoid the policy.

The retainer proposed by the BTE insurer should be checked particularly for hourly rates and compliance with the indemnity principle. Many BTE insurers propose no costs or fixed costs or lower rate costs if a claim is made to the BTE insurer and 'normal costs' (payable by the losing opponent) if the case is won. A partner must sign the bill at the end of the case to confirm that there has been no breach of the indemnity principle. If there has been a breach, the solicitor will be limited only to the costs payable by the BTE insurer.

The retainer with the client might be in the form of a standard private paying client retainer, but with reference to the indemnity from the BTE insurer. However, it might be difficult to explain to the client why they have to pay your 'normal' rates but their insurer will pay nothing or much less towards them. A CFA without a success fee is preferable, which specifies the firm's normal fees if the claim is successful and the lower fees payable by the BTE insurer if the claim fails.

A success fee can be applied to reflect the risk of not recovering full rates[8] although success fees in this context do not sit well with prior insurance from a client care perspective.

If a success fee is sought, then notice of funding must be given to the defendant. If no success fee is sought, no such notice needs to be given.

If the solicitor wishes to render interim bills to the BTE insurer or seek payments on account of disbursements, it is sensible to say so at the outset, although some insurers only provide for payment at the end of the case or after specified periods. In practice, many BTE insurers expressly or impliedly refuse to pay at all if the case is unsuccessful (or at best will agree to pay a very low hourly rate). The BTE insurance is then little more than insurance against third party costs and a referral to a solicitor willing to take a 'no win, no fee' case without a success fee.

If the solicitor is paying the BTE insurer for the referral this should be disclosed to the client in advance. Panel solicitors may accept referrals from legal expenses insurers provided they comply with the provisions of the Code.

10.4.4 Panel Solicitors

The most controversial requirement of BTE insurance is usually panel solicitor restrictions. The Insurance Companies (Legal Expenses Insurance) Regulations 1990[9] provide that the insured has freedom to choose their lawyer 'to defend, represent or serve the interests of the insured in any enquiry or proceedings' whenever recourse is had to BTE with certain exceptions.[10] This has been interpreted as giving freedom of choice once proceedings are imminent or on foot or there is a conflict of interest between the insurer and the insured. The Financial Services Ombudsman has indicated that he would expect a restriction of choice of solicitor to be made clear to the client on inception of the policy. In practice, the insurer rarely does this. However, the Ombudsman has interpreted this more restrictively so that with simple cases (such as low value road traffic accident claims) the insured may be required to use a panel solicitor, but with more substantial claims freedom of choice from the outset may be allowed.[11] However with regard to more substantial claims:

---

8 *Evans v Gloucestershire County Council* [2008] EWCA Civ 21, [2008] 1 WLR 1883.

9 SI 1990/1159.

10 See reg 7 of the Insurance Companies (Legal Expenses Insurance) Regulations 1990, SI 1990/1159.

11 An anonymised decision of the Financial Services Ombudsman described as that of the case of Mrs A and B Company of 10 January 2003.

> 'I would expect insurers to agree the appointment of the policyholder's preferred solicitors in cases of large personal injury and claims that are necessarily complex such as medical negligence . . .'

It is submitted that claims for stress at work will also usually fall into this category and most legal expense insurers will allow choice of representative.

It may also be possible to agree with the legal expense insurer not to make a claim under the legal expenses policy until after proceedings are issued. However, if seeking to recover a success fee from an opponent, it will have to be a reasonable decision to make. If the BTE cover is limited and it is reasonable to reserve this for an opponent's costs, then it may be reasonable.

If the BTE insurer refuses to allow the client's own solicitor to act, a client can still use a CFA instead of BTE. After all the checks and inquiries have been made the solicitor must make clear to the client the contrast between their liability for costs with BTE when compared with proceeding on a CFA with or without additional liabilities and give appropriate advice and costs warnings to his client on the advantages and/or disadvantages of using any BTE policy. After the advice has been given (confirmed in writing) if the client chooses not to use the BTE the solicitor should be able to sign up an enforceable CFA. However, unless the BTE is unsuitable for some reason, recovery from the defendant of the success fee and any ATE premium is doubtful.

10.4.5 Continuing duties to insurer

The solicitor must ensure the client understands the duty of utmost good faith and the importance of full disclosure of material facts, otherwise cover will be avoided. It is irrelevant whether non-disclosure arises from indifference or a mistake. It is irrelevant that the reason for non-disclosure is the client's failure to understand that a fact was material.

Solicitors must themselves, as the client's agent, disclose those material facts which are in their knowledge. They must check the policy for reporting requirements about, for example, costs and the prospects of success. In one case[12] a legal expenses insurer successfully sued a firm of solicitors for misrepresentation. The solicitors had obtained, but not disclosed, an unfavourable counsel's opinion. Also check for warranties about future conduct, for example, to the effect that information is and will remain accurate. Ensure that the client understands that the duty of utmost good faith is continuing. Breach of a warranty will entitle the insurer to avoid the policy and repudiate liability from the date of breach.

---

[12] *DAS Legal Expenses Insurance Co Ltd v Hughes Hooker & Co* (unreported) 1994.

10.5 TRADE UNION FUNDING

The Trade Union movement has been in the forefront of supporting the litigation of stress at work claims by its members. If a client is a member of a trade union then consideration should be given to approaching the union for assistance. Trade unions usually operate a restricted panel of solicitors firms and are very unlikely to consent to another firm acting.

In respect of stress claims in court, union solicitors will normally operate under a collective conditional fee agreement (CCFA) with the union. So far as the individual client is concerned, this operates very much like a normal CFA[13] although there will normally be an express promise that he client will not be charged any solicitor and own client costs.

So far as the liability for the opponent's costs are concerned (in a court claim), the union will either self insure these (and claim a 'notional premium' from the opponent[14]) or fund ATE insurance on behalf of their member.

It should be noted that if the solicitor is prepared to take the case under a CFA (and agree to make no charge to the client whatsoever) and is confident of obtaining ATE insurance (with a deferred premium) for a meritorious case, then there is no particular advantage to the client of trade union funding. A CFA and a union indemnity for adverse costs is equivalent to such a CFA and ATE insurance both in cost to the client (ie nil) and protection from adverse costs orders. The costs implications for the opponent (success fee and ATE insurance premium or notional premium) will also be the same, or roughly equivalent, so the funding choice is not easily attacked by the opponent on assessment.

However, with regard to tribunal claims, support for members in the employment tribunal (funding legal representation) is a key benefit of union membership. As this is free to the member (and legal costs are rarely recoverable in the tribunal) the solicitor should take great care to explain the costs implications of instructing a private firm of solicitors.

That said, it is not uncommon for union members not to choose to use the union. Some may have been refused funding; others may simply not want the union to act for a variety of reasons.

---

13 See **10.5**.

14 AJA 1999, s 30.

10.6 CASES FUNDED WITH CONDITIONAL FEE AGREEMENTS

10.6.1 Statutory requirements

Conditional fee agreements were originally introduced to provide a means of access to justice for 'middle England'. It was argued that only the very rich and the very poor (through legal aid, now known as public funding) had access to the courts. For many years public policy, expressed through the offences of champerty and maintenance and enforced through court decisions and practice rules, had prevented lawyers from having an interest in the outcome of a case. Although the crime was abolished in the 1960s, any such agreement remained unenforceable at law. Fears about an ever-reducing access to justice led to a fundamental change of view. The means by which this policy change was implemented was a very 'English' compromise. Parliament did not want to introduce a US-style system of contingency fees for fear of creating a 'compensation culture'. The 'loser pays' costs rule was to be maintained.

Parliament enacted that the lawyer could charge a percentage increase on his normal fee with a maximum success fee of 100%. The Courts and Legal Services Act 1990, s 58 was not brought into force until 1995.[15] The Access to Justice Act 1999 (AJA 1999) provided that, subject to rules of court, success fees (and indeed any premiums for after the event insurance – see below) should be paid by the loser in the litigation along with other legal costs.[16]

The legality of the CFA regime for all clients, not just the impecunious, was upheld by the House of Lords in *Campbell v MGN*[17] (although not without some regret and not without criticism of some of the effects of Parliament's decision).

It is very important to determine which regulatory framework applies to the CFA as this will have different consequences as to form, advice and effect (eg recoverability of success fee):

- The 1995 Regulations:[18] apply to CFAs entered into between 5 July 1995 and 31 March 2000.

- The 2000 Regulations:[19] apply to CFAs between 1 April 2000 and 1 November 2005.

---

[15] Conditional Fee Agreements Regulations 1995, SI 1995/1675.
[16] Courts and Legal Services Act 1990, s 58A(6) and (7), as amended by AJA 1999, s 27(1).
[17] [2005] UKHL 61.
[18] Conditional Fee Agreements Regulations 1995, SI 1995/1675.
[19] Conditional Fee Agreements Regulations 2000, SI 2000/692.

- The 2003 Regulations:[20] only apply to a 'CFA Lite' which complies with those Regulations and made between 1 July 2003 and 1 November 2005.

- The 2005 Regulations:[21] revoke the 2000 Regulations and the 2003 Regulations for CFAs entered into after 1 November 2005.

10.6.2 The Conditional Fee Agreements Regulations 2000 and the Conditional Fee Agreements Regulations 2005

The Conditional Fee Agreements Regulations 2000 specified in detail the verbal and written information on numerous matters that must be provided to clients before the CFA was made and as the form of the CFA. These Regulations have been the subject of considerable litigation and reported case-law. As these Regulations are revoked by the Conditional Fee Agreements Regulations 2005, it is not proposed to deal with this here. They do, however, remain in effect for CFAs made before 1 November 2005 and specialist texts should be consulted in respect of them as appropriate.[22] The Conditional Fee Agreements Regulations 2005 do not themselves impose any requirements in respect of CFAs after 1 November 2005.

However, this leaves s 58 of the Courts and Legal Services Act 1990 as amended (which provides that a CFA must be in writing) and the Conditional Fee Agreements Order 2005 (which provides that the maximum permitted success fee is 100%) as the only statutory controls on CFAs, with client protections being dealt with by the Solicitors Practice Rules 2007.[23]

10.6.3 Risk assessment

Risk assessment is crucial. Solicitors must go back to the basics: will this case win? Before entering into a CFA this question is fundamental; nothing else matters more. Although there will be many unknowns and it might be easier to shy away from facing this challenge, the issues of the case have to identified and a concerted effort must be made to identify at the outset what proof will be available to clear each of the evidential hurdles. This is the purpose of risk assessment procedures – although this has been somewhat muddied by the use of risk assessment forms to justify success fees before the advent of fixed success fees.

---

20 Conditional Fee Agreements (Miscellaneous Amendments) Regulations 2003, SI 2003/1240.

21 Conditional Fee Agreements (Revocation) Regulations 2005, SI 2005/2305.

22 See, for example, *APIL Personal Injury: Law, Practice and Precedents Looseleaf* (Jordan Publishing Ltd, November 2008) Division D.

23 See **10.2**.

No CFA case should be taken on without the approval of another fee earner, usually a partner and often a panel. No decision to take any case should be taken by one fee earner with no one checking the decision. But the process must be proportionate and effective. Decisions (even if it is to refer back for more investigation) should be made quickly.

As has been seen, stress at work claims are risky and expensive. Very careful risk assessment is warranted.

10.6.4 Success fees

Although not expressly stated in the legislation, the purpose of a success fee is to provide the solicitor with an uplift on normal base costs in successful cases which compensates for the loss of costs in lost or abandoned cases. The CPR originally provided for an assessment process 'without hindsight' in every case to assess whether the success fee reasonably reflected the risk being run. However, it is difficult to assess the required quantum of success fee to enable winners to pay for losers as it is applied to the base costs of the successful case. It is not possible to know whether the lost cases cost on average the same, or more, or less than the successful cases. And success fees must carry some objective element otherwise the bad solicitor who loses many cases would be entitled to a higher success fee than the good solicitor who loses few cases.

For personal injury cases the costs assessment system more or less ground to a halt in the years following the introduction of recoverability of additional liabilities as defendant insurance companies challenged CFAs and success fees. The Civil Justice Council brokered a series of industry mediations which led to fixed success fees being implemented.

'Occupational Stress' is an employer's liability disease claim for these purposes.

The Civil Justice Council commissioned Professors Paul Fenn and Neil Rickman to report. As their report states:

> 'The objective of this study is to assist in the determination of 'reasonable' success fees for Employers' Liability (EL) disease claims. We suggest that one measure of reasonableness is to calculate success fees such that a CFA case yields the same revenue to the solicitor as an hourly fee counterpart (on average) – that is, a success fee which would make the choice between CFA cases and hourly fee cases *revenue-neutral* over a sufficiently large number of EL disease cases. In turn, this requires detailed knowledge of the stages through which a case may proceed, the probabilities of transition between these stages and the costs associated with the transition. A decision tree was constructed to facilitate the calculation of revenue-neutral success fees, and the data we required to populate the tree with costs and probabilities were collected through spreadsheet templates.'

The Fenn and Rickman report contains some interesting background data on the success rates of stress at work litigation in the courts. Table 5 in their Report contains information on failure rates prior to issue of proceedings collected from two claimant solicitors firms (9,000 cases from Firm C and 360 cases from Firm B) and from data collected by the Compensation Recovery Unit (CRU):[24]

	Firm B		Firm C		CRU
	% of total cases	Pre-claim failure rate	% of total cases	Pre-claim failure rate	Post-claim failure rate
Stress	16.94%	67.21%	19.06%	85.19%	72.53%

The CRU data only shows the claim failure rate after notification of the claim to the CRU. The CRU does not capture data as to whether the claim settled before or after issue of legal proceedings. However, by applying the disease-specific pre-claim failure rates for firm B from Table 5 they concluded that the failure rates for stress claims was pre-issue 79.78% and post-issue was 32.64% (with the overall total failure rate being 72.53% as shown above).

The fixed success fee model applied was to have been the same as for other fixed success fees, namely 100% for cases resolved at trial and a different (lower) success fee for pre-trial resolution. However, in the case of stress at work claims, the failure rate was such that a 'revenue neutral' success fee would have been 343.75%. The maximum success fee allowed by the legislation is 100%.

This report and subsequent industry negotiations led to the fixed recoverable success fees for employer's liability disease cases under the CPR.[25] This states:

> **'45.23**
>
> (1) Subject to paragraph (2), this Section applies where—
>
> (a) the dispute is between an employee (or, if the employee is deceased, the employee's estate or dependants) and his employer (or a person alleged to be liable for the employer's alleged breach of statutory or common law duties of care); and
>
> (b) the dispute relates to a disease with which the employee is diagnosed that is alleged to have been contracted as a consequence of the employer's alleged breach of statutory or common law duties of care in the course of the employee's employment; and

[24] The government body which is part of the Department of Work and Pensions established under the under the Social Security (Recovery of Benefits) Act 1997 to which all claims for compensation for injuries or disease must be notified.

[25] CPR 45 Part V.

(c) the claimant has entered into a funding arrangement of a type specified in rule 43.2(1)(k)(i) [ie a CFA or CCFA].

(2) This Section does not apply where—

(a) the claimant sent a letter of claim to the defendant containing a summary of the facts on which the claim is based and main allegations of fault before 1st October 2005; or

(b) rule 45.20(2)(b) applies' [ie a claim which has been allocated to the small claims track; or if not allocated to a track, but for which the small claims track is the normal track].'

Under CPR 45.23(3)(b), an employee is:[26]

> '. . . an individual who has entered into or works under a contract of service or apprenticeship with an employer whether by way of manual labour, clerical work or otherwise, whether such contract is expressed or implied, oral or in writing.'

Under CPR 45.23(3)(d) a stress at work claims is a 'Type B' claim, namely a claim relating to:

> '(i) a psychiatric injury alleged to have been caused by work-related psychological stress;'

And the table annexed to the Practice Direction supplementing Part 45 lists 'occupational stress' as one of the non-exclusive list of diseases within Type B.

The 'percentage increase of solicitors' fees' (ie success fee) allowed under CPR 45.24 is 100% for conclusion at all stages of all 'Type B' claims.[27]

CPR 45 makes similar provision (ie 100% success fee whenever the claim concludes) for counsel's fees.

In theory, CPR 45.26 allows for a lower success fee to be applied on assessment, but only for claims valued at £250,000 or more. For Type B claims, if the court assessed the success fee at less than 75% then the success fee is not 100%, but such success fee as was assessed by the court. If the court would have allowed a success fee of between 75% and 100%, then 100% will be allowed in any event.

It is submitted that this will very rarely apply to stress at work claims unless, for example, there is a full and open admission of liability (including causation) prior to the CFA being made.

---

26 The definition is taken from the Employers' Liability (Compulsory Insurance) Act 1969, s 2(1).

27 CPR 45(1)(a) for claims concluded at trial and CPR 45(2)(b) for Type B claims concluded prior to trial.

10.6.5 Form of the CFA

The Law Society's model CFA can be used.[28]

If it is not certain whether a claim will be brought in the tribunal or in the courts (or indeed both) it might be sensible to amend the CFA to provide for all work.[29]

There is likely to be less danger of homemade variations rendering the CFA unenforceable after the coming into force of the CFA Regulations 2005. However, the indemnity principle still applies, so it is important that nothing is altered that might affect the client's ultimate liability to pay as this might affect recoverability from the defendant (for claims in court).

If the client is to pay disbursements, the model agreement needs to be amended to provide for this.

It is, however, very important to decide at the outset how to deal with a Part 36 offer that is rejected following the solicitor's advice, but which is subsequently not beaten. There are two widely used options – 'the shared risk clause' (where the solicitor waives success fees, but not basic costs after the offer) and 'the ring-fenced damages clause' (where the solicitor waives all costs after the date of the offer). The ring-fenced damages clause is obviously more risky for the solicitor. It is important to check the position with ATE insurance in such circumstances and whether the insurers require a particular clause in the CFA. Barristers will usually not be prepared to accept the ring-fenced damages clause in their CFAs.

10.6.6 Notification

As the winning party to litigation under a CFA is seeking more in costs than would be normally expected (because of the success fee) the CPR provides that notice of the existence of a CFA must be given on issue of proceedings (or, if later, signature of the CFA)[30] and:[31]

> 'A party may not recover as an additional liability—
>
>> "any additional liability for any period in the proceedings during which he failed to provide information about a funding arrangement in accordance with a rule, practice direction or court order;" ...'

---

[28] See precedent at **12.2.1**.
[29] See precedent at **12.2.3**.
[30] CPR Part 19 PD, para 2.
[31] CPR, r 44.3B.

The CPR also provide that similar information should be given pre-proceedings.[32]

If no notice is given, then there is obviously a serious risk that additional liabilities will not be recoverable, although it is possible to apply for relief from sanction.

10.6.7 Counsel

Most of the matters relating to funding covered elsewhere in this section apply equally to counsel as to solicitors. As counsel is usually brought into a case after the solicitor has accepted the case on a CFA basis, different considerations prevail. Counsel should undertake his own risk assessment and not rely upon that conducted by his instructing solicitor. It is recommended that use is made of the APIL/PIBA model[33] CFA.

10.7 AFTER THE EVENT INSURANCE

10.7.1 Selecting a policy

CFAs do not cover the client against exposure to the other side's legal costs. Solicitors should ensure that clients understand this exposure and in most, if not all cases, the client should be advised to take out after the event insurance cover to protect their position. After the event (ATE) insurance is a species of legal expense insurance which is taken out 'after the event', ie when the event which has caused the need for insurance has already incurred, in contrast to pre-purchased 'before the event' cover.

This can include both the usual insurance against the opponent's costs and own disbursements if the case is lost (in personal injury cases, this usually accompanies a CFA) and insurance against both sides' costs (BSC) (own solicitor and opponent's costs). BSC policies were common immediately after the coming into force of the AJA 1999 (especially the 'Claims Direct Protect' policy), but are now rare, most ATE insurers being wary about insuring a lawyer's own costs rather than asking them to take the risk of loss through a CFA. From 1 April 2000, the premium is recoverable from the opponent by way of s 29 of the AJA 1999 as an 'additional liability'.

The solicitor is not required to act as a 'broker' of ATE insurance by the Act, Regulations, CPR, Practice Rules or case-law and should resist any such temptation.

---

32 Practice Direction Protocols 4A.

33 Model CFA agreed between the Association of Personal Injury Lawyers and the Personal Injury Bar Association.

However, note the requirements imposed by the Financial Services Act 1986 and the Solicitors Financial Services (Conduct of Business) Rules 2001 (in force from January 2005). Solicitors need to register with the either the Law Society or the Financial Services Authority direct as 'insurance intermediaries'. And, in particular, a Conduct of Business Rules Statement and Demands & Needs Statement need to be prepared for clients and individual attention and wording needs to be given by each firm to give proper effect to their and each of their client's own situation.

Care should be taken before submitting an application for insurance to ensure that all relevant details have been completed and that the insurer is reasonably likely to take on the case. A turn down by one insurer may significantly damage the prospects of obtaining insurance elsewhere.

Stress and bullying at work claims are not popular with many ATE insurers. Some expressly exclude 'psychiatric injury at work' claims from cover. Others are concerned about the low success rate. Premiums are likely to be high. Some providers do defer the payment of the premium until the end of the case. This is likely to be essential for most clients.

It is rare that a solicitor will be granted delegated authority by ATE insurers to issue a policy. It is likely to require a specific application for a bespoke policy, usually after initial investigation with medical evidence and counsel's advice.

10.7.2 Policy terms

Perhaps the most important point to consider is what happens if there is a Part 36 offer made, rejected on advice, but not beaten with adverse costs consequences. This is particularly important in cases where primary liability is admitted or almost certain as this may be the only real possible adverse costs order the client will face. Some ATE policies will operate in these circumstances to ring-fence damages so that the client does not suffer loss in these circumstances (usually such ATE insurers require the solicitor to include a ring-fenced damages clause in the CFA).[34] This is a valuable protection for the client (and worth incurring the premium for even if liability has been admitted). However, it can lead to client feeling of 'nothing to lose' making it more difficult to obtain rational instructions on a Part 36 offer. The solicitor must also be careful not to imply that the client will lose compensation if the Part 36 offer is not beaten if rejected following advice as this is not true if the policy contains a ring-fence damage clause.

However, other ATE polices are not so beneficial for the client following Part 36 offers which are not beaten. The ATE insurer often will look first

[34] See **10.6.5.**

to the damages to pay the opponent's costs and sometimes may even look to previous costs orders in the client's favour (leaving the solicitor at risk of non-payment).

10.7.3 Premium recovery

So far as bespoke ATE insurance cover is concerned, *Ashworth v Peterborough FC*[35] is instructive. The claimant won acrimonious commercial litigation. The damages awarded were £66,000. The claimant took out BSC cover with an indemnity limit of £125,000. The premium was £46,000 (including insurance premium tax (IPT)). Master Wright allowed the premium and accepted the ATE insurer's evidence that it would not have provided the premium for less.

In *Able UK Ltd v Reliance Security Services Ltd*[36] the claimant sought to recover an ATE premium of £60,000 plus IPT for cover of £200,000. Evidence from the after the event insurer Greystoke was that premiums for contractual disputes 'were fixed within a range of 25-40%' with the position in the range determined by the risk. The defendant produced evidence from four other insurers, suggesting a range of 15-40% of cover and submitted prospects of success were higher than the claimant had assessed them (70%). Master Wright held that with prospects of success of 70%, a premium of 30% of cover was reasonable and the claimant's solicitors had considerable experience of commercial ATE insurance and so did not need to obtain other quotes.

In the *RSA Pursuit Test Cases*[37] policies were considered where the premium was not fixed at the outset, but was instead determined by reference to the final claimed solicitor's base costs and a formula to reflect risk dependent upon anticipated prospects of success and estimation of opponent's costs. Generally the insurer insured difficult, complex cases (including stress at work claims). The defendants argued that the policy was void. Master Hurst held that the policies were not void for uncertainty or champerty. But he also held that the premiums were too high because they were based on claimed, not assessed, base costs and because estimates of opponent's costs at various stages were unrealistic. The premiums were dramatically reduced.

Although dealing with block rated policies, the Court of Appeal in *Rogers v Merthyr Tydfil Borough Council*[38] gave a steer towards staged premiums rather than single rate premiums but if they are used notice of the staging should be given to the defendant. And on assessment:

---

35 FC LTL 4/7/2002.

36 *Able UK Ltd v Reliance Security Services Ltd* [2006] EWHC 90058 (Costs).

37 [2005] EWCA 90003, Master Hurst.

38 [2006] EWCA Civ 1134.

'If an issue arises about the size of a second or third stage premium, it will ordinarily be sufficient for a claimant's solicitor to write a brief note for the purposes of the costs assessment explaining how he came to choose the particular ATE product for his client, and the basis on which the premium is rated – whether block rated or individually rated. District judges and costs judges do not, as Lord Hoffmann observed in *Callery v Gray (Nos 1 and 2)* [2002] UKHL 28 at [44]; [2002] 1 WLR 2000, have the expertise to judge the reasonableness of a premium except in very broad brush terms, and the viability of the ATE market will be imperilled if they regard themselves (without the assistance of expert evidence) as better qualified than the underwriter to rate the financial risk the insurer faces.'

Most importantly, the court considered how proportionality should be applied to ATE premiums:

'. . . the fact that the ATE premium was large compared with the agreed damages of £3,000 did not necessarily mean that it was disproportionate. Under CPR 44.5(1) a court must take into account "all the circumstances". These include the financial risk faced by the insurer.'

10.7.4 Acting under a CFA without ATE cover

It is not compulsory to take out ATE insurance in a case funded under a CFA. It is good practice to do so if insurance is available as the premium is recoverable from the defendant as an 'additional liability'. However, the premium may be large and the client may decide not to incur it. Alternatively, ATE insurance may not be available, because insurers decline to accept the risk. In *Hodgson v Imperial Tobacco and others* the solicitors for the claimants in the tobacco litigation were acting under CFAs but had been unable to obtain ATE insurance. Lord Woolf said:

'There is no reason why the circumstances in which a lawyer, acting under a CFA, can be made personally liable for the costs of a party other than his client should differ from those in which a lawyer who is not acting under a CFA would be so liable. Any suggestion by the defendants' lawyers, and any concern of the plaintiffs' lawyers, that the position of the plaintiffs' lawyers is different from that of any other legal adviser is misconceived. The existence of a CFA should make a legal advisers' position as a matter of law no worse, so far as being ordered to pay costs is concerned, than it would be if there was no CFAs. This is unless, of course, the CFA is outside the statutory protection.'

In *Myatt and Others v National Coal Board (No 2)*[39] the ATE insurance policy had been avoided, because it was dependant upon a valid CFA being in force.[40] The defendants sought a wasted costs order under s51 of the Supreme Courts Act 1981. Dyson LJ held that the solicitors had a significant interest in the appeal where some £200,000 profit costs were at

39 [2007] EWCA Civ 307.

40 The court had previously decided (in *Myatt and Others v National Coal Board (No 1)* that the CFA was unenforceable and so 'outside the statutory protection'.

stake. It had been thought following *Tolstoy-Miloslavsky v Aldington*[41] that a solicitor could not be liable to a wasted costs order in such circumstances unless 'he acts outside the role of solicitor, e.g. in a private capacity or as a true third party funder for someone else'. However, the court held that solicitors could fall within the definition of the third category of funders of litigation in *Dymocks v Todd*,[42] namely a non-party who 'not merely funds the proceedings but substantially also controls or at any rate is to benefit from them'. The defendant had not given prior notification of their intention to seek a wasted costs order and the claimants did themselves have some financial interest in the appeal. The court ordered the solicitors to pay 50% of the defendant's costs. Lloyd LJ did, however add that such an order 'could be common in relation to cases where the enforceability of a CFA is at stake but would be most unusual in any situation'. Brooke LJ agreed 'with both judgments'.

Solicitors should be very wary of themselves promising to indemnify the client against adverse costs orders:

- This additional assumption of risk cannot be rewarded by way of costs recoverable from the defendant.
- It may be difficult to fairly charge the client for this.
- The solicitor may in fact be acting as an insurer and thus subject to registration and regulation under the Financial Services and Markets Act 2000.
- Their position becomes analogous to third party litigation funders and this may have an uncertain impact on their liability for costs and indeed the enforceability of their CFA.[43]

If the client is accepting the risk of an adverse costs order, the advice about the risk being run by the client must of course be carefully recorded.

10.8 CONTINGENCY FEE AGREEMENTS

English law has long frowned on 'contingency fees' for litigation work. A contingency fee is any payment that is contingent upon the result. This includes:

- percentage cuts of the damages won (US-style);

---

41 [1996] 1 WLR 736.
42 [2004] 1 WLR 2807, [2004] UKPC 39.
43 In *Dix v Frizzell Financial Services* [2008] EWHC 90117 the agreement to indemnify the client against adverse costs orders was held to be champertous and the CFA unenforceable.

- uplifts on normal costs if the case is won; and
- normal costs only if the case is won with lower costs only if the case is lost.

However, in common usage it is usually taken to mean a US-style agreement where the lawyer takes a percentage of the damages in lieu of his fee.

The Code defines a contingency fee as meaning:

> '. . . any sum (whether fixed or calculated either as a percentage of the proceeds or otherwise howsoever) payable only in the event of success in the prosecution of any action, suit or other contentious proceeding.'

It has been argued that contingency fees are not prohibited for work done before court proceedings are commenced, as they do not relate to 'the prosecution of any action, suit or other contentious proceeding'. However, the AJA 1999 has also widened the statutory definition of 'proceedings' to catch pre-proceedings work, so this must now be doubtful. CFAs are a statutory exception to the prohibition on contingency fees to litigation. CFAs must strictly comply with the statutory requirements otherwise the agreement with the client will be an unlawful contingency fee agreement.

It had been thought that the common law had also developed to enable fees to be charged contingent upon the result, but without allowing any 'success fee'. However, the Court of Appeal in *Awwad v Geraghty & Co*[44] overturned this and ruled that contingency fees in litigation remain unlawful save as sanctioned by statute. The only safe mechanism for both pre-proceedings and post-proceedings litigation is now a lawful CFA complying with the requirements of the Courts and Legal Services Act 1990 and AJA 1999. Solicitors' Practice Rule 8 prohibits contingency fees where a solicitor is 'retained or employed to prosecute or defend any action, suit or other contentious proceeding' save where permitted by common law or under statute.

However, it is widely accepted that contingency fees are lawful in relation to employment cases in the employment tribunal (because such matters do not constitute an 'action, suit or other contentious proceeding'). If used in an appropriate case, it should be remembered that the client can still ask for a Remuneration Certificate pursuant to the Solicitors (Non Contentious Business) Remuneration Order 1994.

Barristers are not permitted to act under a contingency fee:[45]

---

44 [2001] QB 570, [2000] 1 All ER 608, [2000] 3 WLR 1041, CA.

45 At www.barcouncil.org.uk/guidance/faqs/.

'I have been instructed in an Employment Tribunal case. The solicitor has a contingency (not conditional) fee agreement with the client and would like me to take half of any eventual fee. Can I agree to this?

Answer: No. Owing to an anomaly in the Solicitors' Practice Rules, solicitors are able to take Employment Tribunal work on a contingency fee basis. Barristers may not. Clearly taking half the eventual fee is acting on such a basis. You may agree a conditional fee with the solicitor (i.e. a normal fee with an uplift) but that is all.'

The Department for Business, Enterprise and Regulatory Reform commissioned research into the use of contingency fees in the employment tribunal and the resulting report 'The influence of legal representation at Employment Tribunals on case outcome' was published in July 2007[46] The report's main findings were:

'• There is no statistical difference in the levels of satisfaction with case outcome expressed between those claimants represented on contingent fee arrangements and those who did not have such an arrangement.
- Claimants who were covered by legal expenses insurance and/or members of a trade union were less likely have contingent fee arrangements.
- Claimants with contingent fee arrangements were involved in higher financial value cases and were more likely to be seeking compensation than claimants with other fee arrangements.
- Claimants with contingent fee arrangements were more likely to be advised that they were likely to win their claim than those with other fee arrangements. Tribunal hearing outcomes suggest that this optimism might be misplaced. Claimants with contingent fee arrangements were successful in 48% of cases compared to 56% where normal fee arrangements applied and 56% of all cases (any representation). Note also here the tendency for contingent fee arrangements to be used in higher financial value cases.
- Cases where a contingent fee arrangement existed were more likely to be settled and less likely to be withdrawn. Those cases involving contingent fees were less likely to be ACAS conciliated but twice as likely to be privately settled.
- Large settlements (those over £5,000) were more a feature of contingent fee cases compared to other settled cases.
- Contingent fee payers also have higher salaries on average and more likely to be managers than non-contingent fee payers.
- Claimants entering into contingent fee arrangements do not seem to be responding to cold-calling by persons offering legal representation services when compared to those entering other arrangements with lawyers
- Claimants who eventually enter into contingent fee arrangements are just as likely to have been contacted by Acas and equally aware of their right to some free preliminary advice as claimants in general.

46 Employment Relations Research Series No 84: the influence of legal representation at Employment Tribunals on case outcome by Geraldine Hammersley, Jane Johnson and David Morris, Coventry Business School, Coventry University.

- A multi-variable cluster analysis of the SETA 2003 data suggests that contingent fee claimants had higher than average salaries, had some higher education qualifications, and financial settlements were a the top end of the range reported in SETA 2003.
- There is evidence to suggest that claimants with contingent fee arrangements who settled their case or who rejected an offer of settlement, are more inclined to feel they would have done better at a Tribunal hearing.'

It is likely that stress at work claims (discriminatory harassment) in the employment tribunal would fall within the categories found most likely to be suitable for a contingency fee agreement. However, the solicitor must at the outset analyse the risk of failure, the likely compensation and the anticipated investment in terms of time and expenses. A mathematical model can be prepared to show whether or not the solicitor is likely to make a return on the investment of time.

The solicitor also needs to consider how to structure the contingency fee. A flat percentage fee is simplest to understand, but the greatest investment of time is at the tribunal hearing so some agreements have different percentages dependant upon when the case settles. It is also necessary to clearly explain to the client whether or not VAT is included or on top of the percentage (eg 33% inclusive of VAT produces about 28% of damages as solicitors costs plus VAT; 33% solicitors costs plus VAT is a real percentage of damages of about 40% including VAT).

10.9 RECOVERING COSTS

10.9.1 Costs recovery in the court

10.9.1.1 Indemnity principle

Whatever arrangements may have been made for the client to pay his solicitor, the client and the solicitor have the same interest in maximising the amount of those costs which can be recovered from a losing opponent. The starting point for ensuring that costs are recovered is the 'indemnity principle'. Expressed long ago by the House of Lords in *Gundry v Sainsbury*,[47] this costs principle provides that a successful party cannot recover from the loser more than he has agreed to pay his own solicitor.

In *Bailey v IBC Vehicles Ltd*[48] the question of a trade union's retainer with its solicitors was examined. Following that decision the Chief Taxing Master issued Supreme Court Taxing Office Practice Direction 2/1998. This made it clear that the indemnity principle was alive and well. It

47 [1910] 1 KB 645.
48 [1998] 3 All ER 570.

required solicitors to summarise the terms of their retainer in the bill (or an annexure to the bill) and to certify that there had been no breach of the indemnity principle. Furthermore, in *General of Berne Insurance Co Ltd v Jardine Reinsurance Management Ltd*[49]it was held that not only did the indemnity principle apply to the total amount of costs billed to the client and sought to be recovered from the other side, but also to each individual item of work. In other words, if interim bills are delivered expressly for certain portions of the work then no more than that sum can be recovered from the other side for that work. This is so, even if the totality of the bills to the client exceed the totality of the costs sought from the other side.

The advent of CFAs might seem to obviate the need for such a principle. As the client will not be paying the solicitor anything unless the case is won (triggering an obligation on the defendant to pay costs) it might be argued that the client has very little interest in the headline hourly rate set out in the CFA. The CFA does not, however, breach the indemnity principle because the client's liability to pay the costs on a solicitor and client basis is created if the case is won. However, even if the indemnity principle has been so abrogated (and indeed even if the solicitor has agreed to restrict costs to those recovered, as permitted by CPR Rule 43.2.(3)), it is still necessary (as affirmed by the Court of Appeal in *Hollins v Russell*[50]) for there to be an enforceable retainer (e g a valid CFA complying with the AJA 1999 and the relevant regulations).

10.9.1.2 Loser pays

The court retains an overriding discretion as to '(a) whether costs are payable by one party to another; (b) the amount of those costs; and (c) when they are to be paid' (CPR Rule 44.3(1).

The so-called 'English rule' that the 'loser pays' is retained (CPR Rule 44.3(2)(a)), but 'the court may make a different order' (CPR Rule 44.3(2)(b)). See *Phonographic Performance v AEI Rediffusion*[51], per Woolf MR:

> 'The "follow the event principle" is to be the starting point from which a court can readily depart. The most significant change of emphasis in the new Rules is to require courts to be more ready to make separate orders which reflect the outcome of different issues.'

CPR 44.3 now enables the court to do greater justice where a successful party has caused an unsuccessful party to incur costs on an issue which

49 [1998] 2 All ER 301.
50 [2003] 1 WLR 2487, [2003] 3 Costs LR 423, [2003] 4 All ER 590, [2003] EWCA Civ 718.
51 [1999] 1 WLR 1507, CA.

later fails. In *Johnsey v The Secretary of State for the Environment*[52] Chadwick LJ set out the principles to be applied to the determination of costs post-CPR:

- Costs cannot be recovered except under an order of the court.

- Whether to make a costs order and, if so, what order to make is at the discretion of the trial judge.

- The starting point for the exercise of discretion is that costs should follow the event.

- The judge may make different orders for costs in relation to discrete issues. In particular, he should consider doing so where a party has been successful on one issue but unsuccessful on another and in that event may make an order for costs against the party who has been generally successful in the litigation.

- The judge may deprive a party of costs on an issue on which he has been successful if satisfied that the party acted unreasonably in relation to that issue.

- An appellate court should not interfere with the judge's exercise of discretion merely because it takes the view that it would have exercised the discretion differently.

If the general rule is departed from, it is incumbent on the judge to give reasons for the order that he has made.

Although the CPR indicates that success on issues should be considered, it is usually preferable for the court to make a single order for costs taking this into account rather than a number of cross orders (eg the claimant gets 75% of costs[53], rather than the claimant gets costs of liability issues and 50% of costs of quantum issues, the defendant gets 50% of costs of quantum issues).[54]

Of course, most cases settle and still usually settle on the basis of an agreed sum for damages plus a sum for costs to be assessed. It is submitted that CPR 44.3 is only appropriate for the trial judge as it is only he who has heard the evidence and can make judgments about success or failure on issues. If the case settles with a normal order for costs to be assessed, the district judge, it is submitted, is in impossible position to determine these questions in many cases without evidence, presumably

---

52 (2001) CCS 63, [2001] EWCA Civ 535, [2001] NPC 79, CA.

53 As in *Budgen v Andrew Gardner Partnership* [2002] EWCA Civ 1125.

54 This approach was disapproved of in *Kastor Navigation v AGF MAT (No 2)* [2004] EWCA Civ 277 and *Verrechia v Metropolitan Police Commissioner* [2001] All ER (D) 173 (Mar).

from the parties, which would result in a mini-trial at the detailed assessment. Only in clear cases (eg open abandonment of a head of loss or other issue) is this possible.

10.9.1.3 Basis of assessment and proportionality

The basis of assessment will normally be on the standard basis. The standard basis allows for costs reasonable in amount and reasonably incurred, and adds an additional test that the court will 'only allow costs which are proportionate to the matters in issue' (CPR Rule 44.4(2)(a)).

In *Secretary of State for the Home Department v Lownds*[55] the Court of Appeal, comprising Lord Woolf with the Senior Costs Judge as an assessor, held:

> 'Thus the proportionality of costs incurred by the claimant should be determined having regard to the sum that it was reasonable for him to believe that he might recover at the time he made his claim. The proportionality of the costs incurred by the defendant should be determined having regard to the sum that it was reasonable for him to believe the claimant might recover, should his claim succeed. This is likely to be the sum that the claimant has claimed, for a defendant will normally be entitled to take a claim at its face value.'

The questions to be asked are on a global basis: is the costs claim proportionate having regard to conduct[56], efforts to settle, amount of money (the sum the claimant reasonably expected at the outset), importance, complexity, difficulty or novelty, skill effort, specialised knowledge and responsibility, time spent and place and circumstances in which it was done? If yes, then the receiving party only has to show each individual item was reasonable in amount and reasonably incurred. If no, then he must show each item was necessarily incurred (a standard of competence, without hindsight, and bearing in mind the conduct of the opponent) and was reasonable in amount and reasonably incurred. If disproportionate, the costs will not be disallowed altogether, but will be reduced to a proportionate level. Although disallowed between the parties as disproportionate, if reasonable (but not necessary) the costs might still be recoverable from the client.

10.9.2 Costs recovery in the tribunal

In the employment tribunal, traditionally costs are rarely awarded to either side. This has the advantage that an employee's risk of paying substantial costs if the claim is rejected is limited. However, it also means that even if entirely successful a significant proportion of the compensation will have to go towards paying his own legal fees.

---

55 [2002] LTL 22/3/20.

56 CPR, r 44.5(3).

The intention was that employment tribunals would provide a simple procedure that was inexpensive and could usually be handled without legal representation. However, the employer will normally be legally represented. Also, discrimination claims produce complex issues of law and fact that are rarely suitable for litigants in person.

The tribunal's powers to award costs have been extended. The Employment Tribunals (Constitution and Rules of Procedure) Regulations 2004[57] now provide:

> '38 – (1) Subject to paragraph (2) and in the circumstances listed in rules 39, 40 and 47 a tribunal or chairman may make an order ('a costs order') that –
>
> (a) a party ("the paying party") make a payment in respect of the costs incurred by another party ("the receiving party") . . .'

And:

> '40 – (1) A tribunal may make a costs order when on the application of a party it has postponed the day or time fixed for or adjourned a Hearing or pre-hearing review. The costs order may be against or, as the case may be, in favour of that party as respects any costs incurred as a result of the postponement or adjournment.
>
> (2) A tribunal or chairman shall consider making a costs order against a paying party where, in the opinion of the tribunal or chairman (as the case may be), any of the circumstances in paragraph (3) apply. Having so considered, the tribunal or chairman may make a costs order against the paying party if it or he considers it appropriate to do so.
>
> (3) The circumstances referred to in paragraph (2) are where the paying party has in bringing the proceedings, or he or his representative has in conducting the proceedings, acted vexatiously, abusively, disruptively or otherwise unreasonably, or the bringing or conducting of the proceedings by the paying party has been misconceived.
>
> (4) A tribunal or chairman may make a costs order against a party who has not complied with an order or practice direction.'

However, it still remains the case that costs orders in the employment tribunal are rare.

---

[57] SI 2004/1861.

CHAPTER 11

PRACTICAL CONSIDERATIONS AND TACTICS

11.1 PREPARING THE CLAIM

11.1.1 Seeing the wood for the trees

Almost by definition, in stress at work claims the employee will normally be suffering from a psychiatric condition, most probably moderate or severe depression. As a consequence, many employees will have become obsessed about the circumstances which led to this situation. They become experts in the detail of the documents. They will often have persuaded themselves that they have incontrovertible evidence of breach and causation. It is often difficult to persuade them to the contrary.

Many will also have studied case-law in some detail, usually focussing more on facts than principles, and find it difficult to accept legal advice which differs from their perception of the law.

Litigants in person pursue a significant number of stress at work claims. This is perhaps a reflection of the fact that lawyers often decline to take on such claims under conditional fee agreements (CFAs). It is also a sign that the law may operate counter-intuitively where a claimant with a serious psychiatric condition which developed in the workplace may have no legal remedy (often because foreseeability cannot be established), but the employee is convinced that there must be a legal remedy. It also suggests that some employees are unable to abandon a claim, even when advised that, in law, it will not succeed.

The stress or bullying is likely to have occurred over a period of time, and there are often many individual incidents to analyse. There is also likely to have been a period of absence from work before lawyers are instructed, with criticism of the employer's absence management made by the employee. The employee may focus on issues which are unlikely to provide a legal remedy.

It is essential not to lose sight of the wood for the trees.

Preferably, the letter of claim will not be drafted until the lawyer has all the relevant documents (including medical records).[1] If it must be sent before this, care must taken in drafting the letter to ensure that all matters are adequately evidenced. Whilst the letter of claim must be sufficiently detailed so as to enable the employer to understand the case, the lawyer should take care not to 'throw in the kitchen sink'. The greatest danger is including an unevidenced allegation which the employer can subsequently demonstrate to be untrue or inaccurate. Although the error may be explicable, if the employer can show some of the employee's allegations to be wide of the mark, he will cast doubt in the mind of the court as to whether other allegations might also be without foundation.

Conversely, it is very important to ensure that all of the important causes of action are set out in the letter of claim. The employee is not restricted to pleading the matters set out in the letter of claim. However, causation is such a big issue in most stress and bullying cases that a judge might look askance at a subsequent allegation that a particular breach caused serious psychiatric injury when it was not even mentioned in the letter of claim.

11.1.2 Client credibility and the impact of claims on health

In any stress or bullying claim, at trial the case is likely to rely to a great extent on the credibility of the employee as a witness. If the judge has no sympathy with the employee or does not understand his case then it is likely to fail. A depressive illness can render the employee less plausible as a witness.

In *Ellis v Eagle Place Services Ltd*[2] a solicitor alleged that she had suffered a psychiatric injury caused as the result of bullying by a partner at the office where she worked. The judge found that she had 'improperly manufactured self-certificates' and that her deletion of documents from her computer and apparent misuse of firm notepaper was suspicious. In dismissing her claim the judge said:

> '. . . I have necessarily had regard to the credibility of the parties. I have formed an adverse view of the claimant. I do not believe that she was frank with either psychiatrist when she was discussing her marriage preferring to conceal those problems from them. I am satisfied that she concocted self-certificates intending to mislead her employers . . . Her conduct in deleting some 7 documents where the firm's headed notepaper had been used from her computer on her last day at work causes me to conclude that she knew full well that she should not have used the notepaper as she did . . . of course I bear in mind that the claimant was mentally ill at the time of these events; on the other hand she is a solicitor and prepared a most detailed statement of her case. I did not find her a credible witness and

---

1 See **11.1.4.1**.

2 QBD (Henriques J) 28 June 2002 LTL, 7 October 2002.

> making full allowance for her predicament and her illness and the skill of her cross-examiner there were several occasions when it was difficult to believe her evidence.'

But he did not conclude that she must have been deliberately lying; this may have been a function of her condition:

> 'It is only right that I should record the view of the psychiatrists that the claimant is undoubtedly and genuinely ill. I am quite satisfied that the overwhelming factor giving rise to her illness is the traumatic illness and death of her mother. I believe that her personality traits made her vulnerable to depression when she felt insecure at work . . . I also find that in her depressed state she genuinely believed in the validity of her complaints and may well have convinced herself of the version of events given in her evidence and may genuinely believe that she was bullied. Having found as a fact that the claimant was not bullied her claim must necessarily fail.'

Although most cases will not go to trial, proportionately more stress at work cases are tried than other kinds of personal injury case. No claim should be commenced unless the lawyer is satisfied that the employee is a credible witness. Although it is often difficult to challenge his evidence because of his illness, this must be attempted, sensitively, and an early view of credibility formed.

The other issue that must be explored with the employee at the outset is impact of litigation on his health. The lawyer is not a doctor and cannot give medical advice. However, it is necessary to explain that the litigation is likely to take several years to conclude and will be a constant reminder of the stress and/or bullying that led to his psychiatric condition. Litigation is itself stressful. Some may see the litigation as a mechanism for achieving answers and a 'closure'. Lawyers will be aware that this is rarely the outcome, which is more likely to be an out of court settlement with questions still unanswered. Others may feel that they will only recover when they move on from the issues that led to their psychiatric condition. Litigation might delay recovery by several years.

The employee must be advised of all these matters after which he can decide whether or not to pursue a claim. The decision may be influenced by the extent to which the employee's health has been damaged. If the psychiatric injury is very serious and has had major repercussions on his career, the employee may feel that he has no choice but to pursue the claim whatever the impact on his health. Other employees, particularly those in receipt of income protection benefit (which has largely replaced, and is likely to continue to replace, earnings), may view the stress of litigation as an additional and unnecessary burden.

11.1.3 Stay or go?

In some cases the first question to be considered is whether the employee should resign and claim a constructive dismissal or stay in employment.

First, the lawyer must decide whether the employee is at that time justified in resigning. If, for example, there has been a breach of the duty of mutual trust and confidence by the defendant, the employee has the option of resigning and claiming constructive dismissal.[3] But the difficulty is that the employee has to act promptly in response to that breach. Often an employee chooses to continue with the employment perhaps because he is being paid sick pay. If he resigns later when the sick pay allowed is exhausted, he may be deemed to have affirmed the contract notwithstanding the breach in which case his resignation will be just that; it will not be a (constructive) dismissal. There may be scope for arguing that there has been a 'continuing breach', but this is not straightforward.

If the employee decides to stay in his job, the employer may subsequently seek to use this decision against him arguing that if the conduct complained of was really as serious as he alleges he would surely have left his job.

If the employee decides to leave his job, he gives up the benefit of employment and takes the risk that an employment tribunal may subsequently find that he simply resigned as the alleged breach was not fundamental. The claimant will then have to seek recompense in the courts via a claim for psychiatric injury the outcome of which will be inevitably uncertain.

Unless the employee is certain that he is not prepared to return to that job because of his treatment, the decision to stay or go is a difficult one and the risks of both courses must be carefully explained by the lawyer.

11.1.4 Documents

In stress at work claims the condition generally develops over a period of time rather than from a single incident as in most personal injury claims. They tend therefore to produce much more documentation than most other kinds of personal injury claim. The employee will often arrive at the lawyer's office carrying several carrier bags of papers. These will often relate principally to the management of the claimant's condition after it has developed rather than to the breach that led to the onset of the condition. It is essential to review all the documents in the claimant's possession before forming a preliminary view.

---

[3] See **2.4.3.2** and **5.1**.

It is usually advisable to ask the employee to forward all the documents before the initial meeting if possible so that the lawyer can sift through them beforehand and form an initial view of the likely key issues on which the lawyer can focus questions at the subsequent meeting. It is particularly important to obtain and review all contractual documents, including the contract of employment and ancillary documents such as job descriptions, in order to identify possible breaches by the employer.

11.1.4.1 Medical records

Although the employee may have many documents, he is unlikely to have all the documents that are required to prove the claim. It is essential for the lawyer to obtain and personally review all of the employee's past medical records, particularly GP records.

The lawyer must establish whether the employee is suffering from a recognised psychiatric condition. If there is a referral and diagnosis of clinical depression by a clinical psychiatrist, this is likely to be established. However, mere references to unspecific 'anxiety' and 'stress' in the GP notes should sound warning bells. The lawyer should note how often the employee has seen the GP with regard to the stress-related condition and how often he has seen the GP in the same period without the GP notes mentioning stress at all. Has the GP referred the employee to a psychiatrist? Has he been prescribed anti-depressant medication? Has he been referred for (and taken up) counselling? If the answer to any of these questions is no the lawyer needs to tread warily. However, particularly with regard to counselling, it should be noted that GPs' attitudes towards counselling as a treatment and the local availability of counselling services can be very variable, so this may not be a sign that the employee's illness is mild. The lawyer should review carefully the underlying reasons given for the stress-related illness in the GP notes. The lawyer must consider any other contributory factors (eg marital breakdown, bereavement) recorded by the GP. If there is a long series of GP attendances, are work-related factors recorded each time? It is also important to review copies of the sick notes completed by the GP for the employer. Do these mention work-related stress and depression as the cause of the absence? This can be particularly important in second breakdown cases where it is important to establish that the employer was or ought to have been on notice as to the employee's vulnerability to a relapse.

The GP records must, however, be reviewed in their entirety, not just in relation to the employee's present condition. Past psychiatric history is important. This may indicate whether the employer should have been on notice that the employee was psychiatrically vulnerable. If the employer requested the employee to complete a health questionnaire or attend a medical examination prior to commencing employment was the past history disclosed? If it was, then it may be easier to establish that the employer knew or ought to have known about the psychiatric vulnerability. If it was not disclosed, should the claimant have disclosed it?[4] It is also important to establish whether the employee was vulnerable to psychiatric injury in any event which might lead to 'acceleration' or 'apportionment' arguments in respect of causation. Information provided by the GP in answer to enquiries from occupational health doctors, health insurers or the Benefits Agency is informative as it shows the GP's assessment of the employee when presenting a view to a third party that the GP may have to justify.

The GP records are usually the best independent verification of the psychiatric impact of the stress on the employee. That is not to say that they are always correct. The employee may argue that they are not. If this is the case, the lawyer should explain to the employee that he (the lawyer) does not see the GP records as presenting an alternative version of the truth; the records are another contemporaneous, less subjective, view of what has happened to the employee. However, it must be accepted that judges, like lawyers, are often swayed to a significant degree by contemporaneous documents produced by someone with no axe to grind and the employee should be advised of this. If there is a significant difference between the GP's account and the employee's, the lawyer should consider obtaining a witness statement from the GP to explain the discrepancies.

11.1.4.2 Employment records

The employee will usually have some, but not all, of the documents from his employment. These documents may produce a partial view of the situation. In addition, however, in many cases the employer's knowledge of the likelihood of a possible psychiatric injury may be documented and can be crucial. There are several methods for obtaining these documents from the employer.

First, the employee (or a lawyer on his behalf) can make a 'subject access request' under the Data Protection Act 1998 (DPA 1998) for a complete copy of 'personal data' (documents held by the employer relating to him). In the past, only electronic records were technically caught by this provision, although in practice many hard copy documents on a personnel file would have been produced using word-processing software and stored on a computer. The DPA 1998 now applies to paper records as well. A (statutory) fee which may not exceed £10 (£50 for health records) is payable for the production of such records. The request should be made

---

4 On 16 February 2009, the date as at which the law is stated in this book, the claim brought by Cheltenham Borough Council against their former chief executive, Christine Laird, was being heard in the High Court and expected to last a further 4 weeks. The Council was apparently seeking compensation in excess of £1m from Ms Laird on the grounds that she had misrepresented her state of health on taking up her employment. See, for example, 'Official sued by own council for "lying" on her job application' *Daily Telegraph*, 27 January 2009.

to the employer's 'data controller' as defined by the DPA 1998. The data controller must respond within 40 days. It is important to be reasonably specific about the categories of documents and periods. Whilst it should be straightforward to obtain the employee's complete personnel records, most employees in an office environment will have produced vast quantities of electronic records during their employment (including work-related e-mails and documents) most of which may not be 'personal data' and indeed will be of no relevance to the work-related stress. Disputes over a subject access request can be referred to the Information Commissioner.

Secondly, if the employee may have been the subject of statutory discrimination (on the grounds of sex, race, age, disability, sexual orientation or religious or other belief) it is possible to use the 'questionnaire' procedure under the relevant equality legislation. This enables the employee to ask the employer questions about his treatment and about other matters relating to the employer's practices before he commences employment tribunal proceedings. The employer is required to answer the employee's questions within 8 weeks and if he fails to do so the employment tribunal is entitled to draw inferences from the failure in subsequent tribunal proceedings. As part of the questionnaire process the employee can ask the employer to produce copies of the relevant documents.

Thirdly, the Pre-action Protocol for Disease and Illness Claims[5] requires the employer as the proposed defendant to disclose relevant documents within 3 months and 21 days of receipt. Sometimes this is rather 'chicken and egg': the employee needs the documents in order to fully particularise the claim; the employer refuses to accept the letter of claim as valid because it is too general in its terms. Usually the employer will eventually disclose most documents, if only to avoid an application for pre-action disclosure. If disclosure is not made, then an application can be made to the court under Part 8 of the Civil Procedure Rules (CPR) for an order for disclosure.

Disclosure is, of course, an ongoing obligation once court or employment tribunal proceedings have been issued.

As claims for stress at work involve substantial risk and considerable work under a CFA, unless there are problems with limitation, every effort should be made to obtain and review as much documentation as possible prior to the issue of proceedings.

[5] CPR: Pre-Action Protocols

In any event, the employer should be requested to confirm that all documents will be preserved. In *Green v DB Group Services (UK) Ltd*[6] the employee's solicitors made such a request, but some documents were destroyed. The judge commented:

> 'It is a highly regrettable feature of this case that the claimant's e-mail folders have not been preserved by the defendants. The claimant contends that they would have contained further e-mails of relevance to her claim, e-mails that would be likely to have provided further support for her evidence. The information now available reveals a lamentable failure on the part of defendants.
>
> It now transpires that in breach of the assurance that had been given, rightly understood by the claimant's then solicitors to amount to an undertaking, the claimant's e-mail folders were not saved from her machine. In the course of the trial I sought further explanation as to how this had occurred. It is not necessary for present purposes to rehearse the details. Suffice it to say that in my judgment it was the result of gross incompetence within the Bank, but despite harbouring reservations as to the reasons why the folders were not saved, I do not consider that on the information available to me it would be fair to conclude that they were deliberately deleted.'

11.1.5 Independent witnesses

Independent witness evidence is usually of crucial importance. It provides a more objective overview of how behaviour in the workplace affected the employee. Without it there is a great danger that a judge might conclude that the reality was much less serious than the employee alleges. This is particularly so in court cases. In discrimination claims in the employment tribunal the absence of independent witness evidence may not be so detrimental to the case because of the reversal of the burden of proof.

In many cases the employer will call evidence from numerous members of the management team. There is a danger of the employee appearing to be outnumbered. Even if the direct knowledge of some of the employer's witnesses is rather limited, or the witnesses are suspected of sticking together for business reasons, the judge will be reluctant to find that they are lying or are mistaken in the absence of corroborative evidence from the employee's work colleagues.

In *Green v DB*, for example, the evidence given on behalf of the employee by the head of department clearly weighed heavily with the judge.

It may not be easy to persuade work colleagues to give evidence against the employer. If they are still employed they may be fearful about the effect on their jobs and their career prospects. Although they will have the protection of the anti-victimisation legislation,[7] in practice this will

---

6 [2006] EWHC 1898 (QB), [2006] IRLR 764.

7 See Chapter 5.

involve difficult litigation and a fight for compensation when most would rather have a job. Although some colleagues may have told the employee that they will make a statement in support, they may have second thoughts when they are approached by a lawyer. If they are willing to make a statement, it is best to obtain this as soon as possible to avoid the risk of losing them later. If other matters come to light later on, they can be explored in a supplemental statement. A signed statement from an independent witness will reassure many after the event (ATE) insurers.

Whilst it is most important to find witnesses to support the case on liability, it is equally important not neglect witnesses of fact who can give evidence about the effect of the work-related stress on the claimant. This can have a significant impact on the awards for pain, suffering and loss of amenity, and also on financial loss.[8]

11.1.6 Expert evidence

Good independent expert evidence will be essential in stress and bullying at work claims in court. It may be needed to establish breach of duty and will certainly be required in respect of causation and damage.

So far as breach of duty is concerned, the lawyer should consider whether expert evidence is likely to be required to assist the court. This evidence might come from an occupational or organisational psychologist or an expert in health and safety in the workplace. In *Hatton,* Hale LJ said:

> 'The answer to the foreseeability question will therefore depend upon the inter-relationship between the particular characteristics of the employee concerned and the particular demands which the employer casts upon him. As was said in *McLoughlin v Grovers* [2001] EWCA Civ 1743, expert evidence may be helpful although it can never be determinative of what a reasonable employer should have foreseen. A number of factors are likely to be relevant.'

However, permission will be needed to adduce such evidence. This will normally be sought at a Case Management Conference which will be held after both sides have submitted an allocation questionnaire. The case managing judge may need some persuasion before he gives such permission. Since the Woolf review of civil litigation,[9] judges have been wary of the proliferation of expert evidence. Where the issues are principally issues of fact (eg was there bullying; was there over-work; did the employer know of the employee's vulnerability?) expert evidence is unlikely to assist the judge decide and permission will not normally be

---

8 See Chapter 7.

9 Access to Justice Final Report, by The Right Honourable the Lord Woolf, Master of the Rolls, July 1996, Final Report to the Lord Chancellor on the civil justice system in England and Wales.

given. Where the issues relate to systemic failures and knowledge of industry best practice, an expert may be of use.

In *Heyward v Plymouth Hospital NHS Trust*[10] the Court of Appeal were not prepared to overturn a case management decision allowing expert evidence from a consultant psychiatrist to be adduced, but refusing permission for evidence from an occupational psychologist. The Court of Appeal (Lord Phillips) commented:

> 'The issues as they appear to me are relatively simple. It is common ground that the claimant was vulnerable to stress, that the Trust knew of this, and in these circumstances the experts have identified that there are two possibilities in relation to causation of Mr Heyward's psychiatric injury. One is that he suffered a breakdown caused by stress imposed by the work overload in circumstances where he had already had one spell of psychiatric illness and against the background of which complaint is made in relation to the whistle-blowing incident. The alternative is that he was not subjected to work overload, but that he was unable to cope with what was no more than a normal full-time job and had to retire essentially as a result of his own mental fragility and not because of the work burden that was imposed upon him. Those issues are essentially issues of fact. There is nothing to indicate that if the Trust loses on those issues it will argue that the consequences of work overload could not reasonably have been foreseen, or that nothing could reasonably have been done to avoid the work overload.
>
> There is a possibility, it seems to me – a remote possibility – that the Trust will rely on quasi-expert evidence of a type that needs to be rebutted by an occupational psychologist or physician. Should that happen, it will be, and always would have been, open to Mr Heyward to seek permission to call that additional evidence . . .
>
> On the facts before the deputy district judge and Judge Overend, I can see no criticism that can be made of the case management decision that they reached to limit the expert evidence to one psychiatrist on each side. It seems to me that that was a sensible and proportionate response and one which will cater adequately for the need for expert evidence in the light of any unexpected contingency. Nothing that has been raised before this court causes me to form a different view and for that reason I would dismiss this appeal.'

In all cases it will be essential to adduce evidence from a consultant psychiatrist to establish the employee's present condition and prognosis. The psychiatrist must include a diagnosis of a recognised psychiatric condition in accordance with the recognised international diagnostic criteria if the full range of remedies are to be available to the employee. It is not normally recommended to obtain such an expert report from a treating doctor. The treating doctor may not have the requisite skill in medico-legal reporting (and this may have serious consequences, particularly where establishing causation is crucial). Also, a treating

---

[10] [2005] EWCA Civ 939.

doctor often tends to be rather more positive when it comes to prognosis than an outside expert as, not unnaturally, he hopes his treatment regime will be beneficial to the claimant's health.

The Pre-action Protocol for Disease and Illness Claims does not require the report commissioned by the employee's lawyer to be a report by a single joint expert[11] and normally the lawyer should not instruct the expert on a joint basis. Although the letter of claim should usually suggest several possible experts, and the employer (or their insurer) has the opportunity to object to any of those named (on proper grounds), the report obtained is the employee's report and there is no requirement to disclose it prior to the issue of proceedings.

The independent expert should be asked to report separately on the employee's condition and prognosis and on causation. The condition and prognosis report, which should briefly outline the history, confirm the diagnosis and give the expert's view of the likely prognosis, must be filed and served with the proceedings.[12] The separate report on causation goes to the heart of the case on liability and quantum in a stress at work case and it should be exchanged with the report from the employer's expert as a part of the case management directions set by the court. It is essential that the causation report clearly addresses issues such as whether the employee's injury can be attributed to the breach(es) of duty pleaded. It is necessary to establish whether this can be established on the balance of probabilities and whether the breach(es) were the sole cause or a material contribution.[13] The expert must also deal with issues of acceleration or apportionment.[14] As we have seen, these raise complex issues arising out of the interrelationship between fact and law. Before the report is finalised for service it should clearly deal with these issues and be fully understood and approved by the employee, solicitor and counsel normally at a conference with the expert.

Somewhat different considerations apply in the employment tribunal. The employment tribunal is less familiar with psychiatric injury (or indeed any medical issues).

In the employment tribunal expert medical evidence is usually ordered to be given by a joint expert. Indeed the medical evidence is often limited to a letter from the employee's own GP. It is possible to ask for a direction for separate experts, but it is unusual for such a direction to be given. In *De Keyser Ltd v Wilson*,[15] the EAT gave guidance on expert evidence in the employment tribunal:

---

11 CPR 35.8

12 CPR Practice Direction supplementing Rule 16, paragraph 4.1

13 See **6.1.1**.

14 See **6.1.2** and **6.1.3**.

15 [2001] UKEAT 1438 00 2003.

'(i) Careful thought needs to be given before any party embarks upon instructions for expert evidence. It by no means follows that because a party wishes such evidence to be admitted that it will be. There are valuable observations about expert evidence in *Whitehouse -v- Jordan* [1981] 1 WLR 246 at 256H, H.L.(the expert's evidence should be and be seen to be the independent product of the expert, uninfluenced as to form or content by the exigencies of litigation); *Midland Bank -v- Hett, Stubbs & Kemp* [1979] 1 Ch 383 at 402 c-e per Oliver J. (doubts as to the use of expert evidence when it strays beyond describing accepted standards of conduct within particular professions) and *Re M and R (minors)* [1996] 4 All E.R. 239 at 251-254 C.A. (the need for the Tribunal to keep in mind that the ultimate decision is for it) – see also the very recent cases of *Barings plc -v- Coopers & Lybrand*, The Times 7th March 2001 and Liverpool Roman Catholic Diocesan and Trustees Inc -v-Goldberg, The Times 9th March 2001. Although the Employment Tribunals' practices and rules differ from those of the High Court, guidance may be found on several subjects by way of analogy from the provisions of the Civil Procedure Rules 35.1 to 35.14 and the associated Practice Direction. A prudent party will first explore with the Employment Tribunal at a Directions Hearing or in correspondence whether, in principle, expert evidence is likely to be acceptable;

(ii) Save where one side or the other has already committed itself to the use of its own expert (which is to be avoided in the absence of special circumstances) the joint instruction of a single expert is the preferred course;

(iii) If a joint expert is to be instructed the terms which the parties will need to agree will include the incidence of that expert's fees and expenses. Nothing precludes the parties agreeing that they will abide by such view as the Tribunal shall later indicate as to that incidence (though the Tribunal will not be obliged to give any such indication) but the Tribunal has for the time being no power as to costs beyond the general provisions of Rule 12;

(iv) If the means available to one side or another are such that in its view it cannot agree to share or to risk any exposure to the expert's fees or expenses, or if, irrespective of its means, a party refuses to pay or share such costs, the other party or parties can be expected reasonably to prefer to require their own expert but even in such a case the weight to be attached to that expert's evidence (a matter entirely for the Tribunal to judge) may be found to have been increased if the terms of his instruction shall have been submitted to the other side, if not for agreement then for comment, ahead of their being finalised for sending to the expert;

(v) If a joint expert is to be used, Tribunals, lest the parties dally, may fix a period within which the parties are to seek to agree the identity of the expert and the terms of a joint letter of instruction and the Tribunal may fix a date by which the joint experts' report is to be made available;

(vi) Any letter of instruction should specify in as much detail as can be given any particular questions the expert is to be invited to answer and all more general subjects which he is to be asked to address;

(vii) Such instructions are as far as possible to avoid partisanship. Tendentiousness, too, is to be avoided. Insofar as the expert is asked to make assumptions of fact, they are to be spelled out. It will, of course, be important not to beg the very questions to be raised. It will be wise if the letter emphasises that in preparing his evidence the expert's principal and overriding duty is to the Tribunal rather than to any party;

(viii) Where a joint expert is to be used, the Tribunal may specify, if his identity or instructions shall not have been agreed between the parties by a specified date, that the matter is to be restored to the Tribunal, which may then assist the parties to settle that identity and those instructions;

(ix) In relation to the issues to which an expert is or is not to address himself (whether or not he is a joint expert) the Tribunal may give formal directions as it does generally in relation to the issues to be dealt with at the main hearing;

(x) Where there is no joint expert the Tribunal should, in the absence of appropriate agreement between the parties, specify a timetable for disclosure or exchange of experts' reports and, where there are 2 or more experts, for meetings (see below);

(xi) Any timetable may provide for the raising of supplementary questions with the expert or experts (whether there is a joint expert or not) and for the disclosure or exchange of the answers in good time before the hearing;

(xii) In the event of separate experts being instructed, the Tribunal should encourage arrangements for them to meet on a without prejudice basis with a view to their seeking to resolve any conflict between them and, where possible, to their producing and disclosing a Schedule of agreed issues and of points of dispute between them;

(xiii) If a party fails, without good reason, to follow these guidelines and if in consequence another party or parties suffer delay or are put to expense which a due performance of the guidelines would have been likely to avoid, then the Tribunal may wish to consider whether, on that party's part, there has been unreasonable conduct within the meaning of Rule 12(1) (as to costs).'

It is submitted that in a case where the employee alleges discriminatory harassment causing serious psychiatric injury resulting in 'career loss', this would be grounds to argue that single medical experts would be more appropriate.

However, given the much shorter timescales in the employment tribunal it is essential to consider the practicality of obtaining expert evidence (although this does not have to be filed with the employment tribunal on issue). Tribunals are usually keen to list claims for hearing promptly, but the lawyer may have to argue for delay (at least of the remedies hearing) if the prognosis is unclear, otherwise there is a danger of the tribunal deciding compensation prematurely with the risk that it will either be inadequate or too high.

11.1.7 Counsel

It is most important to involve counsel at an early stage in the case, usually by way of a conference with the client and the independent medical expert. There is, however, little point in doing this before the solicitor has obtained the key medical and employment records. As more stress at work claims are fought to trial than are most other types of personal injury claim, every case must be prepared as though it will be going to trial. The proposed advocate at the trial must be involved in pleading the claim and directing the subsequent evidence gathering.

Furthermore, most ATE insurers will require a positive advice from specialist counsel before agreeing to insure. The solicitor acting under a CFA (which is usually the case) is likely to be risking significant profit costs. It is helpful to have an independent objective verification of the merits and quantum of the claim. It is essential that the solicitor instructs a barrister who has sufficient experience in handling stress at work litigation. The law and practice are both difficult and personal injury counsel used to handling routine accident claims may not have sufficient expertise.

11.2 WINNABLE CLAIMS

Many stress and bullying claims are not pursued at all. Solicitors are cautious about accepting instructions because of the high investigative cost and the low success rate of such claims.

As we have seen, a great many of the claims for stress and bullying that are pursued do not ultimately succeed. Most claims are pursued under a CFA whereby the solicitor will go unremunerated if the claim is abandoned or fails. Even the fixed success fee (of 100%) under the CPR may not be adequate compensation across a basket of similar claims as so many are investigated and abandoned at significant expense. However, some claims do succeed and it is instructive to examine the features they may have in common.

11.2.1 Stress claims

11.2.1.1 There are likely to be good prospects of success where the employee has already suffered a breakdown resulting from stress at work, has returned to work and then suffers a second breakdown. This was the factual matrix in *Walker v Northumberland*,[16] the first successful reported stress at work claim.

[16] [1994] EWHC QB 2, [1995] 1 All ER 737, [1995] ICR 702, [1995] IRLR 35, [1995] PIQR P521.

The employer is in a difficult situation when faced with an employee who wishes to return to work following a first breakdown. If the employer allows the employee to return to work but makes no real effort to manage the return and thereby avoid further injury, as in *Walker*, the employee is likely to establish both breach and, crucially, foreseeability as the employer must have been aware of the employee's vulnerability. Alternatively if the employer does attempt to manage the return, then it is crucial that sufficient resources are put into this to ensure that this is done properly. If not, as in *MG v North Devon NHS Primary Care Trust*[17] and *Young v Post Office*,[18] the employee will establish a breach. However, it is still essential to spell out what it is that the employer has failed to do and the effect. Where the employer and colleagues have made reasonable efforts to facilitate a return to work, the claim will fail as in *Vahidi v Fairstead House School Trust Ltd.*[19]

In many cases the employee will be reluctant to return to the employment where the original psychiatric injury was sustained. If his return is grudging, with numerous conditions sought by the employee, and there is then a swift recurrence of the stress-related absence, it will be more difficult to establish either a breach or causation of significant damage.

If an employer decides not to allow the employee to return to work after the first breakdown (and thereby avoid the risks set out above) he faces two different risks. If he dismisses the employee, he risks a claim for unfair dismissal. Furthermore, if the employee is only able to return to work if adjustments are made to his employment and the employer refuses to make them, or fails to consider them, the employer may be liable under the DDA 1995 if such adjustments are found to be reasonable.

The principal issue in 'second breakdown' cases is likely to be the extent to which the breach(es) of duty were responsible for the injury. The claimant is already vulnerable to a breakdown as a result of the prior non-negligently caused breakdown. The court or tribunal might use this to seek to reduce the compensation payable.[20] However, unless the return to work is very short-lived, the employee can point out that but for the breaches leading to the second breakdown he was fit enough to work. After the second breakdown, the likelihood of returning to similar employment may be small. Certainly in *Walker* the compensation awarded was for career-long loss, although in *MG* and *Young* the court found that both employees could obtain alternative employment albeit

---

17 Where the returning employee was required to cover not only her own workload, but also that of a colleague who had also gone on long-term sick leave ([2006] EWHC 850 (QB)).

18 Where the managers did not know what he was doing on his return and conceded in evidence that some of it was inappropriate ([2002] EWCA Civ 661, [2002] Emp LR 1136, [2002] IRLR 660).

19 [2005] EWCA Civ 765.

20 See **6.1.2** and **6.1.3**.

with reduced earning capacity and future handicap on the labour market because of their vulnerability to future psychiatric injury.

11.2.1.2 First breakdown cases: known pre-existing vulnerability

Where the employee has a pre-existing vulnerability to psychiatric injury which is known to the employer, but which falls short of a stress-related breakdown, it is much harder for the employee to establish that any breach foreseeably caused injury. So, in *Hatton v Sutherland*, previous absence through depression resulting from other stresses was not enough to establish foreseeability. Similarly, in *Cross v Highlands and Islands Enterprise*[21] (referred to by the House of Lords in *Barber v Somerset*[22]) absence from work with depression (which was not expressly attributed to work on enquiry by the employer) was insufficient to establish foreseeability. Nor was becoming tearful and upset in meetings.[23]

However, in *Dickens v O2* the Court of Appeal noted that the judge at first instance had found:

> 'As a consequence of finding that the conversation with Keith Brown was on 23 April 2002, action by the employer should have taken place much sooner than it was. Firstly, it should have been an immediate referral to Occupational Health . . . and secondly the claimant should have been sent home . . . Here was an employee palpably under extreme stress, a valued employee about to crack up, perfectly obviously, she had said so, it was plain to those two gentlemen or should have been and nothing of any substance or of any effect was done.'

The Court of Appeal agreed that this was sufficient to establish foreseeability:

> 'I cannot accept that the judge failed to appreciate the difference between stress and stress-related illness; nor did he fail to understand that the indication of impending illness must be clear before the employer is under a duty to do something about it. The judge held, at his paragraph 39, which I have cited at paragraph 19 above, that on or about 23 April, the respondent was 'palpably under extreme stress' and 'about to crack up' as she had said. That was or should have been plain to her two managers, Allen and Keith Brown, but they did nothing of substance about it. In my judgment, the evidence was quite strong enough for the judge to conclude, as he did, that the appellant had received a clear indication of impending illness.'

Barber v Somerset, the only stress at work case to reach the House of Lords, was a first breakdown case where the Lords declined to interfere with the first instance judge. The judge felt that the employer should have

---

21 [2000] Scot CS 307, (2001) SCLR 547, [2001] IRLR 336.

22 [2004] UKHL 13 , (2004) 77 BMLR 219, [2004] 1 WLR 1089, [2004] 2 All ER 385, [2004] ELR 199, [2004] ICR 457, [2004] IRLR 475, [2004] PIQR P31.

23 *Bonser v RJB Mining (UK) Ltd* [2004] IRLR 164, [2003] EWCA Civ 1296.

paid attention to the unusual absence through stress and depression of a conscientious, long-standing employee.

If a vulnerability that is accepted can be exacerbated through work-place stress is disclosed (eg at interview or on occupational health assessment or subsequent hospitalisation), it is submitted that the Management of Health and Safety at Work Regulations 1999 (the Management Regulations) impose a duty to assess the particular risk and the necessary steps to eliminate or minimise it. This is particularly so in respect of disclosure after 2003 (when breach of the Regulations became actionable at civil law), although of course the duty is a continuing one. Examples might include the development of a heart condition, or neurological conditions such as multiple sclerosis. Even if the employer argues that he is not aware of the specific risk of the impact of stress on the condition, presumably he must be under a duty so as to properly assess risk and to make enquiries of the employee and relevant health professionals.

Evidence that the employer was aware that work-related stress was affecting the health of the employee, but ignores this, is likely to be crucial. It may be difficult for the employee to obtain supportive witness statements from those with the necessary knowledge, as the managers will themselves be subject to criticism. However, contemporaneous documentation, particularly e-mails may be helpfully obtained through protocol disclosure or following an application for pre-action disclosure.

11.2.1.3 First breakdown cases: excessive hours

First it is necessary to establish that the hours were in fact excessive. In the current state of the law, merely working more than the 48 maximum imposed by the Working Time Regulations[24] without an 'opt-out' is not enough, particularly if the hours only just exceed the maximum as in *Pakenham-Walsh v Connell Residential*[25] (or where the hours include on-call working as in *Paterson v Surrey Police Authority*[26]).

In *Six Continents Retail Ltd v Hone*[27] the employee had told the employer that he was working more than 90 hours per week and that this was causing stress. The employer ignored him and it was as much the employer's failure to act having been put on notice that something was wrong, as the number of hours worked by the employee (which was not in fact clearly established) which led to the finding of breach of duty against the employer.

---

24 In *Sayers v Cambridgeshire County Council* [2006] EWHC 2029, [2007] IRLR 29 and *Barber v RJB Mining (UK) Ltd* [1999] ICR 679 two High Court judges have found that there is no civil liability in respect of a breach of the Working Time Regulations per se.

25 [2006] EWCA Civ 90.

26 [2008] EWHC 2693 (QB) (Judge Richard Seymour QC) 7 November 2008 LTL 17 November 2008

27 [2005] EWCA Civ 922.

In *Jones v Sandwell Metropolitan Borough Council*[28] the employer had known that the employee was working excessive hours and was doing the work of more than one person which the employer's manager acknowledged he knew was 'a gamble'. The employee's claim succeeded.

It does seem that hours worked must be very excessive and the risk of injury must have been clearly apparent. In the current state of the law, notwithstanding the apparent protection of the Working Time Regulations and the requirement for risk assessment under the *Management Regulations*,[29] the courts appear reluctant to allow non-compliance with either set of regulations give rise to a stand alone cause of action.

11.2.1.4 First breakdown cases: pressure of work

Sometimes, it is not the number of hours that is the issue, but the demands of the job. This played a part in *Jones v Sandwell.* However, where an employee has been 'over-promoted' or is unable to cope with changes to his role (assuming that the changes are lawful), and the employer's only realistic option was to demote or dismiss the employee, it will be difficult for the employee to succeed.

If the employer has in fact identified a risk to health (whether through a formal risk assessment or otherwise) but failed to act, then it will be easier for the employee to establish liability in negligence (including foreseeability). This is so even if the courts are reluctant to find a breach of statutory duty arising out of non-compliance with the Management Regulations. Where the employee had more than usual stresses and the employer failed to act on the result of his risk assessment it will be hard for the employer to avoid a finding of negligence. Even though the Court of Appeal in *Hatton* were not prepared to find that any particular job rendered employees vulnerable to psychiatric injury, in *Melville v Home Office*[30] the employer had noted the risks, established guidelines but then proceeded to ignore them. The employee's claim succeeded.

Similarly, if there is a systemic problem in a department with a number of employees on sick leave due to stress related illness it is arguable that this state of affairs might put on notice that there could be a risk of health to other employees in similar jobs. This was the case in *Hiles v Gloucestershire PCT*[31] where the managers freely admitted severe problems of stress within the department.

---

[28] One of the conjoined appeals with *Hatton*.

[29] *Paterson v Surrey Police Authority.*

[30] One of the conjoined appeals in *Hartman v South Essex Mental Health & Community Care NHS Trust* [2005] EWCA Civ 6 (2005) 85 BMLR 136, [2005] ELR 237, [2005] ICR 782, [2005] IRLR 293, [2005] PIQR P19.

[31] [2006] EWHC 3418 (QB).

Again witness evidence or (more likely) clear contemporaneous documentary evidence of the knowledge of management is likely to be required.

11.2.1.5 First breakdown cases: breach of procedure

Where the injury has apparently resulted from a breach of procedure, usually the disciplinary or grievance procedure, the court is likely to be reluctant to find in favour of the employee if the claim relies on nothing other than that breach. First, it is necessary to establish that there was a breach, as opposed to merely poor management. Many procedures are expressed to be non-contractual and so a slight error in procedure is unlikely to found a claim for psychiatric injury. However, procedural failings and poor management might lead to a successful unfair dismissal claim in the employment tribunal. Even if there was a contractual breach of procedure, the employee will still have to show that it was so egregious that the breach has caused the damage. If the breach was relatively minor, the court might well find that it was not the cause of the damage.[32]

However, some procedures, particularly in the statutory and third sectors, are long-winded and overly bureaucratic. In the interests of fairness, the process is turned into a parody of a court case. There is a risk that such a process might add to the stress that the employee is experiencing and indeed itself aggravate or cause injury. Indeed an accusation of bullying and harassment is stressful and needs to be carefully handled by the employer to avoid injury to, and a possible claim by, the person accused. An offer of counselling to all involved and a swift resolution of the matter are likely to reduce the risks for the employer. In conclusion, however, the failures in respect of procedures would have to be extreme, or the employer would have to be on notice that the employee had a peculiar vulnerability, for breach of duty and foreseeability to be established in such a claim.

11.2.2 Bullying and harassment claims

Where the bullying and harassment amounts to unlawful discrimination there is likely to be a choice between an employment tribunal claim and a claim in the civil courts. The pros and cons of each are set out at **11.3** but the employee must not fall into the overlap traps dealt with at **8.5**.

Prior to the decision in *Conn v City of Sunderland*,[33] an employee would regularly plead a claim under the Protection from Harassment Act 1997 (PFHA 1997) as an alternative to a claim in negligence. As discussed in Chapter 4, there is no requirement to establish foreseeability of injury

---

[32] As in *Deadman v Bristol City Council* [2007] EWCA Civ 822, [2007] IRLR 888, [2007] All ER (D) 494 (Jul).

[33] [2007] EWCA Civ 1492, [2008] IRLR 324.

under the PFHA 1997. However, following *Conn,* it will be much harder to establish that bullying at work constitutes harassment under the PFHA 1997.

The outcome of a claim will largely depend upon the quality of the evidence about the nature of the bullying and harassment. As much is likely to be verbal, it is usually necessary to have good supportive evidence from colleagues. In *Green v DB*, where the employee's claim succeeded, one of the employee's managers gave evidence as to the workplace culture. Where there is foul and abusive behaviour, witnessed by others, the prospects of establishing liability at common law are good. The intention of such behaviour is to humiliate and distress. Other colleagues can say that they felt this themselves or that they could see how it was affecting the employee. The employer will usually be vicariously liable in this situation.

However, where there was more insidious bullying and abuse of workplace power by a manager, claims will be more difficult to prove. The court may be reluctant to find a breach and, even if they do, it may be impossible to establish that the manager had foreseen that his actions could cause psychiatric injury.[34]

Where the bullying and harassment constitutes statutory discrimination, the claim might be more likely to be successful in the employment tribunal where foreseeability of injury is not required.

11.3 CHOICE OF FORUM

Where the employee has a choice of forum – employment tribunal or civil court – then the issues of timescales, burden of proof, foreseeability, damage, and funding are likely to be the determining factors.

11.3.1 Timescales

Assuming the client is still in time to litigate in the employment tribunal, it is obvious that a decision will usually have to be taken when the extent of the injury is uncertain and the prognosis is unknown. It will often be impossible to get hold of the employee's medical and employment records, let alone obtain an expert's report before the claim has to be lodged with the employment tribunal. Once started, tribunal proceedings generally move quite quickly and a hearing date is often fixed within 6 months. It is possible (indeed quite common) for the tribunal to determine liability and then fix a separate hearing to deal with compensation (assuming, of course, that the employee is successful on liability). In many psychiatric injury cases, the lawyer should seek to agree this with the other side in advance or, failing agreement, apply to the tribunal for an

[34] As in *Barlow v Broxbourne BC* [2003] EWHC 50 (QB).

appropriate direction. Otherwise the lawyer may find himself in the unsatisfactory position of trying to decide on an offer of compensation, or indeed present arguments on compensation in the tribunal, on the strength of a GP report.

However, although initial resolution in the employment tribunal will normally be much faster than in the court, if the case goes to appeal the process can be time-consuming and labyrinthine. Appeals to the Employment Appeal Tribunal (EAT) are common in stress at work cases and can take at least a year to be decided. Appeals to the Court of Appeal are also quite common and may take longer. Following one or more appeals, it is not uncommon for the case to be remitted back to the tribunal for a rehearing or for further determination of specific issues. All these matters should be put to the employee when considering the issue of timescales in connection with the choice of forum.

11.3.2 Burden of proof

In the civil court the burden of proof in a claim for psychiatric injury falls squarely on the claimant. This is not an easy burden to discharge. In their judgment in *Hatton v Sutherland* the Court of Appeal set up no fewer than 16 hurdles for the employee to jump in order to succeed.[35]

In the employment tribunal, once facts giving rise to a potential finding of discrimination are established, the burden of proof shifts to the employer respondent who must then prove that there was no discrimination.[36]

In unfair dismissal claims in the tribunal, the burden of proving the dismissal (eg in respect of a constructive dismissal) falls on the employee. However, once that has been established, the burden of proving fairness falls on the employer.

11.3.3 Foreseeability

The issue of foreseeability (ie whether it is foreseeable that the employer's conduct could cause injury) frequently causes difficulty for employees in court actions for psychiatric injury. When this issue was reviewed by the Court of Appeal in *Hatton v Sutherland* they concluded that the nature of mental disorder made it is harder to foresee than physical injury, but that it might be easier to foresee in a known individual rather than in the population at large. An employer is usually entitled to assume that the employee can withstand the normal pressures of the job unless he knows of some particular problem or vulnerability.[37]

---

35 See further, Chapters 3 and 6.

36 See further at **5.3.2**.

37 See further at **3.4**.

In the tribunal, once the statutory tort of discrimination has been established, injury 'caused' by the discrimination will be compensated. There is no requirement for the damage to be foreseeable. In *Essa v Laing Ltd*[38] a single abusive racist remark by a foreman led to a serious depressive illness on the part of a black worker. The employer argued that it was not reasonably foreseeable that such an incident would cause serious psychiatric injury. The Court of Appeal held (2:1) that in the context of the statutory tort the breach could not be accidental. Once established all losses flowed and were to be compensated, there was no additional test of foreseeability as it was sufficient to prove causation.

11.3.4 Damage

In court proceedings, the client needs to show a recognised psychiatric condition.[39]

In the employment tribunal the award for injury to feelings in discrimination cases is much broader in scope.[40]

If there is any doubt about whether the client has suffered a 'psychiatric injury' (as opposed to distress or hurt feelings) the tribunal will probably be a safer bet.

The county court judge is more likely to be used to determining complex issues arising out of personal injury claims than an employment tribunal. Conversely, an employment tribunal will have experience of making awards for injury to feelings and their perhaps more broad brush approach to this may, in some cases, work in the employee's favour.

11.3.5 Costs and funding

Normal costs rules apply to court proceedings. Costs orders are still rare in the employment tribunal.[41]

Legal aid is no longer available for personal injury claims in the courts. Conditional Fee Agreements can be used.

Legal aid is not available for claims in the employment tribunal (although it might be available for appeals). Contingency fee agreements (allowing the lawyer to take a percentage of the damages) are lawful in the employment tribunal. Conditional Fee Agreements can also be used.

---

38 [2004] EWCA Civ 02.

39 See **7.1**, although this is not necessarily so for a claim under the PFHA 1997.

40 See **7.4.1**.

41 See **10.9.2**.

The employee has to pay no fees in the employment tribunal (although expenses and allowances are available to the applicant and witnesses). Court fees can be very high.

11.3.6 Decisions

Sometimes it is clear whether the claim should be pursued in the court or the tribunal. In many cases it is not. With hindsight it may become apparent that the claim should have been pursued in the alternative forum. The client may use that hindsight to bring a subsequent negligence claim against the lawyer unless there is clear evidence that the options were carefully discussed with the client who made an informed choice and agreed to the forum used.

The table below may be of assistance in choosing the appropriate forum. However, it is for guidance only. It is not advisable to simply count the ticks. The lawyer must look at the case in the round:

Difficulties	**Indicates may be better to bring in**	
	Court	**Tribunal**
Will it be difficult to comply with a 3-month time-limit?	✓	X
Is the prognosis unclear?	✓	X
Is it probably not a recognised psychiatric condition?	X	✓
Will establishing breach of duty of care be problematic?	X	✓
Will establishing statutory discrimination be problematic?	✓	X
Is foreseeability of damage likely to be an issue?	X	✓
Is causation problematic with competing causes?	✓	X
Are there complex quantum issues?	✓	X
Are own costs likely to be high?	✓	X
Is ATE insurance unlikely to be available?	X	✓

There is no doubt that the very short time-limit for employment tribunal proceedings (which means that prognosis is unlikely to be established before the claim has to be commenced) makes the tribunal an unattractive choice in many cases. There will, however, be cases where the employment tribunal is definitely the better forum on the facts of the case.

11.4 SETTLEMENT

11.4.1 Potential payers

When considering settlement of the claim, the lawyer must ensure that all possible sources of compensation are considered. Unless the employer has taken out specific insurance against this risk, most discrimination claims will be handled by the employer himself who will have to pay any award out of his own pocket. By contrast, most claims for psychiatric injury resulting from work-place stress or bullying will be treated as claims under the employer's compulsory liability insurance. If the employee is in receipt of income protection benefit under an insurance policy taken out by his employer, the insurers under that policy may wish to pay a capital sum to buy off future liability as part of a settlement.

11.4.2 Mediation in stress claims

Mediation has been slow to take off for personal injury claims. As the Ministry of Justice minister Vera Baird MP said in answer to a parliamentary question:[42]

> 'As mediation services are provided by a number of local and national commercial mediation organisations, it is not possible to assess the true level of referral to mediation involving personal injury claims across England and Wales. However, the Ministry has recently conducted evaluations of our court-based mediation schemes based at central London, Birmingham, Guildford and Exeter. The results show that, although personal injury claims represent over half of the cases allocated to the fast and multi-track, these claims make up less than 6 per cent. of the cases that undertake the mediation process.'

Whatever the reasons for the low take-up of mediation services in personal injury claims generally, mediation should always be considered as an option in respect of psychiatric injury claims resulting from work-place stress because it has some real advantages. There is often a mix of employment and personal injury claims which can be settled in one go. To resolve the employment claims the employer may have to contribute to a settlement achieved at mediation, which is rare in ordinary personal injury claims. All parties may have an interest in maintaining confidentiality. The employee may wish to preserve some anonymity to

42 *Hansard*, Written Answers, col 1132W (13 June 2007).

enable him to resume a career. The employer may not want the employee's allegations (even if strongly disputed) to become widely known. Insurers may wish to limit 'copy-cat claims'. Creative solutions of real benefit to the employee can be achieved through mediation. These could include continuing use of benefits such as private medical treatment, payment for out-placement services, references and frank apologies. Many employees want their 'day in court'. They want a chance to explain what happened and how it has affected them. A mediation offers an opportunity for the employee to have his say with a neutral 'umpire' present. The employer may not be sympathetic to the claims. Once he has seen how much the employee has been affected there is a chance that his view will soften. Finally, as we have seen, costs will be very substantial and the claims thus carry significant risk for both sides.

In *Vahidi v Fairstead House School Trust Ltd*[43] the Court of Appeal commented:

> 'One shudders to think of the costs of this appeal and of the trial which apparently took as long as 9 days. As the courts have settled many of the principles in stress at work cases, litigants really should mediate cases such as the present. Of course, mediation before trial is infinitely preferable to mediation before appeal. But it is a great pity that neither form of mediation has taken place in this case, or, if it has, that it has not produced a result.'

11.4.3 Tax considerations

When settling claims, it is necessary to remember that the tax treatment of awards in personal injury cases in the courts and of claims before the tribunal is different.

Personal injury lawyers are familiar with the rule in *Gourley's* case[44] that personal injury damages are not a taxable receipt. Claims for lost earnings in tort claims are expressed as claims net of tax and no tax is usually payable on at all the award.[45]

Compensatory awards in the tribunal will normally be taxable[46] and so any claim for lost earnings above £30,000 should be grossed up. It is, however, possible that the 'injury to feelings' element of a discrimination award should be treated in the same way as an award for personal injury, and exempted from tax. Arguably this also applies the financial losses flowing from the discrimination. However, the authority for this is slight.[47] If the sums are to be paid net, the employee should seek an

43 [2005] EWCA Civ 765.

44 *British Transport Commission v Gourley* [1955] UKHL 4, [1956] AC 185.

45 The Income Tax (Earnings and Pension) Act 2003, s 406.

46 Subject to the first £30,000 of an award being exempt from tax: The Income Tax (Earnings and Pension) Act 2003, Part 6, Chapter 3.

47 *Vince-Cain v Orthet Ltd* UK ([2004] IRLR 857, [2004] UKEAT 0801_03_1208, [2005] ICR 374 HHJ McMullen QC. However, in reaching their decision the EAT said 'We are

indemnity for tax from the employer and an agreement that all negotiations on the point with the tax authorities will be at the employer's cost. The EAT in *Vince-Cain v Orthet* said:

> 'We have been referred to no authority and to no authoritative commentary which holds or asserts that tax is payable on such an award. In practice, where a dispute arises between the parties, we accept that it is resolved by an indemnity given by the paying party that if the Revenue attacks the award in the hands of the receiving party, the paying party will make good. Alternatively, as here, a power to seek review can be sought and given at the Employment Tribunal itself.'

Where the benefit of an employer's income protection policy is transferred as part of the settlement, great care must be taken. In *Minto v Revenue and Customs Commissioners*,[48] a decision of the Special Commissioners when, after settlement of his claim against his employer, Mr Minto complained about his payments under a PHI policy being subsequently assessed to tax, the Commissioners explained:

> 'The Compensation Agreement provided that the Appellant agreed to accept the compensation payment and the PI payment in full and final settlement of his claims for compensation for unfair dismissal, redundancy and disability discrimination, and his prospective personal injury claim related to alleged work related stress. The Appellant also warranted that the claims so settled amounted to the entirety of the claims which he believed he had against JLL or any associated company or their directors, etc. arising out of or in connection with his employment including its termination. It confirmed that the Appellant had taken independent legal advice from a named barrister and had raised all issues relevant to his employment and its termination, about which he had a complaint, with the barrister. The Compensation Agreement stated that the consideration given by JLL was given without any admission of liability.'

However, they concluded:

> 'The evidence disclosed no agreement settling a claim for damages for personal injury whereby the damages consisted wholly or partly of the payments under the PHI policy from the RSA and, later, Canada Life. That claim was, as Mr. Charnock submitted, expressly settled by the payments of £12,500 and £47,500 (collectively described as the Compensation Payment and the PI Payment) which were accepted by the Appellant under the Compromise Agreement in full and final settlement of his prospective personal injury claim related to work related stress. Miss Wooderson's evidence confirmed that these provisions of the Compromise Agreement reflected the reality of the position from her viewpoint. In particular she

---

acutely conscious that decisions relating to tax liability may be appealed and determined only by General Commissioners, pursuant to sections 31(1) and 31B of the Taxes Management Act 1970'.

48 SPC00625 (23 April 2007) LTL 4/9/2007: (2008) STC (SCD) 121

> expressly denied that JLL were liable for damages in the amount of £750,000 or any similar sum in discharge of which liability the payments under the PHI policy were made.'

The payments were therefore subject to income tax. This demonstrates how complex the tax consequences of an award or settlement can be. It is essential to take specialist advice and ensure that this is understood. Indemnities may be required.

11.4.4 The compromise agreement

Where an employee's employment is terminated and the employer wishes to ensure that this is in full and final settlement of claims, the settlement agreement will normally be in the form of a compromise agreement. Such an agreement is not binding on the employee without the advice of an independent lawyer. Where tribunal proceedings have been commenced, the settlement is more likely to be in the form of an ACAS COT3 form.

In either case, if the compromise agreement or COT3 form is not drafted carefully, personal injury claims (whether current or prospective) may be caught by the wording. It is very easy to inadvertently settle all claims. When settling employment claims, the lawyer must be very careful to ensure that outstanding claims for personal injury are excluded, if that has been agreed. In *Felix v Department of Social Security*,[49] in rejecting the employee's appeal from the striking out of his stress at work claim against his former employer, the DSS, Hunt J recited the words in the COT3 settlement of his employment tribunal claim:

> 'Without admission of liability the respondent agrees to pay the applicant and the applicant agrees to accept the sum of £11,000 . . . in full and final settlement of all and any claims the applicant may have regarding rights for which a conciliation officer has a duty and where the rights arise under the Employment Rights Act 1996, the Race Relations Act 1996 and all rights relating to the applicant's contract of employment and its termination thereof. This settlement does not affect any rights the applicant may have in relation to industrial injury claims or the Company's pension scheme . . ."

The employee had argued that his right to bring personal injury claims had not been settled as they were intended to be included in the phrase 'industrial injury claims'. The judge held that the settlement included a settlement of all his claims for personal injury:

> 'The words "all rights relating to the contract of employment" can plainly cover personal injury. The two exceptions, namely industrial injury claims and company pension scheme claims were not matters which would be directly litigated between the appellant and the DSS [his employer], which was why they were excepted.

---

49 *Felix v Department of Social Security QBD* (Hunt J) 18 January 2001.

> As to the words "industrial injury claims" the respondent says that they have a specific meaning which is claims under the Social Security and Benefits Act 1992 for rights to benefits (section 94) or in declarations (section 44). That same statute refers to personal injury, underlining that it is not the same thing.'

The judge ended:

> 'I would go on to add that this is not the first case which has come before me on this or a very similar point. It does behove those drafting such settlements as this, in cases before the employment tribunal or elsewhere, to take care that where it is intended to resolve all claims between an employer and an employee which exist, or may exist, it would be better to spell out within such agreements whether it is intended to include all personal injury claims which the employee has or may have, so that litigation such as this is avoided.'

Many employees first consult a lawyer only when their employment has been terminated. Many compromise agreements prepared by employers or their lawyers frequently include personal injury claims within the settlement (either expressly or by implication). Lawyers advising on the compromise agreement for a small fee may overlook the possibility of future personal injury claims which are subsequently barred by the signing of the compromise agreement.

If employment tribunal proceedings have actually been commenced (perhaps by the client or by an advice centre) and it is clear that a claim for psychiatric injury in court should be pursued, even more care needs to be taken in ending the employment tribunal proceedings.[50]

There are potential negligence claims here waiting to entrap the employment lawyer (who may be unaware of how to run a personal injury claim) and the personal injury lawyer (who may be unaware of the possible benefits of the employment claim).

11.5 CONCLUSIONS

Stress and bullying at work claims can be intellectually and emotionally demanding. The law is complex and the claimant will often be suffering from a serious psychiatric illness. Establishing that this was foreseeably caused by a breach of duty or resulted from statutory discrimination is not straightforward. Costs are usually high and there are significant risks that a lawyer acting under a CFA or contingency fee agreement (in the tribunal) will not be paid because the claim fails.

---

50 See **8.5**.

This is a novel area of law which is constantly developing. There are risks of negligence claims because of the problems of overlap between the court and the tribunal.

Many personal injury lawyers prefer to avoid this field of litigation. This is a pity because the work is interesting and there are winnable claims where significant compensation can be recovered for seriously injured employees, whether at trial or through negotiated settlement. It is hoped that this book will provide a route map for successful stress at work litigation.

CHAPTER 12

PRECEDENTS

12.1 CLIENT QUESTIONNAIRE

Stress at work cases: new client instruction sheet

Date	
Client Name	
Client/Matter No.	
Referral source	
Date of birth	
Employer(s)	
Type(s) of claim	Stress
	Harassment
	Bullying
	Sex discrimination
	Race discrimination
	Disability discrimination
	Other (details)
Date employment began	
If ended, date employment ended	
Reason for dismissal or resignation	

Have tribunal proceedings been commenced? What for? When?	
Has there been a compromise agreement or COT 3 relating to employment claims? When? Does it effectively exclude personal injury claims?	
Date of first incident	
Date of latest incident	
Date of first absence from work	
Dates and details of absence(s) from work	
Date latest absence from work began	
Details and dates of the alleged breach(es) of duty	
Does the employer have any occupational health or other counselling service? Was it used? If not, why not?	
Is the client a union member? If yes, which union? Why is the client not consulting the union?	
Is the client overloaded with work compared to others doing the same job?	
Are others doing the same job similarly affected by stress?	
Details and dates of any notification(s) of stress or health problems to the employer, including to whom and whether verbally or in writing	

Details and dates of any GP sick certificates	
Has the client given the employee any reasons other than work-related stress for the health problems?	
What exactly does the client think the employer should have done about it?	
Would that have been practicable and how much would it have cost?	
What medical condition is the client suffering from?	
Has a doctor diagnosed this? Who?	
Has the client ever suffered from a psychiatric condition before? If yes, did the employer know about this?	
Are there any other possible causes (eg divorce, family illness, bereavement, victim of crime, alcohol/drug abuse)?	
Did any other causes contribute to the current illness?	
What is the prognosis?	
What are the likely general damages for psychiatric illness?	
What is/was the client's net salary?	
Any other significant past loss (eg medical expenses, treatment costs)?	
Receiving benefits? How much?	
Rough estimate of past loss to date	
Risk of discount of damages for competing causes/acceleration	

Likely future loss multiplier (including discount for likelihood of non-negligently caused breakdown) or *Smith v Manchester* award	
Rough estimate of future loss	
Rough estimate of total quantum	

Assessment of most relevant forum for claim (if any)

Difficulties	**Indicates may be better to bring in**	
	Court	**Tribunal**
Will it be difficult to comply with a 3-month time-limit?	✓	X
Is the prognosis unclear?	✓	X
Is it probably not a recognised psychiatric condition?	X	✓
Will establishing breach of duty of care be problematic?	X	✓
Will establishing statutory discrimination be problematic?	✓	X
Is foreseeability of damage likely to be an issue?	X	✓
Is causation problematic with competing causes?	✓	X
Are there complex quantum issues?	✓	X
Are own costs likely to be high?	✓	X
Is ATE insurance unlikely to be available?	X	✓
Overall, which forum is indicated?		

Take-on decision summary

	Fee Earner	Date	Partner	Date
Personal injury dept				
Reject personal injury case				
Obtain more evidence? What? Funded how?				
First interview and, if initial instructions corroborated, accept case on CFA				
Referred to employment dept				
Employment dept				
Reject employment case				
Obtain more evidence? What? Funded how?				
First interview and, if initial instructions corroborated, accept case on contingency fee				

12.2 INITIAL ADVICE

12.2.1 Accepted case

Dear

I write further to our meeting and my review of your documents.

I enclose a copy of a statement based on the information you gave me at our meeting. This is an informal document which will not be sent to the Defendant. However, it will be used as the basis of instructions to any expert witness or barrister whom we may instruct, so it is important that it is as accurate as possible. Please read it through carefully and make any corrections or additions you like and then sign and return it to me.

I set out below my preliminary advice in respect of your case. Please note that 'stress at work' cases are notoriously difficult to win. As discussed, the 'success fee' for CFAs in stress claims is fixed by the court rules at 100%. This reflects the fact that far more stress at work claims fail than succeed. At this stage, my preliminary advice is based upon the documents and information I have seen. I need to obtain further information from witnesses, medical experts and evaluate your employer's response to the claim before I can give a more definitive view on the merits of the claim and the amount of any compensation. However, for the reasons set out below, I do think that you have a case which merits further investigation.

1. Psychiatric Injury at Work

Duty of Care

In order to bring a claim for personal injury for the psychiatric illness you have suffered, you need to establish that your employer has been in breach of a duty to you either by breach of contract, breach of a statutory duty or in common law negligence. An employer has a duty of care both under statute and at common law to look after the health and safety of its employees.

An employer is also vicariously liable, or responsible, for the wrongful acts of their employees which were carried out in the course of their employment. [This includes bullying and harassment. This means that it is open for you to claim against your employer in respect of the acts of bullying and harassment committed by [your line manager] as if they had been committed by your employer, subject to overcoming the various hurdles identified below.]

If established, a breach of duty can give rise to compensation for psychiatric injury which is foreseeably caused by that breach.

Breach of Duty

You have to specifically identify breaches of duty. Possible breaches would seem to be:

[set out potential breaches of duty].

In my opinion the points at which your claim is likely to be strongest are in respect of

[set these out with reasons].

I am less convinced that

[set out potential breaches]

although they are unfortunate and poor management are in law a breach of duty by your employer.

Foreseeability

To establish liability for psychiatric injury for any breach of duty on part of your employer you have to show that the breach caused your medical condition and that it was reasonably foreseeable that this might have happened. There is unlikely to be any liability if it was not foreseeable.

In my preliminary opinion, you have reasonable prospects of establishing foreseeability in respect of

[set out potential breach].

Since by this time it would, or should, have been clear to your employer that you were suffering from a psychiatric illness because

[set out reasons].

In my preliminary opinion, you may well not be able to establish foreseeability in respect of

[set out potential breach]

since at this time I think that it will be difficult to establish that it would, or should, have been clear to your employer that you were suffering from a psychiatric illness because

[set out reasons].

[In bullying cases, foreseeability is usually easier to prove than in other cases involving an employer's breach of duty. This is because in such cases an employer is presumed to have the same knowledge as [your line manager] the employee who was subjecting you to bullying and harassment. In my opinion, you have reasonable prospects of establishing that [your line manager] knew or ought to have known the effect his bullying and harassment would have on you as he was the one who subjected you to this.]

Causation

You also need to be able to show that the specific breach of duty caused you damage.

If breach and foreseeability of damage can be established then this appears to have caused very significant damage as [you are unable to return to work for the foreseeable future].

From my review of the medical records there [do not] appear to be any other potential stressors or triggers of your depression. [Or set out other competing causes and their likely impact.]

Damage

It is necessary to establish that you suffer from a recognised psychiatric injury. Your treating psychiatrist has diagnosed [ ].

In terms of compensation, damages for the injury itself are relatively low in England. If liability can be established, my preliminary view (subject to obtaining expert medical evidence) is that compensation for pain, suffering and loss of amenity (general damages) would be in the range of £[ ] to £[ ].

You would also be entitled to recover financial losses caused by the stress. This means that you are entitled to claim for your loss of earnings for your absence from work. You are also entitled to recover your future loss of earnings. This will be based on medical evidence about when you are likely to be able to return to work, and is something that we will explore in more detail in due course when your future prognosis is more certain.

Limitation

Personal injury actions must be brought within 3 years of the breach of duty or, if later, within 3 years of the date of your knowledge that the injuries are significant. However, it is safest to assume the earliest date in respect of each breach.

The limitation date for a negligence claim breach is likely to be [ ]. [This dates from the first recorded diagnosis of depression in your medical notes.]

2. Harassment: (Protection from Harassment Act 1997)

An employer can be vicariously liable for harassment carried out by its employee contrary to the Protection from Harassment Act 1997. This Act was introduced to deal with stalkers, and, as well as criminal sanctions and making provision for injunctive relief, creates a statutory tort that enables the victim to claim damages for the distress caused by the harassment. It has caught the attention of personal injury and employment lawyers in recent years because of the possibility of using it to allow a remedy to those bullied at work (but who do not suffer discrimination) or as an alternative to stress at work claims.

Claims under the Act in respect of bullying which caused psychiatric injury have certain advantages to normal common law or breach of statutory duty claims for workplace stress. Firstly, foreseeability of injury is not an essential ingredient to establish a claim under the Act. As outlined above, this can be a problem in negligence-based claims. Secondly, it is not necessary to establish a medically recognised psychiatric condition. Distress is all that is needed. Thirdly, the limitation period is 6 years and not 3 years (so [ ] not [ ]).

There does have to have been a course of conduct, which must amount to more than a single incident. And as the liability falls to be determined under an Act which also provides for criminal sanctions, a high degree of culpable behaviour will be required to found liability.

[As we discussed at the meeting, I do not think that you will succeed in establishing a case under the Act. This is because whilst it is clear that there was a series of harmful conduct by [your line manager] which was directed at you, I do not think that the behaviour, very serious as it was, amounted to 'quasi-criminal conduct' as it did not involve physical violence or threats of physical violence.]

[In any event, as you can claim to be compensated for your injury and losses in negligence, it is not essential to claim under the Act. In my view, your claim in negligence is stronger than any claim under the Act.]

3. Costs and Funding

Costs of these proceedings are likely to be very substantial. It is very unlikely that if they decide to fight it that it will settle quickly. This would involve experts and a barrister to attend Court which could cost up to £50,000 to £100,000 or even more. If you win the case and recover damages and costs, you will get these costs back on top of your compensation. If you lose, you will have to pay the other side's costs.

I have had sight of your [Home Insurance] Policy and confirm that you do not have Legal Expense Insurance in place. You have advised me that you do not have any other insurance or legal expenses insurance in place which would cover this claim.

As we discussed, I am happy to run your case on a Conditional Fee Agreement, which we both signed at the meeting.

We discussed the basic principles behind a CFA. If you are successful in your claim, you are entitled to recover your costs from the Defendant. [If there is a shortfall between the costs that the Defendant is ordered to pay (or which are agreed), then I will not require you to pay anything towards this shortfall so long as you have co-operated with me throughout your case.]

If you were to lose your case, you will not have to pay anything towards my costs [or your own disbursements], unless you do not co-operate with me throughout your case. However, you are liable to pay the Defendant's costs from the issuing of proceedings. It is for this reason that we discussed at the meeting that I will try, once further investigations have been carried out, to obtain After the Event insurance on your behalf to protect you against the risk of paying the Defendant's costs. I discuss this in more detail below.

4. Next Steps

[Once I have the signed letters of authority, I will apply for your medical records. I need to obtain copies of all your past medical records as these will have to be disclosed in due course and must be reviewed by the independent expert.] When I receive these, I will arrange for you to be examined by an independent medical expert, who will report on your injuries. If the doctor is unable to predict the future for your injuries ('the prognosis'), you may need to be re-examined at a later date.

Once I have received your corrected and signed statement, I will prepare a letter to send to your employer notifying them of your claim and asking them to pass my letter to their insurers. I will ask you to approve the draft before it is sent. In theory, the insurers then have 3 months in which to respond to the claim by accepting or denying responsibility. If they deny that the Defendant is responsible, they must supply reasons and documentation in support. Often insurers do not keep to this timetable and we must press on with your claim regardless.

I will also be obtaining other evidence from witnesses to support your claim.

I will then instruct a barrister with experience in dealing with employment and psychiatric illness claims to advise in conference with you and our independent medical expert on merits and the likely compensation. We discussed at the meeting, and I have summarised above, that on issuing court proceedings, you become liable to pay the Defendant's legal expenses in the event that you are not successful in your claim. We discussed that I will try to obtain After the Event legal expenses insurance to protect you from this risk. It is therefore important that this is in place before proceedings are issued. Whilst stress at work cases are risky and not easy to insure, I have obtained After the Event insurance for cases similar to yours in the past. After the conference, I hope that your barrister will be optimistic about your prospects of success and will prepare a positive written advice to help you obtain After The Event insurance.

It is very difficult to predict how long a stress at work claim will take. As you will appreciate from the above, much depends on the medical situation and on the attitude taken by the insurers, but they tend to be defended strenuously and are complex in respect of fact and law. At present, my 'best guess' is that your claim might take between [ ] and [ ] months to reach a conclusion. However, it is always open to the employer's insurers to negotiate a settlement earlier.

You should be aware that litigation may have an adverse impact on your health. I am not a doctor and so I cannot give medical advice. However, litigation is itself stressful and is likely to take [several years] to conclude. It will be a reminder of the stress and/or bullying that led to your psychiatric condition. You may see the litigation as a mechanism for achieving answers and a 'closure', but you should be aware that it is designed only to obtain financial compensation. Many cases settle out of court with questions still unanswered. You may be advised by your doctors that you will only recover when you move on from the issues that led to your illness and so litigation might delay your recovery. The decision to proceed must be yours in conjunction with your medical advisers.

5. Our Agreement to Act for You

I am a solicitor [and a partner] in the firm. I will have the overall management and responsibility for your case, but may be assisted by an assistant solicitor or a trainee solicitor under my supervision, who will deal with some of the day-to-day work.

The terms of my firm's agreement to act for you are set out in the Conditional Fee Agreement. You have a copy.

We are required by the Law Society to give you an estimate of our legal costs. Of course, this will be of interest to you only if the case is successful, in which case all or most of the costs will be paid by the Defendant's insurers. In stress at work claims it is always difficult to predict the amount of time that will be needed, because much will depend upon the medical situation and the attitude of the insurers. However, I enclose a case plan which shows my best guess of the likely cost, based on the information available at present.

[You were referred to us by [ ]. As I explained when we met, the principal terms of referral are:]

[set out details of any referral arrangement].

Please note that if at any stage in your case we discover that you have committed or intend to commit a criminal offence, the Proceeds of Crime Act 1995 requires us to report this to the authorities.

If you or a third party send us money to hold on your account, that money will be held in your name in a separate bank account. At present, we hold client money in either [ ] or [ ]. In the very unlikely event of a bank failing to repay that money, the Financial Services Compensation Scheme currently provides compensation up to a limit of £50,000. That limit is however an amount set for each individual in total, so if you hold other personal monies in that same banking group, the limit will be reduced accordingly. Whilst we are happy to open and run an account for you, we do so as your agents and we are unable to accept any responsibility for any losses, in the highly unlikely event that that bank fails and you are unable to recover your funds.

If a problem arises at any time, please make an appointment to see me so that we can talk about your concerns. If that does not provide the solution, I will put you in touch with [ ] who is the partner in the firm who handles clients' concerns which cannot be resolved informally. He can provide you with details of our written complaints procedure if you require this.

6. Conclusion

I appreciate that this letter and enclosures contain a great deal to absorb. Please do not hesitate to telephone me if you have any questions.

In the meantime, I look forward to hearing from you with the corrected and signed statement, and signed forms of authority.

If you wish to discuss any matters further, please contact me on [ ].

Yours sincerely

12.2.2 Declining instructions

Dear

I refer to our recent meeting and I write to confirm the advice which I gave you.

I have reached my preliminary view about whether to take on your case on the matters we discussed at our meeting and the limited number of documents you had. If you think that there is crucial evidence on your employer's personnel file, you may be able to obtain this by making a written request under the Data Protection Act 1998 and offering to pay the statutory fee (currently £10). Most written records about employees (and not just computerised ones) should now be disclosed by the employer. However, depending on the number of documents I may have to charge for reviewing them and advising further.

Personal injury claims

An employer can, in principle, be liable to pay compensation to an employee if through their negligence they have caused psychiatric damage to the employee, and it was reasonably foreseeable that their actions or omissions would do so.

There are, however, no occupations considered intrinsically dangerous to mental health. In broad terms, it is therefore necessary to show specific breaches of the employer's duty, specify what could and should have been done instead (and that this was reasonably practicable) and that it was reasonably foreseeable to the employer that what was negligently done or not done might cause psychiatric damage to the employee. (The employer is generally entitled to assume that employees can withstand the normal pressures of the job unless he knows of some particular problem). The employee must then show that the negligence 'caused' (ie that it was, at least, a material contribution to) a 'recognised medical condition' (eg clinical depression). It is then also necessary to consider what compensation a court might award – compensation for injuries is quite low in England, and it is not easy to persuade a judge to award significant compensation for financial loss, particularly if there are other competing or contributory causes, or the employee is particularly vulnerable to psychiatric injury.

It is necessary to get over *all* of these hurdles to succeed (it is not enough to show a breach of duty, if that was not the cause of the illness or that illness was not a foreseeable consequence; it is not enough to show that illness was caused by the work if there is no identifiable breach of duty; it is not enough to show a breach of duty which might foreseeably cause mental illness if it in fact caused only 'injury to feelings' rather than a medical condition or the likely award of compensation is disproportionate compared to the likely cost).

Winning these cases is still very difficult. As you would be asking this firm to accept instructions on a Conditional Fee ('no win, no fee') basis, you appreciate that we have to consider very carefully whether or not to accept instructions to act.

I regret that taking all these matters into consideration, we are not able to accept instructions to act for you. Our decision not to take on your case does not indicate that we are advising that you would not succeed – it is simply that we are not prepared to act for you in this case on a Conditional Fee basis. Another solicitor may take a different view. It is not our policy to give particular reasons for declining to take on an individual case.

Time-limits for bringing personal injury cases of this kind can be strict, so you should seek advice elsewhere immediately if you do wish to pursue matters further.

Employment claims

We also briefly discussed the possible employment problems you might face.

I have briefly discussed your case with our employment law team. You may have claims which could be brought in the employment tribunal. However, once again, the law is complex and you are asking us to act on a 'no win, no fee' basis. I regret that taking all these matters into consideration, we are not able to accept instructions to act for you. Our decision not to take on your case does not indicate that we are advising that you would not succeed – it is simply that we are not prepared to act for you in this case on a 'no win, no fee' basis. Another solicitor may take a different view. It is not our policy to give particular reasons for declining to take on an individual case.

Or

[Possible claims in the Employment Tribunal might include:

[Constructive dismissal]

[Unfair dismissal]

[Sex discrimination]

[Race discrimination]

[Disability discrimination]

[You told me that you were not prepared under any circumstances to return to your employment because of what had happened. You therefore proposed to resign and claim a 'constructive dismissal' (ie that your employer had committed a fundamental breach of contract which you had accepted by bringing the contract to an end). The problem with constructive dismissal claims is that you have to establish the breach of contract and thus the dismissal before any question of unfair dismissal arises. If a tribunal was to decide that you simply resigned, you would have no claim for unfair dismissal. As it is difficult to know what evidence will be before a tribunal and what they will decide on the facts, resigning and claiming a constructive dismissal is always inherently risky. However, if you wait until you are dismissed a claim for unfair dismissal in the employment tribunal will not be straightforward. 'Capability' (ie being incapable of doing the job through illness) is a potentially fair reason for dismissal. The employer should also follow a fair procedure but, provided that the employer does so, and it is not clear when or if you will be able to return to work, such a dismissal may well be held to be 'fair'. Even if you are successful, there is a statutory cap on the compensatory award of £[ ].

[You should be aware that if you do decide to bring proceedings in the employment tribunal for discrimination there is possibility that the tribunal might make an award for 'injury to feelings'. There is a risk that this right might lead an employer to argue that you are not entitled to pursue a personal injury claim in the courts. The law on this subject is complex and not finally decided, but you should think carefully before pursuing an employment tribunal claim for unfair dismissal if you are likely to want to pursue a claim for compensation for personal injury later.]

[I believe that you do have an arguable case for [race] [sex] [disability] discrimination for the reasons set out in my accompanying letter. However, that does not mean that you are bound to win, nor that we are bound to act for you all the way to the tribunal hearing if our views on the merits of the case change (eg once we see the others side's statement of case, documents or witness statements). However, if you choose to commence discrimination proceedings in the employment tribunal you are entitled to an award for injury to feelings. The Court of Appeal has held that this overlaps with damages for personal injury in a claim for psychiatric damage. You are therefore unlikely to be allowed to begin court proceedings once you have brought a discrimination claim in the employment tribunal. In effect, you have to elect at the outset whether to pursue employment law rights in the tribunal or personal injury rights in the courts – as you do not yet know what the other side will say, or your prognosis, this might seem unfair. There cannot be a right or wrong answer at this stage. However, you must make a decision now. I enclose a letter of authority confirming that you understand these issues and that you want me to commence employment tribunal proceedings notwithstanding the fact that you will almost certainly then be barred from bringing proceedings for psychiatric damage in the courts.]

Yours sincerely

12.3 RETAINER

12.3.1 CFA for personal injury claim in court

Conditional Fee Agreement

This agreement is a binding legal contract between you and your solicitors. Before you sign, please read everything carefully. This agreement must be read in conjunction with the Law Society document 'Conditional Fee Agreements: what you need to know'.

Agreement date:

We, the solicitors

You, the client

What is covered by this agreement

- Your claim against your employer for damages for personal injury caused by stress [and bullying] at work between [ ] and [ ].
- Any application for pre-action disclosure.
- Any appeal by your opponent.
- Any appeal you make against an interim order or an assessment of costs.
- Any proceedings you take to enforce a judgment, order or agreement.
- Negotiations about and/or a court assessment of the costs of this claim.

What is not covered by this agreement

- Any counterclaim against you.
- Any appeal you make against the final judgment order.

Paying us

If you win your claim, you pay our basic charges, our disbursements and a success fee. You are entitled to seek recovery from your opponent of part or all of our basic charges, our disbursements, a success fee and insurance premium as set out in the document 'Conditional Fee Agreements: what you need to know'.

[Insert any provision required for payment on account of disbursements]

It may be that your opponent makes a Part 36 offer or payment which you reject on our advice, and your claim for damages goes ahead to trial where you recover damages that are less than that offer or payment. If this happens, we will not claim any costs for the work done after the last date for accepting the offer or payment.

If you receive interim damages, we may require you to pay our disbursements at that point and a reasonable amount for our future disbursements.

If you receive provisional damages, we are entitled to payment of our basic charges our disbursements and success fee at that point.

If you lose you remain liable for the other side's costs.

The Success Fee

The success fee is set at 100% of basic charges. No part of the success fee relates to the postponement of payment of our fees and expenses. The success fee inclusive of any additional percentage relating to postponement cannot be more than 100% of the basic charges in total.

Other points

The parties acknowledge and agree that this agreement is not a Contentious Business Agreement within the terms of the Solicitors Act 1974.

Signatures

Signed by the solicitors:

Signed by the client:

Conditional Fee Agreements: what you need to know

Definitions of words used in this document and the accompanying Conditional Fee Agreement are explained at the end of this document.

What do I pay if I win?

If you win your claim, you pay our basic charges, our disbursements and a success fee. The amount of these is not based on or limited by the damages. You can claim from your opponent part or all of our basic charges, our disbursements, a success fee and insurance premium.

It may be that your opponent makes a Part 36 offer or payment which you reject on our advice, and your claim for damages goes ahead to trial where you recover damages that are less than that offer or payment. Refer to the 'Paying Us' section in the Conditional Fee Agreement to establish costs we will be seeking for the work done after the last date for acceptance of the offer or payment.

If you receive interim damages, we may require you to pay our disbursements at that point as well as a reasonable amount for our future disbursements.

If you receive provisional damages, we are entitled to payment of our basic charges, our disbursements and success fee at that point.

If you win overall but on the way lose an interim hearing, you may be required to pay your opponent's charges of that hearing.

If on the way to winning or losing you are awarded any costs, by agreement or court order, then we are entitled to payment of those costs at that time. If you win overall, we are also entitled to payment of a success fee on those charges at the end of the claim.

What do I pay if I lose?

If you lose, you pay your opponent's charges and disbursements. You may be able to take out an insurance policy against this risk. If you lose, you do not pay our charges but we may require you to pay our disbursements.

Ending this agreement

If you end this agreement before you win or lose, you pay our basic charges and disbursements. If you go on to win, you also pay a success fee.

We may end this agreement before you win or lose.

Basic charges

These are for work done from the date of our instruction until this agreement ends. These are subject to review.

How we calculate our basic charges

These are calculated for each hour engaged on your matter. Routine letters and telephone calls will be charged as units of one-tenth of an hour. Other letters and telephone calls will be charged on a time basis. The hourly rates are:

Grade of Fee Earner	Hourly Rate
1 Solicitors with over 8 years' experience after qualification	£[ ]
2 Solicitors and legal executives with over 4 years' experience after qualification	£[ ]
3 Other solicitors and legal executives and other staff of equivalent experience	£[ ]
4 Trainee solicitors and other staff of equivalent experience	£[ ]

We review these hourly rates periodically and we will notify you of any changes in writing.

Success fee

The success fee percentage set out in the agreement reflects the following:

(a) the fact that if you lose, we will not earn anything;

(b) our assessment of the risks of your case;

(c) any other appropriate matters;

(d) the fact that if you win we will not be paid our basic charges until the end of the claim;

(e) our arrangements with you about paying disbursements.

Value added tax (VAT)

We add VAT, at the rate (now 15%) that applies when the work is done, to the total of the basic charges and success fee.

The insurance policy

We are investigating the possibility that you have an existing contract of insurance which is appropriate. If you do not have such insurance, we believe that it is desirable for you to insure your opponent's charges and disbursements in case you lose. After the Event insurance would be desirable if you are required to commence legal proceedings. However in the circumstances of this case this is unlikely to be available until after a full investigation of the merits of the claim.

Law Society Conditions

The Law Society Conditions below are part of this agreement. Any amendments or additions to them will apply to you. You should read the conditions carefully and ask us about anything you find unclear.

Our responsibilities

We must:

- always act in your best interests, subject to our duty to the court;
- explain to you the risks and benefits of taking legal action;
- give you our best advice about whether to accept any offer of settlement;
- give you the best information possible about the likely costs of your claim for damages.

Your responsibilities

You must:

- give us instructions that allow us to do our work properly;
- not ask us to work in an improper or unreasonable way;
- not deliberately mislead us;
- co-operate with us;
- go to any medical or expert examination or court hearing.

Dealing with costs if you win

- You are liable to pay all our basic charges, our disbursements and success fee.
- Normally, you can claim part or all of our basic charges, our disbursements, success fee and insurance premium from your opponent.
- If we and your opponent cannot agree the amount, the court will decide how much you can recover. If the amount agreed or allowed by the court does not cover all our basic charges and our disbursements, then you pay the difference.

- You will not be entitled to recover from your opponent the part of the success fee that relates to the cost to us of postponing receipt of our charges and our disbursements. This remains payable by you.

- You agree that after winning, the reasons for setting the success fee at the amount stated may be disclosed:
  (i) to the court and any other person required by the court;
  (ii) to your opponent in order to gain his or her agreement to pay the success fee.

- If the court carries out an assessment and reduces the success fee because the percentage agreed was unreasonable in view of what we knew or should have known when it was agreed, then the amount reduced ceases to be payable unless the court is satisfied that it should continue to be payable.

- If we agree with your opponent that the success fee is to be paid at a lower percentage than is set out in this agreement, then the success fee percentage will be reduced accordingly unless the court is satisfied that the full amount is payable.

- It may happen that your opponent makes an offer of one amount that includes payment of our basic charges and a success fee. If so, unless we consent, you agree not to tell us to accept the offer if it includes payment of the success fee at a lower rate than is set out in this agreement.

- If your opponent is receiving Community Legal Service funding, we are unlikely to get any money from him or her. So if this happens, you have to pay us our basic charges, disbursements and success fee.

As with the costs in general, you remain ultimately responsible for paying our success fee.

You agree to pay into a designated account any cheque received by you or by us from your opponent and made payable to you. Out of the money, you agree to let us take the balance of the basic charges; success fee; insurance premium; our remaining disbursements; and VAT.

You take the rest.

We are allowed to keep any interest your opponent pays on the charges.

If your opponent fails to pay

If your opponent does not pay any damages or charges owed to you, we have the right to take recovery action in your name to enforce a judgment, order or agreement. The charges of this action become part of the basic charges.

Payment for advocacy

The cost of advocacy and any other work by us, or by any solicitor agent on our behalf, forms part of our basic charges. Any barrister instructed will have a Conditional Fee Agreement with us, unless we have agreed otherwise with you beforehand.

Barristers who have a Conditional Fee Agreement with us

If you win, you are normally entitled to recover their fee and success fee from your opponent. The barrister's success fee is shown in the separate Conditional Fee Agreement we make with the barrister. If you lose, you pay the barrister nothing.

Barristers who do not have a Conditional Fee Agreement with us

If you win, then you will normally be entitled to recover all or part of their fee from your opponent. If you lose, then you must pay their fee.

What happens when this agreement ends before your claim for damages ends?

(a) Paying us if you end this agreement

You can end the agreement at any time. We then have the right to decide whether you must:

- pay our basic charges and our disbursements including barristers' fees but not the success fee when we ask for them; or
- pay our basic charges, and our disbursements including barristers' fees and success fees if you go on to win your claim for damages.

(b) Paying us if we end this agreement

(i) We can end this agreement if you do not keep to your responsibilities. We then have the right to decide whether you must:
 - pay our basic charges and our disbursements including barristers' fees but not the success fee when we ask for them; or
 - pay our basic charges, and our disbursements including barristers' fees and our and any barrister's success fees if you go on to win your claim for damages.

(ii) We can end this agreement if we believe you are unlikely to win. If this happens, you will only have to pay our disbursements. These will include barristers' fees if the barrister does not have a Conditional Fee Agreement with us.

(iii) We can end this agreement if you reject our opinion about making a settlement with your opponent. You must then:
- pay the basic charges and our disbursements, including barristers' fees;
- pay the success fee if you go on to win your claim for damages.

If you ask us to get a second opinion from a specialist solicitor outside our firm, we will do so. You pay the cost of a second opinion.

(iv) We can end this agreement if you do not pay your insurance premium when asked to do so.

(c) Death

This agreement automatically ends if you die before your claim for damages is concluded. We will be entitled to recover our basic charges up to the date of your death from your estate.

If your personal representatives wish to continue your claim for damages, we may offer them a new Conditional Fee Agreement, as long as they agree to pay the success fee on our basic charges from the beginning of the agreement with you.

What happens after this agreement ends?

After this agreement ends, we may apply to have our name removed from the record of any court proceedings in which we are acting unless you have another form of funding and ask us to work for you.

We have the right to preserve our lien unless another solicitor working for you undertakes to pay us what we are owed including a success fee if you win.

Explanation of words used

(a) Advocacy

Appearing for you at court hearings.

(b) Basic charges

Our charges for the legal work we do on your claim for damages.

(c) Claim

Your demand for damages for personal injury whether or not court proceedings are issued.

(d) Counterclaim

A claim that your opponent makes against you in response to your claim.

(e) Damages

Money that you win whether by a court decision or settlement.

(f) Our disbursements

Payment we make or have made on your behalf such as:

- court fees;
- experts' fees;
- accident report fees;
- agent's fees.

(g) Interim damages

Money that a court says your opponent must pay or your opponent agrees to pay while waiting for a settlement or the court's final decision.

(h) Interim hearing

A court hearing that is not final.

(i) Lien

Our right to keep all papers, documents, money or other property held on your behalf until all money due to us is paid. A lien may be applied after this agreement ends.

(j) Lose

The court has dismissed your claim or you have stopped it on our advice.

(k) Part 36 offers or payments

An offer to settle your claim made in accordance with Part 36 of the Civil Procedure Rules.

(l) Provisional damages

Money that a court says your opponent must pay or your opponent agrees to pay, on the basis that you will be able to go back to court at a future date for further damages if:

- you develop a serious disease; or
- your condition deteriorates;

in a way that has been proved or admitted to be linked to your personal injury claim.

(m) Success fee

The percentage of basic charges that we add to your bill if you win your claim for damages and that we will seek to recover from your opponent.

(n) Trial

The final contested hearing or the contested hearing of any issue to be tried separately and a reference to a claim concluding at trial includes a claim settled after the trial has commenced or a judgment.

(o) Win

Your claim for damages is finally decided in your favour, whether by a court decision or an agreement to pay you damages or in any way that you derive benefit from pursuing the claim.

'Finally' means that your opponent:

- is not allowed to appeal against the court decision; or
- has not appealed in time; or
- has lost any appeal.

12.3.2 Contingency fee (employment tribunal)

Contingency Fee Agreement

This agreement is a binding legal contract between you and your solicitors. Before you sign, please read everything including the conditions carefully.

Agreement date:

We, the solicitors

You, the client

What is covered by this agreement?

Your employment tribunal claims relating to your employment with [Employer's name] (your opponent) and its termination.

What is not covered by this agreement?

- Any counterclaim against you.
- Any appeal you make or any appeal made by your opponent.
- Any reference to the European Court of Justice.
- Representation by a barrister at the hearing.

Paying Us

If you win the case you pay us [40%] of the money we recover from your opponent. This [includes] VAT at the standard rate (currently 15%).

[In addition, if the Employment Tribunal award costs against your opponent you pay us those costs for the work we have done in respect of this for you calculated at our standard rates.]

You also pay us for payments we make or have made on your behalf ('our disbursements').

If you lose the case you do not pay us anything except our disbursements.

For what happens if we end the agreement before the case is won or lost please refer to Condition 5. If you end the agreement before the case is won or lost, you must pay our costs calculated at our standard rates and our disbursements.

'Win' means your claim is finally decided in your favour, whether by a tribunal decision or an agreement to pay you damages or in any way that you derive benefit from pursuing the claim and 'finally' means that your opponent is not allowed to appeal against the tribunal decision, or has not appealed in time, or has lost any appeal. 'Our standard rates' means our time spent calculated in accordance with the hourly rates set out in Schedule 1 plus VAT at the standard rate (currently 15%).

[Non-monetary benefits

If you do not obtain [any compensation] [more than £[ ] in compensation], but do gain non-monetary benefits [set out details] you are liable to pay our costs at our standard rates.]

The Conditions apply to this agreement.

This agreement is a Non Contentious Business Agreement within the meaning of section 57 of the Solicitors Act 1974

Signed for the solicitors **Dated:**

Signed by the client **Dated:**

Conditions

1. Our responsibilities

We must:

- always act in your best interests, subject to our duty to the tribunal;
- explain to you the risks and benefits of taking legal action;
- give you our best advice about whether to accept any offer of settlement.

2. Your responsibilities

You must:

- give us instructions that allow us to do our work properly;
- not ask us to work in an improper or unreasonable way;
- not deliberately mislead us;
- co-operate with us;
- go to any medical or expert examination or tribunal hearing.

3. What happens if you win?

You hereby authorise us to receive the money from your opponent (or any third party) direct. If your opponent (or third party) refuses to accept our receipt, you will pay the cheque you receive to a joint bank account in your name and ours. Out of the money you agree to let us take our costs plus any outstanding disbursements. You keep the rest.

If your opponent does not pay any damages or charges owed to you, we have the right to take recovery action in your name to enforce a judgment, order or agreement.

4. What happens if you lose?

If you lose you do not have to pay us anything except our disbursements.

5. What happens if the agreement ends before the case itself ends?

You can end the agreement at any time. You are then liable to pay us our costs incurred up to the date you end the agreement calculated at our standard rates.

We can end the agreement if you do not keep to your responsibilities in Condition 2. You are then liable to pay us our costs incurred up to the date the agreement ends at our standard rates.

We can end the agreement if we believe that you are unlikely to win and you disagree with us. You do not have to pay us anything.

We can end the agreement if you reject our opinion about making a settlement with your opponent. You must then pay us our costs incurred up to the date the agreement ends at our standard rates [unless you subsequently obtain compensation which is [20%] more than the offer we advised you to accept in which case you do not have to pay us anything].

6. What happens if the agreement ends?

After this agreement ends, we may apply to have our name removed from the record of any tribunal proceedings in which we are acting unless you have another form of funding and ask us to continue to work for you.

We have the right to preserve our lien unless another solicitor working for you undertakes to pay us what we are owed including a success fee if you win.

7. Payment for advocacy

The cost of advocacy and any other work by us, or by any solicitor agent on our behalf, forms part of our basic charges. The costs of any barrister instructed will be paid by you as a disbursement, unless we have agreed otherwise with you beforehand.

8. Costs

If you lose and you are ordered to pay costs to your opponent, then those costs will be payable by you.

Schedule 1

How we calculate our standard charges

These are calculated for each hour engaged on your matter. Routine letters and telephone calls will be charged as units of one-tenth of an hour. Other letters and telephone calls will be charged on a time basis. The hourly rates are:

Grade of Fee Earner	Hourly Rate
1 Solicitors with over 8 year's experience after qualification	£[ ]
2 Solicitors and legal executives with over 4 years' experience after qualification	£[ ]
3 Other solicitors and legal executives and other staff of equivalent experience	£[ ]
4 Trainee solicitors and other staff of equivalent experience	£[ ]

We review these hourly rates periodically and we will notify you of any changes in writing.

These are calculated for each hour engaged on your matter from now until the review date which is one year from the date of this agreement. Routine letters and telephone calls will be charged as units of one-tenth of an hour. Other letters and telephone calls will be charged on a time basis.

VAT at the standard rate (currently 15%) is charged in addition.

The circumstances where orders for costs are made are rare and only arise where the Tribunal is persuaded that one side's conduct has fallen foul of the provisions of the Employment Tribunals (Constitution and Rules of Procedure) Regulations 2004.

12.3.3 CFA (mixed claims)

Conditional Fee Agreement

This agreement is a binding legal contract between you and your solicitors. Before you sign, please read everything carefully. This agreement must be read in conjunction with the Law Society document 'Conditional Fee Agreements: what you need to know'.

Agreement date:

We, the solicitors

You, the client

What is covered by this agreement?

- Your claims against [employer] for damages for [breach of contract and/or disability discrimination and/or personal injury] suffered as a result of harassment for which your employer is vicariously liable and/or personal injury suffered as a result of your employer's negligence, breach of contract or breach of statutory duty between [ ] and [ ] whether pursued in a court, employment tribunal or otherwise howsoever.
- [Any appeal by your opponent.]
- Any appeal you make against an interim order.
- [Any proceedings you take to enforce a judgment, order or agreement.]
- Negotiations about and/or a court assessment of the costs of this claim.

What is not covered by this agreement?

- Any counterclaim against you.
- Any appeal you make against the final judgment order.

Paying us

If you win your claim, you pay our basic charges, our disbursements and a success fee. If you bring court proceedings you are entitled to seek recovery from your opponent of part or all of our basic charges, our disbursements, a success fee and insurance premium as set out in the document 'Conditional Fee Agreements: what you need to know'. If you bring proceedings in the employment tribunal it is unusual to obtain a order for costs. This means that in nearly all cases you will have to pay your own costs.

[Insert any provision required for payment on account of disbursements]

[It may be that your opponent makes a Part 36 offer or payment which you reject on our advice, and your claim for damages goes ahead to trial where you recover damages that are less than that offer or payment. If this happens, we will not claim any costs for the work done after the last date for accepting the offer or payment.]

If you receive interim damages, we may require you to pay our disbursements at that point and a reasonable amount for our future disbursements.

If you receive provisional damages, we are entitled to payment of our basic charges our disbursements and success fee at that point.

If you lose you remain liable for the other side's costs if you bring proceedings in court. If you bring proceedings in the employment tribunal it is unusual to suffer an order to pay your opponent's costs.

The Success Fee

The success fee is set at 100% of basic charges. No part of the success fee relates to the postponement of payment of our fees and expenses. The success fee inclusive of any additional percentage relating to postponement cannot be more than 100% of the basic charges in total.

Other points

The parties acknowledge and agree that this agreement is not a Contentious Business Agreement within the terms of the Solicitors Act 1974.

Signatures

Signed by the solicitors:

Signed by the client:

Conditional Fee Agreements: what you need to know

[Take in the standard Law Society Conditions (see **12.3.1**)]

But under '**Dealing with costs if you win'** consider adding a 'cap' on fees by reference to the damages to deal with a global settlement or no order as to costs:

> 'It may happen that your opponent makes an offer of one amount that includes payment of our basic charges and a success fee ("global offer"). If so, unless we consent, you agree not to tell us to accept the offer if it includes payment of the success fee at a lower rate than is set out in this agreement. However, in these circumstances, if we do so consent then we will limit our claim for base costs and success fee plus VAT payable by you out of the global offer to no more than (25%) of the total amount of the global offer.

> For the avoidance of doubt, this limit applies only to a global offer and not where your opponent pays damages and pays costs in addition.'

and

> 'It may happen that your claim is finally decided with no order to pay your costs (including the success fee) on top of any award of compensation (for example, if your claim proceeds in the employment tribunal only). If so, then we will limit our claim for base costs and success fee plus VAT payable by you out of the global offer to no more than (25%) of the total amount of the compensation awarded to you.'

12.4 LETTER OF CLAIM

12.4.1 Pre-action notification – Letter requesting occupational records including health records

Dear Sirs

We are acting on behalf of the above-named who has developed psychiatric injury caused by occupational stress [and bullying at work].

We are investigating whether this illness may have been caused by breach of duty during the course of his employment.

We are writing this letter in accordance with the Protocol for Disease and Illness Claims annexed to the Civil Procedure Rules.

We seek the following records:

[Insert details, e g personnel/occupational health]

Please note your insurers may require you to advise them of this request.

We enclose a request form and expect to receive the records within 40 days.

If you are not able to comply with this request within this time, please advise us of the reason.

Yours faithfully

12.4.2 Application on behalf of a potential claimant for use where a disease claim is being investigated

This form should be completed as fully as possible

Company

Name

Address

1(a)	Full name of claimant (including previous surnames)	
(b)	Address now	
(c)	Address at date of termination of employment, if different	
(d)	Date of birth (and death, if applicable)	
(e)	National insurance number, if available	
2	Department(s) where claimant worked	
3	This application is made because the claimant is considering:	
(a)	a claim against you as detailed in para 4	YES/NO
(b)	pursuing an action against someone else	YES/NO
4	If the answer to Q3(a) is 'Yes' details of:	
(a)	the likely nature of the claim [psychiatric injury caused by occupational stress [and bullying at work]]	
(b)	grounds for the claim [brief description of alleged breach]	
(c)	approximate dates of the events involved	
5	If the answer to Q3(b) is 'Yes' insert:	
(a)	the names of the proposed defendants	
(b)	have legal proceedings been started?	YES/NO
(c)	if appropriate, details of the claim and action number	
6	Any other relevant information or documents requested	

Signature of Solicitor

Name

Address

Ref

Telephone Number

Fax number

I authorise you to disclose all of your records relating to me/the claimant to my solicitor and to your legal and insurance representatives.

Signature of claimant

Signature of personal representative where claimant has died

12.4.3 Letter of claim

Dear Sirs

Re: Claimant's full name

Claimant's full address

Claimant's national insurance number

Claimant's date of birth

Claimant's clock or works number

Claimant's employer (*name and address*)

We are instructed by the above-named to claim damages in connection with a claim for psychiatric injury caused by occupational stress [and bullying at work].

We are writing this letter in accordance with the pre-action protocol for disease and illness claims.

Please confirm the identity of your insurers. Please note that your insurers will need to see this letter as soon as possible and it may affect your insurance cover if you do not send this to them.

The Claimant [is] [was] employed by you as [job description] from [date] to [date].

The circumstances leading to the development of his psychiatric illness are as follows:

Chronology

No	Date	Event	Comment
1		[Claimant's date of birth]	

2		[Date claimant commenced work for employer]	
3		[Date and description of first incident]	[Detail (including who knew and how evidenced)]
4		[Date and description of subsequent incidents]	[Detail (including who knew and how evidenced)]
5		[Dates and description of complaints]	[Detail (including to whom complaints were made)]
6		[Dates of sickness absences]	
7		[Dates of medical certificates or other indication of stress]	[Details including sick note wording]
8		[Date of 'last straw' if any]	[Detail (including who knew and how evidenced)]
9		[Date of awareness of psychiatric injury]	
10		[Date of diagnosis, if different to 9]	
11		[Date ceased work]	
12		[Date of termination if appropriate]	

Fault

The reason why we are alleging fault is:

1. Breaches of statutory duty

(a) [You have failed to carry out a risk assessment pursuant to the Management of Health and Safety at Work Regulations 1999. If you had carried out your statutory duty then]:
[set out how a risk assessment would have prevented the client's injury].
OR [you carried out a risk assessment dated [ ] but failed to put its recommendations into effect by [details]]

(b) Your client has required our client to work excessive hours contrary to the Working Time Regulations 1998 (from the provisions of which our client has not 'opted out') [give details by reference to the chronology]. The excessive hours have materially contributed to the development of our client's psychiatric injury.

2. Breaches of contract/duty

You are in breach of the following implied terms in our client's contract of employment with you and/or of your duty of care:

(a) [mutual trust and confidence];

(b) [to protect our client from harassment and bullying];

(c) to provide a safe system of work and in particular:
[set out details of the alleged breaches by reference to the chronology].
It was foreseeable that the said breaches of contract and/or duty would cause our client psychiatric injury because:
[set out details by reference to the chronology].

3. Vicarious liability

You are vicariously liable for the actions of [ ] (as set out in numbers [ ] and [ ] of the chronology) [which constitute harassment under the Protection from Harassment Act 1997].

Injury

A description of our client's condition is as follows:

[This should be sufficiently detailed to allow the Defendant to put a broad value on the claim, e g our client suffers from a [major depressive illness of moderate severity]. Our client is currently on anti-depressant medication. He is therefore clinically depressed and cannot presently return to work.]

[The time he has spent off work due to his illness is set out at number [ ] and [ ] of the chronology. His net income is approximately £[ ] per [ ]. [set out any other known financial losses]

Please provide us with the usual earnings details, which will enable us to calculate his financial loss.

Our client is still suffering from the effects of their injury. We invite you to participate with us in addressing their immediate needs by use of rehabilitation.

Expert evidence

[We have obtained a medical report from [name] and will disclose this when we receive your acknowledgement of this letter.]

OR

[Please note that we will be instructing a medical expert in this matter and intend to instruct one of the following experts:

[list experts]

We enclose a copy CV for each expert named. Please let us know within 35 days if you object to any of the experts listed, together with the reasons for any objections.]

Disclosure

[We have the following documents in support of our client's claim and will disclose these in confidence to your nominated insurer or solicitor when we receive their acknowledgement letter.

[Occupational health notes; GP notes]

At this stage of our enquiries we would expect the following documents you hold to be relevant to this action:

1. Our client's complete employment file.

2. Copies of correspondence and e-mails relating to our client.

3. Human Resources Records.

4. Records of complaints or investigations relating to [alleged perpetrator].

5. Communications and correspondence between [employer and insurer] in relation to our client's claim under Permanent Disability Insurance.

6. Documents produced to comply with requirements of the Management of Health and Safety at Work Regulations 1999 including risk assessments.

7. Documents relating to relevant comparators (anonymised as appropriate) showing annual percentage increases in remuneration including bonuses and promotions since [ ].

8 [Other]

[When responding, please expressly confirm that all paper and electronic records held by you relating to our client will be preserved pending resolution of this claim (this should include, without limitation, all e-mail folders maintained on our client's computer or on your servers). We would suggest that an electronic copy is made immediately. As this is likely to contain vital evidence in respect of the claim, if we do not receive an adequate undertaking in this regard we shall have no alternative than to apply to the court for the appropriate order and seek costs.]

Funding

Please note that we have entered into a Conditional Fee Agreement with our client dated [ ] in relation to this claim which provides for a success fee within the meaning of section 58(2) of the Courts and Legal Services Act 1990. [Our client has taken out an insurance policy dated [ ] with [name of insurance company] to which section 29 of the Access to Justice Act 1999 applies in respect of this claim.]

A copy of this letter is attached for you to send to your insurers. Finally, we expect an acknowledgement of this letter within 21 days by yourselves or your insurers.

Yours faithfully

12.5 ORDERS

12.5.1 Compromise Agreement clauses excluding all claims

WITHOUT PREJUDICE AND SUBJECT TO CONTRACT

Dear

Termination of your employment with [employer] ('the Company')

This letter sets out the terms that have recently been discussed and sets out the payments to be made in relation to the termination of your employment with the Company on account of [your disability].

You have or may have potential claims arising from your employment and its termination which include: unfair dismissal and wrongful dismissal ('Employment Claims') and claims for personal injury relating to alleged negligence, breach of statutory duty and harassment ('Personal Injury Claims') and, to the extent not covered by the foregoing, all claims raised by you or your solicitors in correspondence with the Company or any associate including, without limitation, the claims referred to in the draft letter from your solicitors to [ ] dated [ ].

This Agreement settles the claims referred to above. In addition, it reflects the intention of both you and the Company that this Agreement should also settle any other claim(s) made or to be made by you as more fully set out in Clause [ ].

Termination

Your employment with the Company will terminate on [ ] ('Termination Date').

Payments

The Company will pay, without admission of liability, within [ ] days of the later of: the Termination Date and receiving a copy of this Agreement signed by all the parties and your Adviser (as defined below), the following:

a payment of £[ ] as compensation for the termination of your employment ('Compensation Payment').

a payment of £[ ] [specifically on account of the loss of employment due to disability] [by way of damages in respect of the Personal Injury Claims].

Taxation

The payments will be paid [without deduction] of income tax or national insurance by the Company or any Associate.

Company property

[insert provisions]

Confidentiality

[insert provisions]

The Company agrees to also keep confidential the details of this agreement on a 'needs to know' basis within the Company and externally.

Restrictions

[insert provisions]

Claims and warranties

The Company accepts the terms of this Agreement in full and final settlement of all and any claims, costs, expenses or rights of action of any kind against you, whether contractual, statutory or otherwise, arising out of circumstances of which the Company was aware before or on the date of this Agreement.

You accept the terms of this Agreement in full and final settlement of all and any claims, costs, expenses or rights of action of any kind, whether contractual, statutory or otherwise arising out of circumstances of which the parties were aware before, on or after the date of this Agreement, and whether having already occurred or arising in the future in the United Kingdom or in any other country in the world, which you have or may have against the Company or any Associate or its or their partners, members, directors, officers, shareholders, consultants, workers or employees from time to time, which arise out of or in connection with your employment by the Company or any Associate or its termination including (but not limited to) any claim:

- which is an Employment Claim and/or a Personal Injury Claim, and/or has been raised by you or your solicitors in correspondence with the Company including, without limitation, the claims referred to in the letter from your solicitors to [ ] dated [ ];
- in relation to notice or pay in lieu of notice;
- for equal treatment under the Equal Pay Act 1970;
- for direct and/or indirect sex discrimination, discrimination on the grounds of gender reassignment, direct and/or indirect discrimination against married persons, discrimination by way of victimisation, harassment and any other claim under the Sex Discrimination Act 1975;
- for direct and/or indirect discrimination, discrimination by way of victimisation, harassment and any other claim under the Race Relations Act 1976;
- for refusal of employment, action short of dismissal, dismissal and/or other detriment on grounds related to trade union membership, for failure to comply with collective consultation obligations and/or to pay a protective award and/or any other claim under the Trade Union and Labour Relations (Consolidation) Act 1992;
- for discrimination, harassment, failure to make adjustments and any other claim under the Disability Discrimination Act 1995;

- for unauthorised deductions from wages, for detriment in employment (on any ground), for detriment or dismissal or selection for redundancy on grounds related to having made a protected disclosure, for paid time off for ante-natal care, for the right to time off for dependants, for the right to a written statement of reasons for dismissal, for unfair dismissal, for automatically unfair dismissal (on any ground), for a redundancy payment, for automatically unfair selection for redundancy on any ground and any other claim under the Employment Rights Act 1996;
- under the Protection from Harassment Act 1997;
- for the national minimum wage and/or additional remuneration, failure to allow access to records and detriment in employment on grounds related to the national minimum wage under the National Minimum Wage Act 1998;
- for the right to be accompanied and for detriment and/or dismissal on the grounds relating to the right to be accompanied under the Employment Relations Act 1999;
- under the Employment Act 2002;
- for dismissal for reasons related to a relevant transfer, for failure to inform and/or consult, and/or any other claim under the Transfer of Undertakings (Protection of Employment) Regulations 1981 and/or 2006;
- for compensation for entitlement to annual leave, payment in respect of annual leave, refusal to give paid annual leave, daily and/or weekly and/or compensatory rest and/or rest breaks and any other claim under the Working Time Regulations 1998;
- relating to any rights to and/or during any period of parental leave, relating to the right to return after parental leave, detriment relating to parental rights, automatic unfair dismissal on parental grounds, contractual rights to parental leave under the Maternity and Parental Leave, etc Regulations 1999;
- under the Transnational Information and Consultation of Employees Regulations 1999;
- for less favourable treatment, for the right to receive a written statement of reasons for less favourable treatment, automatic unfair dismissal and/or detriment in employment under the Part-Time Workers (Prevention of Less Favourable Treatment) Regulations 2000;

- for less favourable treatment, for the right to receive a written statement of reasons for less favourable treatment, automatic unfair dismissal and/or detriment in employment under the Fixed Term Employees (Prevention of Less Favourable Treatment) Regulations 2002; or

- for any rights to and/or during paternity and/or adoption leave, the right to return after paternity and/or adoption leave, for detriment relating to paternity and/or adoption leave, automatic unfair dismissal and/or contractual rights to and/or during paternity and/or adoption leave under the Paternity and Adoption Leave Regulations 2002 and/or the Statutory Paternity Pay and Adoption Pay (General) Regulations 2002;

- for detriment and/or dismissal or failure to allow the right to be accompanied under the Flexible Working (Procedural Requirements) Regulations 2002;

- for discrimination, victimisation and/or harassment on grounds of religion and/or belief under the Employment Equality (Religion or Belief) Regulations 2003;

- for discrimination, victimisation and/or harassment on grounds of sexual orientation under the Employment Equality (Sexual Orientation) Regulations 2003;

- for discrimination, victimisation and/or harassment on grounds of age under the Employment Equality (Age) Regulations 2006;

- in relation to any breach of your contract of employment including (but not limited to) unpaid wages, unpaid holiday pay and/or unpaid sick pay, permanent health insurance, private medical insurance, bonus or commission or any other contractual or discretionary benefit and any other contractual and/or tortious claim;

- for personal injury and/or negligence;

- in relation to any share option scheme, bonus scheme or other profit-sharing scheme or arrangement between you and the Company or any Associate;

- in relation to the conduct of the Company or any Associate in relation to any retirement benefits scheme (as defined in section 611 of the Income and Corporation Taxes Act 1988) of which you are or claim to be a member including, without limitation, the payment of contributions to, the accrual of benefits under, or the exercise of any powers or discretion in relation to such a scheme;

- in respect of which a Conciliation Officer is authorised to act;
- under European Union law; or
- any other statutory claim or claim for breach of statutory duty,
but excluding any claim for pension rights accrued up to the Termination Date under any occupational pension scheme (as defined in Pension Schemes Act 1993) operated by the Company or any Associate and of which you are a member ('Pension Rights'). You undertake and warrant that, to the best of your knowledge, information and belief, you have no claim against the Company or any Associate in respect of Pension Rights as at the date of this Agreement.

For the purposes of this clause, 'claim' includes (without limitation):

- any claim of which, at the date of this Agreement, neither the Company nor you is aware; and
- any claim of which, at the date of this Agreement, you are aware but neither the Company nor any Associate nor any of its or their partners, members, consultants, directors, employees, officers or workers is aware.

Representation and warranties

[set out provisions]

Reference and Other Matters

[set out provisions]

Please confirm your agreement to the terms set out in this Agreement by signing, dating and returning to me both of the enclosed copies. Please note that it is a condition of this Agreement that your Adviser signs the acknowledgement at Schedule 1.

I look forward to hearing from you.

Yours sincerely

Duly authorised for and on behalf of the Company

I have read and understood and agree to the terms of this Agreement.

....	....
Name of employee	Dated

Adviser's acknowledgement

[set out provisions]

Agreed reference

[set out agreed terms]

12.5.2 COT3

[ ] (Applicant) v [ ] (Respondent)

Claim No.:[ ]

TERMS OF COT3 SETTLEMENT AGREEMENT

WITHOUT PREJUDICE AND SUBJECT TO CONTRACT

Definitions

Claim: the [unfair dismissal] claim brought by the Applicant against the Respondent in the [ ] Employment Tribunal under claim no [ ].

Confidential Information:

[set out provisions]

Termination Payment:

The sum of £[ ].

Agreement

The Respondent agrees to pay and the Applicant agrees to accept the Termination Payment in full and final settlement of all outstanding current and future claims (save for a claim for personal injury arising from the matters asserted in the Claim ('the Excluded Claim')) arising:

- in the Claim
- out of the Applicant's employment with the Respondent or out of its termination,
- whether or not the Applicant currently has knowledge of facts on which such claims would be based and whether or not those claims have already come into existence.

Non Admission of Liability

The Respondent makes the Termination Payment to the Applicant without any admission of liability whatsoever by the Respondent or any of its owners, current or former directors, officers or employees of any of the matters alleged in the Claim or otherwise.

Taxation of the Payments

The Respondent and the Applicant believe that the Termination Payment will be tax free. The Applicant shall be responsible for any further tax and employee's national insurance contributions due in respect of the Termination Payment.

[The Applicant shall indemnify the Respondent on a continuing basis in respect of any income tax or national insurance contributions (save for employer's national insurance contributions) in respect of the Termination Payment (and any related interest, penalties, costs and expenses) save that the Applicant shall not indemnify the Respondent in respect of related interest penalties, costs and expenses due to the default or delay of the Respondent.]

The Respondent shall give the Applicant reasonable notice of any demand for tax which may lead to liability on the Applicant under this indemnity and shall provide him with reasonable access to any documentation and any assistance he may reasonably require to dispute such a claim (provided that nothing in this clause shall prevent the Respondent from complying with its legal obligations with regard to HM Revenue and Customs or other competent body).

Making the Payments

The Respondent agrees to make the Termination Payment to the Applicant; within 14 days of the Respondent's representatives, [ ] Solicitors, receiving this COT3 Agreement signed by or on behalf of the Applicant.

Mitigation Confirmation

The Applicant confirms that as at the date of this Agreement he has not commenced employment nor is he in discussions which are likely to lead to nor has he agreed to accept nor received any offer of employment. The expression 'employment' for the purpose of this clause to include a contract of service, a contract for services, any form of consultancy or self employment and a partnership.

Confidentiality by the Applicant

In recognition of the confidential nature of this settlement and in further consideration of the Termination Payment, and as a condition of the Applicant's retention of the Termination Payment, the Applicant hereby agrees and undertakes:

[set out provisions]

Confidentiality by the Respondent

The Respondent will not make or publish any disparaging remarks about or adverse references to the Applicant save as is required to defend any Excluded Claim.

Withdrawal and Dismissal of Claim

The Applicant consents to the Claim being dismissed upon withdrawal by him and will make an application to the Tribunal as soon as reasonably practicable, but in any event no later than [ ], to withdraw the Claim and shall refrain from instituting or continuing proceedings against the Respondent, or any current or former directors, officers or employees of the Respondent in any Employment Tribunal and/or court in respect of any claim in relation to his employment with the Respondent or its termination. Nothing in this Agreement shall preclude the Applicant from being able to instigate proceedings to enforce its terms or in respect of the Excluded Claim.

The Applicant acknowledges that following the withdrawal of the Claim the Respondent will make an application pursuant to the Employment Tribunals (Constitution and Rule of Procedure) Regulations 2004 to have the Claim dismissed on the basis that there be no order as to costs and the Applicant consents to any such application by his signature on the letter in the attached Schedule.

SCHEDULE

The [ ] Employment Tribunal

[Full address]

Dear Sirs

[ ] v [ ]: Claim No: 2202895/2008

I am the Applicant in this Claim.

Following settlement of my Claim by way of COT3, I wish to now withdraw my Claim (Claim No [ ]) against the Respondent. I consent to the dismissal of this claim on withdrawal pursuant to the Employment Tribunals (Constitution and Rules of Procedure) Regulations 2004 on the basis there be no order as to costs.

Yours faithfully

12.5.3 Consent Order

Upon the parties agreeing the termination of the claimant's employment in accordance with the compromise agreement attached.

By consent

IT IS ORDERED that:

1. All proceeding are stayed save for the purposes of enforcement of the terms set out below, for which there is liberty to apply.

2. The defendant do pay the claimant's costs to be assessed on a standard basis to be assessed if not agreed.

Schedule

1. The defendant do pay the claimant the sum of £[ ] net of CRU in full and final settlement of her claim herein within 14 days of the date of this order

2. Upon payment of the sums set out above the defendant be discharged from all further liability to the claimant in relation to the claim herein.
   [set out any specific additional provisions, eg about confidentiality]

Dated [ ] day of [ ] 20[ ]

We hereby agree to an Order in the above terms.

INDEX

References are to paragraph numbers.